# Competitive Drivers for Improving Future Business Performance

Carlos Martins
*Lusíada University of Porto, Portugal*

Paula Rodrigues
*Lusíada University of Porto, Portugal*

A volume in the Advances in Business Strategy and Competitive Advantage (ABSCA) Book Series

IGI Global
PUBLISHER of TIMELY KNOWLEDGE

Published in the United States of America by
IGI Global
Business Science Reference (an imprint of IGI Global)
701 E. Chocolate Avenue
Hershey PA, USA 17033
Tel: 717-533-8845
Fax: 717-533-8661
E-mail: cust@igi-global.com
Web site: http://www.igi-global.com



Library of Congress Cataloging-in-Publication Data

Names: Martins, Carlos, 1961- editor. | Rodrigues, Paula Cristina Lopes, 1970- editor.
Title: Competitive drivers for improving future business performance / Carlos Martins and Paula Rodrigues, editors.
Description: Hershey, PA : Business Science Reference, [2020] | Includes bibliographical references and index. | Summary: "This book examines conceptual, theoretical, and applied advancements of how to improve competitive performance in an era of uncertainty"-- Provided by publisher.
Identifiers: LCCN 2019034104 (print) | LCCN 2019034105 (ebook) | ISBN 9781799818434 (hardcover) | ISBN 9781799818441 (paperback) | ISBN 9781799818458 (ebook)
Subjects: LCSH: Competition. | Success in business. | Technological innovations.
Classification: LCC HD41 .C6575 2019 (print) | LCC HD41 (ebook) | DDC 658.4/06--dc23
LC record available at https://lccn.loc.gov/2019034104
LC ebook record available at https://lccn.loc.gov/2019034105

This book is published in the IGI Global book series Advances in Business Strategy and Competitive Advantage (ABSCA) (ISSN: 2327-3429; eISSN: 2327-3437)

British Cataloguing in Publication Data
A Cataloguing in Publication record for this book is available from the British Library.



For electronic access to this publication, please contact: eresources@igi-global.com.

# Advances in Business Strategy and Competitive Advantage (ABSCA) Book Series

Patricia Ordóñez de Pablos
Universidad de Oviedo, Spain

ISSN:2327-3429
EISSN:2327-3437

## Mission

Business entities are constantly seeking new ways through which to gain advantage over their competitors and strengthen their position within the business environment. With competition at an all-time high due to technological advancements allowing for competition on a global scale, firms continue to seek new ways through which to improve and strengthen their business processes, procedures, and profitability.

The **Advances in Business Strategy and Competitive Advantage (ABSCA) Book Series** is a timely series responding to the high demand for state-of-the-art research on how business strategies are created, implemented and re-designed to meet the demands of globalized competitive markets. With a focus on local and global challenges, business opportunities and the needs of society, the **ABSCA** encourages scientific discourse on doing business and managing information technologies for the creation of sustainable competitive advantage.

## Coverage

- Business Models
- Globalization
- Ethics and Business Strategy
- Customer-Orientation Strategy
- International Business Strategy
- Resource-Based Competition
- Co-operative Strategies
- Differentiation Strategy
- Competitive Strategy
- Outsourcing

IGI Global is currently accepting manuscripts for publication within this series. To submit a proposal for a volume in this series, please contact our Acquisition Editors at Acquisitions@igi-global.com or visit: http://www.igi-global.com/publish/.

The Advances in Business Strategy and Competitive Advantage (ABSCA) Book Series (ISSN 2327-3429) is published by IGI Global, 701 E. Chocolate Avenue, Hershey, PA 17033-1240, USA, www.igi-global.com. This series is composed of titles available for purchase individually; each title is edited to be contextually exclusive from any other title within the series. For pricing and ordering information please visit http://www.igi-global.com/book-series/advances-business-strategy-competitive-advantage/73672. Postmaster: Send all address changes to above address. 

## Titles in this Series

*For a list of additional titles in this series, please visit: www.igi-global.com/book-series*

***Revolutionizing Institutional Theory Through Stakeholder Capitalism***
Neslihan Aydogan-Duda (UC Berkeley Extension, USA)
Business Science Reference • © 2021 • 300pp • H/C (ISBN: 9781799844921) • US $235.00

***Creating Social Value Through Social Entrepreneurship***
Mine Afacan Fındıklı (Beykent University, Turkey) and Duygu Acar Erdur (Beykent University, Turkey)
Business Science Reference • © 2021 • 369pp • H/C (ISBN: 9781799847274) • US $195.00

***Handbook of Research on International Business and Models for Global Purpose-Driven Companies***
Rafael Ignacio Perez-Uribe (EAN University, Colombia) Carlos Largacha-Martinez (Fundación Universitaria del Área Andina, Colombia) and David Ocampo-Guzman (EAN University, Colombia)
Business Science Reference • © 2021 • 589pp • H/C (ISBN: 9781799849094) • US $345.00

***Cases on Internationalization Challenges for SMEs***
António Carrizo Moreira (University of Aveiro, Portugal)
Business Science Reference • © 2021 • 333pp • H/C (ISBN: 9781799843870) • US $185.00

***Impact of Disruptive Technologies on the Sharing Economy***
Ford Lumban Gaol (Bina Nusantara University, Jakarta, Indonesia) Natalia Filimonova (Vladimir State University, Russia) and Chandan Acharya (City University of New York, USA)
Business Science Reference • © 2021 • 350pp • H/C (ISBN: 9781799803614) • US $245.00

***Innovation Management and Growth in Emerging Economies***
Heather C. Webb (Higher Colleges of Technology, Dubai, UAE) Wendy Wu (Edinburgh Napier University, UK) and Hussain Al Numairy (Higher Colleges of Technology, Dubai, UAE)
Business Science Reference • © 2021 • 288pp • H/C (ISBN: 9781799841951) • US $195.00

***Handbook of Research on Nascent Entrepreneurship and Creating New Ventures***
António Carrizo Moreira (University of Aveiro, Portugal) and José Guilherme Leitão Dantas (CARME, School of Technology and Management, Polytechnic of Leiria, Portugal)
Business Science Reference • © 2021 • 483pp • H/C (ISBN: 9781799848264) • US $295.00

***Reshaping Entrepreneurship Education With Strategy and Innovation***
Ayansola Olatunji Ayandibu (University of Zululand, South Africa)
Business Science Reference • © 2021 • 422pp • H/C (ISBN: 9781799831716) • US $205.00

IGI Global
PUBLISHER of TIMELY KNOWLEDGE

701 East Chocolate Avenue, Hershey, PA 17033, USA
Tel: 717-533-8845 x100 • Fax: 717-533-8661
E-Mail: cust@igi-global.com • www.igi-global.com

# Table of Contents

# Detailed Table of Contents

# Preface

The beginning of the 20th century was characterized by a competitive environment, where there were few competitors, and the cause-and-effect relationships between phenomena were easily identifiable. The future was easily predictable. Changes and speed of change were reduced. The world was linear, predominating long periods of stability that were occasionally shaken by short and fleeting crises. The companies were mainly made up of many workers, who had no training. The disorder was common, thus resulting in organizations with high degrees of inefficiency. The companies object of these studies were, among others, the Erie Railway, Midvale Steel, Bethlehem Steel Company, Yale & Towne Manufacturing Company, Tabor Manufacturing Company, Link Belt Company, Comambault, Western Electric Co.

As already mentioned, the father of scientific management (Taylor), faced a stable competitive environment, but flooded with inefficiencies (ill-defined functions, waste, inadequate incentive systems). The workers were, in many cases, lazy and mischievous. And it was at the beginning of the 20th century that Ford asked, "why is it that every time I ask for a pair of hands they always come with a brain?" It took us a while to realize that Toyota was based on the capabilities of its workers and the responsibility of its leaders. The stable and easily predictable environments that characterized all previous periods until the beginning of the 20th century, were marked by repetitive patterns. The systems were linear, and it was possible to program and predict a future direction. The structures were formalistic, rigid, and predominantly centralist. Progress had been made through continuous improvements. Employees had to be obedient and diligent. In some cases, they were even considered to be efficient automata. In this context it was important:

- The size of organizations (economies of scale and scope);
- The clarity of precise functions and procedures;
- Be specialized in a reduced set of knowledge;
- Concentration and concealment of information, and
- Strong and persistent control.

In the second half of the 20th century, the reigning models that had been so successful in the past, were not the most appropriate. The business environment has seen significant competitive changes since the 1950s. The appearance of Asian Tigers in the 1960s and 1970s (Hong Kong, Singapore, South Korea, and Taiwan) and the subsequent development of neighboring economies such as the Philippines, Indonesia, Malaysia, Thailand, and Vietnam started significant changes in the world's supply. In the 1990s, the BRIC (Brazil, Russia, India, and China) emerged, with an exponential role for China. China's entry into the WTO was another key milestone in international trade. The development of regional economic spaces (CEE, NAFTA; Mercosur…) and the improvement of the transport system, were the initial increments of a new competitive driver for the following years – speed. The development of telecommunications, which, however, began in the 1960s, achieved an improvement and an increased role in the speed of transmission of video and audio signals (at the speed of light). The invention of transistors, semiconductor materials, and microprocessors from the 1970s opened the door to the development of robotics. The first computer produced on a large scale occurred in 1975 (IBM), however it was only in 1995 that Windows 95 was launched. A new revolution was underway.

This is how the 3rd Industrial Revolution (1970s) has brought advances in information technologies (CAD / CAM, MRP / ERP systems), computing and intelligent robotics. In this context, a new set of planetary players appears - the star companies - which are leading companies in the global market and of recent longevity. They emerged in the 1970s - Microsoft and Apple; in the 90s - Amazon, Booking, Google, Paypal, Alibaba; and in the 21st century, Baidu, Facebook, Whatsapp and Uber. Some of these companies appear in the ranking of the most valuable in the world (top 10): Apple, Amazon, Google, Facebook, and Microsoft. As a result of this change, there is an increase in supply in the markets, which also gave rise to changes in consumer profiles. The typical American consumer now has at his disposal more than 260 vehicle models, 400 computer models, 250 thousand software programs, 4.8 million websites, 150 TV channels, 458 new films per year, it's the road for the hyper consumption society. Consumers became more informed, more active, and connected to live-in networks. It is a new society of extremes that started to love luxury, and in contrast everything that is free or low cost. Consumers in these new emerging and developed economies become more unpredictable, and more difficult to understand. In this period between the 60s and today, companies in the USA have lost half of their customers every 5 years, and half of their employees every 4 years. While the percentage of companies that left the top 3 in their industries rose from 2% in 1960, to 14% in 2008. On the other hand, the correlation between being a market leader and being a profit leader has almost ceased to exist. Everything changes faster. And a new cleavage is proclaimed.

The so-called 4$^{th}$ Industrial Revolution democratized the internet and social networks, making available an immense amount of data (Big Data) which can now be obtained through devices that allow the collection of a large amount of information (sensors) and an unusual ability to explore them (Analytics). The IoT (internet of things) will have the ability to network objects, vehicles and equipment through electronic devices, thus allowing the collection of more data. The creation and development of interconnected networks will also enable the development of intelligent factories that can operate autonomously. It will be easy to track and monitor processes according to specific needs in real time. This flexibility represents the possibility for companies to produce according to demand (modularity). This development, together with 3D printing, leads us towards mass customization. The new equipment, in addition to performing automatic tasks, now it also has human interaction capabilities (cobots). This new Digital Revolution will be based on sophisticated algorithms, miniaturization, increased processing speed, and information storage capacity. Quantum computing may also be the driver of this algorithmic society to a new unpredictable level. All these developments throw companies into disorderly, volatile, and chaotic environments.

Stability lost its relevance and business systems evolved into models, where instability and the difficulty of predictability became the norm (McGrath, 2013). Linear models became non-linear, and the programming is no longer appropriate. The order gave way to chaos. Which is not the same as total disorder. Structures need to be more flexible, based on networks, and some models of organizations become self-organizing. Innovation becomes the rule. It is accepted that companies either innovate or die. Only innovation generates wealth. Only creative destruction, based on radical innovations, and on conscious research or creative insights, can lead to incremental leaps in performance. These scenarios also combine moments of relative stability, with moments of disruption and unpredictability. Even when there is some stability, it is recommended from now on to create positive internal crises, which compel the company to strategically look at the "who-what-how" trinomial, stimulating it, through attempts and experimentation. It is through this new succession dynamic that companies can temporarily guarantee acceptable performances. It is an endless race, systematically questioning previous assumptions. Only an organizational culture that promotes this organizational flexibility and agility allows survival. As the Americans say, now, whoever wants order goes to the Marines. A wise combination of evolutionary movements with innovative movements (parallelism) means that not everyone in an organization should follow the same path. Some must be explorers, who identify new advantages during a diffuse and nebulous flow of opportunities, and others, maintain the core business. Opportunities arise outside normal and expected alignments. To this extent, diversity of ideas, opinions, knowledge, and attitudes is required. Adaptation takes place through learning mechanisms. Autocratic leaderships, based on fear and the tyranny of wisdom, are inadequate, leading to despair and business degradation. The agility suggested by some is not a guarantee of success in the future. It becomes essential to combine it with another competence - the ability to resist, and to sustain adverse situations for a longer time compared to its rivals. This capacity is revealed through an adequate financial muscle, the possession of certain tangible and intangible resources (brands, know-how, technologies), and low fixed costs. The new environments require:

- Speed and quickness of decisions;
- Flexibility of general knowledge, (but a good specific "core");
- Integration of teams and knowledge;
- Innovation, information dispersion and feedback;
- Transparency and trust.

Markets and industries are internationalized, making their delimitations more difficult. New economies are emerging, and technologies impose significant changes. Technological changes, and the speed with which they are adopted, give innovation a permanent character. The dissemination of information weakens the resistance and sustainability of companies. This web of complexities also offers a range of emerging opportunities, and new strategic possibilities. The increase in knowledge (information, intelligence, and expertise) represents both a challenge and an advantage. It is the variability of these environmental factors that generates uncertainty and enhances change. The uncertainty will thus be conditioned by changes in environmental factors. Thus, the greater the dynamism and complexity of these factors, the greater the degree of uncertainty (Duncan, 1972). Environmental dynamism is conditioned by the frequency, pace, and amplitude of changes. While complexity is associated with diversity, the interrelation of factors, ambiguity and the degree and sophistication of knowledge required for the analysis and understanding of the context must also be considered. The changes, in addition to being determined by environmental factors, can still be conditioned by the individual decisions of the managers, and thus built by them. Uncertainty is thus a consequence of the speed of change, which can influence the perception of those responsible, thus conditioning the decision-making process. If the competitive environment that the company faces at any given time is stable, uncertainty is low, if the environment is moderate the uncertainty will be moderate, if the complexity and dynamism of the environmental factors are high, the uncertainty is maximum, so the environment will be turbulent and highly unstable. These changes in the environment, and consequently at the level of uncertainty, will require different philosophies and management approaches, thus requiring changes in styles and systems that allow for adequate adaptability. As is well known, one of the tasks of management is to deal with uncertainty in order to avoid it, reduce it or eliminate it. In the absence of information, some decision makers interpret uncertainty with different degrees of tolerance, which conditions the choices that best adapt to the environment.

## COMPETITIVE ADVANTAGE

In stable competitive contexts the competitive advantage stems from the performance of activities different from the competition, or from carrying out the same activities in a different way (Porter, 1985). Superior performance is achieved when the resources that make up its activities are closely linked to form a unique and valuable strategic position, from which managers can increase revenue (differentiation) or decrease costs (cost leadership). The choice of positioning is based on the principles of industrial economy, according to which the structure of the industry / sector conditions strategic choices and, hence, the results. The basic unit is industry, and organizations are open systems where balance and linearity prevail. The environments are considered stable, with the strategy referring to a limited role, namely to the choice of a position within the sector, and later to the configuration of its activities system (Bingham & Eisenhardt, 2008). These activities must consist of strong and complex relationships with each other, to guarantee a sustainable competitive advantage - SCA. The sustainability of competitive advantage is possible and desirable, being achievable through an adequate adjustment (fit) of the chosen activities.

In moderately uncertain environments, managers use resources to create superior performance (Peteraf & Barney, 2003). Leverage logic argues that competitive advantage derives from ownership of specific resources that are rare, difficult to imitate, non-replaceable and highly valuable in various markets (Bingham, Eisehardt, & Furr, 2011). It consists of identifying, building, and exploiting a portfolio of fundamental resources, which are valuable and rare in today's markets, and which can be extended to other markets. The logic of leverage (inside-out view) is based on the economic ideas Chamberlin (1933) and Penrose (1959) that emphasize the importance of the resources, capacities, and internal knowledge of each organization. The basic unit of analysis becomes the company. The heterogeneous distribution of resources, and their imperfect mobility, are the factors that allow organizations to access superior performances. The competitive environment is considered moderately dynamic, and strategy plays a central role, since it must seek to choose and exploit rare, valuable, and inimitable resources, applying them to products in its sector, or in other markets, thus guaranteeing performances above average. The competitive advantage to be sustainable requires the protection of resources through mechanisms that make it difficult to copy, imitate, and replace. Sustainability requires a moderate interconnection between resources that need to be reconfigured according to changes in the environment (Peteraf & Barney, 2003).

When competitive environments are turbulent or highly volatile, competitive advantage and superior performance derive from entrepreneurial action (Bingham, Furr, & Eisenhardt, 2014; Alvarez & Barney, 2007). Superior performance under this strategic logic results from the ability to capture revenues and profits earlier, faster, and in a more effective way than competitors. It consists of choosing one or more organizational processes (e.g., acquisition, alliance, internationalization, and product innovation), which place the company in an abundant flow of attractive opportunities and readjust it in the face of unforeseen events (patching). These environments are characterized by abundant and unpredictable flows, which generate rapid movements and ambiguous opportunities of indefinite duration (Alvarez & Barney, 2007). The logic of opportunity is based on the economic principles of the Austrian School, where processes of change and innovation are the drivers of temporary monopolies (Bingham, Eisehardt, & Furr, 2011). Organizations are interpreted as complex adaptative systems (CAS), where non-linearity and instability find support in theories of chaos and complexity. The environment is recognized as a flow of opportunities, where the capacities of discovery and creation are the most appropriate, to dominate dynamic and highly uncertain environments (McGrath, 2013). The strategy consists of using a set of simple rules, which allow the organization to be placed in a flow of emerging and spontaneous opportunities. The competitive advantage is transitory and is based on processes that are loosely interconnected. Simplicity, improvisation in real time, and timing are the ingredients of temporary advantages (Bingham, Eisehardt, & Furr, 2011).

## COMPETITIVENESS DETERMINANTS

Each company must choose a limited set of activities corresponding to its value proposition. They must constitute activities that allow them to be more efficient or different from the dominant offers. In this way, the competitive advantage results from the configuration of these activities, allowing higher prices to be offered, or lower costs to be obtained. Therefore, the creation of value results from the creation or development of activities that are different from those of the competitors, or from carrying out the same activities in a different way. The integration of this limited set of activities (areas of excellence) establishes the guiding basis for the organization's strategy. Of these areas, some that stand out today seem to be more relevant: the ability to access markets, and innovation. Any of these activities requires resources, capacities and systems that allow to obtain superior performances.

## INTERNATIONALIZATION

The reasons for the need for internationalization of companies can be multiple. It can usually be an evolutionary, gradual, and dynamic process (Johanson & Vahlne, 1992). The degree of knowledge and commitment of the markets determines the evolution of the internationalization process. These involvement in international markets may arise from internal needs: company growth, unique products, unused installation capacities, economies of scale; or external factors: such as small or saturated domestic market, response to competitors, customer follow-up, access to technologies, or lower production costs. These reasons require companies to have certain resources and capabilities. In an initial stage, it may result from the use of assets not fully explored, or from the leverage of management, distribution, or marketing skills. At a later stage, it may be intended to prospect knowledge acquired in these markets, and finally to take advantage of synergies of operations on a global scale (Douglas & Craig, 1985).

The advance towards international production may be conditioned by specific property advantages - innovative products, brands, production, or distribution knowledge - (ownership advantage); location advantages or knowledge internalization advantages, which maximize the results - (internalization advantages). These advantages can determine the type of penetration (license assignment, export, or direct investment) (Douglas & Craig, 1985). These advantages may be dependent on resources that may be controlled by other companies, which raises questions, such as the importance of the company in these connection networks. As stated by Johanson and Mattsson (1988), the internationalization process can thus be developed through partnerships with other companies in these markets, or the participation in existing networks.

## INNOVATION

The innovation model chosen depends on the degree of uncertainty faced in different competitive contexts. As stated by Beal & Yasai-Ardekani (2008:9) "Firms that can align their competitive strategies with the requirements of their environments can cope with these formidable challenges. One approach to coping with environmental requirements is for a firm to identify the stage of its industry's life cycle and then formulate and implement a competitive strategy that effectively responds to the opportunities and threats present in that life cycle stage". This finding must condition the process of continuous or radical innovation. In less demanding environments it will be sufficient to conduct innovations based on improvements or adaptations of products, processes, or methods already on the market (incremental). When competitive contexts present a greater degree of uncertainty, disruptive or radical innovations are the most appropriate. These processes are based on disruptive technologies that transform current businesses and promote new (radical) business models.

The need for constant innovation in most businesses in the future does not focus solely on the presentation of new products or services. This mandatory condition does not seem sufficient. The creation of internal systems that support innovation will also become mandatory. In this line, the identification of new possibilities for innovation can be divided into three broad categories. In the configuration of the activities of the business model (profit model, network development, or process configuration); the most well-known innovation possibility consists of the possibilities of reconfiguring the offer or features of the products / services (offering), - the innovation in the product / service optics consists of the distinction between architectural innovation (maintenance of the core product), changing only the design or the way the components interact, while modular innovation represents a change in the main components of the products while maintaining the entire design (Amit & Zott, 2012; Teece, 2018). Innovation can also occur in the experience offered in terms of service, brand, channels used, or in the mode of interaction with the customer (marketing experience) (Doblin et al., 2013). Therefore, these are some of the main drivers that have conditioned business performance in the future.

## ORGANIZATION OF THE BOOK

The book is organized in five sections. The first one is about strategic orientation, the second is focused on the importance of the market, the third is a brief approach to the international dimension, the fourth is about innovation and the last one presents a view on digital drivers.

A brief description of each chapter follows:

## Section 1: Strategic Drivers

In a world under continuous change, Chapter 1 discusses from the traditional view to sustainable competitive advantage, to a dynamic view of strategy and the consequences of a new approach to gain competitive advantage. Strategy is not dead but must follow new rules in a VUCA world.

Chapter 2 considers that strategic leadership is an important competence in the context of a volatile, uncertain, complex and ambiguous environment (VUCA). This role has an important impact on individuals, teams and at different organizational levels. This chapter also points out the importance of ethical leadership as an imperative for different organizational levels.

Chapter 3 argues that the businesses models are an important question inside innovation, for future businesses. Different business models will have impact on performance and companies' survival.

## Section 2: Market Drivers

Chapter 4 discusses the impact of the fourth industrial revolution on the traditional marketing-mix elements. Digital technologies as a source of low costs, generate business opportunities, at the product level (co-creation, relied on blockchain technology-BT), price (cryptocurrencies), promotion (manifold-marketing) and place (cross-channel experiences) variables.

Chapter 5 debates the market orientation and its consequences on product development and customer satisfaction in the Portuguese wine sector. In this new world with great dynamism and complexity, the importance of customer behavior gave innovation and the development of new products a critical role. Market orientation is positively related to the development of new products and is somehow connected with customer satisfaction.

Chapter 6 explains the foundations of luxury environments and is focused on the adequate key performance indicators to evaluate the customer's experience. Customers expect luxury to be linked to real life experiences, with high customized services.

Chapter 7 considers that the supply chain needs to be optimized and efficient, and this is an important issue at VUCA environments, where speed and agility are also crucial. After the description of the supply chain, the chapter presents and compares different optimization techniques.

## Section 3: International Drivers

Chapter 8 presents an overview of the relevance for the companies regarding the expansion for international markets. The importance of the knowledge (internal and external), networks is fundamental to select new markets. Although several methods can be used to make a better market selection, the holistic view could assure better results.

## Section 4: Innovation Drivers

Chapter 9 discusses the importance to achieve innovation companies must change its business processes to develop new products in the age of digital transformation. The use of information and communication technologies (ICT) is fundamental to SME companies. This chapter tries to answer what factors are important to innovation, and how ICT affects innovation.

## Section 5: Digital Drivers

Chapter 10 considers that e-commerce has a new sales system that could have an influence on customer experience. Some effects on consumer's perceived risk about information shared on this sales process has increased trust, and there is also a positive relation between consumer experience with e-commerce and trust in internet shopping, and a positive relation between social media use and trust at in-commerce.

Chapter 11 enhances the relevance of value to shareholders is a critical issue nowadays. From the classic point of view, to the new competitive contexts, the discussing of value creation tools is still an important topic. This chapter used Siemens as an example to present different value creation and capital allocation tools.

## REFERENCES

Alvarez, S., & Barney, J. (2007). Discovery and Creation: Alternative theories of entrepreneurial action. *Strategic Entrepreneurship Journal, 1*(1-2), 11–26. doi:10.1002ej.4

Amit, R., & Zott, C. (2012). Creating Value Trough Business Model. *MIT Sloan Management Review.*

Beal, R., & Yasai-Ardekani, M. (n.d.). Outperforming the Competition in Each Stage of the Industry Life Cycle. *Journal of Applied Business and Economics.*

Bingham, B., Furr, N., & Eisenhardt, K. (2014). The opportunity paradox. *MIT Sloan Management Review.*

Bingham, C., Eisehardt, K., & Furr, N. (2011). Wich strategy when? *MIT Sloan Management Review*, 71–78.

Bingham, C., & Eisenhardt, K. (2008). Position, leverage and opportunity: A typology of strategic logics linking resources with competitive advantage. *Managerial and Decision Economics, 29*(2-3), 241–256. doi:10.1002/mde.1386

Duncan, R. (1972). Characteristics of organizational environment and perceived environmental uncertainty. *Administrative Science Quarterly, 17*(3), 313–327. doi:10.2307/2392145

McGrath, R. (2013). Transient Advantage. *Harvard Business Review.*

Peteraf, M., & Barney, J. (2003). Unraveling the resource-based tangle. *Managerial and Decision Economics, 24*(4), 309–323. doi:10.1002/mde.1126

Porter, M. (1985). *Competitve advantage: creating and sustaining superior performance.* Free Press.

Teece, D. J. (2018). Business models and dynamic capabilities. *Long Range Planning, 51*(1), 40–49. doi:10.1016/j.lrp.2017.06.007

# Acknowledgment

All the chapters were double-blind review. The editors would like to acknowledge the help of all the people involved in this project and, more specifically, to the authors and reviewers that took part in the review process. Without their support, this book would not have become a reality.

First, the editors would like to thank each one of the authors for their contributions. Our sincere gratitude goes to the chapter's authors who contributed their time and expertise to this book.

Second, the editors wish to acknowledge the valuable contributions of the reviewers regarding the improvement of quality, coherence, and content presentation of chapters. Most of the authors also served as referees; we highly appreciate their double task.

Finally, a special acknowledgement to Isabel Cristina Barbosa, a student of a Master scholarship in Management, of COMEGI (Research Centre in Organizations, Markets and Industrial Management) and Universidade Lusíada – Norte.

*Carlos Martins*
*Lusiada University of Porto, Portugal*

*Paula Rodrigues*
*Lusiada University of Porto, Portugal*

# Section 1
# Strategic Drivers

# Chapter 1
# Is Strategy Dead?
## Moving From Sustainable Competitive Advantage to Transient Advantage

**Raquel Meneses**
*University of Porto, Portugal*

## ABSTRACT

*Traditionally, it was seen as a major goal for companies to achieve sustainable competitive advantage, based on external conditions and/or internal conditions. Firms should seize opportunities and neutralize threats based on their strengths and avoiding their weaknesses. However, nowadays, we live in a volatile, uncertain, complex, and ambiguous context. Markets are very dynamic (hypercompetition), and thus, achieving a sustainable competitive advantage is not possible anymore. In this conceptual chapter, the authors claim that organizations need to be aware of and prepared for this transition. Firms need different tools and frameworks to deal with future situations – design a strategy is not enough; now, to achieve success, firms have to follow a transformational, VUCAS, strategy.*

## INTRODUCTION

The world is continuously changing, market time is shorter, information flows faster, imitators are everywhere, improved versions are almost immediate, consumers are more demanding, and new products and services are a constant. Nothing remains except the textbooks of strategy, which have not changed. As Mack and Kare (2015, 3) claim, [w]*hile the business environment is rapidly undergoing a change, the business tools and frameworks are lagging behind.*

Traditionally, it was considered a major goal for companies to achieve sustainable competitive advantage based on external conditions and/or internal conditions. Firms had to seize opportunities, neutralizing threats based on their strengths while avoiding their weaknesses. As Pröllochs and Feuerriegel (2020, np) note, *strategic management specifically draws on the metrics of SWOT analysis as they—despite their age—still enjoy widespread application in business planning, in management practice, and as a core vehicle for management consulting firms.*

DOI: 10.4018/978-1-7998-1843-4.ch001

According to Porter's (1989) five forces model, firms design their strategy based on market power, whereas Barney's (1991) VRIO model, the existence of valuable, rare, inimitable resources exploited by the organization leads to sustainable competitive advantage. Traditionally, strategy is defined as *the match an organization makes between its internal resources and skills ... and the opportunities and risks created by its external environment* (Grant, 1991, 114), such that strategy is a system that links external and internal analysis at a certain defined moment in time, with a view to constructing the future.

This system is, therefore, static. *In static systems, component parts are constructed from an initial design. Once the system is in place, it usually does not change. Architecture, for example, is a static system. The components of building change very little over time – or at least very slowly. The roof may need to be repaired or replaced, but the level of dynamism is limited. Interdependencies are well defined, and the pace of evolution is slow.* (Wade, Macaulay, Noronha & Barbier, 2019, 27). In many situations when companies do not achieve the desired level of performance, they question implementation, readjust the system, and try again. When they do not reach the desired level of performance after this readjustment, they question the strategy design. However, they often do not realize that the problem is deeper. It is not just the strategy that has to be rethought; it is the entire static logic of the system in which it is processed. *Therefore, these static systems and the interdependencies they encompass form the poor job of describing how most organizations operate today.* (idem). For D'Aveni and Gunther (1995), the world is constantly changing, which implies that companies should be constantly alert to their rivals' moves. This also implies designing and redesigning their strategy whenever required. Moreover, firms must constantly ask themselves who their rivals really are and acknowledge that perhaps the biggest threat may be from outside their sector.

Many companies see transformation as transitory or as an option they have to take at a given moment that will take them to the next level after they have achieved sustainable competitive advantage. We can compare this view to climbing a staircase and passing from one landing to another. The steps serve to move from one stable point to another. However, in a fast-changing world, there are no more landings, only steps. That is, the market is not stable, it does not tend to equilibrium and it is impossible to maintain a sustainable competitive advantage. Thus, managers have become more concerned with carrying out actions and reactions that allow their firms to achieve small advantages, so that cumulatively they are able to achieve competitive advantage over time (Wiggins and Ruefli, 2005). It is in this context that we discuss the VUCA world (see, for example, Bennett & Lemoine, 2014a), hypercompetition (D'Aveni & Gunther, 1995), transient advantage (McGrath, 2013a), and AGILE firms (Leybourn, 2013).

This chapter presents the evolution from the sustainable competitive advantage approach to a transient advantage approach, or put simply, from strategy to transformational strategy. New strategic tools are presented that are more adapted to the world today. We believe that training on Strategy and Competitiveness need this renewal. As McGrath (2013a) states, *strategy is stuck (…) by sticking to the same old playbook* (62). Additionally, we believe that managers and strategists are already changing their mindset and the business world is shifting to a less rigid approach. In this new environment, firms need velocity of action, unusual solutions, clear choices and solid information systems, as well as adaptable options in a stable continuous manner. If changes are abrupt, they will not be accepted. Thus, in this unique environment firms must be VUCAS (the full meaning of which will be explained later).

## BACKGROUND: TRADITIONAL VIEW

To realize the real importance of a new strategic approach, we must understand the traditional one first. Currently, strategy is based on two fundamental pillars: first, firms must develop a sustainable competitive advantage, although the definition of sustainable competitive advantage is ambiguous or, at the very least, problematic (Flint, 2000; Klein, 2002); and secondly, to develop a sustainable competitive advantage, firms must engage in a time-consuming, well-structured process. The rationality behind this approach is *if you take the time and effort to analyze the forces, you will be able to create a roadmap for your business* (Muneer, 2019, 88). These forces refer to the well-known Porterian view of industry, the five forces model, assuming they are stable. However, *inter-industry competition is becoming more prevalent, with barriers to entry rapidly falling and the threat of substitutes growing apace, and traditional industry analysis is too coarse-grained to be effective on its own* (Leavy, 2014, 5).

Another model, the resource-based view, assumes that firms are a bundle of heterogeneous resources which are immovable between firms. These two perspectives, inward-looking and outward-looking, are complementary (Miller, 2019). The traditional strategic process is time-consuming, based on an internal and external picture aimed at obtaining and maintaining a sustainable competitive advantage.

### External Analysis

Interdependency is a reality, as firms operate in an ecosystem with other firms, buyers, suppliers, substitutes, etc. Therefore, firms need to know their external environment to take decisions. The external environment has a great impact on the behavior and performance of firms. Generally speaking, firms do not have any control over the macro-environment, they are only influenced by it. However, they can influence and are influenced by the microenvironment, so it is crucial to know it well. A popular framework to study the microenvironment is Porter's five force model (see Figure 1), which combines *input-output analysis of a specific industry with industry boundaries via entry barriers and substitutes.* (Grundy, 2006, 215). It is, furthermore, a *useful starting point for strategic analysis even where profit criteria may not apply.* (Johnson, Scholes & Whittington, 2008, p. 60).

According to this model (Porter, 2008 [1985]), there are five interconnected forces that impact on industry balance: 1) threat of new entrants, 2) bargaining power of suppliers, 3) bargaining power of buyers; 4) threat of substitute products or services, and 5) rivalry among existing competitors. The goal is not to label an industry as attractive or not attractive, but rather to *understand the underpinnings of competition and the root causes of profitability* (Porter, 2008 [1985], 5). The five forces are described as follows.

The threat of new entrants – new firms in an industry mean more supply and an additional pressure on price, cost, labor and specific raw material. *The threat of entry in an industry depends on the height of entry barriers that are present and on the reaction entrants can expect from incumbents* (Porter, 2008 [1985], 8).

Bargaining power of suppliers – even though these agents, including labor suppliers, are partners throughout the production process, they might have some opposing goals. More powerful suppliers create an extra pressure on firms. *Powerful suppliers capture more of the value for themselves by charging higher prices, limiting quality or services, or shifting costs to industry participants* (Porter, 2008 [1985], 11).

Bargaining power of buyers – even though these agents, consumers or other firms, are the firms' partners, they might have some opposing goals. More powerful buyers create an extra pressure on firms. *Powerful customers – the flip side of powerful suppliers – can capture more value by forcing down prices, demanding better quality or more services (thereby driving up costs), and generally playing industry participants off against one another, all at the expense of industry profitability*. (Porter, 2008 [1985], 14).

Threat of substitutes – although substitutes satisfy the same need, they are products or services from other industries. In some cases, the threat of substitutes from another industry is even more important than inside rivalry. For example, in a small town, the cinema is the biggest threat to the theater (since usually there is only one of each). Another example is when the substitutes satisfy the same need much better. *When the threat of substitutes is high, industry profitability suffers. Substitute products or services limit an industry's profit potential by placing a ceiling on prices. If an industry does not distance itself from substitutes through product performance, marketing, or other means, it will suffer in terms of profitability – and often growth potential!* (Porter, 2008 [1985], 17). The case of the train sector is well-known – mostly concerned about themselves, they have ignored the advances and innovation occurring in other transport alternatives. This marketing myopia could be even more dangerous today, with so-called industry convergence, which is taking place, for example, in the photography sector and telecommunications, or the automobile sector and energy. Initially, Tesla saw itself as an automobile company, whereas currently, its mission is *to accelerate the world's transition to sustainable energy*.[1]

Rivalry among existing competitors – industry rivalry results from combining all the forces mentioned above, but also from the intensity and basis of competition. *Rivalry among existing competitors takes many familiar forms, including price discounting, new product introductions, advertising campaigns, and service improvement*. (Porter, 2008 [1985], 18). This rivalry is strongly related to market structure, market share concentration and dispersion, and to product differentiation, for example.

*Figure 1. The five forces that shape industry competition*
*Source: Porter, 2008 [1985], 4*

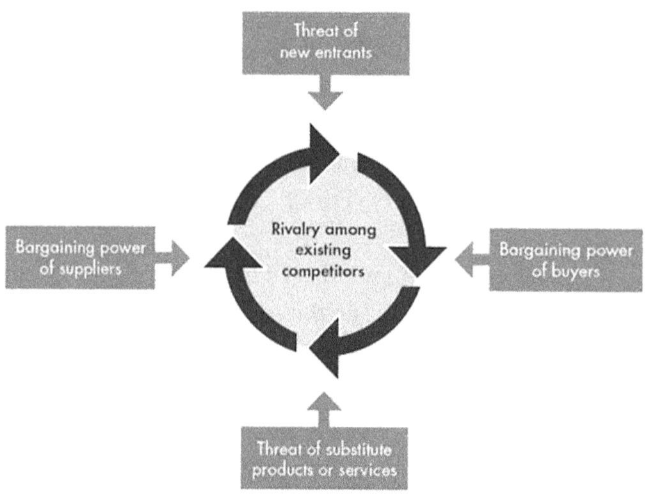

It is therefore important to take into account the circumstances that are associated with high levels of competition, as well as indicators of strong competitive forces that pose an actual or potential threat to industry/sector profits (i.e., making it difficult to achieve high or above-average profits).

One of the major problems of applying this model in practice is the difficulty in defining a specific industry and the adequate boundaries of that industry. Should we study the soft drink industry, the water industry, or the sparkling water industry? The first one is certainly too vague (putting very different forces in the same component of Porter's analysis) and the latter very narrow (excluding too many competitors and artificially increasing the number of substitutes). In a world that does not stop, based on the dichotomy innovate or die, new technologies, new categories, new products appear every day, and it is increasingly more difficult to define what belongs to the same industry or not. Additionally, national borders cease to exist for many industries, whose market is global, and their value and supply chain is completely distributed and spread across several countries. Consider again, for example, what is happening in the automotive industry and the complexity of defining the various players. Moreover, Porter's model does not take into account the effect of time (Dulčić et al., 2012). This means that his Five Forces model is static (Thurlby, 1998), thus, providing only a portrait of what happens at any given moment, not considering the speed of change and current transformation.

Be that as it may, this is an external analysis tool, intended to detect the balance of forces within an industry, so that the company, based on its resources, can design the most appropriate strategy: product differentiation, product segmentation market, or creating greater barriers to entry, for example. Unfortunately, based on this framework, *strategic managers will often rest their decisions on familiar mental models* (Stead & Stead, 2019, 75).

## Internal Analysis

The Resource-Based View (RBV), which has evolved into the Resource-Based Theory (RBT), focuses on the attributes of a company that are unique or the costs to imitate are just too high. The ability of the company to gain and maintain a certain position in the market depends on its ability to access and control strategic resources, i.e., the success of any firm depends on its resources. Thus, RBV *explains how firms achieve competitive advantage and economic rents through ownership and management of assets, capabilities, knowledge, and similar internal resources.* (Miller, 2019, 1). These resources could be tangible, intangible, or human. For example, facilities or knowledge, access to funding or human capital.

Human and intangible resources are often overlooked. For example, culture (which is the most intangible of all) can be very valuable because it includes:

- the way companies work,
- their routines,
- their symbols and *heroes*,
- their values,
- their behavior.

However, when financial analysis is conducted, culture is usually not included.

Reputation, for its part, is all about trust between the company and the community. It is the association that stakeholders establish about the company and its brand. It is the deeper reason why the consumer is willing to pay more for the product or service of a particular company. Undoubtedly, it is an important source of competitive advantage for companies. It cannot be bought or imitated, in other words, you either have it or you don't!

Human capital is a very difficult resource to assess, but on which companies depends completely. Firms can only change continually with motivated, well-prepared human capital. Thus, firms are different because they possess a unique combination of heterogeneous resources: not all resources contribute in the same way to obtaining competitive advantage. *Competitive advantage is the advantage that a firm (a) has over its competitors, (b) develops using its resources, and (c) uses to drive superior performance* (Gupta, Tan, Ee, & Phang, 2018, 2).

However, as Grant claims, RBV is based on two premises: *First, internal resources and capabilities provide the basic direction for a firm's strategy and, second, resources and capabilities are the primary source of profit for the firm* (Grant, 1991, 116).

A consensus has not been reached in the extant literature regarding which resource traits are considered factors of competitiveness in the long term. According to Barney (1991), resources must be valuable (exploit opportunities and neutralize threats with the objective of long-run profit), rare (representing a differential between the company and its competitors), not perfectly imitable and without substitutes (since different resources can generate similar results).

Thus, to achieve sustainable competitive advantage companies must have VRIN resources: Valuable, Rare, Inimitable, and Non-substitutable resources. This framework examines the firm's stock of resources, which means that it is a static analysis. If companies have the right stock of resources, they will obtain sustainable competitive advantage.

Later, Barney (1995) realized that having a stock of the right resources is not enough, so he improved his model and created the VRIO model. It is not enough for firms to have Valuable, Rare, Inimitable and Non-substitutable resources, they must be Organized in order to capture the value of these resources (see figure 2).

*Figure 2. Core competencies as sources of competitive advantage: the VRIO framework*
*Source: https://www.researchgate.net/publication/286622222_Innovation_as_a_source_of_competitive_advantage_the_case_of_Nespresso/figures?lo=1*

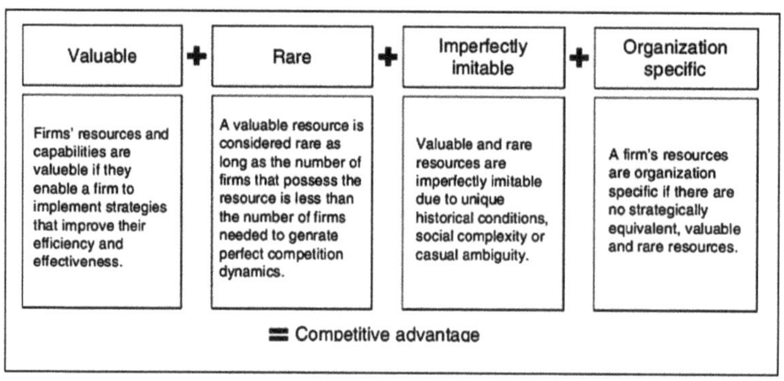


This means that not all resources contribute to competitive advantage as well as not all companies have the organizational capacity to use them. Organizational abilities are the basis of the firm's competitive advantage (Sharma and Vredenburg, 1998; Kusunoki, Nonaka & Nagat, 1998). These abilities are based on the organization of resources to achieve a certain objective (Amit & Schoemaker, 1993; Helfat & Lieberman, 2002).

These criteria could be used as a tool (see Table 1) to evaluate whether companies have adequate resources to achieve sustainable competitive advantage.

*Table 1. The VRIO Model*

| Is the Resource | | | | Competitive Implications |
|---|---|---|---|---|
| **Valuable?** | **Rare?** | **Inimitable?** | **Supported by the Organization?** | |
| No | - | - | No | Competitive disadvantage |
| Yes | No | - | | Competitive parity |
| Yes | Yes | No | | Temporary competitive advantage |
| Yes | Yes | Yes | Yes | Sustainable Competitive Advantage |

Source: Barney and Hesterly (2010)

## Traditional Strategic Paradigm

According to the traditional strategic paradigm, the first step in devising a strategy is making a diagnosis based on internal analysis and external analysis to achieve sustainable competitive advantage (see figure 3).

*Figure 3. Traditional Strategic Paradigm*

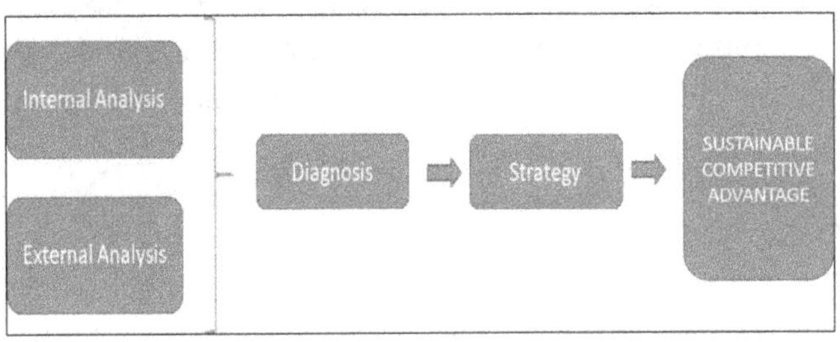


During this process, time never stops. Nevertheless, firms choose options based on a prior analysis and implement their strategy following a preestablished design. Therefore, there are many temporary lags and often the *greatest enemy of tomorrow's success is today's success*. Nokia, Kodak and IBM are notable examples of this situation. They designed a strategy based on their past success, updating their bestselling products and creating new versions, but they never asked themselves how radically the world had changed.

Firms change and the environment changes as well, but it is assumed that, at the end of this process, firms achieve sustainable competitive advantage. Accordingly, firms design a strategy to implement over long time periods (usually years). It is infrequent to restructure or reformulate the designed strategy. If the results do not live up to expectations, it is often assumed that the company did not achieve sustainable competitive advantage because of inadequate execution. However, it is important to understand that:

given the ease with which everything changes; given the uncertainty of what goes on and how it will evolve; given the complexity of the relationships established, both internally and externally; given the subjectivity of the diagnosis, the strategy cannot necessarily be designed with certainty and precision. Similarly, even after designing a strategy, the world is still changing. These changes are neither clear nor predictable, consequently, when the strategy is implemented, it may already be inadequate and outdated. So, *accentuating the previously planned strategy can reduce temporal responsiveness*. (Pina e Cunha, Gomes, Mellahi, Miner, & Rego, 2020, np).

According to Hollingworth (2016, 20), *in seasons of stable weather, this strategy is successful. However, when things become volatile and uncertain — when unexpected events such as unseasonal weather and avalanches and earthquakes occur — the strategy falls apart. The true nature of the strategy is revealed: too linear, too rigid and unable to tolerate the unexpected.* Moreover, *[i]n a world where a competitive advantage often evaporates in less than a year, companies can't afford to spend months at a time crafting a single long-term strategy* (McGrath, 2013a, 67). In this context, Lin, Hsu, Hsu, and Chung (2020) argue that maybe firms cannot enjoy sustainable competitive advantages, but they can pursue consecutively temporary competitive advantages, based on an ambidextrous strategy.

Ambidexterity involves engaging in two apparently conflicting activities at the same time. More usually it is seen as the *ability of an organization to both explore and exploit* (O'Reilly III & Tushman, 2013, 324). Thus, ambidextrous firms are concerned with the present and the future, and they are *aligned and efficient in their management of today's business demands while simultaneously adaptative to changes in the environment* (Raish & Birkinshaw, 2008, 375). In this context, Lin, Hsu, Hsu, and Chung (2020) argue that perhaps firms cannot enjoy sustainable competitive advantages, but based on ambidextrous strategy, they can pursue consecutively temporary competitive advantages. In the same line, Cegarra-Navarro (2005, 3) claims that dynamic capacities *help to renew existing strategies, which foster new adjustments in case of changing environments*. These capacities are based on routines (Eisenhardt & Martín, 2000) or regular actions (Kurtmollaiev, 2020). Therefore, if ambidexterity is based on adaptative changes, and dynamic capacities are based on routines or regular actions, they lack strategic agility.

## THE VUCA WORLD

VUCA is military in origin, an acronym used by the United States Army in the post-Cold War era, defined as follows: *Volatility stands for the speed, magnitude, and dynamics of change, while uncertainty describes the unpredictability of issues and events. Complexity stands for the chaos that surrounds all organizations* (Kornelsen, 2019, 32), and ambiguity describes the unclear, mixed meaning of many situations and conditions (see figure 4). Also, *VUCA describes the nature of the change that the world is currently facing: its parameters describe how change will affect us on a daily basis. We can already see it happening; the business landscape is becoming more volatile and uncertain. It is more ambiguous, especially as the rate of technological innovation increases day by day. This technological innovation is leading to increased interconnectedness across the globe, which is in turn resulting in increased complexity* (Hollingworth, 2016, 8).

It is important to note that these dimensions are not linear, they have multiple interpretations and levels.

*Complexity can be defined as a situation, where interconnectedness of parts and variables is so high, that the same external conditions and inputs can lead to very different outputs or reactions of the system* (Mack & Khare, 2015, 8). Companies have to deal with internal and external complexity. The external complexity may even be higher if companies work with or for different generations (Kornelsen, 2019), and in different countries and cultures. So, complexity is a central concept in the current world.

*Figure 4. What VUCA really means*
*Source: Bennett and Lemoine, 2014b, 27*

| Complexity<br>Characteristics: The situation has many interconnected parts and variables. Some information is available or can be predicted, but the volume or nature of it can be overwhelming to process.<br><br>Example: You are doing business in many countries, all with unique regulatory environments, tariffs, and cultural values. | Volatility<br>Characteristics: The challenge is unexpected or unstable and may be of unknown duration, but it is not necessarily hard to understand; knowledge about it is often available.<br><br>Example: Prices fluctuate after a natural disaster takes a supplier off-line |
|---|---|
| Ambiguity<br>Characteristics: Causal relationships are completely unclear. No precedents exist; you face "unknown unknowns."<br><br>Example: You decide to move into immature or emerging markets or to launch products outside your core competencies. | Uncertainty<br>Characteristics: Despite a lack of other information, the event's basic cause and effect are known. Change is possible but not given.<br><br>Example: A competitor's pending product launch muddies the future of the business and the market. |

Vertical axis: How well can you predict the results of your actions? (- to +)
Horizontal axis: How much do you know about the situation? (- to +)

Uncertainty can be defined as a lack of certainty. Unlike risk, in situations of uncertainty, it is not possible to define a probability distribution for possible outcomes. There are three different kinds of environmental uncertainty: state, effect, and response uncertainty. Uncertainty is a real problem, even more in the decision-making process and when firms are designing and implement their strategy.

Ambiguity is related to the lack of assurance about the right answer. It seems that there are multiple possible solutions to all situations, so everything is ambiguous and undefined. The rationality is limited and it is impossible to know everything. Hence, the most pernicious part is that the decision-makers do not know what they cannot know.

In a volatile world, there is a lot of change and everything is temporary. Thus, volatility is *a dynamically changing social context* (Gupta & Gupta, 2018, 90). It is a *relatively unstable change*, in which information might be available and the situation might be understandable, *but change is frequent and sometimes unpredictable*. (Gupta & Gupta, 2018, 104).

In summary, the problem is not the volatility, the uncertainty, the complexity, or the ambiguity; the big problem is the VUCAlization of the world, with all these four dimensions together.

VUCA is a natural result of three major forces: Technology, People, and Places.

*Volatility is expressed in the need for technological change and speed. Uncertainty as a lack of predictability is a central concern of technology. The complexity surrounding an institution is a constant technological challenge. Ambiguity characterizes the typical context of technology* (Nandram & Bindlish, 2017, 10). This is happening in a new world, where people are interconnected, and they do not live in isolation anymore. It is very important to understand that people and teams are absolutely necessary for change to take place. This new integrative world connects different cultures, different religions, different paths, and different knowledge. This is happening not only virtually, but in the real world too, based on technology.

Knowledge is being shared much faster, hence the capacity for learning and adaptation must be much faster too. For companies, this is a big challenge and sometimes it means misunderstandings and failure. At the same time, firms must be flexible, understanding what is happening and taking action, which means they must have an agility advantage.

So, in a VUCA world companies need to develop VUCA behavior, based on Velocity, Unusualness, Clarity, and Adaptability. Velocity means that firms must understand they cannot stop at any time and must have the capacity to react quickly in an Unusual way. Growing incrementally is no longer an option. Firms must accept that the world is changing, and they must change too in order to adapt to the VUCA world. In brief, firms must develop strategic agility, which means firms must adopt *timely decision-making to execute business strategies in advance of or in reaction to ongoing environmental trends* (Glaister, Ahmad, and Gomes, 2015, 1). To support this idea, researchers (see, for example, Leybourn, 2013) talk about the AGILE Organizations.

The AGILE Model (see Figure 5) considers that it is necessary to Anticipate change, to Generate confidence, to Initiate action, to Liberate thinking, and to Evaluate results. Consequently, a firm with an AGILE leader anticipates the changes and prepares for them. In these organizations *people and capacity can be rearranged and recombined creatively and quickly without major structural change* (Horney, Pasmore, O'Shea, 2010, 4). Wade et al. (2019) further argue that there should be a CTO$^2$ (Chief Transformational Officer). *Leading the continuous shifts in people, processes, technology, and structure requires the capability to sense and respond with actions that are focused, fast and flexible* (Horney, Pasmore, & O'Shea, 2010).

Eisenhardt and Martin (2000) recognize that in rapidly changing dynamic markets it is not possible to sustain a competitive advantage. This leads to *[a] situation in which there is a lot of very strong competition between companies, markets are changing very quickly, and it is easy to enter a new market so that it is not possible for one company to keep a competitive advantage for a long time* (Financial Times). That is, it is no longer possible to sustain a competitive advantage, as the basis for competition is consistently changing, market leadership is being continually threatened, surpassed, and altered, leading to a constant market imbalance.

Today, hypercompetition has spread to practically every sector, to *airline, pharmaceutical, financial services, health care, consumer electronics, telecommunications, broadcasting, auditing, automotive, and computer industries, among many others.* (D'Aveni, 1998, 183). Indeed, the intensity and type of competition has shifted in sectors ranging *from microchips to corn chips, software to soft drinks, and packaged goods to package delivery services* (idem).

*Figure 5. The AGILE Model*
*Source: Horney et al, (2010, 36)*

| THE AGILE MODEL® | | LEADERSHIP AGILITY SKILLS |
|---|---|---|
| FOCUSED | **A**nticipate Change | **VISIONEERING** – creating clarity on the core value proposition of the enterprise engineered into what the workforce does every day to produce desired outcomes for all stakeholders |
| | | **SENSING** – understanding forces of change that influence stakeholder success and creation of early warming systems of impending change that can impact success |
| | | **MONITORING** – having effective processes for tracking performance and trends to identify patterns that impact the organization |
| | **G**enerate Confidence | **CONNECTING** – establishing clear line of sight for all stakeholders with how each can contribute to the enterprise and person success |
| FAST | | **ALIGNING** – establishing and living the congruence of vision, value, priorities and actions |
| | | **ENGAGING** – operating with high levels of inclusion and a climate that delivers the discretionary level of effort from all stakeholders |
| | **I**nitiate Action | **BIAS FOR ACTION** – establishing an execution culture where a sense of urgency around improvement and all stakeholder satisfaction is a basic shared expectation |
| | | **DECISION MAKING** – creating capability for fast, effective decision-making at all levels |
| | | **COLLABORATING** – encouraging ideas and gaining insights across organizational boundaries and from multiple stakeholders |
| | **L**iberate Thinking | **BIAS FOR INNOVATION** – establishing permission and expectations that innovation is a universal requirement for all stakeholders' participation |
| FLEXIBLE | | **CUSTOMER FOCUS** – establishing on-going alignment and understanding of customers to be able to offer business solutions that meet their needs and often identify unrecognized needs |
| | | **IDEA DIVERSITY** – establishing processes to encourage and secure innovation inputs from all levels and stakeholders in the enterprise |
| | **E**valuate Results | **CREATING EXPECTATIONS** – providing clear and measurable priorities and resources that are aligned for all stakeholders and desired outcomes |
| | | **REAL-TIME FEEDBACK** – providing timely and accurate feedback on key success measures for all stakeholders |
| | | **FACT-BASED MEASUREMENT** – using performance metrics grounded in solid information measurement to allow reliable insights and conclusions |

The big problem of this new reality is that any new and innovative product or technology becomes obsolete very quickly: no one can maintain a sustainable competitive advantage. Consequently, markets are always unbalanced. *For decades, firms sought to sustain a competitive advantage, seen as the 'holy grail' of strategy, but they find this impossible in hyper-competitive environments.* (ibidem). In 2000, the GE annual report notes: *We've long believed that when the rate of change inside an institution becomes slower than the rate of change outside, the end is in sight. The only question is when.*

Hypercompetition results from four major forces: more demanding consumers, technology development, falling entry barriers, and deep pockets.

Consumers are well-informed, their knowledge about products and services is significant, so they demand increasingly more developed products immediately. They do not want to wait, and they do not admit being unsatisfied.

Technologies mean firms can improve their products quickly, creating new solutions and improved versions: the window of opportunity is becoming smaller.

*The third force driving hypercompetition is falling entry barriers, both those around nations and those around industries.* This makes competition even more hyper since new solutions, products and versions could come from any other country or sector.

*To make matters worse, a fourth driving force underlying hypercompetition is the use of deep pockets.* (D'Aveni, 1998, 186), which means groups of firms helping one another. Hence, competition is no longer one-on-one.

In this context, it is impossible to sustain a competitive advantage. Long-term advantages no longer exist, and firms must understand this. Long-term advantages result from a series of temporary advantages. McGrath (2013a, 62) goes further, pointing out that *the era of sustainable competitive advantage is over*: only transient advantage exists. *It is through reconfiguration that assets, people and capabilities make the transition from one advantage to another* (idem).

Hypercompetition puts high pressure on the firms' capacity to manage change, to be flexible and adaptive. They must be a changing organism, within a new approach based on reconfiguration (Table 2), combining dynamism and stability.

*Table 2. The new strategy playbook: reconfiguration*

| From | To |
|---|---|
| Extreme downsizing and restructuring<br>Bulk of emphasis on arenas in exploitation phase<br>Stability or dynamism alone<br>Narrowly defined jobs and roles<br>Stable vision, monolithic execution | Continuous morphing and changing<br>Equal emphasis on all phases of a competitive life cycle within an arena<br>Stability combined with dynamism<br>Fluidity in allocation of talent<br>Stable vision, variety in execution |

Source: McGrath, 2013b, 18

This stability is fundamental, for example, in social architecture to limit organizational uncertainty. At the same time, firms must invest in creating a stable vision, culture, and values, creating a *sense* of identity. *Smart companies recognize that continuous training and development is a mechanism to avoid having to fire people when competitive conditions shift* (McGrath, 2013b, 18). All these erase the uncertainty stakeholders could feel in a VUCA world.

With this idea of stability, change and dynamism is a natural thing, not a dramatic one. Whenever we talk about transformation, managers and employees feel some discomfort. However, if the idea is to be natural and continuous, it will not cause shock. Firms do not need to restructure, downsize and fire people – change is embedded in all their daily activities. *They reallocate resources flexibly and on an ongoing basis, rather than going through sudden divestitures or restructurings.* (McGrath, 2013b, 19).

## CONCLUSION: IS STRATEGY DEAD?

*The hierarchical structures and organizational processes we have used for decades to run and improve our enterprises are no longer up to the task of winning in this faster-moving world.* (Kotter, 2012). Moreover, as Hamel (1998, 8) points out, *in a discontinuous world, strategy innovation is the key to wealth creation. Strategy innovation is the capacity to reconceive the existing industry model in ways that create new value for customers, wrong-foot competitors, and produce new wealth for all stakeholders.* Klaus Schwab, founder and chairman of the World Economic Forum, claims that: *In the new world, it is not the big fish which eats the small fish, it's the fast fish which eats the slow fish.* (Holland, 2020, 3).

Big companies have large projects with heavy structures and established routines, which makes them less agile and more complex. It is imperative for these companies to be able to simplify processes, reduce bureaucracy and combat silo mentality, maintaining more cohesive relationships among departments. Communication will be better and information will flow more quickly, leading to a faster and more efficient reaction. These companies, therefore, need to strengthen their internal networks. At the same time, small and medium-sized firms have to deal with the VUCA world and rapid transformation, but they lack many of the required skills and capacities. To solve this problem, they must increase complexity, working in collaborative transformational networks. The firms' flexibility is embodied in evolving networks of interdependence both within the firm and among firms (Qian & Gu, 2020).

Thus, the answer to the question "Is strategy dead?" is: "No"! Nevertheless, a very profound change in the mindset of managers, tools, conventions, and practices is required. As Drucker (1993 [1980], 12) puts it, *[a] time of turbulence is a dangerous time, but its greatest danger is a temptation to deny reality.* Denying reality is to act as if nothing has changed, with the same logic of the past. If firms deny this changing reality, they will be stuck in yesterday. *Currently the field of strategic management is in the middle of a paradigmatic shift similar to the one that took place over 40 years ago when the internal, conceptual model of business policy and planning was questioned and then changed to the externally, focused paradigm of strategic management.* (Stead & Stead, 2019, 67).

Today, strategy, transformational strategy, is even more necessary. However, it is important to note:

1. it is no longer possible to sustain a competitive advantage;
2. firms only achieve a transient advantage;
3. you will not survive alone;
4. being VUCA in a VUCA world is not enough; firms must be VUCAS – Velocity, Unusualness, Clarity, and Adaptability must be Stable characteristics of the firms' identity. Velocity is mandatory. It is no longer possible to develop well-structured, time-consuming analysis processes. In these new circumstances, by the time firms conclude the process, the results are already outdated. Unusualness is fundamental, as replicating the same old models and frameworks will widen the gap between the solution and reality. Clarity is central so that change is accepted inside organizations. Transparency and shared information are needed. If it is not clear why firms are changing, firms will face great resistance internally. Adaptability must be a constant; firms must be prepared to decide and adapt and readapt if necessary. Firms need these four characteristics to be agile. Last but least, stability is the basis of it all. Stability of identity, making all the other characteristics natural and continuous.

As noted by Leavy, *[t]hese sources of stability provide the ballast that allows these successful firms to restructure, realign, reconfigure and redeploy in a continuous, flexible, fast and almost seamless fashion.* (Leavy, 2014, 6). However, this change should not be abrupt so as to avoid inside instability (Botes & Pretorius, 2020). Thus, the non-identical twins – agility and stability – are the basis of this new era. Once again, firms must be ambidextrous. It is fundamental they be stable and agile at the same time; only with agility and stability can firms operate transformation harmoniously. Organizations need to be aware of this transition and prepared for it.

With this chapter, we intended to highlight that firms need different tools and frameworks to deal with future situations, that designing a strategy is not enough. In current times, following a transformational – VUCAS – strategy is crucial to success. In this new context, firms must be increasingly agile, or they will be increasingly fragile (Holland, 2020).

## REFERENCES

Amit, R., & Schoemaker, P. J. (1993). Strategic assets and organizational rent. *Strategic Management Journal*, *14*(1), 33–46. doi:10.1002mj.4250140105

Barney, J. (1991). Firm resources and sustained competitive advantage. *Journal of Management*, *17*(1), 99–120. doi:10.1177/014920639101700108

Barney, J. B. (1995). Looking inside for competitive advantage. *The Academy of Management Perspectives*, *9*(4), 49–61. doi:10.5465/ame.1995.9512032192

Barney, J. B., & Hesterly, W. S. (2010). VRIO framework. *Strategic Management and Competitive Advantage*, 68-86.

Bennett, N., & Lemoine, G. J. (2014a). What a difference a word makes: Understanding threats to performance in a VUCA world. *Business Horizons*, *57*(3), 311–317. doi:10.1016/j.bushor.2014.01.001

Bennett, N., & Lemoine, J. (2014b). What VUCA really means for you. *Harvard Business Review*, *92*(1/2), 27.

Botes, M., & Pretorius, M. (2020). Exploring management perceptions of competitive versus transient advantage. *Journal of Contemporary Management*, *17*(1), 41–63. doi:10.35683/jcm19052.55

Cegarra-Navarro, J. G. (2005). An empirical investigation of organizational learning through strategic alliances between SMEs. *Journal of Strategic Marketing*, *13*(1), 3–16. doi:10.1080/0965254042000328686

D'Aveni, R. A. (1998). Waking up to the new era of hypercompetition. *The Washington Quarterly*, *21*(1), 183–195. doi:10.1080/01636609809550302

D'Aveni, R. A., & Gunther, R. E. (1995). *Hypercompetitive rivalries: Competing in highly dynamic environments*. Free Pr.

Drucker, P. F. (1993). *Managing in turbulent times*. Routledge.

Dulčić, Ž., Gnjidić, V., & Alfirević, N. (2012). From Five Competitive Forces to Five Collaborative Forces: Revised View on Industry Structure-firm Interrelationship. *Procedia: Social and Behavioral Sciences*, *58*, 1077–1084. doi:10.1016/j.sbspro.2012.09.1088

Eisenhardt, K. M., & Martin, J. A. (2000). Dynamic capabilities: What are they? *Strategic Management Journal*, *21*(10-11), 1105–1121. doi:10.1002/1097-0266(200010/11)21:10/11<1105::AID-SMJ133>3.0.CO;2-E

Flint, G. F. (2000). What is the meaning of competitive advantage? *Advances in Competitiveness Research*, *8*(1), 121–129.

Grant, R. M. (1991). The resource-based theory of competitive advantage: Implications for strategy formulation. *California Management Review*, *33*(3), 114–135. doi:10.2307/41166664

Grundy, T. (2006). Rethinking and reinventing Michael Porter's five forces model. *Strategic Change*, *15*(5), 213–229. doi:10.1002/jsc.764

Gupta, D., & Gupta, V. (2018). Effective Policing in a VUCA Environment: Lessons from a Dark Network. In *Flexible Strategies in VUCA Markets* (pp. 89–111). Springer. doi:10.1007/978-981-10-8926-8_7

Gupta, G., Tan, K. T. L., Ee, Y. S., & Phang, C. S. C. (2018). Resource-based view of information systems: Sustainable and transient competitive advantage perspectives. *AJIS. Australasian Journal of Information Systems*, *22*, 22. doi:10.3127/ajis.v22i0.1657

Hamel, G. (1998). Opinion: Strategy innovation and the quest for value. *Sloan Management Review*, *39*(2), 7–14.

Helfat, C. E., & Lieberman, M. B. (2002). The birth of capabilities: Market entry and the importance of pre-history. *Industrial and Corporate Change*, *11*(4), 725–760. doi:10.1093/icc/11.4.725

Holland, S. (2020). Project Management in an Increasingly Fr (Agile). *WORLD (Oakland, Calif.)*.

Hollingworth, P. (2016). *The Light and Fast Organisation: A new way of dealing with uncertainty*. John Wiley & Sons.

Horney, N., Pasmore, B., & O'Shea, T. (2010). Leadership agility: A business imperative for a VUCA world. *Human Resource Planning*, *33*(4), 34.

Johnson, G., Scholes, K., & Whittington, R. (2008). *Exploring corporate strategy: text & cases*. Pearson Education.

Klein, J. (2002). Beyond competitive advantage. *Strategic Change*, *11*(6), 317–327. doi:10.1002/jsc.606

Kornelsen, J. (2019). The quest to lead (with) millennials in a VUCA-world: Bridging the gap between generations. In *Leading in a VUCA World* (pp. 27–41). Springer. doi:10.1007/978-3-319-98884-9_2

Kotter, J. (2012). How the most innovative companies capitalize on today's rapid-fire strategic challenges-and still make their numbers. *Harvard Business Review*, *90*(11), 43–58. PMID:23155997

Kurtmollaiev, S. (2020). Dynamic capabilities and where to find them. *Journal of Management Inquiry*, *29*(1), 3–16. doi:10.1177/1056492617730126

Kusunoki, K., Nonaka, I., & Nagata, A. (1998). Organizational capabilities in product development of Japanese firms: A conceptual framework and empirical findings. *Organization Science*, *9*(6), 699–718. doi:10.1287/orsc.9.6.699

Leavy, B. (2014). Strategy, organization and leadership in a new "transient-advantage" world. *Strategy and Leadership*, *42*(4), 3–13. doi:10.1108/SL-05-2014-0038

Leybourn, E. (2013). *Directing the Agile organisation: A lean approach to business management*. IT Governance Ltd.

Lin, H. E., Hsu, I. C., Hsu, A. W., & Chung, H. M. (2020). Creating competitive advantages: Interactions between ambidextrous diversification strategy and contextual factors from a dynamic capability perspective. *Technological Forecasting and Social Change*, *154*, 119952. doi:10.1016/j.techfore.2020.119952

Mack, O., & Khare, A. (2015). Perspectives on a VUCA world. In O. Mack, A. Khare, A. Krämer, & T. Burgartz (Eds.), *Managing in a VUCA World*. Springer.

McGrath, R. (2013b). Continuous reconfiguration in the transient advantage economy. *Strategy and Leadership*, *41*(5), 17–22. doi:10.1108/SL-05-2013-0039

McGrath, R. G. (2013a). Transient advantage. *Harvard Business Review*, *91*(6), 62–70.

Miller, D. (2019). The Resource-Based View of the Firm. In Oxford Research Encyclopedia of Business and Management. doi:10.1093/acrefore/9780190224851.013.4

Muneer, M. (2019). Knowledge Sharing is Key to Win in the Transient Advantage Era. *NHRD Network Journal*, *12*(2), 87–96. doi:10.1177/2631454119832391

Nandram, S. S., & Bindlish, P. K. (2017). Introduction to VUCA. In *Managing VUCA Through Integrative Self-Management* (pp. 3–14). Springer. doi:10.1007/978-3-319-52231-9_1

O'Reilly, C. A. III, & Tushman, M. L. (2013). Organizational ambidexterity: Past, present, and future. *The Academy of Management Perspectives*, *27*(4), 324–338. doi:10.5465/amp.2013.0025

Pina e Cunha, M. P., Gomes, E., Mellahi, K., Miner, A. S., & Rego, A. (2020). Strategic agility through improvisational capabilities: Implications for a paradox-sensitive HRM. *Human Resource Management Review*, *30*(1), 100695. doi:10.1016/j.hrmr.2019.100695

Porter, M. E. (1989). How competitive forces shape strategy. In *Readings in strategic management* (pp. 133–143). Palgrave. doi:10.1007/978-1-349-20317-8_10

Porter, M. E. (1991). *Michael E. Porter on competition and strategy*. Harvard Business School Press.

Porter, M. E. (2008). *Competitive strategy: Techniques for analyzing industries and competitors*. Simon and Schuster.

Pröllochs, N., & Feuerriegel, S. (2020). Business analytics for strategic management: Identifying and assessing corporate challenges via topic modeling. *Information & Management*, *57*(1), 103070. doi:10.1016/j.im.2018.05.003

Qian, C., Yu, K., & Gu, H. (2020). Flexibility mechanisms in a dynamic distribution network. *Journal of Business & Industrial Marketing*. ahead-of-print.

Raisch, S., & Birkinshaw, J. (2008). Organizational ambidexterity: Antecedents, outcomes, and moderators. *Journal of Management*, *34*(3), 375–409. doi:10.1177/0149206308316058

Sharma, S., & Vredenburg, H. (1998). Proactive corporate environmental strategy and the development of competitively valuable organizational capabilities. *Strategic Management Journal*, *19*(8), 729–753. doi:10.1002/(SICI)1097-0266(199808)19:8<729::AID-SMJ967>3.0.CO;2-4

Stead, J. G., & Stead, W. E. (2019). Why Porter Is Not Enough: Economic Foundations of Sustainable Strategic Management. In *Rethinking Strategic Management* (pp. 67–85). Springer. doi:10.1007/978-3-030-06014-5_4

Thurlby, B. (1998). Competitive forces are also subject to change. *Management Decision*, *36*(1), 19–24. doi:10.1108/00251749810199202

Wade, M., Macaulay, J., Noronha, A., & Barbier, J. (2019). Orchestrating Transformation – How to Deliver Winning Performance with a Connected Approach to Change. Global Center for Digital Business Transformation, IMD, Lausanne, Switzerland.

Wiggins, R. R., & Ruefli, T. W. (2005). Schumpeter's ghost: Is hypercompetition making the best of times shorter? *Strategic Management Journal*, *26*(10), 887–911. doi:10.1002mj.492

## ADDITIONAL READING

Child, J. (2015). *Organization: contemporary principles and practice*. John Wiley & Sons. doi:10.1002/9781119176862

Du, J., & Chen, Z. (2018). Applying Organizational Ambidexterity in strategic management under a "VUCA" environment: Evidence from high tech companies in China. *International Journal of Innovation Studies*, *2*(1), 42–52. doi:10.1016/j.ijis.2018.03.003

Gottschalck, N., & Günther, C. (2017). Lost in Transformation: Strategy Formulation in a Digitized World. In The Palgrave Handbook of Managing Continuous Business Transformation (pp. 67-93). Palgrave Macmillan.

Hall, R., Rowland, C., & Stokes, P. (2015, September). New thoughts on leadership in turbulent times. In *8th Annual Conference of the EuroMed-Academy-of-Business, Verona* (pp. 837-849). Academic Press.

Lyngso, S. (2017). *Agile strategy management: techniques for continuous alignment and improvement*. CRC Press. doi:10.1201/9781351122825

Smith, R. (2013). The end of competitive advantage: How to keep your strategy moving as fast as your business. *Research Technology Management*, *56*(5), 64.

van Tulder, R., Verbeke, A., & Jankowska, B. (Eds.). (2019). *International business in a VUCA world: The changing role of states and firms*. Emerald Publishing Limited. doi:10.1108/S1745-8862201914

Waddell, D., Creed, A., Cummings, T. G., & Worley, C. G. (2019). *Organisational change: Development and transformation*. Cengage AU.

## KEY TERMS AND DEFINITIONS

**Agile Model:** Considers that to leads is necessary to Anticipate change, Generate confidence, Initiate action, Liberate thinking, and Evaluate results. Consequently, a firm with an AGILE leader anticipates the changes and prepares for them.

**Hypercompetition:** Is a situation characterized by a constant imbalance in the sector, with high competition between companies, rapid change, and adjustment, which leads to the impossibility of sustaining a competitive advantage.

**Sustainable Competitive Advantage:** Is a competitive advantage based on a VRIO resource, maintained for a long-time period.

**Transient Advantage:** A competitive advantage obtained for a short-period of time, in a logical of continuous change.

**VRIO Resources:** Resources with four characteristics: Value – creates value to the organization offer or improves efficiency; Rare – it is a unique or rare resource; Inimitability – it is hard to imitate or substitute by other; Organization – the organization should have the capacity to recognize and use this resource in an effective way.

**VUCA World:** Is a world in a rapidly changing: meaning that nowadays, firms face a volatile, uncertain, complex, and ambiguous environment.

**VUCAS:** Means that to respond to a VUCA world firms must have five characteristics: Velocity, Unusualness, Clarity, Adaptability, and Stability. Velocity because it is no longer possible to develop well-structured, time-consuming analysis processes. Unusualness is fundamental, as replicating the same old models and frameworks will widen the gap between the solution and reality. Clarity is essential to making change acceptable inside organizations. If it is not clear why firms are changing, they will face great internal resistance. Adaptability must be a constant; firms must be prepared to decide, and adapt, and readapt if necessary. Stability is central, making all the other characteristics natural and continuous.

## ENDNOTES

1 https://mission-statement.com/tesla/

2 Which actually already exists in many companies

# Chapter 2
# Strategic Leadership for New Competitive Environments

**Isabel Torres**
*Lusíada University of Porto, Portugal*

**Alexandra R. Costa**
https://orcid.org/0000-0001-5053-536X
*Instituto Politécnico do Porto, Portugal*

## ABSTRACT

*The subject of leadership has been addressed by many authors in numerous publications. Nevertheless, the focus has been more on the relationship of middle leaders with their employees than on the role of the strategic leader for the performance of organizations. In this chapter, the authors focus on the importance of top leadership, trying to demonstrate its crucial contribution to organizations. They give special importance to the role of the leader in a changing context characterized by volatility, uncertainty, complexity, and ambiguity – The VUCA environment. They define strategic leadership and highlight its impact on organizational results at the individual, team, and organizational levels. They end by addressing the ethical implications of strategic leadership, which has been given relatively little attention by researchers.*

## INTRODUCTION

The scenarios of uncertainty and the complexity of the changes to which organizations are constantly subject require high flexibility and speed of response. The ability to respond favorably to these challenges is anchored in their human capital. Admitting and retaining talent, maximizing its innovative potential, is only possible through strong leadership, inspiring and intrinsically committed to organizational strategy. Thinking leadership as a key of organizational success is to devise it as a means to deal with new and ambiguous problems, identifying exceptional solutions, through collaborators and teams encouraged to pursue shared goals. Thus, we speak about a process that develops at the rhythm of the capacity to harmonize multiple needs and desires, promoting individual and collective development and well-being, based on ethical behavior.

DOI: 10.4018/978-1-7998-1843-4.ch002

In this environment the role of leadership is crucial. The ability of the leader to influence behaviour and mobilize his employees to make them agents of this change, as can easily be predicted, plays a key role. At an early stage, research highlighted the role of the middle leader by ostracizing the contribution of top leadership. Today, authors believe in the importance of this strategic leadership, namely in its ability to perpetuate the future of the organization, develop a long-term vision and mobilize employees. Nevertheless, the importance of this top leadership is not just about their ability to define long-term strategies but also about their ability to operationalize them.

In the organizational context, particularly in large organizations, a special role is reserved for top leaders, namely the Top Management Team (TMT) headed by the Chief Executive Officer (CEO), who is responsible for defining policies and strategies that will allow the organization to operationalize their vision for the organization. Leadership in general and strategic leadership in particular is considered by many to be a key element in the implementation of organizational strategy (Palladan, Abdulkadir, & Chong, 2016).

In this chapter we will focus on this strategic leadership that some consider playing a key role in organizational performance. We will seek to emphasize their role in a context of major challenges for organizations, with ever-changing and greater diversity including their workforce.

## LEADING IN VUCA ENVIRONMENTS

The importance of leadership in organizations is undisputed. In fact, the performance of an organization can even be dramatically affected by a small group of people who take on leadership roles as, Banzato and Sierra (2016) point out, it is closely linked to the strategic decisions made by the people who work based on their motivations but also on their own circumstances. A huge challenge is now posed to these leaders that relates to the fact that never in the history of humanity has there been such great volatility of circumstances and such a rapid speed of change. In this context, even the most skillful of leaders see their skills become obsolete as the same time the organizations change (Lawrence, 2013).

Some authors, such as Friedman, (2005) argue that this rapidity of change is leading to the emergence of a new organizational environment that has been called VUCA environment. This designation, which originated in military contexts, is intended to describe the dynamic nature of today's world characterized by Volatility, Instability, Uncertaintly, and Ambiguity (Horney, Pasmore, & O'Shea, 2010; Lawrence, 2013).

With Volatility, authors want to highlight the role of market turbulence, a factor more important today than in the past. Organizations today operate in increasingly unpredictable environments where the nature, speed, volume, and magnitude of change do not follow previously established patterns. There are several drivers of this business volatility, including digitalization, market globalization, connectivity, business model innovation, among others (Lawrence, 2013).

On the other hand, changes that occur in organizations are increasingly disruptive. In this context of uncertainty, the past is no longer a good predictor of the future, making predictions is extremely challenging and the process of decision making increasingly difficult. In this environment of uncertainty, it is extremely difficult for organizations and its leaders to foresee and prepare for what will come next (Lawrence, 2013).

Organizations are also increasingly complex and operate in environments at various chaotic levels. Problems often have diverse causes and never tried solutions. An example of the complexity currently facing organizations and their leaders is the increase in diversity as a result of the process of economic globalization, increasing mobility, aging of the working population, intensification and transversely of women's role integration, minority integration and legal imperatives. More than favoring diversity through intercultural management, it is crucial to ensure the psychological experience of inclusion. This means the promotion of feelings of belonging and personal appreciation, the subjective perception of being able to act spontaneously and integration in a fair environment (Ferdman, Barrera, Allen, & Vuong, 2009).

It is easy to understand the imperative of top management to invest in building an inclusive environment, once the underlying competitive advantages are known, such as greater decision robustness in the face of complex problems, the quality of decisions, greater approximation and adjustment to different markets, the increase in creativity and innovation, which eventually mirrors the results (Mazur, 2010). Takayama, Kaplan and Cook-Sather (2017) also highlight the importance of strategic decisions regarding micro, meso and macro organizational levels being committed to a process of change that favors truly inclusive environments.

While recognizing the challenges inherent in diversity-based environments, particularly with regard to conflict potential and decision time (Mazur, 2010), authors such as Mor Barak (2011) highlight the irreversible tendency for a clear increase in diversity of the workforce, which is why it must be given attention by the main organizational decision makers. Based on the ideas of Maxwell et al. and Wilson and Iles, the authors Jonsen, Maznevski and Schneider (2011) highpoints the strategic character of diversity management.

In this context, the leader is expected to be able to foresee and deal with a world characterized by diversity and ever-changing, provoking changes in people and organizational contexts, speed and flexibility in decision making and responsiveness to constant changes in the organizational context. (Horney, Pasmore, & O'Shea, 2010; Lawrence, 2013)

Ambiguity is another feature of this new world. With it the authors intend to refer to the difficulty of clearly defining the meaning of a given event.

In this context the leader's own profile must also be adjusted. Johansen quoted by Lawrence (2013) proposes that the leader VUCA should be characterized by vision, understanding, clarity, and agility.

In a book published in 2012 entitled "Leaders make the future: ten new leadership skills for an uncertain world", Johansen argues that this VUCA environment will be worse in the future, meaning the environment will be increasingly volatile, uncertain, complex and ambiguous; The VUCA world will bring dangers but also opportunities for organizations; In this context, leaders will be asked to develop new skills as a way to prepare for the future and new approaches to leadership development and executive training will be needed (Johansen, 2012). The author conclude that "in order to increase their readiness and ability to make the future, leaders must immerse themselves in the future and return to the present ready to make a better future" (Johansen, 2012, p.3).

In this way, and to be successful in the future, a new leadership profile will be required. Johansen (2012), describes the skills, abilities, competencies, and traits that together create a leadership profile for the future. According to the author, the 10 leadership skillsets needed in the future are as follows:

1. **The Maker Instinct:** The ability to its instinct to build and grow things, as well as connect with others.
2. **Clarity:** The ability to see what others cannot yet see.
3. **Dilemma Flipping:** The ability to turn dilemmas into advantages and opportunities.

4. **Immersive Learning:** The ability to immerse himself in unfamiliar environments, and learn from them.
5. **Bio-Empathy:** The ability to understand, respect, and learn from natures' patterns.
6. **Constructive Depolarizing:** The ability to calm tense situations and bring people from divergent cultures toward positive engagement.
7. **Quiet Transparency**: The ability to be open and authentic about what matters.
8. **Rapid Prototyping**: The ability to create and innovate.
9. **Smart-Mob Organizing:** The ability to create, engage with, and nurture purposeful business or social change networks through intelligent use of electronic and other media.
10. **Commons Creating:** The ability to seed, nurture and grow shared assets that can benefit all players.

## DEFINING LEADERSHIP

Defining the concept of leadership is not a simple task, not only because of the complexity of the concept but also because it is similar to others that may be close or even overlapping. An example of this is the relationship between leadership and management, a recurring theme in the literature that is divided between those who defend the mutual exclusivity of concepts and the proponents of their overlap (Rosinha, 2009). Zaleznik (1977) cited by Rosinha (2009) was the first to propose that leaders and managers are different in terms of their motivations and ways of acting and thinking, with the former using rational techniques focused on tasks and processes, seeking to maintain the status quo, while the seconds use imaginative and visionary techniques seeking to break with the status quo. Leaders are expected to have a long-term vision that allows them to respond to the organization's needs in an original way, implementing and mobilizing their employees for change. The differences are in terms of processes rather than personality characteristics. The management processes are formal and oriented towards the implementation of solutions to everyday problems, while the leadership processes tend to be informal, flexible and oriented towards the future (Rosinha, 2009).

On the other hand, defenders of overlapping concepts such as Mintzberg defend that manager "is a larger label in which the Leader plays a functional role" (Rosinha, 2009, p. 85). Yukl (2002) suggests that supervisory positions integrate the roles of "leader" and "manager", with the manager being associated with planning and organization and problem solving, while the leader is associated with motivation and inspiration, support and advice and conflict management.

Leadership is a complex topic and because that there is not universally accepted definition of that means. There are numerous definitions of the concept, and it is even possible to say that we can find as many definitions as people who dedicated themselves to the study of leadership. Leadership has been defined in terms of traits, behaviors, influence, interaction patterns, role relationships, and occupation of an administrative position (Yulk, 2002).

Winston and Patterson (2006) mention that a search with the term Leadership in scientific databases resulted in 26,000 articles. However, according to the authors, a significant part of these articles did not refer to the study of leadership as a whole, but to the study of isolated dimensions of the global leadership construct. In an effort to analyze leadership as a whole, researchers carried out a systematic review of 160 articles and books, reaching a complex definition containing more than 90 dimensions. The complexity of this definition reflects the difficulty felt by the various authors over time in defining this concept. Despite this, over the years, several authors have defined leadership, emphasizing different approaches and dimensions of the concept.

In a central work in the area of leadership and after conducting a systematic review of the concept, in 1990, Bass defines leadership "as the successful influence of a leader that results in the achievement of goals by the influenced followers" (p.14). Yulk, in turn, argues that "Leadership is the process of influencing others to understand and agree about what needs to be done and how to do it, and the process of facilitating individual and collective efforts to accomplish shared objectives" (Yulk, 2002, p.8).

In 1999 House and collaborators defined leadership as "the ability of an individual to influence, motivate, and enable others to contribute towards the effectiveness and success of the organization (as cited in Yulk, 2002, p. 3)

In these definitions, as in almost all definitions of leadership, three common aspects can be found:

- Influence as a social process used by the leader
- The characteristics of the leader as the main enhancer of leadership
- The importance of context for exercising leadership (McCauley, 2010).

The perpective on leadership has changed dramatically over time. Avery cited by Malewska and Sajdak (2015) refers to 4 paradigms corresponding to different eras, which are supported by different leadership basis. The evolution of these paradigms from classic to transactional, visionary and organic is also analyzed according to criteria such as the involvement of group members and attitudes towards the leader's vision (see table 1).

*Table 1. Leadership Paradigms*

| Leadership Paradigms | Classic | Transactional | Visionary | Organic |
|---|---|---|---|---|
| The most important period of time | From antiquity to the 1970s | From the 1970s to the mid-80s | From the mid-80s to 2000 | After 2000 |
| Leadership basis | The leader's dominance based on respect and authority, based on commands and control | The impact on the group members exerted in face to face contact, with their opinions and feelings taken into account. Creating the right environment for management | Emotions – the leader inspires group members | Shared interpretation of the group environment. Leaders may emerge from the group instead of being formally appointed |
| The source of group members' involvement | The fear of or respect for leaders; an effort made to get a reward or to avoid punishment | Negotiating awards, agreements and expectations | Shared vision; the leader's charisma; individualized approach to group members | Supporting values and processes common to the whole group; willingness to develop self- identification |
| Vision | The leader's vision is not necessary to exact the obedience of group members | The vision is not necessary and may never be articulated | The vision is the most important element; group members can contribute to the leader's vision | The vision is created in the group; the vision is an important element of the organization culture |

Source: Avery as cited in Malewska & Sajdak (2015).

Strategic leadership combines characteristics inherent in visionary and organic leadership and appears to be an excellent solution for organizations operating in markets that require constant change, high employee engagement, and good communication, enabling them to have the speed and efficiency required to implement the strategies defined (Malewska & Sajdak, 2015). In the next topic we will explore this concept

## STRATEGIC LEADERSHIP

Leadership is probably one of the constructs that has received the most attention from researchers in the vast field of study of Organizational Behavior. Nevertheless, there is a clear disproportion between researchers' attention to studying the influence of middle leaders on employee behavior and the results of the organization over the much smaller one that has been given to the study of strategic leadership. The investment by researchers is so much disproportionate that in the last decades of the twentieth century some authors have even shown some skepticism about the impact that top leaders could have on organizational outcomes (Elenkov, Judge, & Wright, 2005).

Hambrick's contribution was essential in overcoming this skepticism. Indeed, the development of upper echelons has provided significant theoretical and empirical support for the impact of strategic leadership within the literature related to the strategic management of organizations (Elenkov, Judge, & Wright, 2005). In fact, the ability to transfer strategic leadership to operational management often determines an organization's success in its marketplace. In the literature this process is called Strategic Leadership (Malewska & Sajdak, 2015)

There is still some disagreement over a formal definition of Strategic Leadership (Jaleha & Machuki, 2018). The vast literature in this area imposes a considerable number of different definitions and perspectives on the concept of strategic leadership. Rowe (2001, p.81), for example, defines "Strategic leadership as the ability to influence others to voluntarily make day-to-day decisions that enhance the long-term viability of the organization". Hambrick (2007) defined strategic leadership as "being concerned with the whole scope of activities and strategic choice of the individual entities at the top of the organization" (Palladan et al., 2016). Malewska and Sajdak (2015, p.45) refer to the "Strategic leadership as the ability to combine visionary operational management, i.e., the spread of ideas, but also the ability to embed these ideas in company operations taking into account their limitations".

While strategic leadership remains focused on the operational oversight of the organization's day-to-day activities, on the one hand, it highlights a set of strategic and long-term responsibilities. Leaders who assume strategic roles are expected to be able to integrate philosophical thinking about organization, operationalized in their vision, beliefs and values with organizational reality (Malewska & Sajdak, 2015). The success or failure of an organization depends on this ability of the strategic leader to think the organization, define a vision of the future and mobilize the resources necessary for its implementation.

If leadership is present at all levels of the organization, strategic leadership refers to the influence exerted by top leaders, such as the chief executive officers (CEO), the Top Management Team (TMT) and the board of directors of the organization the preferred analysis unit (Jaleha & Machuki, 2018; Kriger & Zhovtobryukh, 2013). Strategic leadership research focuses on executive work not only as a relational activity but also as a strategic and symbolic activity while leadership research focuses on the relationship between the leader and his followers (Vera & Crossan, 2004).

The literature review highlights the different roles and unique capabilities that enable strategic leadership to achieve organizational results that are far beyond what a single individual or small group of individuals can play (Jaleha & Machuki, 2018). In this sense, the definition of Ireland and Hitt is integrative, seeking to absorb the importance of the most macro and micro levels of the organization, as well as its context of operation (Jaleha & Machuki, 2018). Thus, the authors consider "strategic leadership as a person's ability to anticipate, envision, maintain flexibility, think strategically, and work with others to initiate changes that will create a viable future for the organization" (Ireland & Hitt, 2005, p.63).

Notwithstanding these conceptual differences, strategic leadership has been given a set of absolutely critical practices for organizations that stand out in defining long-term goals, managing human and social assets, emphasizing the organization's ethical values, ensuring stability, implementing organizational strategy, formulating its vision and developing sustainable cultural values and organizational climate through which it promotes a sustainable competitive advantage (Hunitie, 2018; Ireland & Hitt, 2005; Jaleha & Machuki, 2018). Boal and Hooijberg report that it is evident that there is a significant difference between the roles played by strategic leaders and those held by middle leaders. Some of these roles are identified by the authors and include strategic decision-making, developing core organizational skills, developing organizational structure, creating and communicating organizational mission, and forming new leaders (Boal & Hooijberg, 2000; Hunitie, 2018; Vera & Crossan, 2004).

## THE STRATEGIC LEADERSHIP PROFILE

Strategic leadership has been conceptualized in terms of various dimensions. Davies and Davies (2004) identified two groups of skills related to the strategic leader: the skills required for the development of organizational activities and the personal skills. The abilities related, according to the authors, to the organizational activity are five, namely:

1. Strategic orientation, i.e., having the ability to link the day to day activities of the organization with the long term vision;
2. Strategic execution, translating the strategy into operational actions;
3. Strategic alignment, referring to the coherence of the organizational strategy;
4. Identification of the effective strategic intervention points. This ability allows the identification of critical moments when it is possible to develop new visions and strategies and even orient the organization in new directions;
5. Development of strategic competencies that enable the organization to sustainably develop over time (Davies & Davies, 2004; Hunitie, 2018)

Regarding individual skills, Davies and Davies (2004), state that strategic leaders have:

1. a dissatisfaction or restlessness with the present, that allows them to develop the creative spirit that leads them to a new organizational vision
2. absorptive capacity which can be referred to as the ability to absorb, assimilate and learn new information
3. adaptive capacity or also called strategic flexibility that allows the leader to adapt to new contexts.
4. Wisdom, defined as the ability to do the right thing at the right time.

Contrary to what would be thinkable for many, Rothschild (cit in Schoemaker, Krupp, & Howland, 2013) argues that it is the most unpredictable and unstable environments that create greater opportunities for organizations, as long as there are leadership skills that can leverage innovation and creativity. In this sense, a study conducted by Schoemaker, Krupp, and Howland (2013) with 20,000 executives, identified six leadership competencies that are crucial for success in these environments: 1) ability to anticipate opportunities through information and networking established inside and outside the organization, thus recognizing the potential of those who compete with them and reactions to new business alternatives 2) audacity to challenge the status quo, putting into practice thinking divergent approach, analyzing problems from different perspectives 3) ability to interpret the surrounding data, hypothesize and produce insights from an open mind 4) ability to make decisions considering a multitude of alternatives and risks and balancing the needs of short term to medium and long term results 5) ability to aggregate positions through proactive communication, involving diverse stakeholders and establishing relationships based on trust. 6) developing a systematic learning attitude, not only in successful situations, but also in those that resulted in failure. The authors underline that these are the determining ingredients of strategic leadership, and leaders should be able to identify any weaknesses, since the effectiveness of leadership in current contexts will only be ensured when the six competencies meet find gifts. These six leadership skills are equally recognized by Schoemaker, Heaton and Teece (2018) as members of three dynamic capabilities, which are key determinants of strategic leadership - sensing, seizing and transforming.

Hit and colleagues (1998, cit in Hunitie, 2018) also recognize the ability to scan the environment, dealing with its changes, as one of the core competencies of strategic leadership. In fact, changing contexts put top leaders under greater pressure not only to make critical and effective decisions but also to effectively execute those same strategies across different levels of the organization (Avolio, 2007)

In summary, the potentialities of strategic leadership can be described by the systematization presented by Rowe (2001). This author acknowledges that strategic leadership is able to reconcile the potentialities of visionary leadership and managerial leadership to the extent that: "emphasis on ethical behavior and value-based decisions, oversee operating (day-to-day) and strategic (long-term) responsabilities, formulate and implement strategies for immediate impact and preservation of long-term goals to enhance organizational survival, growth, and long-term viability, have strong, positive expectations of the performance they expect from their superiors, peers, subordinates, and themselves, use strategic controls and financial controls, with emphasis on strategic controls, use and interchange, tacit and explicit knowledge on individual and organizational levels, use linear and nonlinear thinking patterns and believe in strategic choice, that is, their choices make a difference in their organizations and environment (Rowe, 2001, p82).

## STRATEGIC LEADERSHIP AND RESULTS

Moving from the operational to the strategic level of leadership implies, as we have seen, the ability to implement strategies, allocate resources and mobilize competencies that produce long-term results from a sustainability perspective. Equating its impact on results, the literature has been considering strategic leadership as an overall construct. Seeking to fill a gap in the literature, Shao (2019) conducted a study in the IS-Business context and he revealed the role of strategic leadership as an inspirational figure for strategic business alignment, as well as the assimilation of corporate systems.

Indeed, considering the role that decisions made by strategic leadership plays in the overall functioning of the organization, we must address their impact at the individual, team and organizational levels as well as in what concerns their relationship with the environment.

If strategic leadership is the "ability to influence others to voluntarily make day-to-day decisions that enhance the long-term viability at organization, while at the same time maintaining its short-term financial stability" (Rowe, 2001, p. 81), it is up to these top leaders to assume, throughout the hierarchical chain, as ambassadors for the promotion of policies and practices that favor healthy work contexts, as it is well known that work is not just a means of subsistence, but a space for identity construction, development and health and well-being.

Several studies show the effect that leadership has on workers' health and well-being. Research by Gurt, Schwennen and Elke (2011) found that good leadership practices contribute to lower levels of employee strain, namely by reducing role ambiguity, by creating a health-enabling environment. and by practices that aim to promote job satisfaction, which ultimately reflects on organizational performance.

Schmidt et al., (2014), in a research paper with a large sample of 3 331 industry workers, also found a relationship between the negative assessment of support provided by their leaders and the negative assessment of their health.

In 2010 the *Work & Stress* published a special issue aimed at revisiting key studies that show a link between leadership, health, well-being and safety in the organizational context (Kellowaya & Barlingb, 2010). From these results a close link between leadership exercise and indicators of psychological health (such as stress, depression and anxiety), physical health (such as the risks of unsafe heart disease) and safety (such as incidents and accidents at work). This publication particularly highlights the effects of abusive leadership on promoting distress, burnout, reducing self-efficacy, self-esteem, and effective commitment to the organization. For its part, transformational leadership, in which the quality of support provided by leaders is high, has favorable effects in terms of promoting positive emotions, which is reflected in the reduction of perceived stress levels, job strain, burnout and depression.

The literature also emphasizes the role of leadership, namely its exercise with clear ethical concerns regarding the well-being of employees. Leaders who are concerned about the working conditions to which their employees are exposed (such as workload) contribute to higher levels of comfort and satisfaction in teams (Ko, Ma, Bartnik, Haney, & Kang, 2017).

Other studies have sought to understand the impact of leadership virtuosity on organizational dynamics. The results of a survey conducted in the Portuguese context by Araújo and Lopes (2014) suggest that sustained leadership in values, capable of promoting perseverance and maturity in employees, contributes to organizational commitment, which, in turn, is reflected in the individual performance. These results corroborate the various studies that mirror a clear relationship between the exercise of leadership that fosters trust, tolerance, compassion, optimism, meaning of work and equity, and the organizational health of its employees (Rego & Cunha, 2010; Cameron et al, 2004, cit in Araújo & Lopes, 2014, p.4).

The meaning that the work assumes for those who do it has been clearly recognized in the literature, particularly in some francophone authors, such as Davezies (1998), recognizing the latter that it is through work that man can structure their existence, discover himself, test their limits, surpass himself and others. Barsh, Mogelof and Webb (2010) rightly acknowledge that, although the sources of meaning of work may differ, it is crucial that leaders attach high significance to their work, and this will reflect on how they convey their enthusiasm to others. These authors also reflect in their model the importance of a leader, in the current contexts, being able to mobilize positive energy, recognizing in uncertainty opportunities for change and not sources of tension, helping their teams overcome obstacles, remain optimistic, take risks by establishing multiple links and managing the complexity of information. Based on research conducted by McKinsey, authors conclude that leaders who are capable of mastering at least one of the five dimensions are twice as likely to succeed in their business, and when they are able to master the five, quadruple those possibilities, as well as being able to recognize more meaning in their own lives.

Although there is no unanimity regarding the impact that strategic leadership has on organizational performance, contributions emerge that support a clear relationship between them, such as Ireland and Hitt (2005) and Quigley and Hambrick (2015) (cit in Jaleha & Machuki, 2018). For her part, Rowe (2001) argues that if different managers and employees are unaware of the organization's strategic direction, they can inadvertently damage the organization and its relationship with different stakeholders, such as customers, suppliers, communities where they operate. The same author also argues that the fact that strategic leaders focus on the financial stability of the present and also on the future viability, are promoters of the health of their organizations.

Finally, as we will see in the next point, there seems to be some evidence leading to the idea that the exercise of leadership, when sustained by values and ethical behaviour, has an impact on organizational outcomes.

## STRATEGIC LEADERSHIP AND ETHICS

The exercise of strategic leadership and its ethical implications have been relatively poorly studied (Glanz, 2010). The literature seems to be relatively fruitful with regard to ethical leadership, notably highlighting it from other types of leadership, such as charismatic, transnational, transformational, authentic and spiritual, essentially because it is not only focused on the traits and behaviors of the leader, but also linked to value-based management (Ko, Ma, Bartnik, Haney, & Kang, 2017). Thus, Brown, Treviño and Harrison (2005) suggest that ethical leadership involves, on the one hand, the moral person's profile, as being honest, caring, who makes thoughtful and fair decisions and, on the other hand, the moral manager who sets clear ethical standards works as a model and reinforces in his followers a behavioral standard based on ethics. It is precisely this second facet that distinguishes ethical leadership from transformational, authentic or spiritual leadership (Brown & Treviño, 2006).

There are not many publications specifically address the study of ethical behavior by those in top management, that is, those who assume the overall responsibility of organizations (Shin, Sung, Choi & Kim, 2015). Nevertheless, some authors stress the imperative of the whole process inherent in strategic planning to consider its ethical implications for justice and integrity (Bowman 2008, cit in Glanz, 2010, p.79).

Planning and decision-making are key elements of strategic leadership, and they are not disconnected from political components and power (Glanz, 2010). Duffy's model (2003, cit in Glanz, 2010, p. 71) relates precisely how strategic leaders behave, crossing two variables - the degree of power and political behavior and the ethical character of their behavior. At the extremes of a continuum the model considers powerful, political behavior and powerless, apolitical behavior. At the extremes of the other axis the model presents the unethical behavior and ethical behavior. From the intersection of these two axes emerge four quadrants that reflect different behaviors by the leader, participation and diversity of viewpoints and mobilizing people towards achievements focused on ethically responsible behavior. Indeed, if we rely on the Theory of Social Learning (Bandura, 1986), we understand the impact that a leader's ethical behavior has as a reference model for his followers. A good example is the findings of a study conducted in the Chinese context in which Wen and Chen (2016) concluded that ethical leadership is positively related to workers' intention to whistleblowing or misleading practices considered illegitimate. One of the reasons for this phenomenon is that in the context of ethical leadership, followers feel more support and trust in the leader, not fearing retaliation and other negative effects of possible reports of bad practice (Ko, Ma, Bartnik, Haney, & Kang, 2017).

In the military context, Doty and Fenlason (2015) discuss the interesting question of trust and ethics on the part of leaders, questioning whether it should be more associated with competence or character, and its evaluation is always the result of a full exercise of conscience. This refers to the evaluative and cognitive component that is triggered by followers regarding the behavior of their leaders, and this assessment does not leave them indifferent. In fact, ethical leadership has been associated with increased employee involvement with work and the organization, as a result of an assessment of their work context as more fair and meaningful, able to promote trust, gratitude and satisfaction (Ko, Ma, Bartnik, Haney, & Kang, 2017; Shin, Sung, Choi, & Kim, 2015).

Regarding the constant changes that organizations are facing today, Sharif and Scandura (2014) demonstrate the role of leaders with ethical concerns, because they can engage their employees in ongoing processes, thus ensuring greater confidence.

Although it is a relatively unexplored theme, some literature has focused on the *dark side* of unethical leadership, not as the opposite of ethical leadership, but characterized by behaviors that focus only on personal interests, the abuse of power and the encouragement of these same behaviors among the followers. Despite cultural differences in what are considered unethical leadership practices, their impact seems to be visible, not only on organizational performance, but also on the image the organization projects abroad (Midgen, 2015). On the contrary, ethical leadership, namely that of top management, is a good predictor of the ethical climate within the organization, promoting greater organizational citizenship (Shin, 2012) and corporate social responsibility for organizational effectiveness (Choi, Ullah, & Kwak 2015), thus being able to favorably influence organizational performance (Shin, Sung, Choi, & Kim, 2015).

## CONCLUSION

The environment in which modern organizations operate is increasingly challenging and unpredictable, and it is difficult to anticipate the future based on past events and models. In this context, we are led to emphasize the determining role that top leadership plays in the destinies of organizations, which leads us to the need to direct a particular look at it.

Since leadership is one of the issues that has deserved the largest volume of publications in the context of organizational behaviour, the specificities of strategic leadership, namely when we are talking about their relations with individual, team and organizational health and safety are still little worked on.

In this chapter, we reflect on the concept of Strategic Leadership, seeking to highlight its important role in organizations that are inserted in competitive markets, characterized by constant changes and the need to promote employee involvement that allows them the necessary efficiency to implement the defined strategies.

We define the concept of strategic leadership and address its role for organizational results, assuming that when we move from the operational to the strategic level, the impact caused by leadership will imply consistent and long-term changes.

Although little explored, we believe that a chapter on strategic leadership could not be complete if its relationship with ethics was not addressed. Some authors even mention the dark side of unethical leadership, showing the tendency for some leaders to focus on personal interests rather than on organizational interests and behaviors that denote abuses of power.

In this chapter we also argue that there is an evident disproportion between studies and publications on the topic of leadership and strategic leadership. Despite this disproportionality, some evidence emerges in order to prove a clear relationship between strategic leadership and the performance and health of organizations. In this sense, there seems to be some evidence leading to the idea that the exercise of leadership, when sustained by values and ethical behavior, has an impact on organizational outcomes.

We consider crucial to conduct more studies on this topic, namely of a longitudinal nature and using mixed methodologies, to assess how strategic leadership is exercised in organizations, namely how power is mobilized, what concerns exist regarding the health and well-being of members of the organization as well as those of an ethical nature.

Given the impact these concerns have on organizational outcomes as well as on the external image of organizations, it is imperative to recruit and train leaders at various levels, not just strategic ones, whose behaviors are grounded in ethical principles and function as true models in front of their teams.

## REFERENCES

Araújo, M.S.G. & Lopes, P.M.P.R. (2014). Virtuous leadership, organizational commitment and individual performance. *Téckhene – Review of Applied Management Studies*, *12*, 3-10.

Avolio, B. J. (2007). Promoting more integrative strategies for leadership theory-building. *The American Psychologist*, *62*(1), 25–33. doi:10.1037/0003-066X.62.1.25 PMID:17209677

Bandura, A. (1986). *Social foundations of thought and action: A social cognitive theory*. Prentice-Hall.

Banzato, C. R., & Sierra, J. C. V. (2016). Implications of Theory and Research on Strategic Leadership: A Critical Review. *Revista Ibero-Americana de Estratégia*, *15*(03), 119–131. doi:10.5585/riae.v15i3.2331

Barsh, J., Mogelof, J., & Webb, C. (2010). How centered leaders achieve extraordinary results. *The McKinsey Quarterly*.

Bass, B. M. (1990). From Transactional to Transformational Leadership: Learning to Share the Vision. *Organizational Dynamics*, *18*(3), 19–32. doi:10.1016/0090-2616(90)90061-S

Boal, K. B., & Hooijberg, R. (2000). Strategic leadership research: Moving on. *The Leadership Quarterly*, *11*(4), 515–549. doi:10.1016/S1048-9843(00)00057-6

Brown, M. E., & Treviño, L. K. (2006). Ethical leadership: A review and future directions. *The Leadership Quarterly*, *17*(6), 595–616. doi:10.1016/j.leaqua.2006.10.004

Choi, S. B., Ullah, S. M. E., & Kwak, W. J. (2015). Ethical Leadership and Followers' Attitudes Toward Corporate Social Responsibility: The Role of Perceived Ethical Work Climate. *Social Behavior and Personality*, *43*(3), 353–365. doi:10.2224bp.2015.43.3.353

Davezies, Ph. (1998). De la récupération psychique. *Santé et Travail*, *25*, 35–37.

Davies, B. J., & Davies, B. (2004). Strategic leadership, Advancing the Organization from Planning to Reality. *School Leadership, 70*(1), 57–38. doi:10.1080/1363243042000172804

Doty, J., & Fenlason, J. (2015, May-June). It's Not About Trust; It's About Thinking and Judgment. *Military Review*, 78–83.

Elenkov, D. S., Judge, W., & Wright, P. (2005). Strategic leadership and executive innovation influence: An international multi-cluster comparative study. *Strategic Management Journal, 26*(7), 665–682. Advance online publication. doi:10.1002mj.469

Ferdman, B. M., Barrera, V., Allen, A., & Vuong, V. (2009, August). Inclusive behaviors and the experience of inclusion. In B. G. Chung (Chair), *Inclusion in organizations: Measures, HR practices, and climate.* Symposium presented at the 69th Annual Meeting of the Academy of Management, Chicago.

Fitza, M. A. (2014). The use of variance decomposition in the investigation of CEO effects: How large must the CEO effect be to rule out chance? *Strategic Management Journal, 35*(12), 1839–1852. doi:10.1002mj.2192

Friedman, T. L. (2005). *The World Is Flat: A Brief History of the Twenty-First Century.* Farrar, Straus and Giroux.

Glanz, J. (2010). Justice and Caring: Power, Politics and Ethics in Strategic Leadership. *International Studies in Educational Administration, 38*(1), 66–87.

Gurt, J., Schwennen, C., & Elke, G. (2011). Health-specific leadership: Is there an association between leader consideration for the health of employees and their strain and well-being? *Work and Stress, 25*(2), 108–127. doi:10.1080/02678373.2011.595947

Hambrick, D. C. (2007). Upper echelons theory: An update. *Academy of Management Review, 32*(2), 334–343. doi:10.5465/amr.2007.24345254

Horney, N., Pasmore, B., & O'Shea, T. (2010). Leadership Agility: A Business Imperative for a VUCA World. *People & Strategy, 33*(4), 32–38. Retrieved from www.hrps.org

Hunitie, M. (2018). Impact of strategic leadership on strategic competitive advantage through strategic thinking and strategic planning: A bi-meditational research. *Business: Theory and Practice, 19*(0), 322–330. doi:10.3846/btp.2018.32

Ireland, R. D., & Hitt, M. A. (2005). Achieving and maintaining strategic competitiveness in the 21st century: The role of trategic leadership. *The Academy of Management Executive, 19*(4), 63–77. doi:10.5465/ame.2005.19417908

Jaleha, A. A., & Machuki, V. N. (2018). Strategic Leadership and Organizational Performance: A Critical Review of Literature. *European Scientific Journal ESJ, 14*(35), 124–149. doi:10.19044/esj.2018.v14n35p124

Johansen, B. (2012). Leaders make the future: ten new leadership skills for an uncertain world (2nd ed.). San Francisco: Academic Press.

Jonsen, K., Maznevski, M. L., & Schneider, S. (2011). Diversity and its not so diverse literature: An international perspective. *International Journal of Cross Cultural Management, 11*(1), 35–62. doi:10.1177/1470595811398798

Kelloway, E. K., & Barling, J. (2010). Leadership development as an intervention in occupational health psychology. *Work and Stress, 24*(3), 260–279. doi:10.1080/02678373.2010.518441

Ko, C., Ma, J., Bartnik, R., Haney, M. H., & Kang, M. (2018). Ethical Leadership: An Integrative Review and Future Research Agenda. *Ethics & Behavior, 28*(2), 104–132. doi:10.1080/10508422.2017.1318069

Kriger, M., & Zhovtobryukh, Y. (2013). Rethinking strategic leadership: Stars, clans, teams and networks. *Journal of Strategy and Management, 6*(4), 411–432. doi:10.1108/JSMA-09-2012-0051

Lawrence, K. (2013). Developing Leaders in a VUCA Environment. *UNC Executive Development*, 1–15.

Malewska, K., & Sajdak, M. (2015). The Intuitive Manager and the Concept of Strategic Leadership. *Management, 18*(2), 44–58. doi:10.2478/manment-2014-0041

Mazur, B. (2010, November). Cultural Diversity in Organizational Theory and Practice. *Journal of Intercultural Management, 2*(2), 5–15.

McCauley, C. D. (2010). Concepts of Leadership. In E. Biech (Ed.), The ASTD Leadership Handbook (5th ed., pp. 1–13). Campus.

Midgen, T. (2015). (Un)Ethical leadership: What can Educational Psychology Services learn? *Educational and Child Psychology, 32*(4), 81–94.

Mor Barak, M. E. (2011). *Managing diversity: Toward a globally inclusive workplace*. Sage.

Palladan, A. A., Abdulkadir, K. B., & Chong, Y. W. (2016). Strategic Leadership : A Sine Qua Non Toward Revitalizaing Nigerian Public Tertiary Institutions. *International Journal of Economics. Commerce and Management, IV*(9), 253–264.

Quigley, T. J., & Hambrick, D. C. (2015). Has the "cEO effect" increased in recent decades? A new explanation for the great rise in America's attention to corporate leaders. *Strategic Management Journal, 36*(6), 821–830. doi:10.1002mj.2258

Rego, A., & Cunha, M. P. e. (2010). Organisational justice and citizenship behaviors: A study in the Portuguese cultural context. *Applied Psychology, 59*(3), 404–430. doi:10.1111/j.1464-0597.2009.00405.x

Rosinha, A. J. P. E. (2009). *Conhecimento tácito em contexto militar:(inclusões na promoção do desenvolvimento de competências de comando). Conhecimento tácito em contexto militar: Incursões na promoção do desenvolvimento de competências de comando*. Retrieved from http://repositorio.ul.pt/bitstream/10451/967/10/20686_ulsd057394_td_parte2_11.pdf%5Cnhttp://repositorio.ul.pt/handle/10451/967

Rowe, W. G. (2001). Creating wealth in organizations: The role of strategic leadership. *The Academy of Management Executive, 15*(1), 81–94. doi:10.5465/ame.2001.4251395

Schmidt, B., Loerbroks, A., Herr, R., Wilson, M., Jarczok, M., Litaker, D., Mauss, D., Bosch, J., & Fischer, J. (2014). Associations Between Supportive Leadership and Employees Self-Rated Health in an Occupational Sample. *International Journal of Behavioral Medicine*, *21*(5), 750–756. doi:10.100712529-013-9345-7 PMID:24072350

Schmidt, B., Loerbroks, A., Herr, R., Wilson, M., Jarczok, M., Litaker, D., Mauss, D., Bosch, J., & Fischer, J. (2014). Associations Between Supportive Leadership and Employees Self-Rated Health in an Occupational Sample. *International Journal of Behavioral Medicine*, *21*(5), 750–756. doi:10.100712529-013-9345-7 PMID:24072350

Schoemaker, P., Heaton, S., & Teece, D. (2018). Innovation, Dynamic Capabilities, and Leadership. *BerkeleyHaas*, *61*(1), 15–42.

Schoemaker, P., Krupp, S., & Howland, S. (2013). *Strategic leadership: the essential skills. Harvard Business Review*. January-February.

Shao, Z. (2019). Interaction effect of strategic leadership behaviors and organizational culture on IS-Business strategic alignment and Enterprise Systems assimilation. *International Journal of Information Management*, *44*, 96–108. Advance online publication. doi:10.1016/j.ijinfomgt.2018.09.010

Sharif, M. M., & Scandura, T. A. (2014). Do perceptions of ethical conduct matter during organizational change? Ethical leadership and employee involvement. *Journal of Business Ethics*, *124*(2), 185–196. doi:10.100710551-013-1869-x

Shin, Y. (2012). CEO ethical leadership, ethical climate, climate strength, and collective organizational citizenship behavior. *Journal of Business Ethics*, *108*(3), 299–312. doi:10.100710551-011-1091-7

Shin, Y., Sung, S. Y., Choi, J. N., & Kim, M. S. (2015). Top management ethical leadership and firm performance: Mediating role of ethical and procedural justice climate. *Journal of Business Ethics*, *129*(1), 43–57. doi:10.100710551-014-2144-5 PMID:26430288

Takayama, K., Kaplan, M., & Cook-Sather, A. (2017, Summer/Fall). Advancing Diversity and Inclusion. *Liberal Education*, 22–29.

Vera, D., & Crossan, M. (2004). Strategic leadership and organizational learning. *Academy of Management Review*, *29*(2), 222–240. doi:10.5465/amr.2004.12736080

Wen, P., & Chen, Ch. (2016). How Does Ethical Leadership Influence Employee's Whistleblowing Intention? Evidence from China. *Social Behavior and Personality*, *44*(8), 1255–1266. doi:10.2224bp.2016.44.8.1255

Winston, B., & Patterson, K. (2006). An integrative definition of leadership. *International Journal of Leadership Studies*, *1*(2), 6–66.

Yulk, G. A. (2002). *Leadership in Organizations* (5th ed.). Prentice Hall.

# Chapter 3
# Business Model Design:
## Novelty and Efficiency

**Rayssa Quirino**
*Instituto Superior de Gestão, Portugal*

**Alvaro Lopes Dias**
https://orcid.org/0000-0003-4074-1586
*Universidade Lusófona, Portugal & ISCTE, Instituto Universitário de Lisboa, Portugal*

## ABSTRACT

*Business model design refers to the design of transactions operated by an organization represented by the content, structure, and governance of all transactions that occur in an organization in order to create value through exploration of a business opportunity. This study has as objective to analyze the impact of one or more business model design has on the performance. Through the conduct of surveys, a sample of 30 companies was collected between Europe and Brazil. The results showed that it was not possible to obtain correlations to validate the hypotheses, due to the great difficulty of obtaining the data by the companies, thus leading to a reduced number of respondents. This study contributes significantly to the theory of innovation and entrepreneurship, as a response to a latent need on the part of the literature to consistently homogenize the understanding about the theme and clear recommendations and practices for management.*

## INTRODUCTION

The current scenario imposed on companies the modification of their production processes and consequent reduction of costs to become more competitive. According to Casadesus-Masanell and Ricart (2011), the theme: strategy has been the slogan of competitiveness in the last three decades. However, in the future, questions about sustainable competitive advantage will start with the following term: business model design.

DOI: 10.4018/978-1-7998-1843-4.ch003

When Apple released the Ipod, it did more than launch a new music device with good technology and attractive design. Apple combined the digital music distribution hardware, software, and digital music distribution service through a new business model design, giving the customer the task of downloading songs (Johnson et al., 2008).

In its history, Apple was focused on launching innovative hardware and software, but with the Ipod creation, associated with Itunes, this was the first computer company to include music distribution as an activity, linking it to the development of hardware and the Ipod software. By connecting these new activities to its business model (associating legal music distribution with its customers), the company simply radicalized the design of its business model and transformed the music distribution around the world. Rather than just introducing new hardware or software on the market, it has completely transformed its business model in order to achieve a lasting relationship with its customers (Zott and Amit, 2012).

Today, there are many good companies on the market, especially in Europe, and they are constantly adding innovations to their products. But, many of these companies will not survive, even with all their ability to create innovative products. Gassmann et al., 2013 ask themselves how it is possible that companies like Kodak, for example, that remained leader for many years in its branch and worldwide known for its innovations, was simply forgotten and outdated? Faced with this questioning, the authors state that many companies have lost the ability to adapt their business models in a highly volatile business environment. And they say that in the future, business competition will be focused on innovative business models and not on product and service innovations.

The interesting thing about BM is that it has grown substantially both in the academic area and in the business world. However, this growth has not been accompanied by the increase of quantitative empirical evidence capable of relating the different designs of business models with the improvement of companies' performance (Gerdoçi, Bortoluzzi and Dibra, 2017).

Foss and Saebi (2017) also agree that, over the last 15 years, the term BM has gained increasing interest among researchers and entrepreneurs, but despite the fact that it brings up an important phenomenon in the business world, a great lack of knowledge and lack of theoretical support, which has not been accompanied by empirical research. The authors state that there is a latent need on the part of the literature to explore this topic in a more explicit and systematic way, in order to improve this knowledge and to help this research field to develop.

Thus, this study aims to leave its contribution to the literature of business models, providing empirical evidence on the impact of different business models on the performance, and the conflict of choice generated when a company decides to adopt more than one business model.

The rest of this paper is arranged as follows: the second section presents the theoretical background and hypotheses, the third section introduces the research methodology, the fourth section presents the analysis results, and the fifth section discusses the findings, theoretical contributions, managerial implications, limitations, and future research directions.

## THEORETICAL BACKGROUND

For Chesbrough and Rosenbloom (2002), the theme business model is currently the most discussed subject in terms of management and the least understood concept on the web so far. There is a lot of discussion about how the web has changed traditional business models, but little evidence on what exactly the subject means.

This paper adopts the definition of Amit and Zott (2001), which define that a business model describes the design of transactions operated by an organization (which go beyond its barriers), represented by the content, structure and governance of all the transactions that occur in an organization in order to create value through the exploration of a business opportunity. Content is related to the selection of activities performed; the structure describes how these activities are interconnected and governance refers to who will perform each activity. That said, a BM serves to elucidate how an organization is structured and how it engages with its stakeholders, to create value not only for the organization itself, but for all stakeholders.

Regarding the four themes, which are potential value generators of a business model. The authors identified four dimensions or design themes: efficiency; novelty; lock-in and complementarities and they studied the relationship of how each theme affects the performance of companies. These themes are not orthogonal or mutually exclusive; that is, more than one theme may be present in the design of a business model (Amit and Zott, 2001, 2007),

The themes of design elements proposed by Amit and Zott (2001) represent the first drivers of value creation. Not only they capture the essence of what a business model is, but it also facilitates contextualization on the subject and allows better measurement of corporate performance (Hu and Chen, 2016).

That said, Hahn, Speith and Ince (2018) and many other researchers decided to follow the concepts used by Amit and Zott (2001, 2007, 2008, 2010, 2013, 2015) thanks to their large and rich theoretical foundation and their ability to consider the entire enterprise as an activity system. This concept has been widely used and accepted among the literature and is summarized in table 1.

*Table 1. Analytical framework*

| | | | |
|---|---|---|---|
| Activity systems | *Design Themes* (sources of value creation of the system of activities) | *Novelty* | Innovative adoption of content, structure and governance. |
| | | *Lock-in* | Build elements to attract and retain customers. |
| | | *Complementarities* | Build activities to generate more value. |
| | | *Efficiency* | Rearrange activities to reduce transaction costs. |
| | *Design elements* (architecture of an activity system) | *Content* | Which activities are performed? |
| | | *Structure* | How are activities connected and sequenced? |
| | | *Governance* | Who performs the activities and where? |

Source: Hahn *et al.* (2018).

It is important to say that, recently, researchers have focused intensively on NCBMs and ECBMs because these two holistically encompass all the design element configurations initially defined by Amit and Zott (2001) - content, structure, and governance. As a result, business model efficiency focuses more on the use of content, structures and governance of existing transactions in order to improve efficiency, while business model novelty is focused on adopting new content, structures and governance of transactions in order to promote innovation (Hu and Chen, 2016 as cited in Brettel et al., 2017, Hu, 2014, Zott and Amit 2007, 2008, Wei, Zhao and Zhang, 2014).

The NICE framework (novelty, lock-in, complementarities and Efficiency) are defined as the four value-generating dimensions of a business model. However, only two of these design themes (novelty and efficiency) proved to be related to the performance of companies through studies carried out later.

There is still a gap in the literature that studies deeper how the other two issues can affect business performance and the creation of competitive advantage (Kulins, 2016).

In the efforts to contribute to the literature with empirical data that prove the relationship between BMD and performance, Zott and Amit (2007) brought the concepts of two design themes: BMN and BME. In relation to BMN, its essence is focused on "adopting new activities (content), and / or new ways of connecting these activities (structure) and / or new ways of managing these activities (governance)" (Zott and Amit, 2010, 2011).

A NCBM allows companies to be the first to create competitive advantage by being pioneers. These competitive advantages can come, for example, from the purchase of assets, from the exchange of costs between the stakeholders or through the leadership in the technology that it dominates. In this sense, if a company can be the first to market a new business model, it will be able to win new customers and build a reputation before the action of its potential competitors. The greater the company's ability to increase cost sharing with other stakeholders, the new competitors will have to invest more resources to drive them away from the pioneer company. Thus, in addition to representing a source of competitive advantage, an NCBM will also generate a positive impact on company performance (Brettel et al., 2012)

However, often an NCBM connects parties or participants, who once did not work together within the same business model. As a result, there is an increase in the centralization of network power between the parties, since it is the focal company that is aggregating all those involved in the same model. This will represent the potential capacity of the company to acquire and use external knowledge in its favor (Hu, 2014).

In this sense, the greater the capacity to acquire and use this external knowledge, the greater the company's ability to generate open innovation, which will have a positive impact on performance (Chesbrough, 2007).

Thus, the first hypothesis is proposed as follows:

**H1:** BMN positively affects performance.

"An alternative for entrepreneurs to create value is to replicate offers, organizations or business models. In other words, entrepreneurs may choose to imitate rather than innovate - doing things similar to established organizations, but in a more efficient way. " It is then considered that the essence of an ECBM is the reduction of transaction costs through the business model and is not intended to only reduce costs, such as reducing production costs (Zott and Amit 2007: 13).

An ECBM will focus on doing what is already done, but in a better way, giving rise to efficiency and therefore productivity, improving and optimizing the content, structure and governance of transactions. And so, it will help the company make full and mature use of all its systems of activities, participant partnerships and capital resources, enabling the production and marketing of new products with high efficiency at a low cost. The result of this is that technological innovation will become more efficient and better able to respond to the challenges posed by the environment in relation to the pressure to reduce costs and decrease product innovation cycles. (Hu and Chen, 2016).

An ECBM aims to reduce transaction costs across the value chain, improving transparency, reliability and accuracy of the business. These reductions are of great importance to emerging economies as they can help small and medium-sized enterprises attract more affordable customers, boost the size of their market shares and their profitability. It can also drive business to economies of scale, reducing future costs (Pati et al., 2017).

In this way, the second hypothesis is proposed as follows:

**H2:** BME positively affects performance.

As stated earlier, the adoption of an ECBM at the same time as an NCBM is not mutually exclusive. That is, it is possible for a company to operate in the market through more than one business model, as one complements the other, so that the effect of this performance interaction is positive (Zott and Amit, 2007).

The term ambidexterity has been used in the literature to describe the ability of a company to operate with more than one business model and pursue more than one objective at the same time and successfully (Gerdoçi et al., 2017, Hu and Chen, 2016; Markides, 2013, Winterhalter, Zeschky and Gassmann, 2016).

An NCBM makes the business model more unique. This increases the cost sharing with its other stakeholders, and thus allows the company to better position itself to appropriate part of the value created by increasing its efficiency. When an NCBM is also designed as an ECBM, this may attract even more customers (both those who appreciate novelty and those who appreciate lower costs (Zott and Amit, 2007).

Gerdoçi et al. (2017) found a very significant relation in the conclusion of their studies among companies that introduced elements of efficiency in their NCBMs. The elements of efficiency have had an indirect positive effect, moderating innovation and performance. That is, confirming the ambidexterity theory that both models can mutually support each other.

Hu and Chen (2016) argue that it is possible for companies to build ambidextrous business models. Using efficiency elements can make NCBM more attractive in the eyes of the participants and thereby improve their bargaining power while also enabling value creation through efficiency. Another point of view presented is that, empirical studies have shown that companies that operate both business models simultaneously have challenged the traditional thinking of creation and value capture, since they generate many advantages by making the most of all their resources, reducing the entry of other competitors and diversifying their sales and profits.

Zott and Amit (2007) also point out that it may be that companies that want to achieve everything at one time may not have the expected results of their efforts and investments. This can happen because the lack of focus can confuse the participants of the model, taking away their legitimacy, creating both technological and organizational problems, which will ultimately lead to higher costs.

That said, Gerdoçi et al. (2017) draw attention to the fact that more empirical studies are urgently needed to determine whether the concept of ambidexterity is merely academic speculation or whether, in fact, the adoption of more than one business model implies a better performance.

Thus, the third hypothesis is proposed as follows:

**H3:** The use of more than one business model theme positively affects performance.

## METHODOLOGY

### Research Design

Data collection involved a questionnaire administered in 2018. The total sample used was composed of 30 elements according to the following criteria: owners of small and medium-sized companies as well as people who occupy management positions in large companies, that have notoriety about the business of the same. The contacts made by the researcher with the sample were carried out through emails, phone calls, social networks, namely Whatsapp and Facebook Message and LinkedIn. Participants were asked to indicate to which market the company in which they worked belonged.

The sample is composed of 19 companies from Brazil, followed by Portugal with 8 companies, followed by one company from Germany, Spain and England, respectively.

The participants were also asked to indicate the company's year of foundation. From the thirty participating companies, 17 were created in the 2000s and only 4 in the 1950s.

After bibliographic research in qualitative exploratory research in which they were aligned with the same objective of this research, it was verified that the literature has been using the questionnaire developed in the Zott and Amit´s research (2007) in their study to measure the degree of the two independent variables: Business Model Novelty and Business Model Efficiency.

These questions served as a basis for the elaboration of the questionnaire used by this research. In order to avoid any misinterpretation and lack of knowledge about the subject, all questionnaires should be submitted to a pre-test, in a smaller sample, (Gil, 2008). Thus, a pre-test was carried out by a person from the industry segment who occupies the position of project manager and it was verified that there were issues with very prolix or very specific terms of the theme on Business Models, that could be difficult to understand, what resulted in the modification and/or exclusion of some questions.

The final questionnaire was elaborated in blocks of themes; following logic sequence the questions, starting from general questions to more specific questions. The participants were asked to identify their name or company to which they belonged and all the questions required a mandatory response.

Thus, after data collection through Google Forms platform, the data was exported to an Excel spreadsheet and then to the SPSS (Statistical Package for Social Sciences). This software enables the researcher to treat the collected data in a statistical way, having a great variety of techniques and statistical models that allow the interpretation of the same. Data were submitted to the analysis of descriptive statistics and their correlations.

## MEASURES

According to Almeida, Santos and Costa (2010), a good questionnaire should consider its validity and confidentiality. In this sense, Cronbach's alpha coefficient was created by Lee J. Cronbach as a way of estimating the reliability of a research questionnaire. It will measure the correlation between responses through the collected responses by measuring the internal consistency of a scale.

*The minimum acceptable value for alpha is 0.70; below this value the internal consistency of the scale used is considered low. In contrast, the expected maximum value is 0.90; above this value, one can consider that there is redundancy or duplication, that is, several items are measuring exactly the same element of a construct; therefore, redundant items must be eliminated. Usually, alpha values between 0.80 and 0.90 are preferred (Streiner, 2003 cited by Almeida et al., 2010).*

Table 2 shows the coefficients obtained in this investigation. The values are within what is expected. All variables presented values greater than 0.7, with a considerable level of reliability.

*Table 2. Reliability of the variables.*

| Variables | Cronbach's Alpha (α) |
|---|---|
| *Business Model Design* | 0,913 |
| *Business Model Efficiency* | 0,898 |
| Performance | 0,799 |

## Results

As presented in the methodology, the sample collected was very heterogeneous, that is, it consisted of unequal and with quite different elements among them, as regards mainly the year of foundation, number of employees and companies' country of origin.

Below a descriptive analysis with the values is presented for means and standard deviation, in which, due to the heterogeneity of the sample, it showed values of standard deviation that deviate a lot from the mean, being calculated the values in the table 3.

*Table 3. Descriptive statistics.*

| | Number of Employees | BMN | BME | Performance |
|---|---|---|---|---|
| **Sample (n)** | 30 | 30 | 30 | 30 |
| **Mean** | 12817.5 | 3.363 | 3.645 | 3.038 |
| **Standard deviation** | 42804.3 | .452 | .532 | .755 |

The mean presented for the number of employees presented the value of 12817.5 but there was a higher concentration between the values of 0 to 25,000 employees .

Likert items: fully agree; agrees; disagree and totally disagree were used in the questionnaire and the respondents were asked their level of agreement or non-agreement with the statements presented. In this sense, through the SPSS data analysis software, such items were transformed into numbers ranging from 2.00 to 4.50 for the BMN variable and from 2.00 to 6.00 for the BME variable.

The BMN variable has a high concentration of responses near the 3.50 value, close to the mean of 3.36. However, there are two groups with a large cluster of responses, one of which is close to 2.50 and the other is close to the value of 4.50. This means that when asked respondents about this design theme, many of them chose the **agree** option for most questions.

The variable BME has a large accumulation of responses between the values 3 and 4, justifying its average of 3.65. This means that when asked respondents about this design theme, many of them chose the **agree** option for most questions.

When asked about the performance of companies, the performance variable had a large accumulation of answers between values 3 and 4, but presenting an mean of 3.04, closer to the value 3. This means that when asked the respondents about this topic many of them chose the **agree** option for most of the questions.

## Correlations

The study of correlations aims to understand how a variable behaves in an environment where the other is acting, in order to identify if there is any relation between them. This correlation may not imply causality, but the correlation coefficient will be the measure in numbers of the relationship between the variables (Strainer, 2003).

*Table 4. Pearson correlations.*

| | Num_employee | BMN | BMEF | PERF |
|---|---|---|---|---|
| Year | -,649** | -,458* | -,216 | -,246 |
| Num_employee | | ,210 | ,003 | ,019 |
| BMN | | | -,217 | ,402 |
| BMEF | | | | -,061 |

It can be verified that there are very few correlations obtained. For if there is no significance, there is no correlation. As can be seen in table 11, only one has a degree of significance of 99% and another, a degree of significance of 95%. It was also found that the intensity of the correlations is also weak. A positive correlation indicates that the variables tend to increase or decrease together, and a negative correlation indicates that as one variable increases, the other decreases.

The relationship between the variables year and number of employees found a very strong and significant negative correlation at 99% confidence. As the years cannot decrease, it is understood that for this sample, the older the company is, the leaner the number of employees it becomes.

It was only a strong and significant negative correlation at 95% confidence, which occurred between the relationship between the year and the BMN variable. That is, as the years go by, the less innovative the company becomes. In this sense, it could be concluded that the older an organization, the smaller its capacity for innovation.

The variable Country of origin was not considered in terms of data analysis, due to heterogeneity of the sample.

## SOLUTIONS AND RECOMMENDATIONS

Among the main limiting factors of this research, which resulted in a lack of significance of the collected data, were the lack of financial resources to carry out an extensive data collection (it was verified, through the literature review in which the articles that are of qualitative empirical character had the participation of several people for large-scale data collection and analysis) and the difficulty in obtaining answers from companies. It is believed that the size of the sample, in which only a sample of 30 elements was reached, was decisive for the non-significance of the data. A larger sample would give rise to more responses and opinions, further enhancing data confidence. Not only that, but the large heterogeneity of companies that composed the sample of this study associated to the low rate of return obtained to the requests for questionnaire response, greatly influenced the calculation of the results, so that it was not possible to prove correlations between the variables of significantly.

## FUTURE RESEARCH DIRECTIONS

The implications of this study for the science of management are, in a way, relevant for managers and entrepreneurs who want to move forward in this subject, drawing attention to the importance of private participation in academic production, so that it can come to be benefit from the results obtained.

Once more data is collected and analyzed, the greater the conclusions of how to do, avoiding the method of trial and error. Not only as a way of enriching the literature on the subject, a better understanding of it will help entrepreneurs and managers be a step ahead of their competitors.

This study also did not address all the design issues such as Business Model Complementarities and Business Model Lock-in, their performance implications, and even how these two issues can influence Business Model Novelty and Business Model Efficiency, thus leaving interesting issues to be addressed. analyzed in future research.

## CONCLUSION

In the present investigation, we sought to study the implications of NCBMs and ECBMs on company performance, so that this theme is directly related to the survival of companies in the market and how these can create value through new business models.

The present study contributes significantly to the theory of innovation and entrepreneurship, as an attempt to show the effects of the impact of the choice that one or more themes of business models have on the performance of companies, as a response to a latent need on the part of literature to consistently homogenize the understanding about the theme, its development, the lack of clarity of concepts and advice that are clear and practical for the management, correlating its factors of success.

The literature on the subject is full of conceptual articles and in the form of case studies, but this area suffers from a great lack of studies aimed at establishing the impacts of the different design themes on the performance of companies. There is a very small number of articles that have tested the concepts on this subject through empirical studies, allowing a large gap in the production of quantitative studies, which would allow the results to be extrapolated to a larger population.

Due to one of its main characteristics is expansion and multidimensionality, which go beyond the barriers of the company, involving all stakeholders, this topic becomes quite attractive as a subject of study, but rather slippery, given the great limitation of collection of data in the private sector and the difficulty to find research incentives within the academic environment for the social and economic sciences.

And because it is an extremely broad topic and still little explored in an empirical way, there is still much room for progress in literature. The above limitations should be an opportunity to improve this research. These should be analyzed in order to design possible future investigations. In this way, it will be very interesting for future researchers to continue the work that has been started here.

## REFERENCES

Almeida, D., Santos, M. A. R., & dos e Costa, A. F. B. (2010). Aplicação do coeficiente alfa de Cronbach nos resultados de um questionário para avaliação de desempenho da saúde pública. XXX Encontro Nacional de Engenharia de Produção, Anais da Associação Brasileira de Engenharia de Produção, 1 - 12.

Amit, R., & Zott, C. (2001). Value creation in e-business. *Strategic Management Journal, 22*(6/7), 493–520. doi:10.1002mj.187

Amit, R., & Zott, C. (2012). Creating value through business model innovation. *Sloan Management Review, 53*(3), 41–49.

Amit, R., & Zott, C. (2015). Crafting business architecture: The antecedents of business model design. *Strategic Entrepreneur. J., 9*(4), 331–350. doi:10.1002ej.1200

Brettel, M., Strese, S., & Flatten, C. T. (2012). Improving the performance of business models with relationship marketing efforts – an entrepreneurial perspective. *European Management Journal, 30*(2), 85–98. doi:10.1016/j.emj.2011.11.003

Casadesus-Masanell, R., & Ricart, J. E. (2011, Jan.). How to design a winning business model. *Harvard Business Review*, 1–9.

Chesbrough, H. (2007). Business model innovation: It's not just about technology anymore. *Strategy and Leadership, 35*(6), 12–17. doi:10.1108/10878570710833714

Chesbrough, H. W., & Rosenbloom, R. S. (2002). The role of the business model in capturing value from innovation: Evidence from Xerox Corporation's technology spinoff companies. *Industrial and Corporate Change, 11*(3), 533–534. doi:10.1093/icc/11.3.529

Foss, N. J., & Saebi, T. (2017). Fifteen years of research on business model innovation. *Journal of Management, 43*(1), 200–227. doi:10.1177/0149206316675927

Gassmann, O., Frankenberger, K., & Csik, M. (2013). *The St. Gallen Business Model Navigator. Working Paper.* University of St. Gallen.

Gerdoçi, B., Bortoluzzi, G., & Dibra, S. (2017). Business model design and firm performance: Evidence of interactive effects from a developing economy. *European Journal of Innovation Management*. Doi.org/10.1108/EJIM-02-2017-0012

Gil, A. C. (2008). *Métodos e técnicas de pesquisa social* (6th ed.). Atlas.

Hahn, R., Speith, P., & Ince, I. (2018). Business model design in sustainable entrepreneurship: Illuminating the commercial logic of hybrid businesses. *Journal of Cleaner Production, 176*, 439–451. doi:10.1016/j.jclepro.2017.12.167

Hu, B. (2014). Linking business models with technological innovation performance through organizational learning. *European Management Journal, 32*(4), 587–595. doi:10.1016/j.emj.2013.10.009

Hu, B., & Chen, W. (2016). Business model ambidexterity and technological innovation performance: Evidence from China. *Technology Analysis and Strategic Management*, *28*(5), 583–600. doi:10.1080/09537325.2015.1122186

Johnson, M. W., Christensen, C. M., & Kagermann, H. (2008). Reinventing Your Business Model. *Harvard Business Review*, *86*(12).

Kulins, C., Leonardy, H., & Weber, C. (2016). A configurational approach in business model design. *Journal of Business Research*, *69*(4), 1437–1441. doi:10.1016/j.jbusres.2015.10.121

Markides, C.C. (2013). Business model innovation: what can the ambidexterity literature teach us? *The Academy of Management Perspectives*, *27*(4), 313–323.

Pati, R. K., Nandakumar, M. K., Ghobadian, A., Ireland, R. D., & O'Regan, N. (2018). Business Model Design–performance Relationship under External and Internal Contingencies: Evidence from SMEs in an Emerging Economy. *Long Range Planning*, *51*(5), 750–769. doi:10.1016/j.lrp.2018.01.001

Schneider, S., & Spieth, P. (2013). Business model innovation: Towards an integrated future research agenda. *International Journal of Innovation Management*, *17*(1), 1–34. doi:10.1142/S136391961340001X

Wei, Z., Zhao, J., & Zhang, C. (2014). Organizational Ambidexterity, Market Orientation, and Firm Performance. *Journal of Engineering and Technology Management*, *33*, 134–153. doi:10.1016/j.jengtecman.2014.06.001

Winterhalter, S., Zeschky, M. B., & Gassmann, O. (2016). Managing dual business models in emerging markets: An ambidexterity perspective. *R & D Management*, *46*(3), 464–479. doi:10.1111/radm.12151

Zott, C., & Amit, R. (2007). Business model design and the performance of entrepreneurial firms. *Organization Science*, *18*(2), 181–199. doi:10.1287/orsc.1060.0232

Zott, C., & Amit, R. (2008). The fit between product market strategy and business model: Implications for firm performance. *Strategic Management Journal*, *29*(1), 1–26. doi:10.1002mj.642

Zott, C., & Amit, R. (2010). Business model design: An activity system perspective. *Long Range Planning*, *43*(2-3), 216–226. doi:10.1016/j.lrp.2009.07.004

Zott, C., & Amit, R. (2013). The business model: A theoretically anchored robust construct for strategic analysis. *Strategic Organization*, *11*(4), 403–411. doi:10.1177/1476127013510466

# Section 2
# Market Drivers

# Chapter 4
# Marketing-Mix Metamorphosis and New Trusted Business Practices

**Dário de Oliveira Rodrigues**
https://orcid.org/0000-0002-2817-5115
*Escola Superior de Gestão e Tecnologia, Instituto Politécnico de Santarém, Portugal*

## ABSTRACT

*This chapter discusses the impact on the marketing-mix due to the confluence of the internet of things and the internet of value which seems to be made possible by the blockchain technology. This "perfect storm" induces a vortex of reliability and business trust between people ("peer-to-peer") and machines ("bot-to-bot"), without the traditional need of third parties to ensure confidence in a negotiation. This implies innovative business practices and self-executing contracts that will take place in a more decentralized and trustworthy environment, speeding up the metamorphosis of the four marketing-mix elements in such a way that marketers will have to deal with a "product" that is always in a "beta-version"; a dynamic "price" that initially has to be free; an atomized "promotion" of reliable messages found by costumers (not the opposite); and a new virtual secure "place," which is made possible due to augmented reality and blockchain.*

## INTRODUCTION

It is thought that Blockchain Technology (BT) is a game changer that allows the emergence of an Internet of Value (IoV) by making the digital integration of two very different levels of confidence a reality. The first level is necessary to deal with information and to share its value, but it is not enough to deal with transactions which demand a second level of trust. The former lets users deal with information and its "value-of-use" (see Key Terms and Definitions) but the latter goes even further when it comes to business by allowing users to deal with money or its "value-of-exchange" (see Key Terms and Definitions).

DOI: 10.4018/978-1-7998-1843-4.ch004

*This Internet of Everything needs a Ledger of Everything. […] Rather than the Internet of Information, it's the Internet of Value or of Money. It's also a platform for everyone to know what is true—at least with regard to structured recorded information. At its most basic, [the BT] is open source code: anyone can download it for free, run it, and use it to develop new tools for managing transactions online. As such, it holds the potential for unleashing countless new applications and capabilities. (Tapscott & Tapscott, 2016, p.5)*

*[Blockchain technology] offers a way for people who do not know or trust each other to create a record of who owns what that will compel the assent of everyone concerned. It is a way of making and preserving truths. […] The great chain of being sure about things. (The Economist, 2015)*

As it is known, digital reproduction entails very low costs and it is thought that if the problem of the lack of trust traditionally inherent to the virtual world can be overcome, entirely new trusted business practices will arise.

*At the end of the day, bitcoin is programmable money. When you have programmable money, the possibilities are truly endless. We can take many of the basic concepts of the current system that depend on legal contracts, and we can convert these into algorithmic contracts, into mathematical transactions that can be enforced on the bitcoin network. As I've said, there is no third party, there is no counterparty. If I choose to send value from one part of the network to another, it is peer-to-peer with no one in between. (Antonopoulos, 2016, p.27)*

Taking this into account it is thought that the BT can bring a new era of convenience and usability for consumers and "prosumers" (see Key Terms and Definitions), conveying trust between them to the point where they become "trusted prosumers".

*The IoT makes use of the synergies that are generated by the convergence of Consumer, Business and Industrial Internet customer. The convergence creates the open, global network connecting people, data, and things. (Varmesan, 2016, p. 16)*

*Many different features of the marketing function will be transformed by blockchain. Just as blockchain provides ways to obtain information about potential contractors and partners, it will be able to tell you about people or businesses you propose to do business with. (Tapscott, 2017)*

The BT will speed up the digital change of the business paradigm, giving rise to a metamorphosis of the marketing-mix traditional elements (McCarthy, 1960) notoriously referenced for at least fifty years by Philip Kotler (Kotler, 1967), (Kotler, 2017). The metamorphosis of these four marketing-mix elements and the innovative strategies and business practices suggested in the face of such a transformation, are contemplated in this chapter.

## MARKETING-MIX METAMORPHOSIS

### The Fourth Industrial Revolution and the Internet of Things

Today's smart devices have innovative features that can deliver customized services and work regardless of the intelligence of the network where they operate and, according to Antonopoulos (2016), a network's lack of intelligence may even be an advantage.

Considering the previous industrial revolutions, the dominant idea at that time was that smart networks (e.g. phone network) were better not because of the intelligence of peripheral devices. In fact, the less intelligent they were, the easier it would be to evolve network intelligence, because products were developed in-house and the secrecy of their mass launching was seen as the key to the business success. But there is a particular disadvantage with such kind of smart networks, which is especially relevant when intelligence plumps across the market and such secrecy is no longer sustainable.

*[Smart networks] have to be upgraded from the center out. And that means that innovation occurs at the center, [is ruled] by one player, and requires permission. As a result of smart network design, innovation only happens when a feature is needed by all of the subscribers of the network, when it is compelling enough to disrupt the function of the entire network to upgrade it. (Antonopoulos, 2016)*

However, new smart devices are pushing the intelligence to the network's edges and the innovation capabilities are being moved to the prosumer's domains. It is considered that such a distributed intelligence recommends a profound change in the marketing-mix strategies, especially considering the Internet of Things (IoT), an exponentially growing infrastructure that interconnects people with unambiguously identified objects whose associated data can be powerfully processed.

*[Customers are] increasingly surrounded by sensor-based applications and recommender systems using semantic web technologies to represent knowledge in specific domains and these technologies and the Internet of Things (IoT) are being combined in a Semantic Web of Things (Gyrard, 2014, p.1).*

*Overall, the inexorable shift from simple digitization (the Third Industrial Revolution) to innovation based on combinations of technologies (the Fourth Industrial Revolution) is forcing companies to re-examine the way they do business. (Schwab, 2017).*

BT can have a tremendous impact in many business sectors; as stated by Friedlmayer et. al (2016, p.3), "[BT] can be utilized to bypass middlemen in the process of value creations and reduce frictions within systems. It therefore has the potential to be disruptive.".

*In general, blockchain and smart contracts can sustain market equilibria with a larger range of economic outcomes. (Cong et. al, 2017, p. 31)*

## ENTER THE NEW MARKETING-MIX

### Product: Made by Bits, But a Bit at a Time

It is thought that a new digital reality paves the way to a different marketing approach where products and services should not be defined and marketed by companies, but instead developed and promoted by a collaborative work in the community.

*Web 2.0 has made all interactions and conversations concerning "new media "potentially relevant for shaping marketing offers and sales promotions. (Cavallo, 2016, p. 145)*

Therefore, it is thought that customers' contributions can be considered a precious marketing input given by a new kind of "self-service", mostly intellectual, and this is why products will become experiments defined by the community. This is also why databases are probably the most precious assets for companies that want to thrive in this new digital world.

Three decades ago, Langeard and Eiglier (1987) coined the term "Servuction" to designate the process of producing a service. As it is well known, the presence of the customer is always indispensable for a service to take place, unlike the traditional production process that can normally be carried out in production units even in the absence of the customer.

*[Servuction is] the systematic and coherent organization of all the physical and human elements included in the client-company interface necessary for the performance of a service, whose commercial characteristics and quality levels were predetermined. (Langeard and Eiglier, 1987).*

Bearing in mind that the development of competitive products in the digital age must make use of precious market inputs, hereby is first hand suggested the term "self-servuction" (see Key-terms and Definitions) to designate a new type of intellectual self-service. It is thought that such a collaboration must be provided by the prosumers themselves during the process of "self-servuction" of products whose competitiveness is related to their level of innovation and customization.

While in the past the superiority of a product was always established from the outset, namely with advantages derived from branding, pricing, distribution or even through the establishment of legal barriers to entry (patents), currently the competitive advantages may arise from popularity and "crowdsourcing" leverage, mass customization and the sense of ownership or belonging induced in the final consumer.

It is considered important to emphasize the role of the BT when it comes to innovation and product development. As stated by Allen (2016), cited by Kane (2017), "blockchain creates new ways to create".

*[Blockchain] enhances not only the productivity of the system, but harnesses the talents of an open and inclusive community [...] enhancing collaboration and enabling distrust parties working efficiently together in a decentralized and innovative environment. Those powerful crowdsourcing and harnessing features make blockchain the main driver for the fourth industrial revolution. (Chuen, 2017)*

In the second part of the chapter, some related strategies to create innovative products and new value propositions are presented.

## Price: First of All It Has to Be Free or "Tokenized"

In the wake of previous industrial revolutions, the price of goods became largely dependent on production and distribution costs. However, in an increasingly lower transaction cost environment it is thought that the price of a product no longer has to be defined according to its production cost, but instead be formulated taking into account its perceived value.

*Blockchain technology offers a credible and effective means not only of cutting out intermediaries, but also by radically lowering transaction costs, turning firms into networks, distributing economic power, and enabling both wealth creation and a more prosperous future. (Tapscott, 2016)*

Recent technological advances can help companies to comply with new requisites of "price elasticity"; for instance, augmented reality is already taking the "price menu" to an all new level (Brooks, 2015). Thus, it seems that "fixed prices", that once were a very convenient form of setting the price of mass production goods, will give way to an electronically adjusted price.

It turns out that, in the digital market, the marginal cost is equal to zero, and the prices of products made of bits or that incorporate bits as a significant part of its added value, which will be the norm with the growth of IoT, also tend to be so. This way, it is thought to be economically viable to make consumers adopt free products in the first place and once their preference has been won it becomes much easier to propose a premium value afterwards. This could be better than trying to charge early for a commercial offer just for it to be skipped over by many customers and lose a market penetration chance because of free digital copies that can easily arise.

Furthermore this normally happens quickly because the battles for gaining market and wallet share in the virtual world are much faster and more competitive than in the physical world (Chuen, 2007), as is the case of price discovery in a business environment decentralized by the BT. As stated by Ali and others (2017, p. 9), BT can support for sophisticated pricing functions.

*For example, we created a:id names- pace in our implementation [of a pricing function] where (a) the price of a name drops with an increase in name length and (b) introducing non-alphabetic characters in names also drops the price. With this pricing function, the price of john.id > johnadam.id > john0001.id. The function is inspired by the observation that short names with alphabetics only are considered more desirable on namespaces like the one for Twitter usernames. (Ali et.al, 2017)*

In view of the arguments set out above, the future mainstream of business can be based on the supply of free products to many customers in order to be preferred and win something afterwards by selling them related items (e.g. upgrades) with incremental benefits at incremental prices.

When considering incremental prices fitted to pay for incremental benefits of a "long tail" of customized products, it is thought that BT also constitutes a powerful tool to enable the corresponding micropayments since cryptocurrency streamlines such price strategy. Thanks to an unparalleled divisibility, the fractional use of tokens (see Key Terms and Definitions) as a means of payment can track any incremental price increase, which may be as small as the incremental benefits that justify it. The economic viability of such micropayments is also enhanced by disintermediation and the reduction of costs that BT makes possible.

In order to show with some detail how to achieve profitability following a rationale that can somehow be counterintuitive, in the second part of this chapter price strategies and business practices will be presented.

## Promotion: Trusted Inbound Marketing

The increasing availability of new media platforms relates to the empowerment of consumers and "digital technologies have accelerated the prosumer's trend" (Rayna, 2015, p. 93), and it is believed that a new marketing communication paradigm arises marked by the multiplicity of processes to observe and respond to the consumer's needs that are expressed online both directly (e.g. Google searches) and indirectly (*e.g.* Facebook posts).

With this in mind, the author proposed the expression "Manifold Marketing" (Rodrigues, 2012) to designate this new paradigm of marketing communication. This expression results from the author's observation that only an atomized marketing communication, multiplied in time and space in both iterative and interactive ways, can satisfactorily respond to the modern marketing challenges.

*[Manifold Marketing is] the process of creating and providing multiple contents, in multiple forms and formats, intended to be found by multiple customers that seek them in multiple platforms in many occasions during the several stages of their consumption process [which marketers call also "sales funnel"]. (Rodrigues, 2014)*

As in this chapter the expression "Manifold Marketing" is used, it is appropriate to establish a conceptual difference between this expression and another concept, already well established, that is called "Integrated Marketing Communication (IMC)". While the latter expression refers to the combination of the "communication mix" needed to provide clarity, consistency and maximize the impact of marketing communication, in the case of "Manifold Marketing" it is all about creating substantially different content for "buyer personas" (Mattinen, 2016), which are assumed by consumers at different stages of the "sales funnel" (Rose, 2008). Such content should be thought out, not in order to be consistent, but in order to be found by individuals who have different concerns throughout the "sales funnel" and, thus, will search for different keywords.

It is thought that the "atomic unit" of marketing communication in online media is no longer the website or even the web page, but the "post" published on any blog or social network. In fact, the "post" has become the basic unit of social web relations and can aggregate relevant information around itself (e.g. comments). After all, the marketing activity in social media consists of building relationships and dialogues between multiple audiences, and the messages are altered by exchanging perceptions and ideas among participants. As BT works by distributing trust on the Internet (Cachin, 2017) it can be instrumental in freeing individuals from the need to rely on claims made on the social media or even by institutions, about the quality of their own products.

BT has been called 'the trust protocol' because it facilitates trust between people without the need for an intermediary to verify and/or validate identities, funds, or ensure compliance (Hernandez, 2017). For instance, "it seems that provenance tracking along a supply chain could be one of the killer apps of blockchain" (Kim & Laskowski, 2016). On the other hand, in computer science "trust" is also a measure of the quality of a peer in "peer-to-peer" systems (Seppälä, 2016) and it is thought that by using applications based on BT individuals will consider "peer-to-peer" communication more reliable and will use it systematically to make important decisions or even consider it as a general purpose technology to exchange assets and deal with sensitive information. Eventually, in a plausible future no trustful intermediaries or middlemen will be required due to BT.

*Blockchain will be the driver of the fourth industrial revolution as it enhances not only the productivity of the system, but harnesses the talents of an open and inclusive community. There is no lack of capital nor a lack of good technology. But, no amount of capital or technology can do what blockchain does: enhancing collaboration and enabling distrust parties working efficiently together in a decentralized and innovative environment. (Chuen, 2017)*

It is, therefore, important for marketers to make relevant content available, in order for it to be found by consumers and even more users in a networking effect meaningfull to marketing endeavors.

Given the current multiplicity of interaction opportunities (in time and space) afforded by social media, the option to raise "micro-interactions" seems to be the best way to create proximity to consumers who are manifestly volatile and increasingly aware that now they can find what they want by their own means. To explore several ways of doing this, in the second part of the chapter a "Manifold-Marketing Matrix" will be presented.

## Place: Crossing Virtual Reality and Real Virtuality

Considering the existence of a "mixed reality continuum" (Milgram & Kishino, 1994), Ilic and Fleisch (2016) stated that augmented reality (AR) extends the IoT experiences from the physical environment towards the virtual environment. These authors used the term "real" instead of physical, but it is considered that such an adjective is inappropriate because the virtual environment is of course, also real.

*AR extends IoT experiences from the real [i.e. physical] environment towards the virtual environment. In addition to enabling novel user experiences of interacting with objects and the environment, AR also reveals new insights about the user. The same sensing technologies required for high-end AR displays can be used to measure the user. This gives new insights into the behavioral, cognitive, and emotional state of the user. With these insights, product-service interactions can be reshaped on a whole new level. (Ilic & Fleisch, 2016)*

The virtual world should not be considered as separate from the physical world, but instead "tightly integrated into the world around us" (Guenther, 2012, p.365). Whether performed on-line or off-line, a shopping behavior is still real and the eventual developments in augmented reality promises to hit the business mainstream.

*[AR] completely immerses a user in a virtual world or experience, typically through the use of a head-mounted display (HMD) that is often connected to headphones, controllers and other peripherals that let users navigate through that experience. A key characteristic of a great [AR] experience is the feeling of 'presence'—users feel like they are truly in the synthetic environment being presented. (eMarketer, 2016)*

*The basis of [AR] is to display the real environment as faithfully as possible in an artificial virtual environment and work with this environment in real time. [AR] is actually a shift from simple (two-*

*dimensional) human interaction with the machine, to a position where this interaction takes place in three-dimensional environments. (Kaleja, 2016)*

AR provides an exciting new platform for consumer marketing, taking the consumer engagement based on location and interactivity to a new level (Barnes, 2016). Users want to be able to find information and accomplish tasks through multiple channels, and they want to be able to start a task in one channel, such as the physical stacks, and finish the task through another channel, such as a website on a mobile phone. These types of experiences are called "cross channel" experiences and one needs to think about how to integrate all of the different channels in order to move between them easily and seamlessly (NASIG, 2012). For instance, it is thought that the combination of BT with new applications for the retail sector, which are based on digital devices called "beacons", can revolutionize the shopping experience.

*Blockchain and beacon technology are merged together. The result is a smooth and secure shopping experience which fuses the advantages of online and offline worlds in retail. (Frey et. al, 2017)*

On the other hand, the predictable growth of the IoT is believed to further increase the ethical dilemma created by the need to establish a compromise between the convenience of each client and their need for privacy (Rodrigues, 2011). However, BT eventually will allow, for the first time in history, to solve the dilemma that exists when considering the trade-off between convenience and privacy, greatly reducing the perceived risk on the part of consumers. For instance, with a combination of BT and smart devices as the referred "beacons", "the resulting outcome is a recommendation system, a self-checkout system, and a payment system all in one, thereby full anonymity is guaranteed and the customer never loses control on her data" (Frey, 2017, p.1). In the second part of the chapter (section 2.2.4.), this system will be detailed.

## NEW TRUSTED BUSINESS PRACTICES

### The Blockchain Technology and the Internet of Value

An idea visualized by Jarvis (2010), cited in (Rodrigues, 2012, p. 315), may be useful for understanding the phenomenon of value creation in business networks, not only during the third industrial revolution, as this author seems to believe, but also in today's shifting paradigm *due to BT* which is itself considered a fourth industrial revolution (Chuen, 2017). *According* to Jarvis, it is a matter of imagining the economic agents as inserted in "a cloud of connections that lights up every time a new connection is created so that the cloud grows bigger and becomes denser, more luminous, more valuable". It turns out that this value can be subdivided into "value-of-use" and "value-of-exchange", two important concepts covered in this chapter (see also Key terms and Definitions).

The "value-of-use" created by digital networks has increased considerably and has been distributed by its users. However the "value-of-exchange", which is not so well spread as the former, is being distributed asymmetrically in favor of companies such as GOOGLE and FACEBOOK that are appropriating all of it. This asymmetry can be dramaticaly injust when it is known that the corresponding market value is essentially formed by assets derived from data provided by their own users.

Instead of being quantified by using "likes", as happens with the value-of-use, the correspondent value-of-exchange is quantified by using money (*e.g.* euros). Interesting enough, due to BT, some companies (e.g. Steemit) can not only distribute the former but also the latter kind of value to their users (in the form of tokens and cryptocurrencies) and still profit from the process.

*Steemit is a publishing and a social networking platform [based on its own blockchain], whose principle is to favor and remunerate the contributions of its users using a virtual currency. These contributions can take many forms, that range from publishing original content (blog posts, videos, images, etc.) to the active curation of the platform through the appreciation of content submitted by other users. (De Fillipi, 2016, p.9)*

BT uses the combination of peer-to-peer networks, cryptographic algorithms, distributed data storage and decentralized consensus mechanisms (Wright & De Fillippi, 2015), to enable new decentralized forms of allowing individuals (and even objects) to make trusted contracts between each other or collaborate with one another with no need for a middleman nor any kind of central coordination.

*[BT] is a remarkably transparent and decentralized way of recording lists of transactions […] particularly well suited to situations where it is necessary to know ownership histories. […] Blockchains shift some control over daily interactions with technology away from central elites, redistributing it among the users. (Boucher, 2017, p. 5)*

*The basic economics of blockchain can be thought of the case for why decentralized solutions to ledgers, now technically possible, are likely to become increasingly cost effective compared to centralized solutions as they run down three exponential cost curves: (1) Moore's law (cost of processing digital information, i.e. speed, halves every 18 months); (2) Kryder's Law (cost of storing digital information, i.e. memory, halves every 12 months); and (3) Nielsen's Law (cost of shipping digital information, i.e. bandwidth, halves every 24 months). (Davidson et. al, 2016)*

As it is stated by Wright & De Fillippi (2015), cited by Pazaitis (2017, p.14), "[BT] serves as a means to record, in a secure and verifiable manner, a particular state of affairs which has been agreed upon by the network". This "general purpose technology" (Davidson et al, 2016, p.2) is the first native digital medium for value (Tapscott & Tapscott, 2016), allowing "mutualised productive resources that are central to the capacity for any kind of production, including physical goods" (Pazaitis, 2017, p.11). For the first time, by allowing peers to operate through "smart-contracts" (see Key Terms and Definitions), BT can change social perceptions and even the current value system. It is early to know if a radical transformation of today's economic society is coming, but BT is already considered prominent in shaping the business environment in the near future.

*Property, contracts, and identity management are only a few examples of how a peer-to-peer, open, and frictionless [BT system could change how we conduct business in the future. (Wan, 2014, p. 2)*

*What we should expect is for Blockchain to eventually exhibit the key characteristics of a General Purpose Technology to such a great degree that it will seem obvious that it is a major innovation capable of bringing long term growth and change. (Kane, 2017)*

As stated by Pilkington (2016), cited by Kane (2017), we are still in the early stages of BT acceptance as a disruptive new technology. However, looking into the speed of adoption of such paradigms as the mainframe computer, the PC, and the Internet, whose influence was spread by mobile and social networking, it is true that "due to the current widespread global Internet and cellular connectivity, [BT] could be deployed much more quickly than any of previous paradigms" (Crosby et al., 2016, 8).

BT is showing the ability to spread into areas that involve even more complex issues such as justice and governance, which is believed to be a fertile area for academic research in the coming years. It is thought that if the principles of openness, collaboration, and sharing are politically framed and legitimized, more interest and investigation in BT should be expected.

*There is an emergence of a hybrid economy composed, on the one hand, of the capitalist market and, on the other hand, of the economy [based on] community sharing of common collaborative goods. (Rifkin, 2014, p. 11)*

*The main political binary of the last half of the twentieth century was communism versus capitalism. In the 21st century, this binary is open versus closed. (Ross, 2016, p. 233)*

It is important to understand how the new standards of openness, that can be fully trusted due to BT, contribute to the notion of "shared ideas" and should be taken into account for marketing success.

*Traditionally, the predominance of secret or closed programming standards made impossible for third parties to program interfaces between programs and applications created by different organizations. These entities and respective applications remained stagnant because secrecy was considered to be "the heart and soul" of any business. Apparently, this is no longer true and the generalization of open code software and opened APIs (Application Programming Interfaces) clearly specify the details of the interaction between independent programs belonging to independent companies or programmers. (Rodrigues, 2011, p. 320)*

It is believed that co-opting third parties contributing to this value-creation process may not be as difficult to achieve as one might think, and as it will be seen, it is considered very important indeed to be able to integrate their contributions into the development process of innovative products.

*The most important motivators for users' participation are knowledge acquisition and intrinsic motivations. Socialization with other users sharing common interests, also emerged has a relevant determinant while being rewarded for their participation was not among the most important [motivators]. [Although] participants collaborate mostly in a free and voluntary way, our research concludes that engagement in creating with peers may not purely be a function of altruism, but also of benefits that participants, reasonably, expect to attain, and perceived CCv [Co-Creation Value] within the engagement process. (Fernandes, 2015, p.11)*

In keeping with Fernandes (2015), one can take an interesting conclusion: it seems that this kind of collaboration through users' participation can be more motivating when it occurs more frequently and extensively.

All these changes seem to pave the way for an entirely new set of marketing-mix strategies and innovative business practices as will be observed in the next pages.

## THE NEW MARKETING-MIX GUIDELINES

### The New "Product": "Self-Servuction" Architecture

When it comes to the products considered in this chapter, we refer to a whole "long tail" (Anderson, 2006) of products whose digital component is increasingly responsible for their functionality, stressing that, in the so-called "Internet-of-Things (IoT), "bits" are the components that will give greater value to products, much more than the atoms that physically make them up.

As it was seen in the first part of this chapter, the "prosumers" should add value to products through a new kind of self-service that was then designated "self-servuction" (*e.g.* user-generated content on social media) which it is thought that can intellectually add much more value to products when compared to the added value of its manual counterpart of the previous industrial eras.

*Products become experiments and we shouldn't design an experiment with only that experiment in mind; it is necessarily linked to many other experiments that we must take into account with our design. [...] Experiments become cross channel experiences – Cross channel experiences will be ubiquitous [and] users are becoming more and more involved with content creation. (Bacon, 2012, p.1).*

The architecture of a "self-servuction" process should allow a continuous and gradual increase of the global value of products and services, added in each time they are used by each client. Therefore, it must be an interactive and iterative process, unfolding in a spiral of knowledge in which the company learns from the client's interactions (business inputs), which should be integrated in future product features. This is the case of "Google Translator" platform among other products or services that use similar algorithms.

*Our framework makes it possible for human collaborators not only to detect and correct some errors, but also to identify detectable errors that aren't correctable given the current information. We designed an interface to support this collaborative monolingual translation protocol. (Hu et. al, 2010, p. 8)*

On the other hand, technological progress in the realm of virtual reality (VR) and 3D printing can further increase the autonomy and involvement of the prosumers in the aforementioned "self-servuction", making participation experiences more immersive and appealing, having a positive impact on their viral marketing potential.

*Within research and development, 3D modeling is already commonplace in the consumer segment [...] VR also enables customers and representatives to design their own customized products. For example, the Lowe in-store Holoroom application allows consumers to design a kitchen or bathroom, explore it in VR, and share it on YouTube. (Morris 2016)*

*Experiential marketing content can be convincing, immersive, and also potentially social and participatory, creating a potential for virality. (Barnes, 2016)*

Finally, as stated by Pazaitis et. al (2017), BT is enabling a new system of value that will better support the dynamics of social sharing. For instance, in the matter of privacy, a potential customer can allow a company to apply a recommendation algorithm without disclosing his or her personal data (Frey, 2016) and it is believed that this BT feature can increase the consumers' appetite to share and collaborate.

## The New "Price": "Freemium" and Micropayments

It is known that a "free" offer can increase the value of other complementary offerings which can be charged if the former creates a perception of their scarcity. Hence, it is thought that, when dealing with digital products, the marketer should manage the commercial offerings by thinking first about what abundance is more interesting to create in order to get some type of profit from the scarcity that follows.

According to this rationale, certain price models are exhibited in table 1, which are useful to address the challenges settled by the BT.

*Table 1. Free-based price models*

| Types | Price Models | Examples |
|---|---|---|
| Free 1 | Direct Cross-Subsidy: get one thing free, pay for another. | The smartphone is free, but only when accompanied by a chargeable signed-in plan... |
| Free 2 | Ad Supported: the free product or free service is supported by ads (a third party subsidizes the second party). | The daily newspaper is free but contains ads... (the journal does not sell newspapers to readers, it sells the readers to advertisers) |
| Free 3 | Freemium: when the company offers many products and sells premium versions (the traditional ratio of samples is reversed) | The Skype calls on terrestrial lines are free, but the Skype mobile call service is paid...<br>(a few people subsidize everyone else) |
| Free 4 | Gift-Economy: people give away things for non-monetary rewards (to fulfill belonging, self-esteem, or self-realization needs). | Wikipedia (if someone offers their work voluntarily to many, later on, many will be grateful and some of them will donate). |

Source: adapted from Anderson (2009)

Specifically regarding the model of type 3, there are several possibilities that can even be combined: (i) to offer free use of the product for some time but after that exhausted time start cashing in; (ii) to offer a limited number of free features but demand payment to activate extra features; (iii) to offer a certain number of units of products for free but charge for selling extra units; (iv) to offer a free product to clients who meet certain requirements or have a certain profile but request payment from other customers.

It is thought that the impact of BT in the operationalization of these price models will be particularly interesting, especially when applied to type 3 and type 4 price models. Concerning the latter, which is the price strategy followed by Wikipedia, it is believed that, like it was seen in relation to the aforementioned redistributive behavior of the company Steemit, it will also be possible to distribute tokens to any users who want to give their attention, reputation and knowledge in what used to be a non-paid voluntary work. It should be noticed that these tokens can be given or exchanged between users, obviously being offered first by those who purchased them following an Initial Coin Offering (ICO), generally doing this with the hope that these tokens will increase in value in the future, thanks to the popularity of their use (depending on the models used by the issuing companies, these tokens may or not be subject to the inflation resulting from eventual new issuings).

If BT really changes the business game, future prosumers can prefer to collaborate with those companies that choose to share their wealth with whom ultimately originated it. As for the type 3 model, it is thought that BT and cryptocurrencies will also allow faster payments for using premium features and even to make micropayments to buy single features, because the cryptocurrencies "are better for microtransactions and micropayments with very fast resolution" (Antonopoulos, 2016, p.135). Therefore, it is thought that BT will facilitate the adoption of an "as-a-service" approach (e.g. pay-as-you-go) and perhaps people will start to prefer "using" instead of "owning".

*"Services that let customers access goods, such as car-sharing, are increasing relevance as an alternative to ownership. These access-based services allow consumers to avoid the "burdens of ownership", i.e., risks and responsibilities that come with owning a good [...] a higher usage of an access-based service increases the likelihood that consumers subsequently reduce ownership." (Schaefers, 2016, p. 569)*

In fact, it is thought that there might be a tendency of substitution, on the part of the prosumers, of the feeling of individual property for an ecological feeling of shared use, is an important subject that deserves to be investigated from the marketing point of view and beyond.

## The New "Promotion": "Manifold-Marketing"

In the first part of this chapter it was stated that marketing communication works better with a "Manifold-Marketing" approach. Although without intending to generalize or extend to other sectors the results obtained in a pharmaceutical marketing study conducted by the author (Rodrigues, 2012), it is thougth that one can take it as an example on how to identify different segments of customers as well as their preferred communication channels and the best marketing conducts to be undertaken online. Therefore, the following "Manifold-Marketing Matrix" is presented:

*Table 2. The Manifold-Marketing Matrix*

| | **The Curious** | **The Criterious** | **The Communitarians** |
|---|---|---|---|
| Consumers | *Circa* 50% of users | *Circa* < 20% of users | *Circa* > 30% of users |
| Channels | Prefer Web Content | Prefer Websites | Prefer Social Media |
| Conducts | Social Bookmarking | Search Engine Marketing | Social Media Marketing |

Source: adapted from Rodrigues et. al, (2013)

Observing table 2 it is possible to distinguish three market segments:

- "The Curious" are the users that consider search engines a preferred tool to search for information because they think first about content and related keywords in order to search and be able to find what they want. This is the segment with the largest number of potential consumers and the marketing effort should be based on content marketing and content aggregation through social bookmarking (see Key Terms and Definitions) making content fully searchable and ready to be found by users.

- "The Criterious" are the users that give high importance to the public and private institutional websites. The most suitable procedure in this case is to increase the likelihood of an institutional website to be found online, raising their conspicuity on the web through search engine marketing aiming to capture the customer's attention and help them to find their way to products and services.
- "The Communitarians" are the users that value interacting and sharing content on the Internet. Therefore the marketing effort must embrace the participation in the social networks, emphasizing the creation of "posts" and their comments, not forgetting about other network functionalities which are available in the social media ecosystem, including interactions via chats, video and photo sharing, micro-blogging, etc..

Therefore, the marketers' focus on Search Engine Marketing isn't a marketing panacea or even a business procedure as relevant as one can think, which discourages what seems to be a common practice for the majority of marketers, which is comprehensible because for both companies and customers this is considered one of the most important keys for business success.

*The majority of marketing spend is derived from online marketing where Search Engine Marketing is the largest spend category [...] The majority of marketing spend today is on Search Engine Marketing. (Delloite, 2015)*

Further studies are therefore needed in order to understand whether it is possible to extrapolate the results expressed in the presented "Manifold-Marketing Matrix" and verify their applicability to other business sectors.

## The New "Place": Omni-Channels of Augmented Reality

Regarding the "Place" element of the marketing-mix, its metamorphosis is underway and the modern distribution should ensure that an organization can keep delivering on its promises in the presence of "omni-channel" customers that are and will be emancipated as never before. For this purpose, specific "Place" strategies must be set in place.

*[The omni-channel customers] think of shopping as one experience, whether online (including on a mobile device) or in-store and so must businesses. [...] Consumers now expect the same experience across multiple shopping channels, including the same products being available both online and in-store. (Worldpay, 2015)*

The double entry matrix presented in Table 3 shows the possible buying situations when shopping either on-line or off-line.

To facilitate the management of the "Place" element when it involves an "omni-channel" perspective, specific customer relationship management (CRM) strategies can be established to facilitate the seamless marketing integration of various distribution channels. However, such systems are complex and their articulation can be difficult to implement and maintain. This is why it is thought that BT can empower many applications to coordinate such integration, notably by facilitating the articulation of multiple decentralized databases from the retailer's perspective, enabling reporting to a trusted public ledger and the use of "smart contracts" to reduce friction from the customer's perspective.

*Table 3. The multi-channel shopping experiences*

| | *Buy In-Store* | *Buy On-line* |
|---|---|---|
| *View In-Store* | Traditional Shopping (Bricks-and-Mortars) | "Showrooming" and "Self-Checkout" |
| *View On-line* | In-store inventory is visible through e-Commerce. | Digital Shopping (Pure Players) |

Source: adapted from Worldpay (2015) and Frey (2017)

Several marketing studies proved that personalized offers are more successful than non-personalized ones and increase the customer satisfaction (Smutkupt et. al, 2010). Thanks to the use of BT, the privacy of customers becomes cryptographically guaranteed which is of great interest to facilitate the use of "smart-contracts" and the creation of a new purchasing system where the customer can invoke and customize such contracts stipulating which data can be used and by whom.

*"An apparel company gets access for computing recommendations for clothes based on the customer's body measurements. The company has never access to the measurements and the customer is even able to completely block other sensitive data like detailed textures resulted from a 3D body scan. All involved data are permanently encrypted. There is no need for a trusted-third party.". (Frey et. al, 2012, p. 2)*

On the other hand, as stated by Çadırcı & Köse, (2016, p. 281), augmented reality "is a valuable tool that can be used to enhance the online shopping experience in a way that wasn't possible before". The following situation is an example of this:

*"She then uses an augmented reality feature in the application to see how it looks at her, and sends it to her friends for feedback. Her friends give a positive review and she places the order online, to have it delivered to her home in the next few hours" (Mishra, 2014, p. 10)*

Looking into an innovation in retail, recently made possible by the combination of BT and the "beacon" technology, which is based on low energy devices that broadcast a Bluetooth signal to nearby mobile devices equipped with an application that pushes marketing notifications and displays them on the user's screen (Andriulo, 2015), it seems to be clear that this evolution allows a seamless shopping experience as is detailed in the following example:

*When she approaches the store, the Beacon sends a signal to her smartphone and triggers two actions. First, the app computes a new blockchain address for the upcoming transactions. Second, an encrypted message, including the personal data and its permissions is automatically sent into the blockchain network to the company's address. [Then] the company gets a notification and starts the recommendation algorithm. [...] When the company receives the results, the recommendations are forward to the user's address. Finally, the app decrypts/visualize the recommendations. [After that] the customer may decide to buy one of the recommended products. She selects the product on her smartphone and put it into a virtual shopping basket. Then she directly pays with a transaction into the blockchain network to the address of the company. After completion, she may terminate all data access and computation permis-*

*sions. During the whole process, the full anonymity for the customer is guaranteed and the company never received customer's personal data. (Frey et. al, 2017, p. 2)*

It is known that the processing costs of payments can be up to 5 percent per transaction, decreasing the already short margins of e-commerce players (Deliotte, 2015). When incurred by other players of the physical world these costs can be even higher and, interestingly enough, BT can reduce them considerably (Antonopoulos, 2016). It is believed that this will lead to a technological substitution and new business practices. This evolution was announced a few years ago, having been detailed how BT simplifies payment systems (Nakamoto, 2008).

Finally, the aforementioned use of augmented is already in place thanks to companies such as Nestle, Unilever and Cadbury, and has enabled better shelf layout and increased sales (Rutgers Online, 2014). On the other hand, the socially-connected nature of mobile devices (and other computing devices) means that instead of providing augmented reality in stores, companies are increasingly likely to change their distribution strategy and distribute downloadable apps for consumers (Barnes, 2016).

Due to BT's decentralized structure and to the discretionary privacy that can be guaranteed to those who use it, the public availability of information about the supply chain provenance of goods is now a reality and such monitorization gives to all stakeholders the ubiquitous opportunity to track products from the place of origin to the end consumer (Dickson, 2016). Blockchain startups like provenance.org and skuchain.com are working on the supply chain provenance (Kim, 2016). These are examples on how the cryptography-based and immutable nature of the ledgers based on BT will bring security and trust to the business practices related to this marketing-mix element.

## CONCLUSION

Digital reproduction entails very low costs and means business opportunities, in particular through the use of innovative forms of collaboration based on openness and decentralization which is the case of blockchain technology (BT). The basic economics of blockchain are a good example of a network effect, revealing the greater efficiency of decentralized solutions when compared to centralized ones. Because relying on algorithms of mathematical trust seems to be much cheaper than relying on trusted third parties, BT is becoming increasingly competitive against the mature technology of centralized ledgers and this is driving a technological substitution. On the other hand, the current competitive environment calls for creativity and for a cross-fertilization of projects and ideas which are coming from different minds and different owners. This is making the legal framing of intellectual property obsolete and leading to the emergence of less restrictive approaches. It is thought that these and other fundamental changes, determine the following metamorphosis of the marketing elements.

Starting with the "Product", it is known that a growing part of the value proposition of innovative products is related to their customization which is tendentiously based and formed by bits instead of atoms. These bits are coming from databases whose value is correlated with their capability of collecting information that leads to product innovation and customization - it is for this very reason that user data is so coveted and valued in the market, even giving rise to cases as scandalous as those involving the companies Facebook and Cambridge Analytics (Cadwalladr & Graham-Harrison, 2018). Accordingly, the "Product" will be constantly changing (bit by bit, but a bit at a time) and will look like a permanent and pervasive "beta" experiment carried out jointly with the users. In order to do this, for co-opting third parties to work as an external resource is increasingly important and such contribution corresponds to a new "self-service" paradigm in the information age. To designate it, the "self-servuction" neologism was first hand created. It is considered that product management will become, to a large extent, a matter of encouraging users to co-create value and that such contributions can be increasingly relied upon BT, enhancing the safety and productivity of a decentralized and collaborative work (e.g. peer-to-peer).

As for the "Price", it is thought that it is also in a deep metamorphosis mainly due to a deflationary digital environment by virtue of the extremely low costs associated with the digital reproduction. It is increasingly easy to obtain information about prices and to know the global availability of products and services, which makes it increasingly difficult to create value based on the traditional way of doing business. New price models can use digital features to increase the popularity of products and services rather than managing the product´s scarcity and it is possible to turn this digital abundance into a passport for profitability, often in ways that can be counterintuitive. Moreover, the BT allows the creation of "[cryptocurrencies] that are better for microtransactions and micropayments with very fast resolution" (Antonopoulos, 2016, p.135), contributing to the growing of a "long tail" of products. As the BT allows businesses to release their own tokens, for instance through an Initial Coin Offering (ICO), these can later be exchanged for products, services or money. For this reason the price strategies should allow such advanced payments.

Regarding the marketing-mix element "Promotion", the author uses the expression "Manifold-Marketing" to designate a new marketing communication paradigm that starts from the premise that multiple messages must be searched and found by customers rather than being thrown against them. Taking into account that a new paradigm of trust (BT) seems to be coming to the Internet and even reliability could become searchable, a new set of multiple trusted messages will be marketable. Trying to elucidate how to deal with the element "Promotion", a "Manifold Marketing Matrix" was introduced and different types of preferred digital marketing tools and communication channels were presented.

Finally, considering the "Place", it seems to be clear that only an ubiquitous distribution can satisfy omni-channel customers that want to find information and be able to buy through "cross-channel" experiences. As it was seen, this can influence the technological progress and new applications will be created on top of BT. It is thought that trusted transactions are on their way and a more decentralized distribution of value is perhaps, not so far away.

## REFERENCES

Ali, M. R., Nelson, J., & Freedman, M. (2017). *Blockstack: A Decentralized Internet*. Retrieved from https://blockstack.org/whitepaper.pdf

AllenD. (2016). *Discovering and Developing the Blockchain Cryptoeconomy*. Retrieved from https://ssrn.com/abstract=2815255

Anderson, C. (2006). *The Long Tail: Why the Future of Business is Selling Less of More*. Hyperion.

Andriulo, S., Elia, V., & Gnoni, M. G. (2015). Mobile self checkout systems in the FMCG retail sector: A comparison analysis. *International Journal of RF Technologies: Research and Applications*, *6*(4), 207–224. doi:10.3233/RFT-150067

Antonopoulos, A. (2016). *The Internet of Money*. Merkle Bloom LLC.

BarnesS. (2017). Understanding Virtual Reality in Marketing: Nature, Implications and Potential. doi:10.2139srn.2909100

Boucher, P. (2017). *How blockchain technology could change our lives*. European Parliamentary Research Service. Retrieved Apr 13, 2017, from https://www.europarl.europa.eu/RegData/etudes/IDAN/2017/581948/EPRS_IDA(2017)581948_EN.pdf

Brooks, J. (2015). *Virtual Reality: Advancing Marketing Research… and Visualizing a Better World*. Lieberman Research Worldwide.

Cachin, C. (2017). *Blockchain, cryptography, and consensus*. Retrieved from https://www.zurich.ibm.com/~cca/talks/20170622-blockchain-ice.pdf

Çadırcı, T. O., & Köse, Ş. G. (2016). Augmented reality as a tool to enhance the experiential value of online shopping: The future of fashion retailing. In *Handbook of research on global fashion management and merchandising* (pp. 280–304). IGI Global. doi:10.4018/978-1-5225-0110-7.ch012

Cadwalladr, C., & Graham-Harrison, E. (2018). Revealed: 50 million Facebook profiles harvested for Cambridge Analytica in major data breach. *The Guardian, 17*, 22.

Cavallo, M. (2016,). *Accueil: IMODEV - Improving public policies. Sharing economy, sharing information. Are open data addressing us towards a new wikieconomy?* Retrieved on March 12th, 2017, from http://ojs.imodev.org/index.php/RIDDN/article/view/145/201

Caywood, C., Schultz, D. E., & Wang, P. (1991). *Integrated Marketing Communications*. Northwestern University Medill School of Journalism.

Christidis, K., & Devetsikiotis, M. (2016). Blockchains and smart contracts for the internet of things. *IEEE Access: Practical Innovations, Open Solutions, 4*, 2292–2303. doi:10.1109/ACCESS.2016.2566339

Chuen, K., & David, L. E. E. (2017). *Fintech Tsunami: Blockchain as the Driver of the Fourth Industrial Revolution*. Academic Press.

Cong, L. W., He, Z., & Zheng, J. (2017). *Blockchain Disruption and Smart Contracts*. Rtetrieved from https://papers.ssrn.com/sol3/Data_Integrity_Notice.cfm?abid=2985764

Crosby, M., Nachiapan, P., Verma, S., & Kalyanaraman, V. (2016). Blockchain Technology: Beyond Bitcoin. *Applied Innovation Review*. Retrieved from: http://scet.berkeley.edu/wp-content/uploads/AIR-2016-Blockchain.pdf

Davidson, S., De Filippi, P., & Potts, J. (2016). *Economics of blockchain*. Retrieved from https://papers.ssrn.com/sol3/papers.cfm?abstract_id=2744751

De Filippi, P., & Reymond, M. (2016). *La Blockchain: comment réguler sans autorité*. Retrieved from https://archive-ouverte.unige.ch/unige:90735

Deloitte. (2015). *Omni-channel retail A Deloitte point of view*. Retrieved from https://www2.deloitte.com/content/dam/Deloitte/se/Documents/ /Omni-channel-2015.pdf

Editora, P. (2016). *Dicionário da Língua Portuguesa*. Porto Editora.

eMarketer. (2016). *Virtual Reality Is an Immersive Medium for Marketers: Marketers should start experimenting sooner rather than later*. Retrieved February 10, 2017 from: https://www.emarketer.com/Article/Virtual-Reality-Immersive-Medium-Marketers/1013526

Fernandes, T., & Remelhe, P. (2015). How to engage customers in co-creation: Customers' motivations for collaborative innovation. *Journal of Strategic Marketing*, *24*(3-4), 311–326.

Frey, R., Wörner, D., & Ilic, A. (2016). *Collaborative Filtering on the Blockchain: A Secure Recommender System for e-Commerce*. Retrieved from https://aisel.aisnet.org/amcis2016/ISSec/Presentations/36/

Guenther, M. (2012). *Intersection: How Enterprise Design Bridges the Gap between Business, Technology, and People*. Newnes.

Gyrard, A. (2014). *Domain knowledge Interoperability to build the Semantic Web of Things*. W3C Web of Things Workshop, Berlin, Germany

Hernandez, K. (2017). *Blockchain for Development–Hope or Hype?* Retrieved from https://opendocs.ids.ac.uk/opendocs/handle/123456789/15

Ilic, A., & Fleisch, E. (2016). *Augmented Reality and the Internet of Things*. Retrieved from https://www.research-collection.ethz.ch/bitstream/handle/20.500.11850/128476/eth-50534-01.pdf

Kaleja, P., & Kozlovská, M. (2016). Virtual reality as marketing tool for developer projects. *Czech Journal of Civil Engineering.*, *2016*(1), 64–70.

Kane, E. (2017). *Is Blockchain a General Purpose Technology?* Retrieved from https://ssrn.com/abstract=2932585

Kim, H., & Laskowski, M. (2016). *Towards an ontology-driven blockchain design for supply chain provenance*. Retrieved from https://papers.ssrn.com/sol3/papers.cfm?abstract_id=2828369

Kotler, P. (1967). *Marketing Management: Analysis, Planning, and Control*. Prentice-Hall.

Kotler, P., & Keller, K. (2017). *Marketing Management, Student Value Edition* (15th ed.). Pearson.

Langeard, E., & Eiglier, P. (1987). *Servuction: Le marketing des services*. John Wiley & Sons.

Levine, R., Locke, C., Searls, D., & Weinberger, D. (2011). *The cluetrain manifesto*. Basic books.

Mattinen, J. (2016). *Intensifying buyer personas using an inbound marketing strategy*. Academic Press.

McCarthy, E. (1960). *Basic Marketing: A Managerial Approach*. Lisa Firth.

Mishra, R. (2014). *Omni-channel Retailing: When it becomes a commodity, what then?* Academic Press.

Morris, C. (2016). *Virtual reality and the new sales experience*. Retrieved from: https://www.campaignlive.com/article/virtual-reality-new-sales-experience/1392253

Muniz, A., & Schau, H. (2007). Vigilante Marketing and Consumer-created Communications. *Journal of Advertising*, *36*(3), 187–202.

Nakamoto, S. (2008). *Bitcoin: A Peer-to-Peer Electronic Cash System*. Retrieved from https://bitcoin.org/bitcoin.pdf

NASIG. (2012). *NASIG Communication. Newsletter*. Retrieved from http://tigerprints.clemson.edu/cgi/viewcontent.cgi?article=1385&context=nasig

Newman, N. (2014). Apple iBeacon technology briefing. *Journal of Direct, Data and Digital Marketing Practice*, *15*(3), 222–225.

Pazaitis, A., De Filippi, P., & Kostakis, V. (2017). *Blockchain and Value Systems in the Sharing Economy: The Illustrative Case of Backfeed*. Academic Press.

Perelman, M. (1994). Retrospectives: Fixed capital, railroad economics and the critique of the market. *The Journal of Economic Perspectives*, *8*(3), 189–195.

Pilkington, M. (2015). *Blockchain technology: principles and applications*. Retrieved from https://papers.ssrn.com/sol3/Papers.cfm?abstract_id=2660

Rayna, T., Striukova, L., & Darlington, J. (2015). Co-creation and user innovation: The role of online 3D printing platforms. *Journal of Engineering and Technology Management*, *37*, 90–102.

Rifkin, J. (2014). *A Sociedade do Custo Marginal Zero*. Bertrand.

Rodrigues, D. (2011). Cyberethics of Business Social Networking. In M. Cruz-Cunha, P. Gonçalves, N. Lopes, E. Miranda, & G. Putnik (Eds.), *Handbook of Research on Business Social Networking: Organizational, Managerial, and Technological Dimensions* (pp. 314–338). Business Science Reference.

Rodrigues, D. (2012). Cyberethics of Business Social Networking. In Information Resources Management Association (Eds.), E-Marketing: Concepts, Methodologies, Tools, and Applications (pp. 756-781). Hershey, PA: IGI Global.

Rodrigues, D. Tavares, J. Lopes, J. (2014). Manifold-Marketing: A new marketing archetype for the information age, applied to the adoption of oral contraceptives and other drugs by end-users. Lusíada. *Economia & Empresa, 2*(17), 59-80.

Rodrigues, D. F., Lopes, J. C., & Tavares, J. F. (2013). Manifold Marketing: A New Marketing Archetype for the Information Age, Applied to the Adoption of Oral Contraceptives and Other Drugs by End-Users. *Proceedings of the Third Annual Conference of International Network of Business & Management Journals (INBAM 2013).*

Rose, D. (2008, June). The information-seeking funnel. In *National Science Foundation workshop on Information-Seeking Support Systems (ISSS)* (pp. 32-36). Academic Press.

Rubino, J. (2014). Bricks and clicks. *CFA Institute Magazine*, *25*(4), 30–32.

Schaefers, T., Lawson, S. J., & Kukar-Kinney, M. (2016). How the burdens of ownership promote consumer usage of access-based services. *Marketing Letters*, *27*(3), 569–577.

Schwab, K. (2016). *The fourth industrial revolution: a Davos reader*. Council on Foreign Relations.

Schwab, K. (2017). *The fourth industrial revolution*. Crown Business.

Smutkupt, P., Krairit, D., & Esichaikul, V. (2010). Mobile Marketing: Implications for Marketing Strategies. *International Journal of Mobile Marketing*, *5*(2), 126–139.

Snow, C. C., Fjeldstad, Ø. D., Lettl, C., & Miles, R. E. (2010). Organizing Continuous Product Development and Commercialization: The Collaborative Community of Firms Model. *Journal of Product Innovation Management, 28*(1), 3–16.

Tapscott, D., & Tapscott, A. (2016). *Blockchain Revolution: How the technology behind Bitcoin is changing money, business, and the world.* Penguin.

The Economist. (2015, Oct. 31). Blockchains: The great chain of being sure about things. *The Economist.*

Varmesan, O., & Friess, P. (Eds.). (2016). Internet of Things: Converging Technologies for Smart Environments and Integrated Ecosystems. River Publishers.

Wan, T., & Hoblitzell, M. (2014). Bitcoin's promise goes far beyond payments. *Harvard Business Review.*

Worldpay. (2015). *The Store of the Future and the Role of Omni-Channel Payments in Driving Business Growth.* Retrieved 21 Mar. 2017 from https://www.worldpay.com/sites/default/files/WPUK-Omni-channel-payments-store-of-the-future.pdf

## KEY TERMS AND DEFINITIONS

**Manifold Marketing:** The process of creating and providing multiple contents, in multiple forms and formats, intended to be found by multiple customers that seek them in multiple platforms in many occasions during the several stages of their consumption process.

**Prosumer:** A proactive consumer that voluntarily and when stimulated to do so, participates in the design, creation or improvement of products and services.

**Self-Servuction:** The process of production of a service carried out in a strategic partnership and close collaboration with the prosumers.

**Smart Contracts:** Software programs that code business arrangements and that execute themselves automatically under pre-determined circumstances which are also coded.

**Social Bookmarking:** Web services that perform the indexation and the tagging of content in a socially intelligible way, allowing to organize that content in order to facilitate access and sharing.

**Token:** An object (either in hardware or software) which represents the right to perform some operation. Currencies are "tokens" of the physical world and cryptocurrencies are tokens of the virtual world.

**Value of Exchange:** The value that can be obtained by trading something.

**Value of Use:** The value that can be obtained when using something.

# Chapter 5
# The Consequences of Market Orientation on Performance, New Product Success, and Customer Satisfaction in Traditional Sectors:
## The Case of the Portuguese Wine Sector

**Paulo Matos Graça Ramos**
*Universidade Lusíada Norte, Portugal*

## ABSTRACT

*The market orientation concept used has been used as a way to measure the implementation of marketing strategies and tactics. Although it is still widely accepted and used as a framework for various researches, it is still open for debate as there is not yet a consensus on its consequences on business performance and in other consequences such has new product development and customer satisfaction. This chapter discusses the application of market orientation in a traditional sector (the Portuguese wine sector) using a market orientation model that integrates both the cultural and the behavioural streams. The results of the research lead us to conclude that market orientation favours in a moderate ways new product success and customer satisfaction and that it is not directly related with business profitability.*

## INTRODUCTION

The concept of Market Orientation (MO) has attracted a great deal of attention since the early 1990's because it made a significant contribution to the measurement of the marketing concept (Foley & Fahy, 2009). In recent years MO has been shown to provide a valuable resource-based advantage in domestic markets on the level of export performance (He, Brouthers & Filatotchev, 2018). Some of the main expected MO outputs are, therefore, related to business performance, sustained by authors such

DOI: 10.4018/978-1-7998-1843-4.ch005

as Narver and Slater (1990), Ruekert (1992), Deshpandé Farley and Webster (1993), Diamantopoulous and Hart, (1993), Greenley, (1995). These are still a matter of debate since many did not find this direct connection between MO and business performance (Langerak, 2001; Dobni & Luffman, 2003; Gray & Hooley, 2002). More recent studies in a similar context (Ho, Nguyen, Adhikari, Miles & Bonney, 2018) indicate that there was no significant relationship between market orientation and performance, but related constructs such as customer orientation and inter-functional coordination were positively related to innovation. Also a positive relationship between innovation and financial performance was found. Han, Namwoon and Rajendra (1998) found that innovation has a mediating role in the MO and corporate performance relationship. What seems less questionable is the link between MO and the impact on new product success (Lukas & Farell, 2000; Hult, Hurley & Knight G. 2004; Baker & Sinkula, 2005; 2007). Although less explored, the relationship between MO and customer satisfaction was sustained by Kohli and Jaworski (1990) and Gray, Matear and Boshoff (1998) and by Morgan and Vorhies (2018). This paper will evaluate some of the main outcomes of MO in a traditional environment were production orientation may still prevail: the Portuguese wine sector. This paper initially presents the MO construct and its main streams. The expected outcomes of the MO are further discussed and three main hypotheses are formulated. Finally, the results are discussed and recommendations for future research are made.

## THE PORTUGUESE WINE SECTOR

According to OIV (2018) Portugal is the 5th producer in the Europe and the 11th in the world in 2018 with a production around 6.7 million hectolitres. In terms of consumption it is the 12th biggest market in the world with 5.2 million hl with the highest *per capita* consumption of around 54L per year (OIV, 2018). In 2017 it amounted to around 1,5% of Portugal's total exports and 11,5% of all agri-food sector exports and amounts to 66% the share of Portuguese wines within the export of all Portuguese beverages, spirits and vinegar products (ViniPortugal, 2018). As for the exports Portugal is the 9th biggest exporter with 3 million hl which represents 0.8 billion euros and exports 45% of its wine production. In terms of imports is 12th biggest importer with 2.1 million hl. (ViniPortugal, 2018). In recent years the production of wine stabilized significantly at around 6 million hectolitres (OIV, 2018). From January to September de 2019 the wine exports increased 3,6% in volume and 5% in value and increase the average price by 1,3% to 2,66 €/l. (ViniPortugal, 2019; IVV, 2018).

On the Ramos, Martins and Barandas (2012) research on the market orientation within the Portuguese wine sector, it was suggested that producers and wine intermediaries tend to over appreciate their own self concept of being "Market Oriented". They tended to overemphasize the MO cultural aspects (values and beliefs) without fully implementing most of the MO activities, namely the necessary and organized systems of information gathering and flow. This research also suggested that both wine producers and intermediaries were still in an embryonic stage of market orientation. The most critical aspect was the obvious information gap between wine consumer's and the supply side (producers and intermediaries). This made clear a need for a more market oriented approach in this sector.

## MARKET ORIENTATION CONCEPT AND DIMENSIONS

Levitt (1975) proposed that marketing myopia is the opposite of being market oriented, thus defining more what is not being "market oriented". It was only with the promotion of the 1987 Marketing Science Institute (MSI) conference under the topic "Developing a Market Orientation" that the concept gained the shape it holds today. The main issues raised there were: how to measure it, its optimal level and the need to think of it as the basis for innovation. These were then developed at another MSI conference in 1990 (Deshpandé, 1999) were three main different groups of researchers (Kohli & Jaworski, 1990; Narver & Slater, 1990; and Deshpandé, Farley & Webster, 1993) emerged with slightly different proposals.

Kohli and Jaworski's (1990) research into the understanding of MO led them to propose a concept divided into three dimensions: (1) intelligence generation (2) intelligence dissemination and (3) responsiveness. The first dimension means, not only identifying the customers' needs, but also the analysis of the exogenous factors that influence them, the competitors, suppliers and distributors, as well as the ways in which they react to market changes. The second dimension refers to spreading this information into every department of a corporation. Lambin (1999) claims that dissemination of market information is the best way to develop a market-orientated culture, suggesting a kind of feedback effect between business culture and dissemination. However, according to Deshpandé, Farley and Webster (1993), this dimension seems to be strongly conditioned by the corporate cultures of the organizations, and according to Harris (1999), it is the most serious obstacle to MO. The third dimension, implies turning the previously acquired knowledge into concrete actions, which may involve transformations in the way of using the marketing mix as a means to improve the market performance of the company. The MO is only complete when the company uses the generated and disseminated intelligence in order to refine its actions in the market.

Trying to propose a wider concept of MO, Narver and Slater (1990) defined it as "*the organizational culture that effectively and efficiently creates the necessary behaviours for the creation of superior value for buyers, and, thus, continuous superior performance for the business*" (p. 21). The model proposed by Narver and Slater (1990) identifies three different behavioural dimensions: *customer orientation, competitors orientation and interfunctional coordination,* which constitute the activities related to the acquisition and dissemination of market information and to the creation of customer value (making it possible to detect a parallelism with Kohli and Jaworski's perspective). The first dimension, customer orientation, implies the understanding of the present and future needs of the target clients, in order to create products and services of greater value. This means becoming conscious of the customer's chain of value, so as to concentrate on activities that either increase the benefit or diminish the costs for the customer. The second dimension, competitor orientation, means that the corporation should acquire information about all its competitors, both existing and potential and should compare its resources and capabilities with those of the competition. The third dimension, interfunctional coordination, is the coordinated use of the resources at the disposal of the corporation in order to create higher value for the customers. So that this may occur, the authors claim that all the information should be shared by all sectors of the corporation, making it possible for the decisions to be taken in an interfunctional manner, to increase efficiency in the creation of value for the customer. This implies that the intelligence dissemination proposed by Kohli and Jaworski (1990) is a fundamental condition for the organization's interfunctional coordination. The interfunctional coordination also requires an integrated and coordinated vision of all marketing functions. Narver and Slater (1990) consider the market organization to be likewise determined by an organizational culture, which may create the behaviours necessary to supply a superior value for the customers, and, consequently, a higher business performance.

Sharing a similar perspective Deshpandé, Farley and Webster (1993) claim that the understanding of the MO concept varies according to different cultural contexts. These authors assessed the variation of the concept of MO by measuring the connections between corporate culture, customer orientation, innovation, and business-related performance. The core dimension is the organizational culture as "*the pattern of shared values and beliefs that help individuals understand organizational functioning and thus provide them with the norms for behaviour in the organization*" (Deshpandé & Webster, 1998, p.4). This perspective of organizational culture views the organization as systems and focuses on managerial information processing, somewhat similar with the intelligence dissemination dimension of Kohli and Jaworski (1990). Nonetheless, this central corporate culture dimension can is also considered more of an antecedent of the MO concept, were it creates the proper climate where it can prosper (Henderson, 1998). Kohli and Jaworski (1990) view customer orientation and MO as synonymous where the market is just a set of potential customers of a firm. For them MO should not include the competitor orientation dimension as they consider it the opposite of customer orientation (Deshpandé et al., 1993). They defined customer orientation as the set of beliefs that put the customer's interests first, before other stakeholders such as owners, managers and employees. In their opinion, customer orientation is a component of the overall corporate culture that does not just imply information collecting activities about the needs of actual and potential buyers. For their proposed third dimension, organizational innovativeness and performance, they adopt Drucker's (1954) vision that there are only two basic business functions: marketing and innovation and that innovation has a positive impact on business performance.

Proposing a more consensual definition of market orientation, Ruekert (1992) argues that the MO definition relies on three basic points: information collection, strategy development and implementation of that strategy. Therefore, this constitutes a broader perspective that is also related with the marketing concept and process (analysis, planning, implementation and control) as proposed by Kotler (1996). A different view of the main dimensions of MO is put forward by Homburg and Pflesser (2000), who proposed eight different dimensions of market-oriented values and norms (i.e. success, innovativeness and flexibility, openness of internal communication, quality and competence, speed, inter-functional cooperation, responsibility of employees, and appreciation of employees). Although these alternatives have been proposed, most of the subsequent literature on MO is based on the propositions of Kohli and Jaworski (1990), Narver and Slater (1990) and, to a lesser extent, Deshpandé et al. (1993). Table 1 compares the main authors' MO concepts.

*Table 1. Comparison of the dimensions of the concept of Market Orientation*

| Authors | Dimensions | | |
|---|---|---|---|
| Kohli & Jaworski (1990) | Intelligence Generation | Intelligence Dissemination | Responsiveness |
| Ruekert (1992) | Information collection | Strategy development | Strategy implementation |
| Narver & Slater (1990) | Customer orientation Competitor orientation | Interfunctional coordination | |
| Deshpandé et al (1993) | Central dimension: Corporate culture | | |
| | Customer orientation | | Business Performance and Innovation |

Despite proposing these different approaches to the MO construct, a convergence among these main dimensions is sustained by Jaworski, Kohli, and Sahay (2000): (1) knowledge of market development, (2) sharing this information with the organisation's management, and (3) adaptation of the offer according to the changes in the market (Table 1.). Summarizing the main levels of MO, Deshpandé (1999) stated that market orientation operates at 3 basic levels: culture (shared values that lead to putting the customer first), strategy (allowing the creation of a superior value for the customers) and tactics (the set of cross functional processes and activities that aim at customer satisfaction).

Analysis of these similarities and a particular understanding of the early efforts of founders of the modern concept of MO can prevent some generalizations and misinterpretations (Hult et al, 2004) as there are also some differences between them. Customer focus (when not considered as synonymous with market orientation) is a narrower dimension than market intelligence. The customer orientation proposed by Narver and Slater (1990) and by Deshpandé et al. (1993) is, in fact, part of this intelligence generation dimension (confirmed by Narver and Slater (1990) measures of information use and collection in their own scale). However, the intelligence generation dimension proposed by Kohli and Jaworski (1990) goes beyond a simple information collection. It considers external factors and actors that affect the present and future consumer preferences (Kohli and Jaworski, 1990), also implying a specific business culture (Deshpandé et al., 1993). Customer orientation, when used interchangeably as synonymous with market orientation (Shapiro 1988; Deshpandé et al., 1993) constricts the scope of MO itself and creates confusion between both concepts. The MO cannot be simply reduced to customers, as it is a fact that external actors (Kohli & Jaworski, 1990) have to be considered. The second dimension found by Jaworski et al. (2000), information sharing (dissemination), is more behavioural in nature and does not include the cultural elements that either favour or constrain it and neglects the full use of resources that create customer value (Narver & Slater, 1990). Nevertheless, the behavioural elements in the interfunctional coordination are also linked with the Kohli and Jaworski (1990) responsiveness dimension (Ruekert, 1992).

The inclusion of the competitor orientation dimension in the measurement of MO proposed by Narver and Slater (1990) and Slater and Narver (1994) is challenged by Deshpandé et al. (1993), as previously stated, and the authors even state that this dimension is antithetical to customer orientation because it would distract the firm from the focus point of the customer's needs.

Consequently, although there are some basic similarities amongst these dimensions, there are also some relevant differences. Even if these can be considered more of emphasis than substantive in nature (Ruekert, 1992), such differences have to be evaluated when a MO scale is proposed. This leads to the suggestion that a blend between the Narver and Slater (1990) and Kohli, Jaworski and Kumar (1993) dimensions is a more robust approach to measuring the MO concept and its key dimensions.

Also although it is broadly recognized in the literature that MO is the implementation of the marketing concept (Foley & Fahy, 2009; Elg, 2007), only Kohli and Jaworski (1990) developed in detail the link between these two concepts. For them, MO means implementing the marketing concept so as to translate it in terms of action/tactics. There is a parallel here between these three dimensions and the operational definitions of the marketing concept that Kohli and Jaworski (1990) adopted. Such parallel is based on the marketing definition provided then by Kotler (1988), which suggests that in order to achieve organizational goals, an organization has to determine and satisfy the needs and wants of the target markets more effectively than its competitors. The main dimensions of the marketing concept for Kotler (1988) are target markets, customer needs (both previously under the single label of *customer focus*), integrated marketing and profitability.

According to Kohli and Jaworski (1990), this communality is in consonance with many other marketing definitions (i.e. Felton, 1959; Levitt, 1969; McNamara, 1972, cit in Kohli & Jaworski, 1990). However, it had severe practical measurement limitations, hence the market orientation *raison d'etre* as the operational measurement of the marketing concept and its behavioural nature. The overlap between these two concepts is proposed in Table 2.

*Table 2. Similarities between Market Orientation and the marketing concept*

| Concept | Dimension 1 | Dimension 2 | Dimension 3 |
|---|---|---|---|
| **Market Orientation** | Intelligence generation (K-J)<br>Information collection (R)<br>Customer orientation (N-S; D-F-W)<br>Competitor orientation (N-S) | Intelligence dissemination (K-J)<br>Strategy development (R)<br>Interfunctional coordination (N-S) | Responsiveness (K-J)<br>Strategy implementation (R)<br>Business performance and innovation (D-F-W) |
| **Marketing Concept**<br>Kotler (1988;1996) | Customer focus:<br>Customer needs & Target markets | Integrated marketing | Profitability |

Notes: K-J (Kohli & Jaworski, 1990); N-S (Narver & Slater, 1990); D-F-W (Deshpandé et al, 1993) R (Ruekert, 1992).

## CULTURAL, BEHAVIOURAL AND SYSTEMIC PERSPECTIVES OF MARKET ORIENTATION: OPPOSITE OR COMPLEMENTARY APPROACHES?

There are arguments that the cultural dimension may not be an active dimension of MO concept, as it is the case of Kohli and Jaworski (1990), who implied that there may be divergent perspectives of its different dimensions and also in the general concept, that have critical implications on its the measurement level. Helfert, Ritter and Walter (2001), building on an earlier discussion by Ruekert (1992), pointed out the existence of three different perspectives towards the concept of MO. The first one is a behaviour-based perspective (management practice according to Ruekert, 1992), which, according to the author, has Kohli and Jaworski (1990) as its representatives, and claims that MO is related with the behaviours and activities in a corporation. Therefore, it implies the behaviour concerning the information to be collected and disseminated, and the behaviour concerning market response. Although Helfert, et al. (2001) include Narver and Slater on the cultural side, Ruekert (1992) considers that Narver and Slater (1990) included behavioural components as they measure activities (i.e. information collection) in their scale. The second perspective is the cultural one, stated by Narver and Slater (1990), and by Deshpandé et al. (1993). From this point of view, culture is a condition for the MO to prosper, since it depends on behavioural components: competitors and customers' orientation and interfunctional coordination within the corporation (Narver & Slater, 1990). Deshpandé et al. (1993) had already acknowledged these two opposite perspectives.

A third perspective is that of Helfert et al. (2001), who assumes that, besides these two major outlooks, there is a third one, based on management systems. Becker and Homburg (1999) define the management of MO according to the level of design of the management systems, as a means to promote the company's customer and competitor orientation. According to this approach, the management system is divided into five subsystems: organization, information, planning, control and system of human resources, all contributing to the organization's market orientation.

Despite this distinction between behavioural, cultural and system-based cultures, there is an overlap between the theories (Helfert et al., 2001). The leading perspective appears to be the behavioural one, since all the other outlooks include it, and that culture and management systems exist to favour market oriented behaviours. Considering the Narver and Slater's (1990) outlook exclusively cultural seems likewise arguable, since it settles in three behavioural components, of which two have substantial parallels with Kohli and Jaworski's (1990) outlook, as discussed earlier.

When distinguishing the cultural and behavioural perspectives of MO, an important question regarding the measurement of the construct is posed. As this measure is based on a self-reported attitude scales applied to the managers, what is actually measured is the cultural component that underlies their attitude and their perception of being greater or lesser market oriented. Behaviours are measured indirectly through queries that question the practice of certain actions, as well as their periodicity, which lacks accuracy regarding time limits, as it will further discussed here. Therefore Kirca, Cavusgil, and Hult (2009) argue that there should be an integration of the behavioural and cultural perspectives in market orientation.

Being the core dimension of MO the organizational culture as stated before in the Deshpandé and Webster (1998) definition, the findings of Morgan and Vorhies (2018) indicate that the organizational culture domain of MO is as critical important in explaining firm performance. They suggest that researchers need to re-visit the conceptualization, and perhaps more importantly the operationalization, of MO as a central construct in strategic marketing thought.

## The Relationship Between Market Orientation, Business Performance, New Product Success and Customer Satisfaction

Although assumed as a major consequence of MO (Deshpandé & Farley, 1998), the link between MO and business profitability needs to be carefully assessed. Narver and Slater (1990) demonstrated that the connection between MO and the return on investment was non-linear. Ruekert (1992) also established this relationship but by contrasting the worst performing SBU against the best performing one in his sample. However, a similar approach by Diamantopoulous and Hart (1993) and Greenley (1995) could not find sufficient evidence to support this link. Other studies such as Langerak (2001), Dobni and Luffman (2003), Gray and Hooley (2002), and Hunt and Lambe (2000), contradicted this proposition by not finding a link between MO and business performance. This question is also acknowledged by Narver and Slater (1990), who were not able to fully identify how MO has a positive relationship with profitability. This may be due to the fact that there seem to be other variables involved, such as the company's strategic definition or the nature of the industry itself. If two industries with traditionally different ROI are being compared, that would bias the results. The wine industry is widely recognized as having a very low ROI, where financial results will only come after 8 to 10 years. A more recent research (Ho, et al., 2018) also could not find a significant relationship between market orientation and performance.

Therefore, if MO can't always prove its relationship with business profitability and it is considered an implementation of the market concept, what are the consequences in terms of marketing? Henderson (1998) discussed the nature of the synergistic effect of the MO and the marketing concept on business profitability. This author challenges the link between satisfying the costumers' needs and wants and business profitability, stating that there is no implicit promise of above industry average profit for a market or marketing orientated company. Additionally, since some measurements of MO consider it a form of organizational culture (Narver & Slater, 1990; Deshpandé et al. 1993), this could contribute to the fact that the connection between MO and business performance might not be straightforward. A market oriented culture seems to be an antecedent to market oriented behaviours, but may not be sufficient to explain them (Matsumo, Mentzer & Rentz, 2005) as other factors may also contribute to it (business structure and strategy, resources, size and market share). MO seems to act more on mediating role in the link between entrepreneurial intention and business performance (Vega-Vázquez, Cossío-Silva & Revilla-Camach, 2016) Jaworski and Kohli (1993) defend the idea that profitability is a consequence of market orientation and not its component, as it seems to be the case of the marketing concept. Other measures of business performance topically used in market orientation studies are: sales growth, size (Slater & Narver, 1994; Deshpandé et al., 1993), and market share (Deshpandé et al., 1993; Baker & Sinkula, 2005). However, these measures present the same basic difficulties: they may not depend solely on the self-reported levels of market orientation. Ho et al. (2018) gave a recent argument of this by not finding a direct relationship between market orientation and performance. The arguments presented above show that there might not be a direct link between market orientation and business profitability. Hence, and according to the arguments exposed above, state the first hypothesis is stated as a null hypothesis:

**H1:** Market orientation doesn't have a direct and positive effect in business performance.

One of the initial questions raised in the 1987 MSI's conference was the need to think of market orientation as the basis for innovation. This link is initially defended and empirically tested by Deshpandé et al. (1993). Lukas and Farell (2000) studied the impact of market orientation on product innovation. They tested the propositions of Deshpandé et al. (1993), Kohli and Jaworski (1990), and Slater and Narver (1994) that a higher degree of marketing orientation would favour a superior innovation and consequently a greater success in business innovation. Bennett and Cooper (1979) don't agree with this assumption, suggesting that a strong market orientation may originate a higher degree of imitation of the competitor's products and, consequently, a lesser degree of innovation being introduced in the market. Nevertheless, the research conducted by Lukas and Farell (2000) determined that a higher customer orientation favours new product development and reduces the introduction of me-too products. The same happens with an effective interfunctional coordination that increases the product line extensions. A high competitor orientation increases the copy of products and reduces the new product launch and line extensions. Lukas and Farell (2000) suggest that future research should focus on the comparison of the market orientation perceptions between managers and customers to evaluate if market orientation and its effect on new product development varies.

The positive relationship between market orientation and new product success is also sustained by Hult et al. (2004) and by Ho et al. (2018), who suggest that innovation is an intervening variable, linking the Narver and Slater (1990) dimensions of market orientation to business performance. They define innovativeness as the capacity to introduce a new process, product or idea in the organization. This implies that one of the main outcomes of innovativeness is the ability to achieve success with the new products developed by the organization, which in its turn reinforces the innovativeness of the organization's culture (Hult et al., 2004).

According to Narver et al. (2004), the relationship between MO and new-product success has been neglected due to the fact that it has been measured too narrowly. He believes the measure of MO has been focused on behaviours related to satisfying customers' expressed needs rather than satisfying their latent needs as well. The concept of MO implies both a responsive market orientation (to the expressed needs of customers) and a proactive market orientation (the latent needs of customers and opportunities for increasing customer value). The Narver et al. (2004) study extends the measurement of MO to new product success in order to match the full scope of the concept. The study findings imply that a responsive MO is not sufficient for any business to create and sustain new-product success and that, thus, a proactive market orientation is required in order to achieve a positive role in the new product success. This assumption goes back to the Kohli et al. (1993) study, which argued that MO requires a certain level of risk tolerance that allows for businesses to respond to market developments with new products.

Baker and Sinkula (2007) also showed that optimal new product development programs require a balance between customer-led (adaptive learning inspired incremental innovation) and lead-the-customer innovation practices (generative-learning-inspired radical innovation). This brought along clear implications for the intelligence generation activities, which should not only access the actual needs but also propose new products that still have to be tested by customers. Latter Ngo and O'Cass (2012) also sustained that that MO significantly contributes to customer and innovation related performance outcomes via marketing and innovation capabilities. According to Baker and Sinkula (2007), some believe that a strong MO causes firms to overemphasize customer-led incremental innovations. Baker and Sinkula (2007) suggest that the abandonment of traditional conceptualizations and measures of MO are premature, although arguing that its single construct operationalization needs to be complemented by new dimensions. These authors sustain that new product success seems a better and more reliable measure than innovation, as innovation capabilities can feedback negatively on new product success. Therefore the alternative hypothesis is proposed:

**H2** There's a positive and significant impact of market orientation on new product success.

The link between MO and customer satisfaction as a consequence was never much explored individually. Consumer satisfaction is found to be determined by a pre-experience comparison standard and disconfirmation (Yi, 1990). Two main streams appeared divided between those who defend satisfaction as a process of evaluations (or consequence) and those who defend it is a response (Yi, 1990). On the first side is Oliver's (1977) expectancy/disconfirmation theory, where satisfaction is the result of initial expectancy that will be confirmed or exceeded by the actual performance of a product or service. As for the cognitive perspective, it implies that satisfaction is an interpretation and a cognitive and affective response to the products and services that are bought or used (Gomez, McLaughlin & Wittink, 2004).

Kohli and Jaworski (1990) proposed the beneficial effect of MO on customer satisfaction as a result of the valued added effect. This link was developed by Gray et al. (1998), who proved that MO has beneficial effects on customer satisfaction and loyalty. This was also sustained by Ramos et al. (2012) that proved a positive connection between MO and customer relationships. The reason why this relationship does not seem to be frequently explored lies in the fact that it is considered mainly an outcome in the acquisition of competitive advantages (Sanzo, Santos, Vásquez, & Álvaréz, 2003), rather than a direct consequence of MO. If MO is the implementation of the marketing concept (which implies satisfying customers), the value creation and the relationship management would have to evolve customer satisfaction. Guo and Wang (2015) found that customer orientation and competitor orientation influence customer relationship outcomes, but that interfunctional coordination does not. Although it is odd that competitor orientation has a slightly stronger impact on customer satisfaction than customer orientation does, it only has an indirect relationship with customer retention, but only through customer satisfaction. Morgan and Vorhies (2018) suggested that MO culture's indirect effect on customer satisfaction is due to its positive impact on firms' MO behaviors. In fact, and from a MO perspective companies should have a deep knowledge of customer needs and satisfaction levels in order to differentiate their offers and obtain a sustainable competitive advantage (Sanzo et al., 2003) that will allow a higher degree of customer satisfaction. Therefore the third hypothesis is proposed:

**H3:** There's a significant and positive relationship between market orientation and customer satisfaction.

## Methods

The procedure to build the scale adopted a blended approach, using the procedure suggested by Rossiter (2002) and adopting it to a limited extent due to constrains pointed out by Diamantopoulos (2005). This approach was useful particularly for the initial development of the scale. The performance scale used in this research is an adaptation of the Slater and Narver (1994) scale augmented to 9 points, with the scale descriptors they used in the business competitive environment ("decreased a lot" to "increased a lot"). The consequences of MO, namely the performance indicators are based in Narver and Slater (1990), Customer Satisfaction and New Product success as suggested in Lambin (1999) and Gabarino and Johnson (1999).

*Table 3. Design and characteristics of the research work*

| | |
|---|---|
| Survey type | E-mail Survey, Portuguese wine producers |
| Geographical scope | Portugal |
| Sample size | 112 wine companies that completed the performance indicators. |
| Data collection method | E-mail structured personally with a link to an online survey sent by the main wine producers representatives to their e-mail databases |
| Sampling procedure | Convenience sample: all the producers and members of the main wine boards were asked to reply to the survey. |

The research hypotheses are analyse using the statistical partial least square (PLS) method using SmartPLS™ (Ringle, Wende & Will, 2005). This approach, developed by Wold (1966), allows using structural equations that are less demanding regarding lower sample sizes and non-normal distributed data and the possibility of the existence of multicollinearity (Tenenhaus, Vinzi, Chatelin, & Lauro, 2005). The PLS algorithm produces loadings between reflective constructs that are similar to the ones of a principal component analysis (Duarte & Raposo, 2010), providing a good measure to confirm the content validity. The Average Variance Extracted (AVE) values can also provide a good measure to confirm the discriminant validity (Fornell and Larker, 1981). Although the PLS method does not provide significance levels, these can be achieved by using the Bootstrap resampling method. Consequently, the t-values were obtained by performing a bootstrapping procedure consisting of 500 runs (Tenenhaus et al, 2005).

*Table 4. Average variance extracted, composite reliability, and Cronbach α*

| Dimensions | AVE | Composite Reliability | Cronbach α |
|---|---|---|---|
| CUST | .404178 | .820826 | .783 |
| ID | .494636 | .850705 | .837 |
| IG | .585434 | .869767 | .839 |
| RES | .564457 | .866065 | .847 |
| PERF | .719562 | .927404 | .903 |

*Figure 1. Impact of MO on Performance P Ramos*

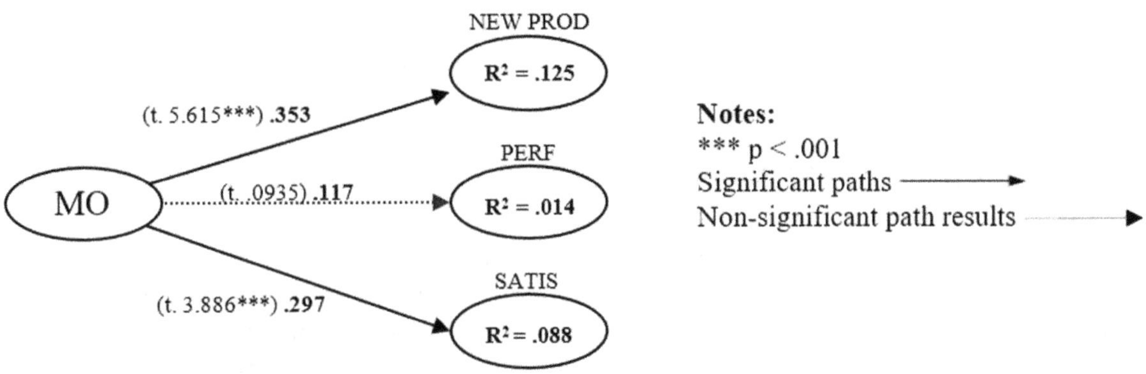


## RESULTS, DISCUSSION AND CONCLUSION

The internal consistency is assessed by Cronbach alpha and the composite reliability values. No items if deleted presented a significant increase in the alpha of the proposed scale and all values are satisfactory according to Nunnally and Bernstein's (1994) and Hair, Black, Babin, and Anderson (2010) cut of point of .7. Regarding the Average Variance Extracted (AVE) for each construct, if the values are above .5 it means the variance explained by indicators exceeds the variance explained by error. One dimension (CUST) was below this cut of point, but looking at the composite reliability, the dimension loadings and the Cronbach alpha of the dimension, the dimension was kept as it was believed to reflect the respondents' degree of cultural customer orientation. The significant levels suggest that the hypotheses (one null -H1- and two alternative hypothesis -H2; H3) could be accepted. Although only the second hypothesis $R^2$ is above .1 (Falk & Miller, 1992), the third hypothesis is quite close to this .9 value and can therefore be accepted as it is significant at a 99.9% level.

The results of the research lead us to conclude that MO favour, although not very strongly, new product success and customer satisfaction. The hypotheses test lead us to conclude that the relationship between MO and business performance is not significant confirming the findings of Langerak, 2001; Dobni and Luffman, 2003; Gray and Hooley, 2002 and of Hunt and Lambe, 2000. However these results can also be influenced by some of the factors mentioned before (the measurement nature of the performance, the natural bias of the managers to highly rate their organization's MO).

The second hypothesis is confirmed leading to the corroboration that one of the MO's outcomes is the success in the development of new products. These results are in consonance with Hult et al. (2004). Therefore, in the Portuguese wine sector, the implementation of MO procedures and, consequently, a higher knowledge of the customer leads to the development of new wines that will have better market acceptance. The third hypothesis is the least explored as an outcome of MO, but our results demonstrated that this is as path that should be further explored. It is a natural consequence that if MO implies the knowledge of the market, its disseminations and market response, it will be more directly related to customer satisfaction. Likewise, the fact that the companies that present higher levels of MO have more knowledge of the satisfaction levels, favours this relationship. The moderate results from both the $R^2$ and the path coefficients suggest that MO is only one of the factors that favour these consequences. The relationship between MO and customer satisfaction should be developed in future research. Moreover, it should also explore the possibility of customer satisfaction mediate the relationship between MO and new product development, as well as performance. The hypothesis may be that companies with a higher perception of their customer satisfaction may be more willing to develop more successful products.

## LIMITATIONS AND SUGGESTIONS TO FUTURE RESEARCH

Several caveats need to be recognized: due to the sector's secretive nature, some respondents in the pre-test refused to give exact figures of some of their performance measures (such as ROI; sales growth, revenue; profits, etc.) leading to a more vague measurement of performance variables. The sample had to be a convenience sample, although all the wine producers listed in the board's e-mail list had a chance to reply. The research is a cross sectional study, so it is affected by the contingency factor at the time of the data collection. The scale validity may be only applicable to the wine sector or to similar agricultural product contexts.

The relationship between market orientation and customer satisfaction should be developed in future research. Moreover, it should also explore the possibility that customer satisfaction mediates the relationship between market orientation and new product development, as well as performance. The hypothesis may be that companies with a higher perception of their customer satisfaction may be more willing to develop more successful products.

Market orientation needs to be further validated by evidence on other subjective and perceptual measures. Likewise, it needs to be confronted with real measures such as comparing the perceptions of producers and intermediaries of their own market orientations and its non-financial consequences as, for example, their business relations. Future researches should try to confirm the consistency of all the factors and to evaluate the impact of each of the MO dimensions found here in other business contexts.

Future researches should also try to confirm the consistency of all the factors and to evaluate the impact of each of the MO dimensions found here in other business contexts. This is in line with what Morgan and Vorhies (2018) suggest that researchers need to re-visit the conceptualization, and perhaps more importantly the operationalization of MO as a central construct in strategic marketing thought, namely enhancing the role of culture.

## REFERENCES

Baker, W., & Sinkula, J. (2005). Market orientation and the new product paradox. *Journal of Product Innovation Management, 22*(6), 483–502. doi:10.1111/j.1540-5885.2005.00145.x

Baker, W., & Sinkula, J. (2007). Does market orientation facilitate balanced innovation programs? An organizational learning perspective. *Journal of Product Innovation Management, 24*(4), 316–334. doi:10.1111/j.1540-5885.2007.00254.x

Becker, J., & Hamburg, C. (1999). Market oriented management: A system based perspective. *Journal of Market Focused Management, 4*(1), 17–41. doi:10.1023/A:1009804011447

Deshpandé, R. (1999). *Developing a Market Orientation*, MSI. *Sage (Atlanta, Ga.).*

Deshpandé, R., & Farley, J. (1998). Measuring market orientations: Generalization and synthesis. *Journal of Market Focused Management, 2*(3), 213–232. doi:10.1023/A:1009719615327

Deshpandé, R., Farley, J., & Webster, F. Jr. (1993). Corporate culture, customer orientation and innovativeness in Japanese firms: A quadrat analysis. *Journal of Marketing, 75*(1), 23–37. doi:10.1177/002224299305700102

Deshpandé, R., & Webster, F. Jr. (1989). Organizational culture and marketing: Defining the research agenda. *Journal of Marketing, 53*(1), 3–15. doi:10.1177/002224298905300102

Diamantopoulos, A. (2005). The C-OAR-SE procedure for scale development in marketing: A comment. *International Journal of Research in Marketing, 22*(9).

Diamantopoulos, A., & Hart, S. (1993). Linking market orientation and company performance: Preliminary evidence on Kohli and Jaworski's framework. *Journal of Strategic Marketing, 1*(2), 93–121. doi:10.1080/09652549300000007

Dobni, C. B., & Luffman, G. (2003). Determining the scope and impact of market orientation profiles on strategy implementation and performance. *Strategic Management Journal, 24*(6), 577–585. doi:10.1002mj.322

Elg, U. (2007). Market orientation processes in retailing: A cross-national study. *European Journal of Marketing, 41*(5/6), 568–589. doi:10.1108/03090560710737615

Foley, A., & Fahy, J. (2009). Seeing market orientation through a capabilities lens. *European Journal of Marketing, 43*(1/2), 13–2. doi:10.1108/03090560910923201

Fornell, C., & Bookstein, F. L. (1982). Two structural equation models: LISREL and PLS applied to consumer exit-voice theory. *JMR, Journal of Marketing Research, 19*(4), 440–452. doi:10.1177/002224378201900406

Gabarino, E., & Johnson, M. (1999). The different roles of satisfaction, trust, and commitment in customer relationships. *Journal of Marketing, 63*(2), 70–87. doi:10.1177/002224299906300205

Gomez, M., McLaughlin, E., & Wittink, D. (2004). Customer satisfaction and retail sales performance: An empirical investigation. *Journal of Retailing, 80*(4), 265–278. doi:10.1016/j.jretai.2004.10.003

Gray, B., Matear, S., Boshoff, C., & Matheson, P. (1998). Developing a better measure of market orientation. *European Journal of Marketing*, *32*(9/10), 884–903. doi:10.1108/03090569810232327

Gray, B. J., & Hooley, G. J. (2002). Market orientation and service firm performance – a research agenda. *European Journal of Marketing*, *36*, 980–988. doi:10.1108/03090560210437280

Greenley, G. E. (1995). Market orientation and company performance: Empirical evidence from UK companies. *British Journal of Management*, *6*(1), 1–13. doi:10.1111/j.1467-8551.1995.tb00082.x

Guo, C., & Wang, Y. (2015). How manufacturer market orientation influences B2B customer satisfaction and retention: Empirical investigation of the three market orientation components. *Journal of Business and Industrial Marketing*, *30*(2), 182–193. doi:10.1108/JBIM-03-2012-0042

Hair, J., Black, W., Babin, B., & Anderson, R. (2010). *Multivariate Data Analysis: International Version*. Prentice Hall.

Han, J., Namwoon, K., & Rajendra, K. (1998). Market Orientation and Organizational Performance: Is Innovation a Missing Link? *Journal of Marketing*, *62*(4), 30–45. doi:10.1177/002224299806200403

Harris, L. (1993). Benchmarking against the theory of market orientation. *Journal of Marketing*, *57*(3), 537–545.

He, X., Brouthers, K., & Filatotchev, I. (2018). Market orientation and export performance: The moderation of channel and institutional distance. *International Marketing Review*, *35*(2), 258–279. doi:10.1108/IMR-09-2015-0194

Helfert, G., Ritter, T., & Walter, A. (2001). How does market orientation affect business relationships. *17th IMP conference*.

Henderson, S. (1998). No such thing as market orientation – a call for no more papers. *Management Decision*, *36*(9), 598–609. doi:10.1108/00251749810239487

Ho, L. P. K., Nguyen, C. N., Adhikari, R. P., Miles, M. P., & Bonney, L. (2018). Exploring market orientation, innovation, and financial performance in agricultural value chains in emerging economies. *Journal of Innovation and Knowledge*, *3*(3), 154–163. doi:10.1016/j.jik.2017.03.008

Homburg, C., & Pflesser, C. (2000). A Multiple-layer model of market-oriented organizational culture: Measurement issues and performance outcomes. *JMR, Journal of Marketing Research*, *37*(49), 449–462. doi:10.1509/jmkr.37.4.449.18786

Hult, G., Hurley, R., & Knight, G. (2004). Innovativeness: Its antecedents and impact on business performance. *Industrial Marketing Management*, *33*(5), 429–438. doi:10.1016/j.indmarman.2003.08.015

Hunt, S. D., & Lambe, C. J. (2000). Marketing's contribution to business strategy: Market orientation, relationship marketing and resource-advantage theory. *International Journal of Management Reviews*, *2*(1), 17–43. doi:10.1111/1468-2370.00029

IVV. (2018). Instituto do Vinho e da Vinha I. P. *Anuário*. Retrieved from: http://www.ivv.min-agricultura.pt/np4/Anuário

Jaworski, B., & Kohli, A. (1993). Market orientation: Antecedents and consequences. *Journal of Marketing, 57*(3), 53–57. doi:10.1177/002224299305700304

Jaworski, B., Kohli, A., & Sahay, A. (2000). Market-driven versus driving markets. *Academy of Marketing Science Journal, 28*(1), 45–54. doi:10.1177/0092070300281005

Kirca, A., Cavusgil, S., & Hult, G. (2009). The effects of national culture on market orientation: Conceptual framework and research propositions. *International Business Review, 18*(2), 111–118. doi:10.1016/j.ibusrev.2009.02.003

Kohli, A., & Jaworski, B. (1990). Market Orientation: The Construct, Research Propositions, and Managerial Implications. *Journal of Marketing, 54*(2), 1–18. doi:10.1177/002224299005400201

Kohli, A., Jaworski, B., & Kumar, A. (1993). MARKOR a measure of market orientation. *JMR, Journal of Marketing Research, 30*(4), 467–477. doi:10.1177/002224379303000406

Kotler, P. (1988). *Marketing Management*. Prentice Hall.

Lambin, J. J. (1999). *Marketing Estratégico*. McGraw Hill.

Langerak, F. (2001). Effects of market orientation on the behaviours of salespersons and purchasers, channel relationships, and performance of manufacturers. *International Journal of Research in Marketing, 18*(3), 221–234. doi:10.1016/S0167-8116(01)00040-4

Lukas, B., & Farrell, O. (2000). The effect of market orientation on product innovation. *Journal of the Academy of Marketing Science, 28*(2), 239–247. doi:10.1177/0092070300282005

Matsumo, K., Mentzer, J. T., & Rentz, J. O. (2000). A refinement and Validation of the MARKOR Scale. *Journal of the Academy of Marketing Science, 28*(4), 527–539. doi:10.1177/0092070300284005

Morgan, N., & Vorhies, D., (2018). The business performance outcomes of market orientation culture and behaviors. *Innovation and Strategy, 15*, 259-286.

Narver, J., & Slater, S. (1990). The effect of a market orientation on business performance. *Journal of Marketing, 54*(4), 20–35. doi:10.1177/002224299005400403

Narver, J., Slater, S., & MacLachlan, D. (2004). Responsive and proactive market orientation and new-product success. *Journal of Product Innovation Management, 21*(5), 334–347. doi:10.1111/j.0737-6782.2004.00086.x

Ngo, L., & O'Cass, A. (2012). In search of innovation and customer-related performance superiority: The role of market orientation, marketing capability, and innovation capability interactions. *Journal of Product Innovation Management, 5*(5), 861–877. doi:10.1111/j.1540-5885.2012.00939.x

Nunnally, J. C., & Bernstein, I. H. (1994). *Psychometric Theory* (3rd ed.). McGraw-Hill.

OIV. (2018). *OIV Statistical Report on World Vitiviniculture*. Retrieved from: ttp://www.oiv.int/fr/normes-et-documents-techniques/analyses-statistiques/situation-annuelle

Pattanayak, D., Koilakuntla, M., & Punyatoya, P. (2017). Investigating the influence of TQM, service quality and market orientation on customer satisfaction and loyalty in the Indian banking sector. *International Journal of Quality & Reliability Management*, *34*(3), 362–377. doi:10.1108/IJQRM-04-2015-0057

Ramos, P., Martins, F. V., & Barandas, H. (2012). Differences in the market orientation impact on business relationships between wine producers and intermediaries: a PLS application. *Proceedings of the 41st EMAC Conference, 172.*

Ringle, C. M., Wende, S., & Will, A. (2005). *SmartPLS 2.0*. www.smartpls.de

Rossiter, J. (2002). The C-OAR-SE procedure for scale development in marketing. *International Journal of Research in Marketing*, *19*(4), 305–335. doi:10.1016/S0167-8116(02)00097-6

Ruekert, R. (1992). Developing a market orientation: An organizational strategy perspective. *International Journal of Research in Marketing*, *9*(3), 225–245. doi:10.1016/0167-8116(92)90019-H

Sanzo, M., Santos, M., Vásquez, R., & Álvaréz, L. (2003). The effect of market orientation on buyer–seller relationship satisfaction. *Industrial Marketing Management*, *32*(4), 327–345. doi:10.1016/S0019-8501(01)00200-0

Slater, S., & Narver, J. (1994). Does competitive environment moderate market orientation-performance relationship? *Journal of Marketing*, *58*(1), 46–55. doi:10.1177/002224299405800104

Tenenhaus, M., Amato, S., & Esposito, V. (2004). *A global goodness-of-fit index for PLS structural equation modelling*. Paper presented at the XLII SIS Scientific Meeting, CLEUP, Padova.

Tenenhaus, M., Vinzi, V. E., Chatelin, Y.-M., & Lauro, C. (2005). PLS Path Modelling. *Computational Statistics & Data Analysis*, *48*(1), 159–205. doi:10.1016/j.csda.2004.03.005

Vega-Vázquez, M., Cossío-Silva, F.-J., & Revilla-Camach, M.-A. (2016). Entrepreneurial orientation–hotel performance: Has market orientation anything to say? *Journal of Business Research*, *69*(11), 5089–5094. doi:10.1016/j.jbusres.2016.04.085

Viniportugal. (2018). *Viniportugal Estatísticas*. Retrieved from: https://www.viniportugal.pt/Estatisticas

Wold, H. (1966). Estimation of principal components and related models by iterative least squares. In P. R. Krishnaiah (Ed.), *Multivariate Analysis* (pp. 391–42). Academic Press.

# Chapter 6
# How to Ensure an Ideal Omnichannel Client Experience With Key Performance Indicators:
## Focus on Personal Luxury Goods

**Anne-Flore Maman Larraufie**
*SémioConsult, France & ESSEC Business School, France*

**Lucile Arsov Gouriou**
*ESSEC Business School, France*

**Cécilia Goutran**
*SémioConsult, France*

## ABSTRACT

*By 2025, electronic sales (e-sales) of luxury goods are expected to triple, reaching about €74 billion and standing for one-fifth of total luxury sales. This mix of online and offline client journeys increases the number of digital points and touchpoints. Thus, the journey of the omnichannel client is worth a deep focus. The omnichannel client experience (CX) requires key performance indicators (KPIs) to assess and understand disruption, enhance the experience, and present the "wow" factor. To get fresh insights on CX in luxury/digital retail, a qualitative study (with focus groups) on the omnichannel luxury client journey was conducted to identify specific pain points and KPIs. Results from an online survey quantitative study on poorly or uncovered omnichannel KPIs are disclosed. Ultimately, an overall list of relevant KPIs for CX in the luxury omnichannel retail industry is provided as a guideline for managers.*

DOI: 10.4018/978-1-7998-1843-4.ch006

## INTRODUCTION

Online sales of personal luxury goods (i.e., apparel, footwear, accessories, jewelry and watches, leather goods, and beauty products and perfume) account for 8% of the €254 billion global luxury market (about €20 billion). According to McKinsey (2018), by 2025, luxury goods online sales could triple to about €74 billion. One-fifth of luxury sales will be made online. Affordable luxury sales, including the beauty segment, are also growing online. To answer clients' newest demands, more scalable, agile, and technology-savvy electronic retailers (e-retailers) are emerging in the online luxury industry. This group maximizes digital points thanks to a higher number of touchpoints along the client journey (Achille, Marchessou, & Remy, 2018).

However, clients do not neglect physical stores. In fact, 73% of clients explicitly value their physical shopping trips (Ramirez, 2018). Online retail has not replaced the sensory and social experiences that come with shopping at physical stores. Consequently, the typical luxury client follows a mixed online/offline journey.

There are more similarities than differences among traditional and online store shoppers. Only a few unique shopper types are present on online stores, attracted by distinctive characteristics and attributes of the online retail environment (Ganesh, Reynolds, Luckett, & Pomirleanu, 2010). Clients who shop across multiple transaction channels provide higher revenues and a higher share of wallet. In addition, they have higher per client value and higher likelihood of being active as compared to other clients (Kumar & Venkatesan, 2005; Mathwick, Malhotra, & Rigdon, 2001; Neslin et al., 2006).

In 2015, multichannel retailing moved to omnichannel retailing (Verhoef, Kannan, & Inman, 2015). In this omnichannel journey, the typical client increasingly seeks memorable experiences instead of tangible, material goods (Homburg, Jozić, & Kuehnl, 2017; Limayem & Hirt, 2003; Mitchell & Harris, 2005). Through this experience, the client aspires for a status, a differentiation, and a sense of quest in a unique moment (Batat, 2017).

Store space will become predominantly experiential and lifestyle-oriented (Achille et al., 2018). Online-offline integration (OI) leads to a competitive advantage and channel synergies rather than channel cannibalization (Herhausen, Binder, Schoegel, & Herrmann, 2015). Today, the client expects a seamless and coherent relationship with brands across these different touchpoints, even as they travel between countries. Creating this consistent omnichannel seamless experience is a challenge for brands that are still organized around channels and geographies (Achille et al., 2018).

Luxury 4.0, a luxury with increased speed and agility, is enhanced using client data, design, and partnerships across the luxury ecosystem. For most modern luxury brands, reverse omnichannel started when stores began matching the quality of the online experience. However, it is a challenge to avoid the dilution of the following essential DNA of luxury products: craftsmanship, unique design, and personalization (Achille et al., 2018). Brands can enhance the client relationship and restore the authentic personal experiences that defined luxury when it was confined to a small elite. Finally, the trajectory of digitalization will likely bring further disruption for which players in the luxury market should prepare.

According to research, one-third of clients separately distinguished experiences on each channel (Kaczorowska-Spychalska, 2017). For many firms and brands, the omnichannel client experience (CX) lacks fluency and relevance. Factors that impact relationship building with the client must eliminate causes of dissatisfaction while delighting by exceeding expectations (Powaga, 2008). The omnichannel CX requires key performance indicators (KPIs) to assess and understand disruption in order to enhance. This chapter creates a comprehensive list from the clients' perspective.

First, the chapter defines CX and luxury CX (or "luxperience"). A list of KPIs from the literature is presented. This is followed by a methodology to refine, delete, or add KPIs. Then, the findings are discussed. Finally, the chapter presents recommendations for managers.

## BACKGROUND

### A Definition of Client Experience (CX), 'Luxperience' and Client Journey

CX is subjective, intangible, cumulative, and memorable (Batat, 2017). The experience is subjective and intangible because it depends on interaction through "lived" dimensions in a social and cultural context. As a result, experience is highly personal and individual (Pine & Gilmore, 1999). Experience is felt, sensed, and interpreted. Guests (i.e., clients living an experience) cocreate their experience as they engage in a participatory role (Pine & Gilmore, 1999).

Experience is also transformative as the individual engages in a self-accomplishment process (Batat, 2017). His/her experience depends on their previous state (e.g., state of mind, mood, experiences). Experience is cumulative as it depends on touchpoints before, during, and after purchase (indirect and direct contacts). Finally, experience is memorable, creating either good or bad memories (Lindgreen, Vanhamme, & Beverland, 2009). By triggering true emotions, the experience solicits short-term memory. When the experience is moving, the client will crystallize it into his/her long-term memory. The client brings back indelible impressions (Maman, 2011). Nevertheless, a CX evaluation is both rational (the quality of the product) and emotional or irrational (Arnould & Price, 1993).

Although the two concepts are different, CX is often confused with client service. Client service (or client care) is not specifically related to the client's view on the firm. CX notably includes the visit (i.e., store, Website), checkout experience, product (quality), service quality, brand image, company values and engagements, or client service (including contact center services). Therefore, client service is only a part of the CX (Bouchet & Pulh, 2006).

Today, the luxury industry faces two challenges related to the digital revolution and social, ethical, and environmental issues (Batat, 2017). Firstly, clients' behaviors mutate, resulting in an evolution on their perception of luxury. Secondly, the "new client" is characterized by expectations and needs beyond functional benefit and luxury ownership. He/she retrieves for meaningfulness.

Therefore, luxperience relies on five items (Batat, 2017):

- **Client Values:** Functional, ideological, social, and experiential
- **Product or Luxury Brand:** Brand content and experiential brand, storytelling, and story-doing
- **Environment:** Immersion, multisensorial, hyper-real, thematizing
- **Human Resources:** Personnel, training, and emotional capital
- **Education on Luxury Consumption:** Initiation and exploration

These five items are the basics to leverage luxperience. For instance, the product or brand fosters values, emotions, and experiences through relevant content to immerse the client (i.e. Barneys New York The Window). Its physical and digital environment solicit a hypersensorial experience, theme, and hyper-reality to immerse the client both inside and outside the store (including pre- and post-purchase). Of course, this is only possible with a dedicated team of ambassadors.

To conclude, CX gathers many dimensions and preconditions to trigger long-term memory. The luxury industry intensifies these states to "wow" the new client and imprint on his/her impressions.

CX assembles moments and situations along the client journey. The client journey can be mapped through digital and/or physical touchpoints. For example, a client can start his/her journey browsing a catalog and searching the Web, asking friends for recommendations on social media, visiting the retail store, ordering online, and getting the order at the store (Solis, 2015). CX is studied along the client journey regardless of whether it is visible through the client's eyes (Barwitz & Maas, 2018; Richardson-Greenfield, 2016). In addition, new technologies have brought multiple touchpoints and channels. As a result, nearly half of touchpoints are digital. The current client journey is omnichannel, fragmented, highly personalized, nonlinear, and complex (Hachin, Dubois, Jourda, & Besse, 2014). Moreover, client journeys are individualistic and lack frequent patterns (Achille et al., 2018; Dholakia et al., 2010).

Clients are generally satisfied with the convenience, quality, selection, and value provided by current retailers (Burke, 2002). In fact, new technologies offer interesting insights on clients, collecting data regarding preferences, digital journeys, and digital identities. Mobiles devices, "bots" imitating sellers, intensive use of social platforms, and the Internet of things (IoT) collect client data and big data (Eroglu, Machleit, & Barr, 2005). Big data encompasses client behavior and transactions, allowing real-time access and the sharing of information to answer who, how, where, and, in some instances, why (Kaczorowska-Spychalska, 2017).

## Key Performance Indicators (KPIs)

A specific and reliable indicator is proposed with each promise to the client (Hachin et al., 2014). The promise can be expressed (for instance, through marketing) or unexpressed. The unexpressed promise can be expected or unexpected (for instance, a quick delivery of the purchase). KPIs can be key dissatisfiers or key enhancers.

CX KPIs found during the literature review can be organized along the client journey. The cross-phase KPIs are kept aside due to cross-relevancy.

The following interphase definitions are used to organize KPIs in its related phase:

1. **Awareness-to-Prepurchase:** When the client is engaging proactively with the brand or product (Website research, a visit to the store, clicking on an online advertisement)
2. **Prepurchase-to-Purchase:** Fruitful purchase intention (client is entering the buying process)
3. **Purchase-to-Postpurchase:** Purchase is complete (not including physical store's validation, delivery, pick up, out-of-the-box, returns, after sales client service, etc.)

A detailed list of KPIs is summarized in the Box 1. Each of them is then explained, sorted by CX phase. Authors and sources are conjointly listed (we did not include them in the table for ease of reading).

## Cross-phases KPIs

Many KPIs are cross-phase KPIs. These KPIs are relevant to more than one channel or one phase in the client journey. Thus, the following KPIs have been classified as cross-phase KPIs. These cross-phase KPIs are necessary in some situations. In essence, cross-phase KPIs can be used to track client feedback at critical touchpoints like sales transactions, client service calls, or problematic situations (Powaga, 2008).

*Box 1. List of KPIs according to CX phase (NB: No consistent KPIs have been found in the literature for the awareness step)*

| **Cross-phases KPIs** | |
|---|---|
| Product KPIs | • Assortment (Brand and Product choice): availability and variety of products<br>• Product information: product quality |
| Sustainability KPIs | • Brand transparency (on processes) |
| Ownership flexibility KPIs | • Renting<br>• Purchasing experiences and emotions: continuous excitement |
| Channel choice and spillover KPIs | • Usage and overall perception of quality: Ease of use, Enjoyment, Search convenience and search effort, Speed of purchase<br>• Content and aesthetic design: Assortment, Information quality, Information comparability, Aesthetic appeal<br>• Privacy, risk, and security<br>• Service After-sales, Service<br>• Convenience: Ability to shop from home, Ability to shop any time of day or night, Ability to avoid crowds, Ability not to travel from store to store.<br>• Channel assessment: Clients occurrences, Frequency of interaction, Proportion of returns |
| Online and offline fluency KPIs | • Client's perceptions of effort and time needed to complete a task: task fluency itself, content fluency, interaction fluency, cognition fluency and feeling fluency<br>• Relevance of the source |
| Consistency KPIs | |
| Channel integration quality KPIs | • Channel service transparency, channel choice breadth, content consistency, and process consistency |
| Control KPIs | • Decisional control: attractivity of alternatives, freedom of choice |
| Education KPIs | • Knowledge and skill sets: learning about luxury craftsmanship, good manners, history, and knowing how to spot counterfeit goods. |
| Client comfort and fun KPIs | • Convenience and shopping fun |
| Client intimacy KPIs | • Personalization: contextual marketing for each client, moment and occasion<br>• Brand authenticity |
| Privacy and data security KPIs | • GDPR compliance |
| **Pre-purchase phase KPIs** | |
| Research-shopping phenomenon | • Attribute-based decision-making, lack of channel lock-in, and cross-channel<br>• Showrooming, Webrooming<br>• Time-saving: well-structured website, convenience, waiting delivery time, information availability<br>• User experience: usefulness and ease of use<br>• Recommendation agents rated as highly professional |
| Peer observation | • Perceived majority opinion |
| **Purchase phase KPIs** | |
| Service KPIs | • Level of service: personal shopper |
| In-store experience KPIs | • Sensory experience |
| Checkout KPIs | • Mobile scanning: preference for unassisted one<br>• Digital payment possibilities |
| **Post-purchase phase KPIs** | |
| Physical store's validation | • Checking of the client by the security service: validation process, inconvenience, mistrust, and privacy intrusion. |
| Delivery | • Convenience, security, and related services |
| Out-of-the-Boxing (Unboxing) KPIs | • Creativity and surprise: authenticity card, handwritten notes, smells |
| Returns KPI | • Easiness |
| Aftersales client service KPIs | • Value provided, service, convenience, and perceived risk |

## Product KPIs

Product KPIs are directly related to the product. Product KPIs in the literature are related to assortment and product information.

In a general way, assortment (and product selection) is a recurring KPI in the literature (Burke, 2002; Huang & Dubinsky, 2014). A positive experience connected with buying online is linked to the availability of products (Kaczorowska-Spychalska, 2017). Multibrand platforms offer a wide choice of brands and products, especially instabrands posted on Instagram (Achille et al., 2018). For instance, in 2017, Tmall.com launched a luxury pavilion with labels like Saint Laurent and Farfetch (Achille et al., 2018). It offers a centralized site where clients can shop in boutiques around the world. In fact, Chanel signed a five-year partnership with Farfetch.

As far as product KPIs are concerned, they are mostly related to information cost and focused on product quality (Burke, 2002; Huang & Dubinsky, 2014). The most popular client request is "better products" (Ramirez, 2018). However, there is no scientific definition of the term "better" (e.g., more resistant material, sustainability of the product, country of production, know-how, etc.). Therefore, authors use quality as a KPI, maintaining the same definition subjectivity.

## Sustainability KPIs

Sustainability will matter more as digital platforms enhance transparency into brand product processes for clients (Achille et al., 2018).

## Ownership Flexibility KPIs

Renting is becoming trendy. In 2016, Rent the Runway served 6 million clients, generating about €1 billion in revenue (Achille et al., 2018). Clients are no longer simply buying a product. They are purchasing experiences and emotions offered by the brand. Digital access has trained clients to expect continuous excitement.

## Channel Choice and Spillover KPIs

Many parameters define channel choice (Neslin et al., 2006). As they support channel choice, these parameters are linked to the likelihood of spillover.

- KPIs related to usage and overall perception of quality (Yu, Niehm, & Russell, 2011):
    - Ease of use (Keen, Wetzels, De Ruyter, & Feinberg, 2004; Neslin et al., 2006) and Enjoyment (Neslin et al., 2006; Verhoef, Neslin, & Vroomen, 2005),
    - Search convenience and search effort (Neslin et al., 2006; Verhoef et al., 2005),
    - Speed of purchase (Neslin et al., 2006; Verhoef et al., 2005),
- KPIs related to content and aesthetic design:
    - Assortment (Neslin et al., 2006; Verhoef et al., 2005),
    - Information quality (Neslin et al., 2006) (Montoya-Weiss 2003)
    - Information comparability (Neslin et al., 2006; Verhoef et al., 2005),
    - Aesthetic appeal (Neslin et al., 2006) (Montoya-Weiss 2003)

- KPIs related to privacy, risk, and security (Burke, 2002; Neslin et al., 2006; Verhoef et al., 2005),
- KPIs related to service:
  - After-sales (Jiang & Rosenbloom, 2005; Neslin et al., 2006; Verhoef et al., 2005),
  - Service (Neslin et al., 2006; Verhoef et al., 2005),
- KPIs related to convenience (encouraging the online shopping) (Ganesh et al., 2010):
  - Ability to shop from home,
  - Ability to shop any time of day or night,
  - Ability to avoid crowds,
  - Ability not to travel from store to store.

Moreover, channel experience effects occur when using the channel increases the likelihood that the client will use the same channel on the next occasion (Gensler, Verhoef, & Böhm, 2012). The assessment of touchpoints impacts positively as compared to frequency (Baxendale, Macdonald, & Wilson, 2015).

Spillover occurs if the client changes channels (the term "spillover" is defined in the glossary at the beginning of this thesis). The strongest spillover effect occurs between the search and purchase stages (Gensler et al., 2012). Spillover effects explain a portion of clients' channel choices. However, they are less important than experience effects. Research has established that the adoption of a second or third channel depends on various parameters. A second channel adoption is linked to the frequency of the interaction, whereas a third channel adoption is linked to the proportion of returns (Venkatesan, Kumar, & Ravishanker, 2007).

## Online and Offline Fluency KPIs

The perceived fluency (i.e. ease of processing information) deals with the client's perceptions of effort and time needed to complete a task. It can be online and / or offline. This is a rather subjective concept with an impact moderated by expectations and attribution (Reber, Schwarz, & Winkielman, 2004). The perceived fluency relies on the task fluency itself, the content fluency, the interaction fluency, the cognition fluency and the feeling fluency (Shen, Li, Sun, & Wang, 2018).

Many visual parameters play a role in the perceived fluency: the goodness of form, the symmetry, the figure-ground contrast and the perceptual and conceptual priming procedures (Reber et al., 2004).

Past research has shown that fluency has a particularly strong positive impact when its source is unknown and comes as a surprise (Reber et al., 2004). On the contrary, the source of relevant information can be discounted when perceiver attributes experience to an irrelevant source (Reber et al., 2004).

The more the information is perceived as pleasing and easy to absorb, the more the clients consider their thoughts and feelings associated with this task as more enjoyable and less effortful (Mosteller, Donthu, & Eroglu, 2014). Consequently, the client's evaluations of the shopping outcome are more positive regarding his/her aesthetic pleasure and his/her judgement (Mosteller et al., 2014; Reber et al., 2004).

## Consistency KPIs (Staw, 1981)

Justification and consistency influences are found in the literature to override more objective elements of the situation (Staw, 1981).

## Channel Integration Quality KPIs (Shen et al., 2018)

Channel integration is the completion of a channel with another (Shen et al., 2018). The integration quality of parallel channels relies on object-based beliefs like technological features and functionalities. KPIs identified by Shen et al. (2018) include channel service transparency, channel choice breadth, content consistency, and process consistency. Channel integration quality KPIs are redundant with channel choice and consistency KPIs.

## Control KPIs (Reinders, Frambach, & Dabholkar, 2007)

Control KPIs deal with decisional control (Reinders, Frambach, & Dabholkar, 2007). Decisional control is defined as whether individuals are free to choose to use the technology. The following situations can occur:

- If a client perceives that there are no or few alternatives, then he/she feels forced to use available alternatives.
- If a client does not perceive the alternatives as more attractive than the current alternative, the client is likely to stay with the current mode of service. If alternatives are less attractive, people will feel forced to use the self-service option.

The cost of switching to another channel is too high and the current investment is perceived as too valuable. Switching barriers has a negative effect on perceived client control. The client feels a lack of freedom of choice, negatively affecting his/her attitude.

## Education KPIs (Batat, 2017)

Education KPIs deal with the knowledge and skill sets of consuming personal luxury goods. These include learning about luxury craftsmanship, good manners, history, and knowing how to spot counterfeit goods.

## Client Comfort and Fun KPIs (Burke, 2002)

The literature has shown that convenience and shopping fun are important to the client. However, the "fun of shopping" KPI may not be applicable to every luxury client.

## Client Intimacy KPIs (Achille et al., 2018)

Trendy client intimacy KPIs are labeled by researchers as Luxury 4.0. Personalization can occur through three-dimensional- (3D) printed products, machine learning, and the use of big data and advanced analytics to interpret the desires and needs at an early stage. The goal is to proactively tailor products to each client, moment, and/or occasion through contextual marketing. As a result, brands appear as authentic (c.f., Vuitton's notes).

### i. Privacy and Data Security KPIs

The respect of privacy and security is a KPI for clients (Burke, 2002). Moreover, the European Union General Data Protection Regulation (GDPR) now empowers clients to inform, access, rectify, erase, or restrict access to and process their data (European Parliament, 2016). Notably, the regulation sets the minimization of stored data, imposing a proportionality to its storage duration.

## Pre-Purchase KPIs (Huang & Dubinsky, 2014)

The awareness phase is part of the client journey in the luxury industry (D'Arpizio, Prete, & de Montgolfier, 2019). Nevertheless, no consistent KPIs have been found in the literature. A few references have been noticed, giving some clues on successful awareness KPIs. As an example, Burberry has excelled on the online experience whereas Hermès has been found disappointing, being qualified as 'it doesn't feel luxury' (despite the 360 view of the products).

Owing to a growing clients' desire for smoothness and effortlessness when engaged in the shopping process, luxury companies have set a goal to reach a trouble-free client journey (Huang & Dubinsky, 2014). The literature has shown that clients pay attention to elements in the pre-purchase process, evaluating many elements prior to making a purchase. These include:

- Perceived service quality (accessibility and speed)
- Purchase intention quality (response to clients' needs)
- Loyalty intention quality
- Return process

Clients use various means to gather information before a purchase. Several trends are observed, including the research-shopping phenomenon and peer observation. Most sales (80%) are influenced by online research. This result often depends on product category (Achille et al., 2018). Moreover, the mobile channel has become the main source of information and, increasingly, the way luxury goods are purchased. By 2018, clients' time on mobile devices will be four times higher than desktops. Therefore, mobile research (m-research) is strategic for luxury retailers. Additionally, pre-purchase satisfaction is likely to affect post-purchase evaluations like purchase intention and loyalty (Gardial, Clemons, Woodruff, Schumann, & Burns, 1994; Huang & Dubinsky, 2014).

## Research-Shopping Phenomenon

A frequent observation, research-shopping phenomenon, includes clients who take online information about a product and visit a traditional shop for its purchase. Reverse phenomenon is equally high (Kaczorowska-Spychalska, 2017). This can only occur when several conditions are met, including attribute-based decision-making, lack of channel lock-in, and cross-channel synergy (Verhoef, Neslin, & Vroomen, 2007). Furthermore, showrooming (i.e., in-store research, online purchase) and Webrooming (i.e., online search, in-store purchase) trends are a part of the research-shopping behavior (Brynjolfsson, Mohammad, 2013).

The research-shopping phenomenon is encouraged by a well-structured Website or another digital media to make clients feel like they are saving time (Castañeda, Muñoz-Leiva, & Luque, 2007; Gupta,

Su, & Walter, 2004). This convenience, although less important than in the purchase and post-purchase phases, can drive choice of channel for research (Gensler et al., 2012). For instance, the waiting time for delivery can be a driver for a final offline choice (Gupta et al., 2004).

Moreover, the user's experience (UX) of the Website, including via smartphone, and the usefulness and ease of use perception take part in the research-shopping phenomenon. This translates into the likelihood of a visit. However, a direct link is not found regarding purchase (Burke, 2002; Castañeda et al., 2007; Gefen, Karahanna, & Straub, 2003; J. Kim & Lennon, 2013). The least experienced users tend to give credit to the ease of use KPI. More experienced users perceive usefulness as more important. In both cases, the better the visit, the more likely the user is to purchase (S. S. Kim, Malhotra, & Narasimhan, 2005).

During the research phase on digital media, clients may use recommendation agents (RAs). Wang et al. (2016) found that RAs significantly enhance users' cognition-based trust (Wang, Qiu, Kim, & Benbasat, 2016). RA avatar interfaces have a significant positive impact on users' affect-based trust. However, this is only for those who rate the avatar as highly professional. Cognition-based trust delivers the utilitarian value (perceived usefulness); affect-based trust contributes to the hedonic value (perceived enjoyment) of using a RA. This is particularly relevant for luxury because well-established luxury brands show a strong interest in chatbots (Arthur, 2019).

To conclude, attribute-based decision-making, lack of channel lock-in, cross-channel synergy, well-structured digital media (ease of use and usefulness), convenience via Ras, and availability of information regarding delivery time are considered in this chapter as KPIs in the research phase (Burke, 2002; Castañeda et al., 2007; Gefen et al., 2003; S. Gupta et al., 2006; Verhoef et al., 2007; Wang et al., 2016).

### Peer Observation

Clients may seek outside advice to make up their mind and assess a product (Reynolds, 1965). This is especially true when products are perceived as high priced or produce enough anxiety for the uninformed client to seek advice before buying. The client tends to abide by the perceived majority opinion. Such peer observation is significant both in physical and digital worlds (Baxendale et al., 2015). Clients seek advice of peers on social media or look for suggestions from trusted bloggers before entering a store (Achille et al., 2018).

## Purchase KPIs

Purchase KPIs are related to the purchase phase in the client journey. Several KPIs were found in the literature, including KPIs related to service, in-store experience (i.e., sensory experience, new technology, surroundings, image), browsing and searching during the purchase, and the checkout.

### Service KPIs

Various levels of service are suggested in the literature (Burke, 2002). The personal shopper is a new service offered both offline (in store) and online. For instance, Net-a-Porter and Mr. Porter allow their "extremely important people (EIPs) to call a personal shopper to select their items (Ramirez, 2018).

### In-Store Experience KPIs

Despite the rise of online shopping, brick-and-mortar retail maintains its attraction in the luxury industry thanks to its related experience (D'Arpizio et al., 2019). The luxury boutique can provide a specific sensory experience enhanced by new technology (Kaczorowska-Spychalska, 2017). However, some parameters cannot be controlled by the retailer. These include crowding, surroundings, and image (Huang & Dubinsky, 2014; Terblanche & Boshoff, 2006). Indeed, stores display sensory attributes (i.e., touch, smell, seen in real life) which are not offered by digital channels (D'Arpizio et al., 2019). As a result, retailers face the challenge of bridging the gap between the real world and the virtual one without losing everything represented by luxury. To keep the client's interest, retailers create experiences like spectacular openings of new stores and art investments through foundations (Atwal & Williams, 2009).

### Checkout KPIs

Check-out KPIs addressed by the literature deal with scanning (Aloysius, Hoehle, & Venkatesh, 2016) and digital payment issues (Kaczorowska-Spychalska, 2017). However, there is no evidence in the literature whether luxury clients find mobile scanning to be enjoyable or to have utilitarian benefit. However, mobile unassisted scanning is preferred over mobile assisted scanning. From the consulted sources, mobile assisted scanning with mobile assisted payment is the least preferred checkout mode. Zaczorowska-Spychalska as found that there is a slow adoption of client mobile checkout in the retail store. However, digital online payment is more positively welcomed if the client is offered more payment means like online bank transfer, instant transfers (PayU), or cash.

## Post-Purchase KPIs

The post-purchase phase begins when the property (and the use of the product) is transmitted to the client. The evaluation of the post-purchase phase depends on the perceived value and the assessment of the evaluation (confirmation or disconfirmation) of the newly purchased product (Gardial et al., 1994).

### Physical Store's Validation (Hoehle, Aloysius, Chan, & Venkatesh, 2018)

The physical store's validation is the checking of the client by the security service. The literature shows that clients have a higher tolerance for validation when mobile technologies are used in the checkout processes rather than the traditional self-service option with no mobile technology. Validation depends on the clients' tolerance for changes in the validation process, inconvenience, mistrust, and privacy intrusion.

### Delivery

KPIs related to delivery include convenience, security, and related services (Burke, 2002). Delivery differences between channels appear to affect client channel switching for many products (Gupta et al., 2004). Clients tend to choose one channel (for example, an online channel) to select various delivery possibilities (Kaczorowska-Spychalska, 2017).

### Out-of-the-Boxing (Unboxing) KPIs

The out-of-the-boxing experience is gaining importance due to the increase of online purchases. Brands compete on the most creative and surprising out-of-the-box-experience. The popularity of this KPI is witnessed by numerous videos on YouTube[1] showcasing the creativity of brands (i.e., ribbons, magnet boxes, a folder with the authenticity card and a handwritten note, care booklet). Dior sales associates even spray the packaging with one of the Maison's perfumes.

### Returns KPI (Kumar & Venkatesan, 2005)

A nonlinear relationship between returns and multichannel shopping has been demonstrated in the literature. This nonlinear relationship shows positive synergy toward multichannel shopping when clients are contacted through various communication channels. Easy returns are appreciated by clients.

### Aftersales Client Service KPIs

Research has listed few aftersales service KPIs. These include value provided, service, convenience, and perceived risk (Gensler et al., 2012).

## METHODOLOGY

The red line of this methodology is to refine, delete, or add KPIs from the literature review's list along the client journey. It focuses on the experiential journey rather than the purchase journey (Batat, 2017). However, due to the omnichannel context, many cross-channel and cross-phase KPIs may be relevant.

### Main Conceptualization

The proposed methodology is based on client research. The methodology involved a qualitative exploratory phase (focus groups) and a quantitative survey phase (questionnaire). As the literature suggested, a preliminary assessment of potential sources of bias was performed during the research setting (Podsakoff, MacKenzie, Lee, & Podsakoff, 2003).

### Phase One: Exploratory Qualitative Study with Focus Groups

The first phase of this methodology was the client-centric qualitative exploratory research (Corbin & Strauss, 2008). This exploratory study aimed at understanding regular or new consumption behaviors (Maison, 2018). It required the moderator to structure and guide the interview to elicit rich information from participants. Mitchell and Harris' (2005) protocol was followed. The overall objectives of this exploratory qualitative phase were: (1) create a "journey-in-the-day" client journey map of the buying process, touchpoints, and pain points (key dissatisfiers); (2) identify critical moments of truth (i.e., moments on which a special focus was performed); (3) assess the brand promise (goal met or not); and (4) identify microexperiences where people enter or exit the client journey, identifying why and how (motivated by an information search, a new action, or a new purchase; (Mitchell & Harris, 2005).

The sampling of participants used a theoretical sampling method, focusing on buyers of personal luxury goods. Purchases were made in less than one year; shopping had been completed. The two focus groups consisted of four to five people in each group. This offered each respondent the opportunity to be more active (Maison, 2018). Special attention was paid to the representativity and the reliability of the participants (Batat, 2017). This ensured the pertinence of the exploratory study, especially a mix of digital natives and digital migrants in each focus group. Prior to the focus group, the moderator ensured that none of the participants had been involved in several focus groups or had worked or studied in the luxury industry (Guelfand, 2013). The two-hour focus groups took place in a closed room in a business school executive campus in Paris (none of the respondents were studying at this location).

The focus groups were recorded with an IC recorder. A discussion guide was prepared by the moderator and used as a guideline during the focus group. The discussion guide gathered the main topics and set the direction of the discussion. Typically, a four- to five-person focus group of two hours duration allows four to five topics (Maison, 2018). Topics follow a logical order. However, the discussion guide served as a frame. Therefore, flexibility was encouraged to avoid word-by-word. In addition, it promoted the sharing of opinions through open-ended questions. The guide set the direction, asking informative (for specific information) and motivating questions (How did the respondent maintain and/or enhance his/her motivation?).

At the beginning of the session, each participant was invited to fill in a small form. The form collected demographics, asking participants to briefly describe their best and their worst luxury good purchase experience.

After each group, the qualitative verbal data was transcribed for analysis. This generated a total of 36 pages of verbatims.

## Phase Two: Quantitative Study with a Survey

Considering the great amount of KPIs generated through the qualitative study, a selection was performed based on the following criteria: (1) the KPI was not already covered by the literature; (2) it focused on the omnichannel experience; and (3) it was easy to interpret and implement by luxury professionals.

The questionnaire method was chosen due to its convenience in gathering a high amount of precise data. It helped quantify a result and validate a hypothesis. Often used in applied research, the questionnaire results, as well as analysis, support decision making (Harris, 2014).

The methodology suggested by Harris (2014) helped to plan and write the questionnaire. Based on the qualitative research results and collected data, the research plan focused on which KPIs to identify for an ideal CX (Churchill Jr., 1979). Various constraints were applied to the questionnaire design to facilitate respondents' answers. The most difficult or sensitive questions were located at the end of the questionnaire. In doing so, the respondents felt more at ease. Moreover, the limited number of questions were organized from general to more specific. The questions had transition statements between main categories to support the cognitive effort of the respondent. Rating scales estimated each aspect of the shopping experience, including unipolar (3 to 6) or bipolar (4 to 7) scale lengths. Demographic questions ended the questionnaire. The survey answers remained anonymous.

The survey was deployed online via SurveyMonkey. A pretest using survey data was performed on Thursday, March 7, 2019 to ensure proper understanding, time of completion, and data collection (Wixom & Todd, 2005). This pretest validated the format and wording. One respondent from the qualitative study (focus group) was asked to pretest the questionnaire and discuss it with the author. Attention to design, as well as the application of reliability and validity checks, ensured robust study results. The online survey was distributed widely after validation and readjustments to reduce the questionnaire length and decrease the time of completion. Data collection took place via a social media post (LinkedIn and Facebook) and e-mails using the intranet of the author's company and friends. The survey was reshared on social media and forwarded e-mails to friends, colleagues, and relatives of the author. This used a snowball sampling technique.

The data was collected from Saturday, March 9, 2019 through Sunday, April 7, 2019. The raw data was cleaned using the screening questions. Data meeting the two constraints (having no experience in luxury and having purchased within the last 18 months) was used for the data analysis. A total of 149 respondents answered the survey. After screening questions (no professional or academic experience with luxury and being the buyer of the personal luxury good from the last 18 months), 104 respondents were filtered into the study. Unfortunately, many respondents dropped from the survey before the end (46% of 149 respondents). This led to a 73-respondent relevant sample size.

## FINDINGS

### Step 1: Findings from the Qualitative Study with Focus Groups

The qualitative study, based on focus groups, stressed numerous KPIs. The most relevant KPIs were deduced from the revealed pain points (key dissatisfiers) of clients. In addition, respondents from various nationalities provided insight regarding their preferences.

Analysis of the two focus groups, as well as the verbatims, identified clients' pain points (key dissatisfiers) along the client journey. See the tables in the Appendix: Table 6 presents pain points for awareness and motivation phase, Table 7 those from purchase phase, Table 8 those from payment and shipping, Table 9 those from collection phase, and finally Table 10 those from use phase. A list of KPIs along the client journey emerged from the list of pain points, content analysis of the verbatims, and overall shared CX. In addition, a KPI for cross-phases was identified as "the overall rapidity of the purchase."

They are all presented below: Table 1 deals with KPIs in awareness and motivation phase, Table 2 with purchase phase, Table 3 payment and shipping phase, Table 4 collection phase, and Table 5 use phase.

### Step 2: Selected KPIs for the Quantitative Study

Step 1 led to numerous KPIs. Considering the literature and need for an efficient, shorter questionnaire, this study focused on the Research, Wrapping, Packaging of the Purchase, and Collection/Delivery phases as part of the quantitative study.

### Step 3: Results from the Survey

The retailer from the respondents' last purchase was mostly physical (78% physical and 22% digital). However, no significant appreciation of experience was found depending on the purchase location (an average rating of 4 out of 10). The difference between the average and median was less than 0.5, suggesting the ratings were homogeneous. These results show a low standard deviation. However, a difference of one point (out of 10) was observed when comparing the customer experience average and median ratings of the physical and digital retailers.

*Table 1. KPIs from the qualitative study: awareness and motivation phase*

| Awareness and Motivations Phase | Research Phase |
|---|---|
| • Consistency of the message through advertising and the product<br>• Sophistication of the message and visual channel in the advertisement<br>• Advice, opinions, and purchases from friends, family, or colleagues<br>• Advice and opinions from social media (including YouTube) and blogs<br>• Corporate social responsibility (CSR) of the company selling the product<br>• Location of the manufacturer<br>• Reputation of the brand (common knowledge and friends and family), including quality and sustainability of the product<br>• Trust in the brand regarding quality and sustainability of the product (> 10 years) | • Information on the Website regarding the unavailability of the item (stock for e-commerce purchase)<br>• Information on the Website regarding the availability of the item in the store (in-store stock)<br>• Information on the Website regarding the physical store in which the item can be purchased<br>• Personal advice from the vendor, for the buyer, or for a gift<br>• Color choice on the Website<br>• Fairness of the color on the Website vs. real life<br>• "Mental projection" of the item on the e-commerce site, fitting the client<br>• Exclusivity of the product (only in some countries, etc.)<br>• Aesthetics of the product<br>• Genuine opinions about the product<br>• Information on the Website regarding the CSR of the company selling the product<br>• Information on the Website regarding product traceability<br>• Information on the Website and the product regarding the materials (e.g., fur)<br>• Personalization of the products (fitting the client's taste)<br>• Quality of the product |

*Table 2. KPIs from the qualitative study: purchase phase*

| Purchase Phase | |
|---|---|
| Store Specifics | General |
| • Educated and trained personnel<br>• Welcome of the client as a guest<br>• Polite social distance from the vendor (physical and relational distance)<br>• Availability of the vendor<br>• Advice and added value provided (for example, assortment)<br>• Same person taking care of the client, whatever the client service task (salesperson and cashier)<br>• Time for the client to choose<br>• Year-long client service (sales vs. regular collection)<br>• Perfume of the client's choice<br>• Product presentation<br>o Simplicity<br>o Sophistication<br>o Beauty<br>o Choice<br>• Clear information, especially for holiday specials<br>• Products included<br>• Exchange options<br>• Store location (thoroughfare)<br>• Product visibility (especially products for men)<br>• Try on during sale<br>• Try on products previously listed by the client<br>• Attractiveness of the store's design<br>• External advice from someone other than the salesperson<br>• Store decorations (thick carpet)<br>• Client database<br>o Validation of data privacy policies (on the app)<br>o Availability of client profile listing all purchase invoices (proof in case of burglary)<br>• Availability of the product on CE (Comité d'Entreprise) channel (i.e., collaborative discount offered in some companies) | • Speed of the purchase<br>• Try on product at home without traveling to the store |

*Table 3. KPIs from the qualitative study: payment and shipping phase*

| Payment Phase | Shipping |
|---|---|
| • Initiative to purchase product other than the exposure model<br>• Credit card payment terminal performance<br>o Possibility to pay by different means (deferred payment service credit card, usual credit card [immediate payment], check, phone, gift card)<br>o Possibility to pay with cash<br>• Clear information<br>o Regarding phone payment thresholds<br>o Regarding compatibility of credit cards for phone payment | • External appearance of the box<br>• Shipping costs (€3-4 vs. €12 euros vs. > €12) |

*Table 4. KPIs from the qualitative study: collection phase*

| Collection (Pickup) Phase | Out-of-the-Box Phase |
|---|---|
| • Storage points availability (two to three hours)<br>• Giving perfume and cosmetics samples fitting the client's tastes and wishes<br>• Getting closer to the client to give the package (turning around the counter) or is this too common?<br>• Packaging and wrapping of the product for collection (pick-up)<br>o Wrapping free of charge for gifts<br>o In front of the client<br>o Sustainability of the bags<br>o Beauty of the bags<br>o Reusability of the bags<br>o Bag size<br>o Number of wrapping and packing levels<br>o Bag fastening (closure) systems and silk ribbons<br>• Treat (high-quality tea and macarons)<br>• Returns<br>o Unused make-up returns<br>o Easy return for clothes<br>• Shipping and return costs | • The "wow" factor<br>• Wrapping or packing the purchase invoice in a folded envelope |

*Table 5. KPIs from the qualitative study: use phase*

| Use Phase |
|---|
| • Mechanical resistance of the product (containing material)<br>• Application of salesperson's advice<br>• Influence of social media and/or blogs<br>• Rituals (perfume)<br>• Practical (smaller) packaging, especially for travelling and packing when have a choice<br>• Sustainability of the product by its resistance and design (safe bet)<br>• Hands-free, resistant, "difficult to steal" bags (for public transport)<br>• Adapted size and weight for walking in a city<br>• Sensitive skin products |

## Overall Customer Experience Appreciation

Figure 1 shows a variation of customer experience ratings regarding product categories. Notably, the Belts category customer experience rating was low (2 out of 10). This rating was based on one respondent, which is not significant. When gathering product categories, customer experience ratings show a lower (around 0.2) average for perfumes, cosmetics, make-up, and skincare. For other categories, customer experience ratings are lower (around 0.35) than the median. This difference suggests a higher standard deviation and more diverse ratings for other categories although the median is the same (around 4 out of 10).

*Figure 1. Customer experience by category*

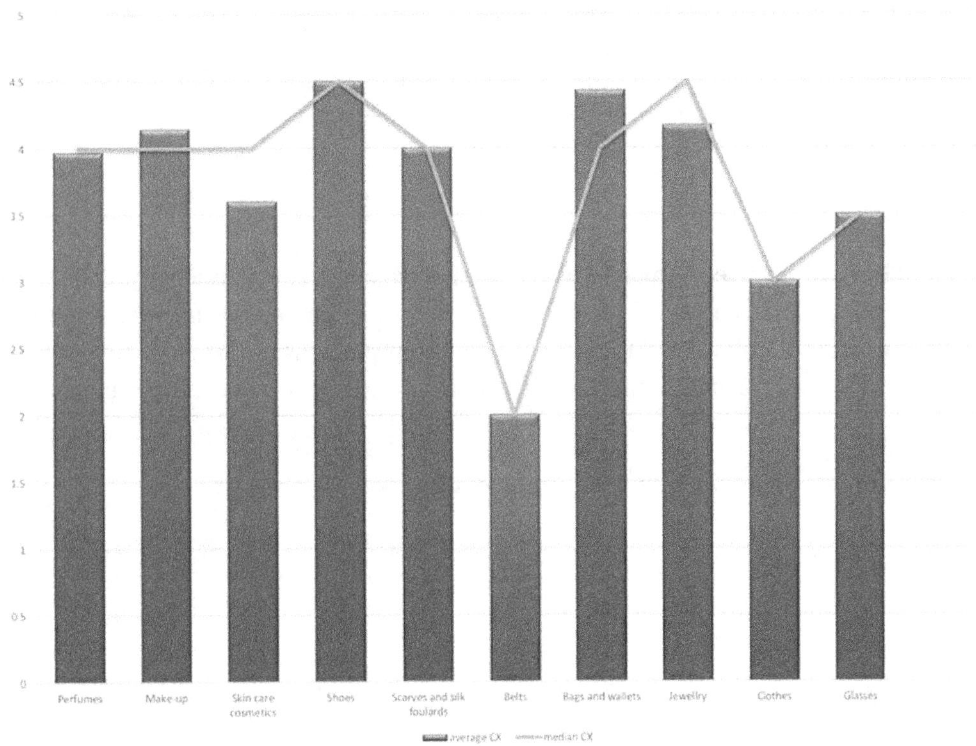


The question "Please rate the ease to find information regarding your LAST personal luxury good purchase" displayed a rating around 4.2 out of 10 on average. As the median is around 4 out of 10, the difference between the median and the average is around 0.2. This suggests a low standard deviation and homogeneous responses.

Figure 2 shows the average "ease to find information" ratings and its median regarding product categories. The difference between the average and the median is low (less than 0.5). Results suggest the responses are mostly homogeneous. When compared to customer experience ratings, the difference between the information availability rating and the customer experience rating is low (less than 0.5). This result suggests that the overall customer experience may be correlated to the information availability.

*Figure 2. Information availability and client experience ratings and categories*

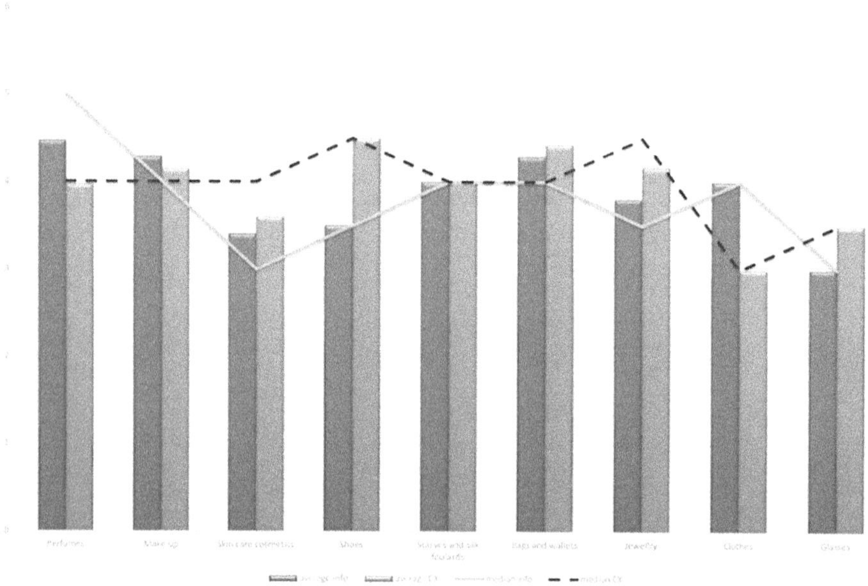

The question "Have you ever recommended your LAST personal luxury experience (research, purchase, payment, collection and use) to someone?" displayed 48% of respondents answering "yes," 42% answering "no," and 10% answering "don't know." Figure 3 shows the proportions of responses regarding product. Respondents tended to recommend categories other than perfumes, cosmetics, make-up, and skincare.

*Figure 3. Recommendations and customer experience ratings and categories*

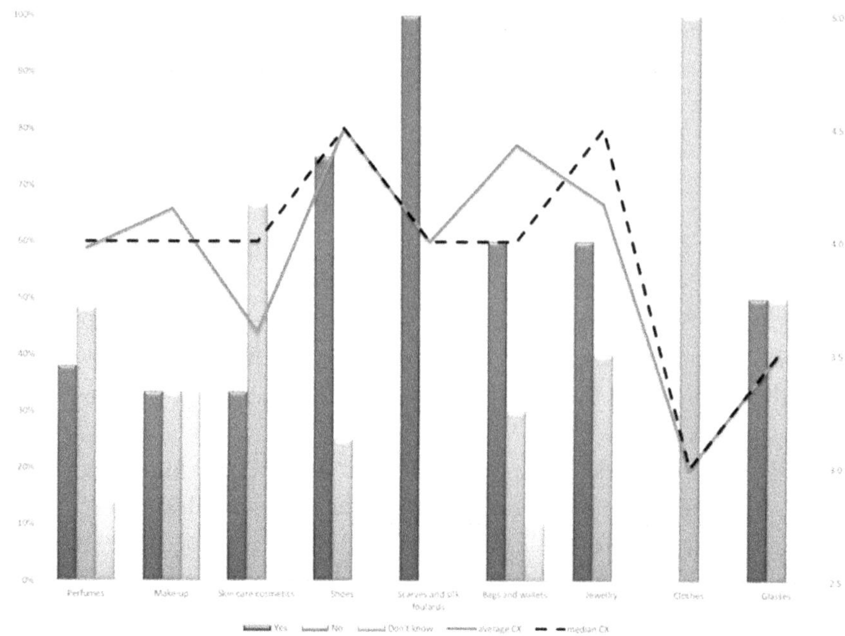

## Research Phase

### Information

The information rating is expected to be associated with the information cost. The Website visit is a channel in which the difference between the average information rating and its median is the highest (0.64 out of 10). This observation suggests that most respondents who visited the Website or application rated the parameter with a score close to 5. Moreover, the respondents who used social media rated "ease to find information" as 4.5 (the average is equal to the median). Consequently, it can be interpreted that visiting the Website, application, or social media brings a higher feeling of completion of information for those who consult these channels. The information channels with the highest scores are friends and relatives (average 4.5 and median 4.75 out of 10). The second highest is digital channels (average 4.29 and median 4.5 out of 10). Traditional channels come in last (average 4.03 and median 4 out of 10).

The most researched information is quality (28%) and shape/style (28%). This is followed by price (15.5%). Researched information varies regarding channel information. For instance, shape/style is more researched through the Website or application channels (47%) as compared to visiting the store (around 33%). On the contrary, quality was more researched during a store visit (around 31%). Respondents who researched information by asking someone they personally know were more interested by the quality (50%) than other information (shape/style 33% and price 17%). Digital channels are used to assess shape/style (39%). On the other hand, traditional channels are used for quality (30%) and price (18.5%). Respondents ask friends and relatives for information about the quality (62.5%). Moreover, the 50 to 59 age range shows that the price is the most important parameter to check prior to purchase (40%).

From the qualitative study, the store or digital visit has been mentioned as a way to research information for respondents. The reasons are various and focused on more than research. However, the results show that the main reason for store or digital visits remains part of a research process (48.5% and 50%, respectively). The question "Thinking about your last personal luxury good purchase, what are the reasons why you visited the store?" results in the most important reason to visit a store is to see, touch and/or smell, and try on the product (48.5%). The second reason is to get the product without waiting (18.2%). In addition, a gathering of the reasons shows that store visits are due to the characteristics of the store. This result demonstrates the importance of the physical experience for most respondents.

To compare with the reasons for digital visit, the question 'What are the reasons why you visited the website or the smartphone/tablet application?' was asked. Answers show that the most important reason for digital visits is to get all the info without having to go to the store' (50%), far followed by a willingness to avoid travelling to the city' (9%). In addition, like the store visit, a gathering of the reasons was performed, showing that the reasons for store visit are mostly due to the characteristics of the digital channels. This shows the importance of the provided information in digital channels for most of the respondents, using the convenience of avoiding travelling to the store.

### Choice

The most important reason to choose a product is because it better suited the respondent (43%). This was followed by a decision during the research phase (24%) and then because it was on a list of products the respondent found to be of interest (11%). This result shows the importance of the personalization of products. A gathering of the individual reasons was performed, showing that fit is the highest determinant for the respondents' choice (around 43%). This was followed by the Previous Choice selection (around 35%).

Most respondents who answered the categories and choice questions bought perfumes and cosmetics (54%). For this category, the most important reasons for the respondents' choice was the fit with desires and needs ("You chose this product because it suited you better"), especially for perfumes (45%) and make-up and skincare cosmetics (67%). Nevertheless, this reason was met in other categories, including bags and wallets (29%), skincare cosmetics (6.4%), jewelry (6.4%), shoes (6.4%), and glasses (3%). In addition, many respondents made their choice prior to purchase (34.7%). They anticipated a favorite product or a short list of products (i.e., scarves and silk foulards, jewelry and glasses categories). Nevertheless, those categories were linked to smaller samples (5 or fewer respondents).

Previous Choice and Fit were not linked to a category. Nevertheless, Service Influence was important when purchasing make-up. About 67% of respondents who purchased make-up selected "You followed the advice of the customer service (salesperson in the store or phone customer service or chatbot" as the most important reason for choice.

## Wrapping of the Purchase

Wrapping is the coverage of the product (for example, gift paper for Christmas). A high number of respondents preferred wrapping (30%); paper was the favorite wrapping material (44%). Furthermore, silk (14%) was preferred over satin (11%). There is no significant difference in the results depending on the nature of the retailer when taken individually. When regrouping retailers regarding physical or digital characteristics, the only significant observations are a wider preference for paper for digital retailers (61.5%), a slightly larger preference for no wrapping for the physical retailer (33.3%), and a slight preference for satin (15%) for the physical retailer.

Similarly, there is no significant difference between categories. Age did not play an important role in wrapping preferences. Males slightly preferred the absence of wrapping (41% vs. 31% for females). On the contrary, females preferred paper (53% vs. 41% for males). Income did not impact the wrapping preferences.

## Fastening Tool for the Purchase

A fastening tool seals the package. Results show that ribbon made of satin or silk (46.5%) was the most preferred fastening (closing) tool among respondents. No fastening (closing) was also attractive (34%). The sticker option was preferred by about 10% of respondents. No specific observation can be made on the fastening (closing) preferences regarding the retailer or product category or respondents' income.

However, younger respondents preferred no fastening (54% of ages 30 to 39), as well as the 70 or older. Results also show that females preferred "ribbon made of satin or silk" (55%); half the amount (25%) of males preferred this option. Males preferred no fastening (40%) and stickers (males, 25%; females, 4%).

## Packaging of the Purchase

Results show that respondents' favorite packaging was "cardboard material with a logo" (49%). Nevertheless, "no packaging at all" is an attractive option for 26% of respondents. "Cardboard without a logo" comes in third with about 18%. For most users (physical or digital retailers), the preference of respondents went to cardboard with a logo. However, a wider range opted for no packaging material for the department store Website (50%) and multibrand physical store (45%, no packaging material; 30%, cardboard with a logo).

When gathering retailers along the digital/physical dimension, results show a wider preference for "carboard with a logo" when the retailer is digital (67%) vs. physical (5%). "Carboard without a logo" was preferred for a physical retailer (21% vs. 7% for digital retailers). Furthermore, the "no packaging" option was slightly preferred for physical retailers (28%) vs. digital (about 20%).

No significant difference was found for age, income, or product categories.

### a. Pick-up and delivery

Most respondents (77%) preferred getting their purchase immediately at the physical store. Only 7% preferred that the store kept their purchase for a few hours. Seven percent preferred home delivery.

Results show that the favorite collection and delivery means depend on the retailer. In a general way, physical retailers are linked to a significant preference for an immediate collection at the store (88%). The Websites (brand Website and multibrand platform Website) show a greater preference for the home delivery or in another place, respectively 28.6% and 25%. Multibrand platform application and marketplace Website counted for a single respondent in each category. For these retailers, a consistent interpretation cannot be drawn. The favorite pick-up and delivery channel do not depend on the category, except for skincare cosmetics. The latter suggests a dislike for the regular collection at the physical store.

Older respondents preferred an immediate collection or delivery, respectively 90% for ages 50 to 59 and 100% for ages 60 to 69 and 70 or older. In a general way, the older the respondent, the more the respondent prefers immediate collection or delivery at the physical store.

Immediate collection or delivery at the physical store remains the favorite option for respondents regardless of gender (females, 76.5%; males, 80%). However, the remaining 23.5% of females show a variety of answers that are not seen in male answers. The second choice for females was delivery at home (9.8%). Their third choice was delivery at the physical store if the store keeps the purchase a few hours (7.8%). On the contrary, apart from immediate collection or delivery at the physical store (80%), males preferred delivery in another place (10%) or another means (10%).

## SOLUTIONS AND RECOMMENDATIONS

From the literature review and the applied methods in this thesis, several KPIs have been identified to enhance the customer experience in an omnichannel context. These KPIs were extracted from a wide literature review, a qualitative study, and a quantitative study.

## General KPIs

The overall customer experience with digital retailers is, in a general way, better than physical experiences. However, digital channels are not perceived as personalized. Nevertheless, the store keeps this attractive channel for quality service thanks to skilled and proactive personnel, atmosphere (sophistication with a "cozy" twist), and a real-life experience. In particular, the ability to see, touch, and smell the product allows the customer to determine if it fits their needs. They can also review the product's quality.

The studies demonstrate the importance of coherence and reliability between channels. While some customers like the impulsivity of the purchase, many customers prepare for their visit. The customer experience rating is linked to the "ease of finding information" (or information availability).

## Research KPIs

To do their research, customers check brand reputation and product characteristics (mostly shape, style, and quality, as well as price and quantity in stock) on digital media (Websites, applications, social media). Customer satisfaction is determined by the level of information available through digital channels. Meanwhile, gathering information from friends and relatives is the most trusted information channel regarding the quality of the product. Furthermore, the absence of recommendations tends to be associated with low customer experience ratings.

Generally, customers look for personalization of products and services. Yet, many perfumes and cosmetics customers continue to buy the same product because they like it and it fits their needs and desires.

## Wrapping, Fastening, Packaging and Collection and Delivery KPIs

Further along the customer journey, several KPIs were determined and their importance assessed.

There is no clear trend in the wrapping of products. Paper is the most preferred material. No wrapping is also successful, especially for physical retailers, older respondents, and ecology-friendly individuals. In a general way, silk wrapping is preferred to satin.

Regarding the fastening material, satin or silk ribbons were selected by about half of respondents. Nevertheless, no fastening is more attractive to males (20 to 39 age range) and the oldest age range (70 to older).

Regarding packaging, the overall favorite is cardboard with a logo. This followed by no packaging and cardboard without a logo. Only the 50 to 59 age range appears to prefer plastic bags with a logo. The survey results show a dislike of cardboard with a logo for the 30 to 49 age range. When customers use a physical retailer, they prefer cardboard without a logo for discretion. Furthermore, no packaging is slightly more attractive when customers purchase from physical retailers (28%) vs. digital (20%).

Lastly, concerning collection and delivery, a vast majority of respondents prefer immediate collection at the physical store. The older the customer, the more they tend to prefer this option. This preference is greater for users of physical retailers. However, this observation may be due to the limited experience of respondents. Delivery is a successful option for digital retailers (at home or in a place chosen by the customer). This KPI may merit more investigation in the future. Respondents are annoyed by unsuccessful deliveries and problematic collections. Consequently, they demand an immediate collection to avoid problems.

## Perspectives

To conclude, customers demand attention and flexibility. They expect tailored customer journeys and real-time communication (Baxendale et al., 2015). Digital retailers had the highest customer experience ratings thanks to their high level of information, flexibility, and capacity to leverage technology (Ganesh et al., 2010).

To become better omnichannel retailers, they can pick the best of physical and digital retail to enhance customer experience as they link the two retail options. The store can extend through an online experience (Lipskier, 2018). CX management is a higher resource of cultural mindsets toward CX. Strategic directions for CX design and businesses capabilities are meant to renew CX as they work to achieve and sustain long-term customer loyalty (Homburg et al., 2017). CX must be aligned and coherent across the business, sharing a definition of key concepts and KPIs (Lipskier, 2018). For instance, the choice of a lack of wrapping and packaging may be due to long-term environmental concerns (CSR, see the qualitative survey's findings). This is also a key part of the digital native vertical brands' strategy.

The endless development of technology supports the omnichannel vision of business. Technology can leverage the omnichannel customer experience by placing both customers and employees in a business vision (Lipskier, 2018). Inspiration can come from digital native vertical brands as fully customer-centric businesses. Complementing innovation, technology, and business, they have long-term goals based on effective and flexible logistics and supply, big data, artificial intelligence, and predictive algorithms.

## LIMITATIONS

Considering the high number of potential KPIs, this chapter first used a qualitative study to investigate KPIs along the customer journey. Second, KPIs were selected for additional inspection if they were neither covered by the literature nor stressed during the qualitative study. Finally, the quantitative study went through the reduced amount of KPIs.

The survey was in English because it is intended for an international population. The qualitative study demonstrated that respondents did not have difficulty with the English language. Nevertheless, English is not the native language of most respondents. The used language, as well as its vocabulary, may have been an impediment to respondents. This may have led to uncertainties in their answers. The quantitative study's survey was also performed in English, bringing potential impediments. Moreover, some respondents told the author that the software pages changed too fast, questioning whether their answers were saved.

The participation rate of the quantitative study was about 50%. To avoid misinterpretation of collected data, filters were systematically set on the data to ensure a double check of analyzed data. The multiple choice tool from the online survey was meant to let respondents choose several answers in a single question. Unwillingly, the multiple choice was a single check box among several answers. This readjustment in the survey brought more robust answers. A single check box encouraged the respondent to select the most relevant answer rather than check every idea that would match their experience.

Lastly, the applied methodology measured what it intended to measure (i.e., customer experience KPIs regarding personal luxury goods in an omnichannel context) from the customers' point of view. Thus, the validity is limited by the applied boundary conditions.

## CONCLUSION AND FUTURE RESEARCH DIRECTIONS

To conclude, customers expressed the desire to be offered both personalized choices and a range of choices for their omnichannel customer journey. These choices impact the desired "wow" effect. Customers expect luxury stores to focus on real-life experiences as they differentiate themselves from regular stores without being intimidating. Customers have an inclination for stores that offer personalized services not found through a digital channel or retailer. For instance, the possibility to try on, see, touch, and smell the product allows customers to assess quality. This, together with highly skilled and flexible customer service, can retain customers' interest in physical retailers. Nevertheless, digital channels complement physical channels, bringing coherence, information, and convenience of staying at home or browsing from another location. Purchasing online or offline, as well as receipt of the purchase by delivery, does not excuse a retailer from offering thoughtful and personalized services like wrapping, fastening, and packaging with quality materials to enhance the out-of-the-boxing experience.

The qualitative study revealed interesting pathways for further investigation, including environmental and CSR concerns like country of production, traceability, craftsmanship, and environmental impact. Other possibilities for study include quick, free, and flexible delivery, easy returns, customer data management, travel-size luxury products for easy transport, and third-party reviews. The quantitative study also showed trends like the preference of older customers for easily opened products.

## REFERENCES


Achille, A., Marchessou, S., & Remy, N. (2018). *Luxury in the Age of Digital Darwinism*. Academic Press.

Aloysius, J. A., Hoehle, H., & Venkatesh, V. (2016). Exploiting big data for customer and retailer benefits: A study of emerging mobile checkout scenarios. *International Journal of Operations & Production Management*, *36*(4), 467–486.

Arnould, E. J., & Price, L. L. (1993). River Magic: Extraordinary Experience and the Extended Service Encounter. *The Journal of Consumer Research*, *20*(1), 24–55. doi:10.1086/209331

Arthur, R. (2019, April 18). Louis Vuitton Becomes Latest Luxury Brand to Launch a Chatbot. *Forbes*.

Atwal, G., & Williams, A. (2009). Luxury brand marketing–the experience is everything! *Journal of Brand Management*, *16*(5-6), 338–346. doi:10.1057/bm.2008.48

Barwitz, N., & Maas, P. (2018). Understanding the omnichannel customer journey: Determinants of interaction choice. *Journal of Interactive Marketing*, *43*, 116–133. doi:10.1016/j.intmar.2018.02.001

Batat, W. (2017). *Luxe et expérience client*. Dunod.

Baxendale, S., Macdonald, E. K., & Wilson, H. N. (2015). The impact of different touchpoints on brand consideration. *Journal of Retailing*, *91*(2), 235–253. doi:10.1016/j.jretai.2014.12.008

Bouchet, P., & Pulh, M. (2006). *L'expérience Vécue: Un Autre Regard sur l'Analyse du Comportement du Consommateur*. Paper presented at the 5èmes Journées Normandes de Recherche sur la Consommation: Société et consommations, Caen.

Burke, R. R. (2002). Technology and the customer interface: What consumers want in the physical and virtual store. *Journal of the Academy of Marketing Science*, *30*(4), 411–432. doi:10.1177/009207002236914

Castañeda, J. A., Muñoz-Leiva, F., & Luque, T. (2007). Web Acceptance Model (WAM): Moderating effects of user experience. *Information & Management*, *44*(4), 384–396. doi:10.1016/j.im.2007.02.003

Corbin, J., & Strauss, A. (2008). Basics of Qualitative Research (3rd ed.). Thousand Oaks: Sage.

D'Arpizio, C., Prete, F., & de Montgolfier, J. (2019). *Luxury Goods Worldwide Market Study, Fall-Winter 2018*. Academic Press.

Dholakia, U. M., Kahn, B. E., Reeves, R., Rindfleisch, A., Stewart, D., & Taylor, E. (2010). Consumer behavior in a multichannel, multimedia retailing environment. *Journal of Interactive Marketing*, *24*(2), 86–95.

Eroglu, S. A., Machleit, K., & Barr, T. F. (2005). Perceived retail crowding and shopping satisfaction: The role of shopping values. *Journal of Business Research*, *58*(8), 1146–1153. doi:10.1016/j.jbusres.2004.01.005

European Parliament. (2016). Regulation (EU) 2016/679 of the European Parliament and of the Council. *Regulation*, *679*, 2016.

Ganesh, J., Reynolds, K. E., Luckett, M., & Pomirleanu, N. (2010). Online shopper motivations, and e-store attributes: An examination of online patronage behavior and shopper typologies. *Journal of Retailing*, *86*(1), 106–115. doi:10.1016/j.jretai.2010.01.003

Gardial, S. F., Clemons, D. S., Woodruff, R. B., Schumann, D. W., & Burns, M. J. (1994). Comparing consumers' recall of prepurchase and postpurchase product evaluation experiences. *The Journal of Consumer Research*, *20*(4), 548–560. doi:10.1086/209369

Gefen, D., Karahanna, E., & Straub, D. W. (2003). Inexperience and experience with online stores: The importance of TAM and trust. *IEEE Transactions on Engineering Management*, *50*(3), 307–321. doi:10.1109/TEM.2003.817277

Gensler, S., Verhoef, P. C., & Böhm, M. (2012). Understanding consumers' multichannel choices across the different stages of the buying process. *Marketing Letters*, *23*(4), 987–1003. doi:10.100711002-012-9199-9

Guelfand, G. (2013). *Les études qualitatives: fondamentaux, méthodes, analyse, techniques*. Éditions EMS. doi:10.3917/ems.guelf.2013.01

Gupta, A., Su, B.-C., & Walter, Z. (2004). An empirical study of consumer switching from traditional to electronic channels: A purchase-decision process perspective. *International Journal of Electronic Commerce*, *8*(3), 131–161. doi:10.1080/10864415.2004.11044302

Hachin, G., Dubois, B., Jourda, M.-C., & Besse, J. (2014). *Expérience Client: les clés pour réussir la transformation*. Academic Press.

Harris, D. F. (2014). *The complete guide to writing questionnaires: How to get better information for better decisions*. I & M Press.

Herhausen, D., Binder, J., Schoegel, M., & Herrmann, A. (2015). Integrating bricks with clicks: Retailer-level and channel-level outcomes of online–offline channel integration. *Journal of Retailing*, *91*(2), 309–325. doi:10.1016/j.jretai.2014.12.009

Hoehle, H., Aloysius, J. A., Chan, F., & Venkatesh, V. (2018). Customers' tolerance for validation in omnichannel retail stores: Enabling logistics and supply chain analytics. *International Journal of Logistics Management*, *29*(2), 704–722. doi:10.1108/IJLM-08-2017-0219

Homburg, C., Jozić, D., & Kuehnl, C. (2017). Customer experience management: Toward implementing an evolving marketing concept. *Journal of the Academy of Marketing Science*, *45*(3), 377–401. doi:10.100711747-015-0460-7

Huang, W. Y., & Dubinsky, A. J. (2014). Measuring customer pre-purchase satisfaction in a retail setting. *Service Industries Journal*, *34*(3), 212–229. doi:10.1080/02642069.2013.778249

Jiang, P., & Rosenbloom, B. (2005). Customer intention to return online: Price perception, attribute-level performance, and satisfaction unfolding over time. *European Journal of Marketing*, *39*(1/2), 150–174. doi:10.1108/03090560510572061

Kaczorowska-Spychalska, D. (2017). Consumer perspective of omnichannel commerce. *Management*, *21*(2), 95–108. doi:10.1515/manment-2017-0007

Keen, C., Wetzels, M., De Ruyter, K., & Feinberg, R. (2004). E-tailers versus retailers: Which factors determine consumer preferences. *Journal of Business Research*, *57*(7), 685–695. doi:10.1016/S0148-2963(02)00360-0

Kim, J., & Lennon, S. J. (2013). Effects of reputation and website quality on online consumers' emotion, perceived risk and purchase intention: Based on the stimulus-organism-response model. *Journal of Research in Interactive Marketing*, *7*(1), 33–56. doi:10.1108/17505931311316734

Kim, S. S., Malhotra, N. K., & Narasimhan, S. (2005). Research note—two competing perspectives on automatic use: A theoretical and empirical comparison. *Information Systems Research*, *16*(4), 418–432. doi:10.1287/isre.1050.0070

Kumar, V., & Venkatesan, R. (2005). Who are the multichannel shoppers and how do they perform?: Correlates of multichannel shopping behavior. *Journal of Interactive Marketing*, *19*(2), 44–62. doi:10.1002/dir.20034

Limayem, M., & Hirt, S. G. (2003). Force of habit and information systems usage: Theory and initial validation. *Journal of the Association for Information Systems*, *4*(1), 3. doi:10.17705/1jais.00030

Lindgreen, A., Vanhamme, J., & Beverland, M. B. (Eds.). (2009). *Memorable Customer Experiences - A Research Anthology*. Gower Publishing Limited.

Lipskier, V. (2018). *D.N.V.B.: Les surdouées du commerce digital (Digitally Natives Vertical Brands)*. Maxima Laurent du Mesnil.

Maison, D. (2018). *Qualitative Marketing Research: Understanding Consumer Behaviour*. Routledge. doi:10.4324/9780429467028

Maman, A.-F. (2011). Memorable Customer Experiences–A Research Anthology. *Journal of Consumer Marketing*, *28*(3), 241–242. doi:10.1108/07363761111127680

Mathwick, C., Malhotra, N., & Rigdon, E. (2001). Experiential value: Conceptualization, measurement and application in the catalog and Internet shopping environment☆. *Journal of Retailing*, *77*(1), 39–56. doi:10.1016/S0022-4359(00)00045-2

Mitchell, V.-W., & Harris, G. (2005). The importance of consumers' perceived risk in retail strategy. *European Journal of Marketing*, *39*(7/8), 821–837. doi:10.1108/03090560510601789

Mosteller, J., Donthu, N., & Eroglu, S. (2014). The fluent online shopping experience. *Journal of Business Research*, *67*(11), 2486–2493. doi:10.1016/j.jbusres.2014.03.009

Neslin, S. A., Grewal, D., Leghorn, R., Shankar, V., Teerling, M. L., Thomas, J. S., & Verhoef, P. C. (2006). Challenges and opportunities in multichannel customer management. *Journal of Service Research*, *9*(2), 95–112. doi:10.1177/1094670506293559

Pine, B. J. II, & Gilmore, J. H. (1999). *The Experience Economy: Work is Theatre & Every Business a Stage*. Harvard Business Press.

Podsakoff, P. M., MacKenzie, S. B., Lee, J.-Y., & Podsakoff, N. P. (2003). Common method biases in behavioral research: A critical review of the literature and recommended remedies. *The Journal of Applied Psychology*, *88*(5), 1939–1854. doi:10.1037/0021-9010.88.5.879 PMID:14516251

Powaga, K. (2008). Integrated customer measurement. *Marketing News*, *42*, 26–31.

Ramirez, S. (2018). *Shoppers Want More Personalised Technology In-Stores and Online*. Luxury Society.

Reber, R., Schwarz, N., & Winkielman, P. (2004). Processing fluency and aesthetic pleasure: Is beauty in the perceiver's processing experience? *Personality and Social Psychology Review*, *8*(4), 364–382. doi:10.120715327957pspr0804_3 PMID:15582859

Reinders, M. J., Frambach, R. T., & Dabholkar, P. A. (2007). Forced adoption of self-service technologies: An exploration of antecedents and consequences of consumers' perceived decisional control. *Marketing Theory and Applications*, 85.

Reynolds, W. H. (1965). A stochastic-model of opinion solidification. *Journal of Advertising Research*, *5*(3), 20–23.

Richardson-Greenfield, P. (2016). *Force Usage of Self-Technology (SST) in a Retail Service Setting and the Moderating Effect of Shopping Value*. Paper presented at the AMA Summer Educators Conference, Atlanta, GA.

Shen, X.-L., Li, Y.-J., Sun, Y., & Wang, N. (2018). Channel integration quality, perceived fluency and omnichannel service usage: The moderating roles of internal and external usage experience. *Decision Support Systems*, *109*, 61–73. doi:10.1016/j.dss.2018.01.006

Solis, B. (2015). *X: The experience when business meets design*. John Wiley & Sons.

Staw, B. M. (1981). The escalation of commitment to a course of action. *Academy of Management Review*, *6*(4), 577–587. doi:10.5465/amr.1981.4285694

Terblanche, N. S., & Boshoff, C. (2006). A generic instrument to measure customer satisfaction with the controllable elements of the in-store shopping experience. *South African Journal of Business Management, 37*(3), 1–15. doi:10.4102ajbm.v37i3.603

Venkatesan, R., Kumar, V., & Ravishanker, N. (2007). Multichannel shopping: Causes and consequences. *Journal of Marketing, 71*(2), 114–132. doi:10.1509/jmkg.71.2.114

Verhoef, P. C., Kannan, P. K., & Inman, J. J. (2015). From multi-channel retailing to omni-channel retailing: Introduction to the special issue on multi-channel retailing. *Journal of Retailing, 91*(2), 174–181. doi:10.1016/j.jretai.2015.02.005

Verhoef, P. C., Neslin, S. A., & Vroomen, B. (2005). *Browsing versus buying: determinants of customer search and buy decisions in a multi-channel environment.* University of Groningen, Groningen, working paper.

Verhoef, P. C., Neslin, S. A., & Vroomen, B. (2007). Multichannel customer management: Understanding the research-shopper phenomenon. *International Journal of Research in Marketing, 24*(2), 129–148. doi:10.1016/j.ijresmar.2006.11.002

Wang, W., Qiu, L., Kim, D., & Benbasat, I. (2016). Effects of rational and social appeals of online recommendation agents on cognition-and affect-based trust. *Decision Support Systems, 86*, 48–60. doi:10.1016/j.dss.2016.03.007

Yu, U.-J., Niehm, L. S., & Russell, D. W. (2011). Exploring perceived channel price, quality, and value as antecedents of channel choice and usage in multichannel shopping. *Journal of Marketing Channels, 18*(2), 79–102. doi:10.1080/1046669X.2011.558826

## KEY TERMS AND DEFINITIONS

**Information Cost:** Mental inputs as needs to exert mental effort to acquire the needed information (desire of information: price, availability, physical attributes or performance characteristics).

**Key Dissatisfiers:** Chief causes of dissatisfaction: core needs that most affect customer dissatisfaction when expectations are not met. A poor performance increases the risk of defection.

**Key Enhancers:** Delight factors that lead to strong loyalty strengthening emotional and rational bonds. The key enhancers prevent competition and promote a positive word of mouth.

**Omnichannel:** Customers move freely between channels (online, mobile devices, and physical store) all within a single transaction process.

**Research-Shopping Phenomenon:** The 'research-shopping phenomenon' is occurring when a customer uses multiple channels for search, and sometimes another channel in a physical store (brick-and-mortar store), subsequently retaining one of these for the actual purchase.

**Showrooming:** A practice whereby consumers visit a physical store (brick-and-mortar retail store) to evaluate products or services firsthand and use mobile technology while in-store to compare products for potential purchase via any number of channels. Visiting a store in order to examine the product before buying it online at a lower price.

**Spillover:** Spillover effects result when the likelihood of using a channel in one stage of the buying process affects the likelihood of choosing that channel in another stage.

## ENDNOTES

1 BONJOURAIKA. 2019. "Our first family luxury haul/unboxing 2019 | BonjourAika - YouTube.": https://www.youtube.com/watch?v=iZb5vIB9VLo.
BRALY, K. 2019. "Luxury unboxing! | Dior, Louis Vuitton - YouTube.": https://www.youtube.com/watch?v=zedaCQ4sSw4.
CHANEL AMBROSE. 2017. "£800 Luxury Gucci Bag Unboxing - YouTube.": https://www.youtube.com/watch?v=YU9WqQShcc4.
DEE LAVIGNE. 2017. "Van Cleef & Arpels Surprise Luxury Unboxing First Look + Try-On! - YouTube.": https://www.youtube.com/watch?v=_ETVj-sMgCA.
WHITNEY, S. 2017a. "Gucci, Chanel & Christian Louboutin Unboxings (Part One) | Shea Whitney - YouTube.": https://www.youtube.com/watch?v=glL2xd_DP30&list=PL9LApalSdMt4MYpnsqJJuqOPzYV8sCW
Vz&index=2.
WHITNEY. 2017b. "Huge Louis Vuitton Haul & Unboxings (Part Two) | Shea Whitney - YouTube.": https://www.youtube.com/watch?v=MDAnMqlOHSs&list=PL9LApalSdMt4MYpnsqJJuqOPzYV8s CWVz&index=1.
WHITNEY. 2017c. "Louis Vuitton Unboxing Gone Wrong | Shea Whitney - YouTube.": https://www.youtube.com/watch?v=l3xrc-Mf3P4.
WHITNEY. 2017d. "Louis Vuitton Unboxing Take 2! | Modeling Shots & Bag Details | Shea Whitney - YouTube.": https://www.youtube.com/watch?v=T1Upr2khkFQ.

# APPENDIX

*Table 6. Pain points from the qualitative study: awareness and motivations phase*

| Awareness and Motivations Phase | Research Phase |
|---|---|
| • Chemicals presence, especially in cosmetics<br>• Number of brands around (feeling of being overwhelmed). | • Unavailability of the item for e-commerce purchase,<br>• No information on the website of the availability of the item in the store (stock in the physical store for the item),<br>• No information on the website of the physical store where the item could be purchased,<br>• Unfaithful color of the item on the e-commerce website,<br>• Difficulty projecting the item worn by the client,<br>• Absence of personalization of the internet. |

*Table 7. Pain points from the qualitative study: purchase phase*

| Purchase Phase | |
|---|---|
| **Store Specifics** | **General** |
| • Ignorance of the client by the client service in department stores,<br>• Close-distance or pressuring salesperson,<br>• Different employees depending on the client service task (different salesperson and cashier),<br>• Poor trust in the salesperson's honesty regarding the product fitting on the client,<br>• Crowding in the store,<br>• Intimidating store (sophistication of the store itself and attitude of the personnel),<br>• Security service following the clients,<br>• Difficulty to find a store (for a specific brand). | • Forced travelling to the store,<br>• Online: no possibility to touch and smell,<br>• Client data base: Uneasy validation of data privacy policies on the app,<br>• Exchange options not provided,<br>• Clearly labelled products,<br>• Giving any perfume and cosmetics samples, whoever the client.<br>• Different client service regarding the time of the year (sales vs. regular collection). |

*Table 8. Pain points from the qualitative study: payment and shipping phase*

| Payment Phase | Shipping |
|---|---|
| • Slow credit card payment terminal,<br>• Impossibility to pay by check,<br>• Impossibility to pay by phone,<br>• Impossibility to pay by cash on the company' choice, leading to management long discussions,<br>• No clear information:<br>• about the phone payment thresholds,<br>• about the compatibility of the credit cards for phone payment. | • Shipping to a 'Point Relais' very impersonal,<br>• No branded name on the box causing theft,<br>• Shipping costs over 12 euros. |

*Table 9. Pain points from the qualitative study: collection phase*

| Collection (Pickup) Phase | Out-of-the-Box Phase |
|---|---|
| • Client service:<br>o Giving any perfume and cosmetics samples, whoever the client,<br>o Incomplete wrapping and packing:<br>• Refusing the wrapping and packing of the purchase (gift and/or Christmas),<br>• Cumbersome bags,<br>• Asking the client to wrap the gift himself,<br>• Returns:<br>o impossible for make-up (even if unused),<br>o complex return for clothes,<br>o unclear shipping and returns costs on the e-commerce website. | • No special attention (handwritten note of thanks…) thanking the client who purchased a product through the e-commerce website. |

*Table 10. Pain points from the qualitative study: use phase*

| Use Phase |
|---|
| • Heavy and cumbersome packaging for perfumes and some cosmetics,<br>• Sustainability of the products,<br>• Risk in public transports due to obviously luxury products. |

# Chapter 7
# A Review of Optimization Techniques for Supplier Selection and Order Allocation

**Bruno A. S. Ferreira**
https://orcid.org/0000-0003-2362-5399
*Lusíada University of Porto, Portugal*

**Rui G. Silva**
*Lusíada University of Porto, Portugal*

## ABSTRACT

*Supply chain is an integrated process in which a group of several organizations, such as suppliers, producers, distributors, and retailers, work together, and where activities such as procurement, production, distribution and demand planning must be addressed. The selection of suppliers is one of the most crucial activities in supply chain management and is conditioned to factors such as lead time, responsiveness, and capacity. This chapter presents an overview of the state of art techniques regarding optimization of supply chain management focussed on the selection of suppliers and order allocation as well as optimization objectives and includes some practical applications. Apart from presenting some of the most common problem categories and optimization techniques, a comparison is provided suggesting the growing importance of heuristic and metaheuristic-based artificial intelligence techniques, given the increased complexity of supply chains and its non-deterministic nature.*

## INTRODUCTION

Optimization, in simple terms, is a mathematical discipline that focusses on finding the extreme (minimum and maximum) of functions or systems (Motta Toledo et al. 2014). It is undeniable the fact that all of us are optimizers, as we all make decisions for the sole purpose of maximizing our quality of life and productivity as well as our welfare. Since this is an ongoing struggle, optimization was, is and will

DOI: 10.4018/978-1-7998-1843-4.ch007

always be the core requirement of human life and this fact yields the development of a massive number of techniques, starting from the early ages of civilization until now (Kiranyaz 2014). Additionally, the development of computers, around the 60', boosted the science of optimization due to the fact that calculations with higher complex level and large scale could be done in much less time (Theodossiou, Karakatsanis, and Kougias 2014). This began a new era for optimization, with the presentation of new and more accurate techniques like: heuristic and metaheuristic (Zare-Reisabadi & Hamid Mirmohammadi, 2015), belonging to categories such as: linear programming (Jung, Jeong, and Lee 2008), multi-objective programming (Varsei and Polyakovskiy 2015), stochastic programming (Theodossiou et al. 2014), among others. Those techniques were applied on a wide variety of cases such as: supply chain (Garcia and You 2015), energy efficiency (Wu, Xia, and Wang 2015) and financial (Pan 2012).

A supply chain (SC), can be viewed as an integrated and synchronized system with ordered processes: acquisition of raw materials, transformation of raw materials into finished products and the distribution of these products (Fahimnia, Farahani, and Sarkis 2013), where the selection of suppliers has an critical impact on the performance, considering that it is an important component of production and logistics management for many organizations (Setak, Sharifi, and Alimohammadian 2012). In today's competitive world the success of an organization is highly dependent on the selection of proper suppliers, also, the supplier's capacity constraints demand that buyers order quantities from multiple suppliers being the total demand split. So, they should decide what to buy or make, from who and how many (order allocation), as well as when, being either single or multi-period (Setak et al. 2012) actions. More recently and corresponding to a global trend (United Nations Development Programme 2017), the supply chain management (SCM) has matured from a field that was only addressed from an operational and economic perspective to one that integrate and consider the broader environmental and social issues, giving rise to the green supply chain management (Zinciri et al. 2018).

The main purpose of this chapter is to provide a review of the literature on the optimization field and how it is applied to supply chain management, more specifically to supplier selection and order allocation. The chapter firstly presents a description of supply chain and green supply chain management, including objectives and methods followed by the scope of optimization, history and management techniques. After, a review is given on the applications of optimization techniques in the fields of supply chain management with a focus on supplier selection and order allocation. Additionally, considerations regarding the different optimization techniques are addressed, compared and discussed. This review considers published research in the last five years from indexed databases and with high impact factors, focussed in optimization techniques applied to supplier selection.

## OPTIMIZATION TECHNIQUES USED IN SCM

The concept of Supply Chain Management (SCM) is credited to Oliver & Webber (1982) given that they have helped to integrate procurement, operations and distribution into a more unified field giving rise to an increased interest in the field. Since its beginning, there have been some theory development, however there is a crucial point that might be a large omission and oversight in the conceptualization and emerging theories of Supply Chain (SC) (Eskandarpour et al. 2015). The current perspective of SC is usually oversimplified whether we think of it as a chain or a network. The SC can be defined as an integrated system synchronizing a series of interrelated business processes in order to: acquire raw materials and parts, transform the raw materials and parts into finished products and distribute these products to either retailers or customers (Fahimnia et al. 2013). The omission in the conceptualization is that there is a tendency to think of SC as products physically flowing and this generally fail to explicitly take into account the many additional parts of the SC that play a vital but indirect supportive role in the movement, storage and transformation of the product across organizations (Carter, Rogers, and Choi 2015).

The main goal of SCM is the optimization (maximization) of the organization profitability and customer satisfaction through integrated planning and control decisions (Mafakheri, Breton, and Ghoniem 2011), which also allowed the SCM to become an integral component of global operations strategy in the 21st century global market, with organizations around the world setting up SC operations in order to take advantage of the global resources and market (Gunasekaran and Ngai 2014). Moreover, globalization has increased the challenges of SCs to remain competitive by focusing on reducing operational costs, increasing the overall profit and integrating the activities of partnering firms around the globe (Guo and Li 2014; Hamdan and Cheaitou 2017). Along that, the environmental protection became one of the big current concerns for the society and consequently to SCM where the leading global organizations have recognized the urgency and need to take measures for environmental protection and have begun to change their own policies and practices to conform to this goal (Lo et al. 2018). The ambition behind green SCM is to integrate logistical, financial and environmental information, increase the competitiveness of SC units, products or services, resulting in sustainable organizational development and improved environmental protection (Sarkar et al. 2017; Wan, Xu, and Dong 2017).

## Supply Chain Optimization Objectives

In optimization, the objectives must be decided before the process itself because all the developed optimization models consider minimization or maximization of objective or a combination of both (Zinciri et al. 2018). The most common objectives are: Maximizing Product Rate (Chandra 1993), Maximizing Revenues (Weraikat, Zanjani, and Lehoux 2016), Maximizing Benefits (Jung, Frank Chen, and Jeong 2008), Minimizing Costs (Choudhary and Shankar 2013; Fahimnia, Sarkis, and Davarzani 2015; Keskin 2015; Paksoy and Chang 2010; Shiguemoto and Armentano 2010), Maximizing Service Level or Customer Satisfaction (Lucas et al. 2001) and Minimizing Environmental Impact (Zhang et al. 2014). However, some of the studies are multi-objective such as: (Selim, Araz, and Ozkarahan 2008) concerned on Maximizing Benefits, Minimizing Costs and Maximizing Service Level or Customer Satisfaction or (Zhang et al. 2014) concerned on Minimizing Costs, Maximizing Service Level or Customer Satisfaction and Minimizing Environmental Impact.

## Supply Chain Optimization Aspects

The SC optimization can be categorized according to mainly nine topics: SC network, Facility Location, Supply Planning, Production Planning, Distribution Planning, Inventory Planning, Capacity Planning, Lot Sizing and Supplier Selection (Zinciri et al. 2018). Some of these topics are studied on an isolated way like: Capacity Planning (Lucas et al. 2001), SC Network (Paksoy and Chang 2010; Varsei and Polyakovskiy 2015), and the Facility Location (Kanani Nezhad, Roghanian, and Azadi 2013). However, the trend and the majority of the studies are focused on integrated approaches such as: the integration of Production, Distribution and Inventory Planning (Fahimnia et al. 2015), the integration of Lot Sizing and Supplier Selection (Bhuiyan, Choudhury, and Dahari 2014) and the integration of Supply and Distribution Planning (Keskin 2015). Almost every decision made in SCM is affected by supplier evaluation and selection (Brandenburg et al. 2014; Fazlollahtabar 2016; Ghadimi and Heavey 2014). Besides the supplier selection, the lot sizing problem, introduced by (Wagner and Whitin 1958), which deals with sourcing decisions, is also among the most important challenges that organizations are facing, and actually, some researchers tried to combine the supplier selection and order allocation problems in order to, align and analyse the available strategies (Azadnia, Saman, and Wong 2015; Bhuiyan et al. 2014; Ghadimi, Dargi, and Heavey 2017; Ghadimi, Ghassemi Toosi, and Heavey 2018; Sodenkamp, Tavana, and Di Caprio 2016).

### Supplier Selection

In today's competitive environment in which customer expectation have increased (Hamdan and Cheaitou 2017), organizations are trying to attain the goals of: low cost, high quality, flexibility and consequent loyalty. So, in order to remain competitive, it is crucial for organizations to work and have a long relationship with its SC partners. The success of an organization is highly depended on the selection of proper suppliers and it is considered a critical task the achievement of different objectives on the SC (Setak et al. 2012). The supplier selection activity, is recognized as the most important and prominent part of the purchasing function, as contributes to enhancing competitive strategy and global market share by reducing operational costs, offering high-quality products, increasing total SC profit and improving total SC performance (Hamdan and Cheaitou 2017; Zhang and Zhang 2011)

### Order Allocation

Due to the increased customer expectations, in today's competitive world, acceptable cost and quality are not enough to determine appropriate suppliers (Hamdan and Cheaitou 2017). Therefore, different factors such as lead time, responsiveness, warranties, capacity, among others, have been taken into account (Gören 2018). The supplier's capacity constraints make buyers order quantities from multiple suppliers and the total demand is split among them. Decisions on what to buy (buy or make), from who and how many (order allocation) and when (single or multi-period) (Setak et al. 2012) have to be made.

## Optimization Techniques

The process of maximizing or minimizing a desired objective function while satisfying the prevailing constraints is called optimization (Belegundu and Chandrupatla 2011). Its foundations were created by the great ancient philosophers and mathematicians, which defined the optimum as an extreme, maximum or minimum, over several domains such as astronomy, geometrical shapes optics, quality of human life, physics, among others. The era of optimization started with the Greek philosopher Pythagoras of Samos (569 BC to 475 BC) who made essential developments in mathematics and astronomy (Kiranyaz 2014). Over the time, philosophers and mathematicians have worked a lot with minimization and maximization problems inspired many times by natural observations (Kiranyaz 2014), such as the ribs near the base of tall trees, the honeycomb structure and the genetic mutation (Belegundu and Chandrupatla 2011).

I. Newton (1660) and G.W. von Leibniz (1670) were responsible for the foundations of modern optimization techniques/methods with their systematic study on differential equations. Some of the first examples are: in 1687, Newton solved the problem of defining the minimum resistance during the movement of a solid body within a liquid; in 1696, Johann and Jacob Bernoulli studied the *brachistochrone* curve, which is the path that will carry a body from one place to another, in the shortest time possible; and in 1758, Euler solved a chess problem according to which a knight must move to each square only once, which later serve as the basis to solve the "traveling salesman problem" (Biggs, Lloyd, and Wilson 1986). The history of optimization techniques and its applications is very rich where many scientists, through the centuries, were occupied with the problem of finding the best, among many solutions. Some, among those who have offered significant contributions to this area are: J.L. Lagrange (1736-1813), J.C.F. Gauss (1777-1855), J.B.J. Fourier (1768-1830), John von Neumann (1903-1957) and H. Markowitz (1927-). The development of computers, since 1960, boosted the science of optimization, due the fact that became possible to solve complex and large-scale calculations in amazingly short times. This represents the beginning of a new era for the science of optimization with the presentation of new and more accurate techniques (Theodossiou et al. 2014).

In order to choose and apply optimization techniques it is necessary to understand the theory supporting the algorithms as well as an understanding of the problem since it requires adjusting the algorithmic parameters, scaling and even modifying the techniques for the specific application. Moreover, the user may have to try several optimization techniques to find one that can be successfully applied to the problem (Belegundu and Chandrupatla 2011). There is a wide variety of optimization techniques and to distinguished them it is necessary to categorize them according to the procedure used for problem solution. Some of the most important categories/concepts on optimization are the Linear and Non-Linear Programming, Multi-Objective Programming, Stochastic Programming, and Heuristic and Metaheuristic Methods (K.L. Katsifarakis 2012; Theodossiou et al. 2014; Zelinka, Snasel, and Abraham 2013).

## Classification Based on the Nature of the Equations Involved

Based on the nature of expressions for the objective function and the constraints most optimization problems can be classified as linear or non-linear problems.

Linear Programming: This category includes techniques, such as the Simplex Method, Integer or Mixed Programming and the Transport Problem, for the solution of linear models, which are described with a linear objective function and linear constraints (Theodossiou et al. 2014).

Non-Linear Programming: Unlike the linear programming techniques, the non-linear ones, include problems where either the objective function or the constraints are of non-linear form (Theodossiou et al. 2014). Some of the most common techniques are: Dynamic Programming, the Neutral Point Technique and a large number of techniques based on Differential Equations.

## Classification Based on the Deterministic Nature of the Variables

Under this category the optimization problem can be classified as deterministic or stochastic programming problems.

Deterministic Programming: The factor that distinguishes deterministic techniques from the stochastic ones is that, in deterministic methods the introduction of input data leads always to the same results, because these approaches take advantage of the analytical properties of the problem to generate a sequence of points that converge to a global optimal solution, while in the stochastic methods this does not happen (Lin, Tsai, and Yu 2012). Some of the most relevant deterministic techniques are: Integer Programming, Network Algorithms, Dynamic Programming and Approximation Algorithms (Lee et al. 2013).

Stochastic Programming: The stochastic optimization does not always ensure that the total optimum will be reached, however, the repetitive application of a stochastic techniques, particularly in complex problems, is more probable to reach the total optimum than a single application of a deterministic one (Theodossiou et al. 2014). Some of the most common techniques are the Decision Making Theory, the Game Theory and the Markovian Theory.

### Classification Based on the Number of Objective Functions

Under this category the objective functions can be classified as single or multi-objective programming problems.

Single-Objective Programming: The single-objective programming techniques, including Calculus-Based, Enumerative and Random Techniques, only can handle problems that needs to optimize only one objective function (Bandyopadhyay and Saha 2018).

Multi-Objective Programming: These techniques, which include Multi-Targeting Optimization, Pareto Analysis and Fuzzy Optimization, can handle problems that simultaneously need to optimize more than one objective function (Bandyopadhyay and Saha 2018).

### Heuristic and Metaheuristic Methods

As stated by C. K. H. Lee (2018) the majority of the decisions in SCM belong to the class of non-deterministic problems, and thus heuristic methods have been applied to improve decisions. These methods define a completely new approach on optimization. Their characteristic is that they scan the area of potential solutions searching for the overall optimal one, testing and evaluating solutions along the way. The simplest form of such a procedure is to test and evaluate all possible combinations. Since this option is not efficient, they usually use a strategy for accelerating the whole procedure. This strategy is often inspired by a natural phenomenon (Theodossiou et al. 2014). In this way there are methods that simulate the theory of Darwin for the evolution of species (Holland 1975), music harmony (Zong Woo Geem, Joong Hoon Kim, and Loganathan 2001), the behaviour of flocks of animals (Kennedy and Eberhart 1994), the social structure of ants (Colorni, Dorigo, and Maniezzo 1992) or bees (Colorni et al. 1992). These methods are considered the most modern tools of research as far as optimization is concerned.

## Optimization Techniques for Supplier Selection and Order Allocation

Optimization techniques are used to operate SC processes effectively, due to the fact that they can handle the complexity of SC, which integrate the procurement, production, distribution and demand planning (Zinciri et al. 2018). There are many optimization techniques used in SC processes, however they are related with certain categories, such as Linear Programming (Jung, Frank Chen, et al. 2008; Paksoy and Chang 2010; Selim et al. 2008), Multi-Objective Programming (Choudhary and Shankar 2013; Varsei and Polyakovskiy 2015), Stochastic Programming (Gupta and Maranas 2003) and Heuristics (Fahimnia et al. 2015; Kanani Nezhad et al. 2013; Keskin 2015; Shiguemoto and Armentano 2010). Each category, has techniques associated with it, and some of the most common (Gören 2018; Setak et al. 2012) are: the Analytic Hierarchy Process (AHP) (Deng et al. 2014; Hamdan and Cheaitou 2017; Li, Wong, and Kwong 2013; Mafakheri et al. 2011), Technique for Order Preference by Similarity to Ideal Solution

(TOPSIS) (Hamdan and Cheaitou 2017; Kilic 2013; Liao and Kao 2011; Lo et al. 2018; Rouyendegh (Babek Erdebilli) and Saputro 2014), Decision-Making Trial and Evaluation Laboratory (DEMATEL) (Gören 2018; Keskin 2015; Sarkar et al. 2017).

## Applications of Optimization Techniques for Supplier Selection and Order Allocation

The selection of suppliers has a decisive effect on the performance of SCs. Therefore, in literature, numerous approaches have been proposed for solving supplier selection and order allocation problems. Some examples of it are: Li et al. (2013) proposed a two-stage mathematical model to deal with an material supplier selection and order allocation. They applied a fuzzy extended AHP to generate risk weights for different suppliers among five factors: cost, quality, risk, profile and service performance; A. H. I. Lee, Kang, Lai, & Hong (2013) constructed an integrated lot sizing model with multi-period supplier selection, to minimize the cost with all-unit and incremental quantity discounts. They adopted two approaches based on the size of the problem: mixed-integer programming (MIP) used for small-scale problems, while a genetic algorithm (GA) was applied for complex and large-scale problems; and Ware, Singh, & Banwet (2014) developed mixed-integer non-linear programming to minimize the total cost of purchasing (TCP) in a dynamic supplier selection problem in a multi-product and multi-period situation.

Besides those, Gunasekaran & Ngai (2014) published a work concerning to expert systems and artificial intelligence in the 21st century logistics and SCM, where a review about some works on the field were made, such as: Deng et al., 2014 which, based on a feasible representation of uncertain information, called D numbers, proposed and demonstrated the effectiveness of a D-AHP method for the supplier selection problem, which extends the classical AHP method; and W. Zhang & Xu (2014) designed an optimal logistics network including suppliers and retailers by taking into account the order quantity of products under an uncertain consumer demand pattern. They proposed a mixed-integer bi-level programming model and employs an iterative-optimization method. With their work, they showed that, if there were a large number of suppliers in the logistics system, retailers could order the product with relatively low price being the largest profit for the retailer who could sell the commodity at the highest price.

Moreover, C. K. H. Lee (2018) made an attempt to review the applications of Genetic Algorithms (GA) in operation management. The reviewed literature from 2007 to 2017 was categorized into three themes, process and product design, operations planning and control, and operations improvement. The three themes contain nine different decision areas, which are facility layout design, supply network design, job design and work, forecasting, capacity planning, inventory control, scheduling, maintenance and risk management; J. L. Zhang & Zhang (2011) developed a MIP model to minimize the total cost, including the product cost and fixed cost, with stochastic demand; Du, Guo, Huang, Li, & Guo (2015) proposed a hybridization of the Pareto Genetic and investigated the supplier selection problem while taking into consideration life-cycle cost using a bi-objective model that accounts for operational cost in addition to the purchasing cost, as minimizing purchasing cost might only lead to more equipment failures resulting in increased maintenance cost; Kumar, Vrat, & Shankar (2006) formulated and used fuzzy mixed-integer goal programming (GP) to solve the vendor selection problem with a fuzzy nature; Amorim, Curcio, Almada-Lobo, Barbosa-Póvoa, & Grossmann (2016) proposed an MIP model for stochastic supplier selection in the food industry; Moghaddam (2015) applied Monte Carlo simulation with fuzzy GP to solve an supplier selection problem; S. H. Amin, Razmi, & Zhang, 2011 were the first to consider strategic perspectives by developing a two-stage integrated quantified ´Strengths, Weaknesses,

Opportunities and Threats´ SWOT analysis technique with fuzzy linear programming to deal with the supplier selection problem; and W. Y. Wu, Sukoco, Li, & Chen (2009) used the Delphi method, the analytic network process (ANP) and the multi-objective mixed-integer programming (MOMIP) model for the supplier selection problem, in which criteria are generated by experts using the Delphi method, then these criteria serve as input for ANP, and finally the MOMIP model is used to select the best suppliers and the associated quantities.

Furthermore, A. H. I. Lee, Kang, & Chang (2009) used fuzzy AHP and fuzzy multiple goal programming to select the suppliers for the thin-film transistor liquid-crystal display; Liao & Kao (2011) developed a two-stage model that uses fuzzy TOPSIS and multi-choice GP for supplier selection and order allocation in watch manufacturing; Rouyendegh (Babek Erdebilli) & Saputro (2014) applied fuzzy TOPSIS and multichoice GP in a fertilizer and chemicals company; Kilic (2013) applied fuzzy TOPSIS with mixed-integer linear programming (MILP) to select the best suppliers for multi-item in a multi-supplier problem; Ghorbani, Bahrami, & Arabzad (2012) used SWOT analysis and entropy to evaluate suppliers and the integer linear programming (ILP) model to select and determine the quantities; and Sodenkamp et al. (2016) used group decision making with different voting power and linear programming in supplier selection.

Similar to the classic supplier selection problem, Green Supplier Selection has attracted the attention of many researchers and a number of works related to green SC have been developed, such as: Mafakheri et al. (2011) introduced a two-stage dynamic programming model for a single-product and multi-period green vendor selection and order allocation problem. Firstly, they used AHP to rank the potential suppliers using four main criteria: price performance, delivery performance, environmental performance and quality. The objectives were to maximize a utility function and to minimize the purchasing and inventory holding cost, which they later combined into one objective function and solved using a dynamic programming algorithm; Hamdan & Cheaitou (2017) provided a decision-making tool to solve a multi-green supplier selection and order allocation problems, they used the fuzzy TOPSIS to rank potential suppliers on the basis of two sets of criteria: traditional and green; Lo et al. (2018) proposed a novel model that integrates the best-worst method (BWM), the TOPSIS and a fuzzy multi-objective linear programming (FMOLP) to solve problems in green supplier selection and order allocation; Ghadimi et al. (2018) proposed a multi-agent system (MAS), which was successfully proven by conducting a comprehensive experiment inspired by a scenario adopted from a real case study in the medical device sector SC. The proposed system aimed to improve the process of sustainable supplier selection and order allocation in terms of adding values such as: less human interaction, facilitated communications and structured information exchange between all participating members of the SC; and Gören (2018) presented a decision framework for the sustainable supplier selection and order allocation problem. The decision framework consists of a hybrid approach, by integrating fuzzy DEMATEL and Taguchi loss function, and bi-objective mathematical model. The hybrid approach, in the first stage, is related to evaluating and ranking the suppliers and the second stage, proposing a new bi-objective mathematical model to deal with optimal allocation of orders among selected suppliers, considering the issue of lost sales.

## Comparison of Optimization Techniques

As the number of optimization techniques and implementations of those techniques has increased researchers have pursued comparative studies, generally referred as optimization benchmarking, to evaluate their performance. When well done, those studies can be valuable in helping end-users choose the most suitable optimization techniques for their problems (Amin and Habib 2015). Comparing or benchmarking of optimization algorithms is a complicated task that involves many subtle considerations to yield a fair and unbiased evaluation, and besides that there are some challenges such as: how to compare optimization algorithms that are different in nature (Gillard and Kvasov 2016; Kvasov and Mukhametzhanov 2018), for example, a deterministic with a non-deterministic method; or, how to compare algorithms that approach the same problem from fundamentally different points of view (Regis and Wild 2015) for example, infeasible point with interior point method, one assumes an infeasible starting point and the other assumes a feasible starting point.

Some of the optimization benchmarking studies are: Saleh, Mohamed, Hemeida, & Ibrahim (2018) made an comparison of three optimization algorithms: Whale Optimization Algorithm (WOA), Dragonfly Algorithm (DA) and Moth-Flame Optimization (MFO) to identify the optimal location and sizing of distributed generation (DG) in radial distribution systems considering minimization of network power losses. The results of this study has shown that MFO algorithm is better than DA and WOA algorithms; Okati, Mosavi, & Behroozi (2017) applied different meta-heuristic methods to find the suboptimal solution for power allocation problem. The results proved that meta-heuristics methods like Genetic Algorithm (GA), Partial Swarm Optimization (PSO) and Teaching-Learning-Based Optimization (TLBO), that rely more on the whole population to improve the solution, have better solution quality than those which do it based on single individuals like Bee Algorithm (BA), Tabu Search (TS) and Simulated Annealing (SA). Hence, they proved that GA, PSO, TLBO and TS have the lowest CPU time among other methods; and Chase & Rademacher (2008) conducted a benchmark study that compared the performance of single-objective optimization algorithms, Adaptive Simulated Annealing (ASA), GA, Systematic Human Error Reduction and Prediction (SHERPA) and Non-Linear Programming by Quadratic Lagrangian (NLPQL), on a broad set of test problems. It was observed that on all of the test problems, SHERPA outperformed the other algorithms in terms of efficiency measure and quality of solutions. The authors also stated that, the superior behaviour of SHERPA is attributed to its hybrid and adaptive formulation.

## CONCLUSION

Finding an alternative solution with the most cost effective or highest achievable performance, under the given constraints, by maximizing desired factors and minimizing undesired ones, is interpreted as optimization. Decision making is broadly an application of optimization and in fact it represents one of the most important aspect for the economy and society development, such as in the supply chain management. Further, the SCM and green SCM, play an important role for organizations due the fact that it has the potential to provide financial benefits (such as increased revenue and reduced costs); environmental benefits (such as reduced waste, increased energy efficiencies, and reduced air and water emissions); and social benefits (such as better health and safety), enhancing in this way, the reputation of organizations. However, in order to remain competitive in today's environment, it is crucial for organizations to have a long-term relationship with its partners, because the success of an organization depends on the correct selection of suppliers. Supplier selection is not a simple task since it depends on a significant number of factors such as lead time, responsiveness, warranties and capacity. The supplier's different constraints demand that organizations are able to swiftly perceive their need to buy or make, from who and how many (order allocation) and when.

This chapter presents a comprehensive literature review on applied optimization techniques used in SCM as well as their advantages and disadvantages. It provides an insight to the success factors pertaining to the application of different techniques taking into account the different case studies analysed providing a wide-ranging guide to different approach scenarios given that, where possible, detailed comparisons are made concerning the performance of the SCM. This work demonstrates that supplier selection and order allocations are critical aspects of SCM and that optimization techniques have an important role in its enhancement. Some of the most used techniques are de AHP, TOPSIS and DEMATEL. As the competitive environment evolve to a more complex system, it becomes essential the use of metaheuristic and heuristic techniques. The major factors influencing the performance, or otherwise compromising results, on the performance of SCM have been found to be related to problem formulation when characterising suppliers since different measures and models are used to define their dominant features. The comparison of optimization techniques is a difficult activity because it is fundamental to ensure identical conditions and, in addition, there are some challenges such as how to compare different types of techniques or how to compare techniques from different perspectives. For those reasons the comparison should be undertaken for each specific problem under the range of some factors, such as time, quality of results, types of approach, among others.

The necessity of optimization techniques in SCM should be emphasized given the growing complexity of the market as well as the emergence and evolution of the optimization techniques field. This field of research concerning the application of optimization techniques to the SCM still lacks the development of a comparable framework so that it would be possible to extrapolate comparable results.

## REFERENCES


Amin, M. N., & Habib, A. (2015). Comparison of Different Classification Techniques Using WEKA for Hematological Data. *American Journal of Engineering Research*, (43), 2320–2847.

Amin, S. H., Razmi, J., & Zhang, G. (2011). Supplier Selection and Order Allocation Based on Fuzzy SWOT Analysis and Fuzzy Linear Programming. *Expert Systems with Applications*, *38*(1), 334–342. doi:10.1016/j.eswa.2010.06.071

Amorim, P., Curcio, E., Almada-Lobo, B., Barbosa-Póvoa, A. P. F. D., & Grossmann, I. E. (2016). Supplier Selection in the Processed Food Industry under Uncertainty. *European Journal of Operational Research*, *252*(3), 801–814. doi:10.1016/j.ejor.2016.02.005

Azadnia, A. H., Muhamad, Z. M. S., & Wong, K. Y. (2015). Sustainable Supplier Selection and Order Lot-Sizing: An Integrated Multi-Objective Decision-Making Process. *International Journal of Production Research*, *53*(2), 383–408. doi:10.1080/00207543.2014.935827

Bandyopadhyay & Saha. (2018). *Unsupervised Classification*. Academic Press.

Belegundu, A. D., & Chandrupatla, T. R. (2011). *Optimization Concepts and Applications in Engineering* (2nd ed., Vol. 34). doi:10.1017/CBO9780511975905

Bhuiyan, M. S. H., Choudhury, I. A., & Dahari, M. (2014). Monitoring the Tool Wear, Surface Roughness and Chip Formation Occurrences Using Multiple Sensors in Turning. *Journal of Manufacturing Systems*, *33*(4), 476–487. doi:10.1016/j.jmsy.2014.04.005

Biggs, Lloyd, & Wilson. (1986). Graph Theory, 1736-1936. Clarendon Press.

Brandenburg, M., Govindan, K., Sarkis, J., & Seuring, S. (2014). Quantitative Models for Sustainable Supply Chain Management: Developments and Directions. *European Journal of Operational Research, 233*(2), 299–312. doi:10.1016/j.ejor.2013.09.032

Carter, C. R., Rogers, D. S., & Choi, T. Y. (2015). Toward the Theory of the Supply Chain. *The Journal of Supply Chain Management, 51*(2), 89–97. doi:10.1111/jscm.12073

Chandra, S. K. (1993). Sustainability of Social Service Sector Programmes in India. *The Indian Journal of Public Administration, 39*(3), 498–502. doi:10.1177/0019556119930329

Chase & Rademacher. (2008). A Benchmark Study of Optimization Search Algorithms. *Red Cedar,* 1–15.

Choudhary, D., & Shankar, R. (2013). Joint Decision of Procurement Lot-Size, Supplier Selection, and Carrier Selection. *Journal of Purchasing and Supply Management, 19*(1), 16–26. doi:10.1016/j.pursup.2012.08.002

Colorni, Dorigo, & Maniezzo. (1992). An Investigation of Some Properties of an 'Ant Algorithm.' *Ppsn, 92*, 509–20.

Deng, X., Hu, Y., Deng, Y., & Mahadevan, S. (2014). Supplier Selection Using AHP Methodology Extended by D Numbers. *Expert Systems with Applications, 41*(1), 156–167. doi:10.1016/j.eswa.2013.07.018

Du, B., Guo, S., Huang, X., Li, Y., & Guo, J. (2015). A Pareto Supplier Selection Algorithm for Minimum the Life Cycle Cost of Complex Product System. *Expert Systems with Applications, 42*(9), 4253–4264. doi:10.1016/j.eswa.2015.01.056

Eskandarpour, M., Dejax, P., Miemczyk, J., & Péton, O. (2015). Sustainable Supply Chain Network Design: An Optimization-Oriented Review. *Omega (United Kingdom), 54*, 11–32. doi:10.1016/j.omega.2015.01.006

Fahimnia, B., Farahani, R. Z., & Sarkis, J. (2013). Integrated Aggregate Supply Chain Planning Using Memetic Algorithm – A Performance Analysis Case Study. *International Journal of Production Research, 51*(18), 5354–5373. doi:10.1080/00207543.2013.774492

Fahimnia, B., Sarkis, J., & Davarzani, H. (2015). Green Supply Chain Management: A Review and Bibliometric Analysis. *International Journal of Production Economics, 162*, 101–114. doi:10.1016/j.ijpe.2015.01.003

Fazlollahtabar, H. (2016). Integration between Fuzzy PROMETHEE and Fuzzy Linear Program for Supplier Selection Problem: Case Study. *Journal of Applied Mathematical Modelling and Computing, 1*(1), 8.

Garcia, D. J., & You, F. (2015). Supply Chain Design and Optimization: Challenges and Opportunities. *Computers & Chemical Engineering, 81*, 153–170. doi:10.1016/j.compchemeng.2015.03.015

Geem, Z. W., Woo, Z., Kim, J. H. J. H., & Loganathan, G. V. (2001). A New Heuristic Optimization Algorithm: Harmony Search. *Simulation, 76*(2), 60–68. doi:10.1177/003754970107600201

Ghadimi, Dargi, & Heavey. (2017). Making Sustainable Sourcing Decisions: Practical Evidence from the Automotive Industry. *International Journal of Logistics Research and Applications.*

Ghadimi, P., & Heavey, C. (2014). Sustainable Supplier Selection in Medical Device Industry: Toward Sustainable Manufacturing. Procedia CIRP. doi:10.1016/j.procir.2014.06.096

Ghadimi, P., Toosi, F. G., & Heavey, C. (2018). A Multi-Agent Systems Approach for Sustainable Supplier Selection and Order Allocation in a Partnership Supply Chain. *European Journal of Operational Research, 269*(1), 286–301. doi:10.1016/j.ejor.2017.07.014

Ghorbani, M., Bahrami, M., & Mohammad Arabzad, S. (2012). An Integrated Model For Supplier Selection and Order Allocation; Using Shannon Entropy, SWOT and Linear Programming. *Procedia: Social and Behavioral Sciences, 41*, 521–527. doi:10.1016/j.sbspro.2012.04.064

Gillard, J. W., & Kvasov, D. E. (2016). Lipschitz Optimization Methods for Fitting a Sum of Damped Sinusoids to a Series of Observations. *Statistics and Its Interface, 10*(1), 59–70. doi:10.4310/SII.2017.v10.n1.a6

Gören, H. G. (2018). A Decision Framework for Sustainable Supplier Selection and Order Allocation with Lost Sales. *Journal of Cleaner Production, 183*, 1156–1169. doi:10.1016/j.jclepro.2018.02.211

Gunasekaran, A., & Ngai, E. W. T. (2014). Expert Systems and Artificial Intelligence in the 21st Century Logistics and Supply Chain Management. *Expert Systems with Applications, 41*(1), 1–4. doi:10.1016/j.eswa.2013.09.006

Guo, C., & Li, X. (2014). A Multi-Echelon Inventory System with Supplier Selection and Order Allocation under Stochastic Demand. *International Journal of Production Economics, 151*, 37–47. doi:10.1016/j.ijpe.2014.01.017

Gupta, A., & Maranas, C. D. (2003). Managing Demand Uncertainty in Supply Chain Planning. Computers and Chemical Engineering. doi:10.1016/S0098-1354(03)00048-6

Hamdan, S., & Cheaitou, A. (2017). Supplier Selection and Order Allocation with Green Criteria: An MCDM and Multi-Objective Optimization Approach. *Computers & Operations Research, 81*, 282–304. doi:10.1016/j.cor.2016.11.005

Holland, J. H. (1975). *Adaptation in Natural and Artificial Systems*. Academic Press.

Jung, H., Chen, F. F., & Jeong, B. (2008). Decentralized Supply Chain Planning Framework for Third Party Logistics Partnership. *Computers & Industrial Engineering, 55*(2), 348–364. doi:10.1016/j.cie.2007.12.017

Jung, H., Jeong, B., & Lee, C.-G. (2008). An Order Quantity Negotiation Model for Distributor-Driven Supply Chains. *International Journal of Production Economics, 111*(1), 147–158. doi:10.1016/j.ijpe.2006.12.054

Katsifarakis, K. L. (2012). *Hydrology, Hydraulics and Water Resources Management: A Heuristic Optimization Approuch*. WIT Press.

Kennedy, J., & Eberhart, R. (1994). Particle Swarm Optimization. *Proceedings of ICNN'95 - International Conference on Neural Networks, 4*(10), 1942–48.

Keskin, G. A. (2015). Using Integrated Fuzzy DEMATEL and Fuzzy C: Means Algorithm for Supplier Evaluation and Selection. *International Journal of Production Research*, *53*(12), 3586–3602. doi:10.1080/00207543.2014.980461

Kilic, H. S. (2013). An Integrated Approach for Supplier Selection in Multi-Item/Multi-Supplier Environment. *Applied Mathematical Modelling*, *37*(14-15), 7752–7763. doi:10.1016/j.apm.2013.03.010

Kiranyaz, S., Ince, T., & Gabbouj, M. (2014). Optimization Techniques: An Overview. *Adaptation, Learning, and Optimization*, *15*, 13–44. doi:10.1007/978-3-642-37846-1_2

Kumar, M., Vrat, P., & Shankar, R. (2006). A Fuzzy Programming Approach for Vendor Selection Problem in a Supply Chain. *International Journal of Production Economics*, *101*(2), 273–285. doi:10.1016/j.ijpe.2005.01.005

Kvasov, D. E., & Mukhametzhanov, M. S. (2018). Metaheuristic vs. Deterministic Global Optimization Algorithms: The Univariate Case. *Applied Mathematics and Computation*, *318*, 245–259. doi:10.1016/j.amc.2017.05.014

Lee, A. H. I., Kang, H. Y., Chun, M. L., & Wan, Y. H. (2013). An Integrated Model for Lot Sizing with Supplier Selection and Quantity Discounts. *Applied Mathematical Modelling*, *37*(7), 4733–4746. doi:10.1016/j.apm.2012.09.056

Lee, A. H. I., Kang, H. Y., & Ter Chang, C. (2009). Fuzzy Multiple Goal Programming Applied to TFT-LCD Supplier Selection by Downstream Manufacturers. *Expert Systems with Applications*, *36*(3), 6318–6325. doi:10.1016/j.eswa.2008.08.044

Lee, C. K. H. (2018). A Review of Applications of Genetic Algorithms in Operations Management. *Engineering Applications of Artificial Intelligence*, *76*(May), 1–12. doi:10.1016/j.engappai.2018.08.011

Li, Z. (2013). An Integrated Model of Material Supplier Selection and Order Allocation Using Fuzzy Extended AHP and Multiobjective Programming. *Mathematical Problems in Engineering*, 1–14.

Liao, C. N., & Hsing, P. K. (2011). An Integrated Fuzzy TOPSIS and MCGP Approach to Supplier Selection in Supply Chain Management. *Expert Systems with Applications*, *38*(9), 10803–10811. doi:10.1016/j.eswa.2011.02.031

Lin, M.-H., Tsai, J.-F., & Yu, C.-S. (2012). A Review of Deterministic Optimization Methods in Engineering and Management. *Mathematical Problems in Engineering*, *2012*, 1–15. doi:10.1155/2012/756023

Lo, H. W., Liou, J. J. H., Wang, H. S., & Tsai, Y. S. (2018). An Integrated Model for Solving Problems in Green Supplier Selection and Order Allocation. *Journal of Cleaner Production*, *190*, 339–352. doi:10.1016/j.jclepro.2018.04.105

Lucas, C., Mirhassani, S. A., Mitra, G., & Poojari, C. A. (2001). An Application of Lagrangian Relaxation to a Capacity Planning Problem under Uncertainty. *The Journal of the Operational Research Society*, *52*(11), 1256–1266. doi:10.1057/palgrave.jors.2601221

Mafakheri, F., Breton, M., & Ghoniem, A. (2011). Supplier Selection-Order Allocation: A Two-Stage Multiple Criteria Dynamic Programming Approach. *International Journal of Production Economics*, *132*(1), 52–57. doi:10.1016/j.ijpe.2011.03.005

Moghaddam, K. S. (2015). Fuzzy Multi-Objective Model for Supplier Selection and Order Allocation in Reverse Logistics Systems under Supply and Demand Uncertainty. *Expert Systems with Applications*, *42*(15–16), 6237–6254. doi:10.1016/j.eswa.2015.02.010

Nezhad, Abbas, Roghanian, & Azadi. (2013). A Fuzzy Goal Programming Approach to Solve Multi-Objective Supply Chain Network Design Problems. *International Journal of Industrial Engineering Computations*.

Okati, Mosavi, & Behroozi. (2017). A Comparison between Different Meta-Heuristic Techniques in Power Allocation for Physical Layer Security. *Iranian Journal of Electrical and Electronic Engineering*.

Oliver & Webber. (1982). Supply-Chain Management: Logistics Catches up with Strategy. *The Roots of Logistics*.

Paksoy, T., & Ter Chang, C. (2010). Revised Multi-Choice Goal Programming for Multi-Period, Multi-Stage Inventory Controlled Supply Chain Model with Popup Stores in Guerrilla Marketing. *Applied Mathematical Modelling*, *34*(11), 3586–3598. doi:10.1016/j.apm.2010.03.008

Pan, W.-T. (2012). A New Fruit Fly Optimization Algorithm: Taking the Financial Distress Model as an Example. *Knowledge-Based Systems*, *26*, 69–74. doi:10.1016/j.knosys.2011.07.001

Regis, R. G., & Wild, S. M. (2015). CONORBIT: Constrained Optimization by Radial Basis Function Interpolation in Trust Regions. *Mathematics and Computer Science Division*, (October), 1–29.

Rouyendegh, Daneshvar, & Saputro. (2014). Supplier Selection Using Integrated Fuzzy TOPSIS and MCGP: A Case Study. *Procedia: Social and Behavioral Sciences*.

Saleh, A. A., Al Attar, A. M., Hemeida, A. M., & Ibrahim, A. A. (2018). Comparison of Different Optimization Techniques for Optimal Allocation of Multiple Distribution Generation. *Proceedings of 2018 International Conference on Innovative Trends in Computer Engineering, ITCE 2018*. 10.1109/ITCE.2018.8316644

Sarkar, S., Lakha, V., Ansari, I., & Maiti, J. (2017). Supplier Selection in Uncertain Environment: A Fuzzy MCDM Approach. *Advances in Intelligent Systems and Computing*, *458*, v–vi.

Selim, H., Araz, C., & Ozkarahan, I. (2008). Collaborative Production-Distribution Planning in Supply Chain: A Fuzzy Goal Programming Approach. *Transportation Research Part E, Logistics and Transportation Review*, *44*(3), 396–419. doi:10.1016/j.tre.2006.11.001

Setak, M., Sharifi, S., & Alimohammadian, A. (2012). Supplier Selection and Order Allocation Models in Supply Chain Management: A Review. *World Applied Sciences Journal*, *18*(1), 55–72.

Shiguemoto, A. L., & Armentano, V. A. (2010). A Tabu Search Procedure for Coordinating Production, Inventory and Distribution Routing Problems. *International Transactions in Operational Research*, *17*(2), 179–195. doi:10.1111/j.1475-3995.2009.00741.x

Sodenkamp, M. A., Tavana, M., & Di Caprio, D. (2016). Modeling Synergies in Multi-Criteria Supplier Selection and Order Allocation: An Application to Commodity Trading. *European Journal of Operational Research*, *254*(3), 859–874. doi:10.1016/j.ejor.2016.04.015

Theodossiou, Karakatsanis, & Kougias. (2014). The History of Optimization. Applications in Water Resources Management. *Conference of the Hellenic Hydrotechnical Association (H.H.A).*

Toledo, M., Fabiano, C., De Oliveira, L., Rodrigo, D. F. P., França, P. M., & Morabito, R. (2014). A Genetic Algorithm/Mathematical Programming Approach to Solve a Two-Level Soft Drink Production Problem. *Computers & Operations Research, 48*, 40–52. doi:10.1016/j.cor.2014.02.012

United Nations Development Programme. (2017). *Background of the Sustainable Development Goals*. United Nations Development Programme.

Varsei, M., & Polyakovskiy, S. (2015). Sustainable Supply Chain Network Design: A Case of the Wine Industry in Australia. *Omega (United Kingdom), 66*, 236–247.

Wagner, H. M., & Whitin, T. M. (1958). Dynamic Version of the Economic Lot Size Model (Vol. 5). Academic Press.

Wan, Xu, & Dong. (2017). Supplier Selection Using ANP and ELECTRE II in Interval 2-Tuple Linguistic Environment. *Information Sciences, 385–386*, 19–38.

Ware, N. R., Singh, S. P., & Banwet, D. K. (2014). A Mixed-Integer Non-Linear Program to Model Dynamic Supplier Selection Problem. *Expert Systems with Applications, 41*(2), 671–678. doi:10.1016/j.eswa.2013.07.092

Weraikat, D., Zanjani, M. K., & Lehoux, N. (2016). Two-Echelon Pharmaceutical Reverse Supply Chain Coordination with Customers Incentives. *International Journal of Production Economics, 176*, 41–52. doi:10.1016/j.ijpe.2016.03.003

Wu, W. Y., Sukoco, B. M., Chia, Y. L., & Shu, H. C. (2009). An Integrated Multi-Objective Decision-Making Process for Supplier Selection with Bundling Problem. *Expert Systems with Applications, 36*(2), 2327–2337. doi:10.1016/j.eswa.2007.12.022

Wu, Z., Xia, X., & Wang, B. (2015). Improving Building Energy Efficiency by Multiobjective Neighborhood Field Optimization. *Energy and Building, 87*, 45–56. doi:10.1016/j.enbuild.2014.10.079

Zare-Reisabadi, E., & Hamid Mirmohammadi, S. (2015). Site Dependent Vehicle Routing Problem with Soft Time Window: Modeling and Solution Approach. *Computers & Industrial Engineering, 90*, 177–185. doi:10.1016/j.cie.2015.09.002

Zelinka, I., Snasel, V., & Abraham, A. (2013). *Handbook of Optimization: From Classical to Modern Approach* (Vol. 38). doi:10.1007/978-3-642-30504-7

Zhang, J. L., & Ming, Y. Z. (2011). Supplier Selection and Purchase Problem with Fixed Cost and Constrained Order Quantities under Stochastic Demand. *International Journal of Production Economics, 129*(1), 1–7. doi:10.1016/j.ijpe.2010.08.003

Zhang, Q., Shah, N., Wassick, J., Helling, R., & Van Egerschot, P. (2014). Sustainable Supply Chain Optimisation: An Industrial Case Study. *Computers & Industrial Engineering, 74*(1), 68–83. doi:10.1016/j.cie.2014.05.002

Zhang, W., & Xu, D. (2014). Integrating the Logistics Network Design with Order Quantity Determination under Uncertain Customer Demands. *Expert Systems with Applications*, *41*(1), 168–175. doi:10.1016/j.eswa.2013.07.019

Zinciri, Çalışmaları, Literatür, Sınıflama, Kocaoğlu, Gümüş, & Kocaoğlu. (2018). *Supply Chain Optimization Studies: A Literature Review and Classification* (Vol. 19). Academic Press.

# Section 3
# International Drivers

# Chapter 8
# From Systematic to Mimetic Behavior in the International Market Selection

**Maria do Rosário Correia**
https://orcid.org/0000-0001-5381-0611
*German University in Cairo, Egypt*

**Raquel Meneses**
*University of Porto, Portugal*

## ABSTRACT

*Traditionally, the international market selection is a systematic process, based on predefined criteria. This process is, however, very time- and cost-consuming, and only a small number of firms have sufficient resources to do it. So, according to the Uppsala Model, firms tend to internationalize to the closest markets (psychic distance), managing uncertainty in a very gradual process based on experiential knowledge. The second-hand knowledge that flows in the firm's network could help firms select the market, helping them to expand gradually. Independently from the source (experiential or second hand), knowledge seems to be a mandatory resource to internationalize. However, a lot of firms imitate other firms' behavior, selecting the international market according to others' selections, believing that they must have superior information. In this situation, firms could imitate the leader (a successful firm) or the herd (a big number of firms). This international market selection is not based on knowledge; it is a mimetic process.*

## INTRODUCTION

In an increasingly globalized marketplace, expansion to international markets is no longer a luxury or even an option but a need for most business firms (Ohmae, 1989). In other words, international expansion became an imperative to grow and to sustain profits (Ozturk, Joiner and Cavusgil, 2015). Nevertheless, entering in new foreign markets comes with inherent risks and uncertainties due to new and relatively unknown surroundings (Astley & Brahm, 1989). Notwithstanding the difficulties, it is crucial that firms

DOI: 10.4018/978-1-7998-1843-4.ch008

select the adequate market as this decision has a profound impact on performance and firm growth. "The selection of an international market affects the entire operational setup of a firm, as it influences the production dispositions as well as financial, organizational and managerial issues adapted to existing business activities" (Andersen & Strandskov, 1997, 66). As a firm's knowledge of a new market is limited, the degree of perceived risk is greater and managers might be cautious about committing scarce resources to the foreign market (Erramilli & Rao, 1990; Johanson & Vahlne, 1977). A means to overcome this lack of knowledge and perceived risk is to adopt an international market selection approach that best fits firm's characteristics namely the previous experience, the resources owned and the existing network (Silva, Meneses & Radomska, 2018). Traditionally, international market selection (IMS) literature argues that systematic and direct knowledge of cross-border markets is mandatory to internationalize. Thus, Andersen and Buvik (2002) and Ozturk, Joiner and Cavusgil (2015) propose structured processes that manager should follow to obtain crucial information regarding foreign markets potential and opportunities for international expansion.

However, in practice several authors defend that companies can obtain valuable information by relying on existing network system (e.g. Agndal & Axelsson, 2002; Moen et al., 2014; Andersen & Buvik, 2002) or by observing other's behavior and the outcomes that follow from this behavior (e.g. Bikhchandani, Hirshleifer & Welch, 1998; Michailova & Wilson, 2008). The former is conventionally known by the relational approach while the latter is traditionally referred to as the mimetic approach. Both these approaches have been proposed by the literature as means by which firms select and develop their business strategy. Generally, the mimetic approach has been defended by two different strands of literature. On one hand, there are theories that relate the mimetic approach to information-based learning processes. On the other hand, a broad category of research relates the mimetic approach to the need to maintain competitive parity or to limit rivalry. These are conventionally known by rivalry-based theories. The information-based theories can be further divided into three categories: informational cascade, social learning process and social legitimacy requirements.

## SYSTEMATIC AND OPPORTUNISTIC APPROACHES (DIRECT DATA COLLECTION AND EXPERIMENTAL APPROACHES)

According to Papadopoulos & Dennis (1988) and Musso & Francioni (2014) firms can gain knowledge and evaluate the attractiveness of potential markets by following a formalized process of data collection and standardized statistical methods that underpin the data analysis.

This formalized and structured process is known as the systematic approach. According to Andersen and Buvik (2002) it includes six stages:

1. Problem definition, which implies that international market selection must be analized as an independent issue not dependent on any other decision (as, for example, entry mode selection);
2. Identify the choice criteria i.e. "the decision-maker should identify all relevant criteria or objectives against which the alternatives will be evaluated" (Andersen & Buvik, 2002, 348).
3. Weight the criteria, providing different relevance to diverse criteria.
4. Generate the alternatives and in this case "at least two strategies could be used: 1) an extensive search, generating a complete list of all alternatives (countries, portfolios); 2) an optimal search,

continuing to generate alternatives until the cost of search outweighs the value of the added information" (Andersen & Buvik, 2002, 349).

5. Rate each alternative on each criterion. According to Andersen and Buvik (2002) this step is very important and must already consider the long range impact of each alternative.
6. Compute the optimal solution, which could be done using several models.

Examples of these models are for instance: compensatory models where to each different criterion different weight is allocated, so that the absence of one criterion can be compensated by the presence of another; or non-compensatory models – these can either be disjunctive models or conjunctive models. In the disjunctive models a minimum level of some criteria or criterion is defined and only countries below these criteria are considered. In the conjunctive models the countries are sorted into acceptable and non-acceptable clusters (Andersen & Buvik, 2002). "While the compensatory models require complete information about the alternatives, the non-compensatory models allow decisions to be made based on the partial information" (Andersen & Buvik, 2002, 349).

Based on systematic approach Ozturk, Joiner and Cavusgil (2015) propose a new tool - Foreign Market Opportunities Analysis (FMOA) - to guide managers in the decision process of selecting the best markets for entry. FMOA allows for a systematic screening of potential countries of entry while simultaneously providing an assessment of the industry market potential. To this extent, FMOA establish a practical three steps methodology (see figure 1) which managers should follow to acquire essential information regarding the firm's internationalization opportunities. The first step of FMOA methodology introduces a new concept, the concept of country responsiveness, which is a measure of elasticity and "reflects the proclivity of consumers to spend, in a specific product category, in a response to a rise in their income. If the tendency to spend is high, then this country is classified as responsive" (Ozturk et al, 2015, 121) otherwise the country is classified as unresponsive. In this way, the methodology considers the specific industry factors that are relevant in the decision-making process.

*Figure 1. Building Blocks for the FMOA tool*
*Source: Osturk et al, 2015, 128*

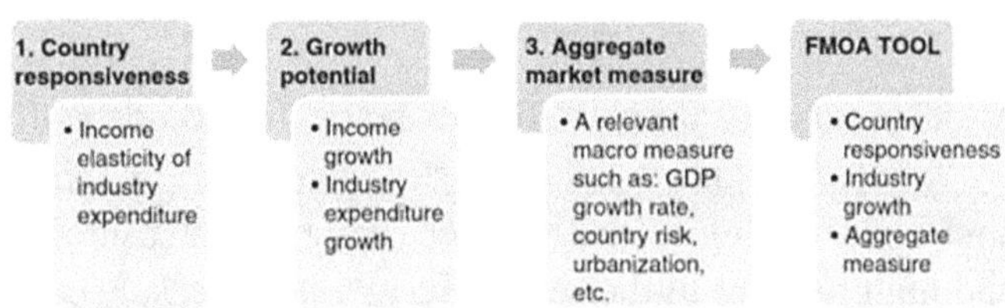


It is fundamental, indeed, to understand the specificities of industry/product in each country. Ozturk et al., (2015) point out that when the consumer purchasing power rises, part of the additional income received is used to buy a specific product. However, the amount of income apportioned to each product is quite different from one country to another. This is the rationality behind the first step, implying that the starting point of any decision regarding IMS should rely on the computation of country responsiveness to increases in industry-specific consumer expenditure.

However, the past is history! Firms should not decide on the best market to internationalize based only on past information. In the second step proposed by Ozturk et al., (2015), firms must forecast the growth potential of each country in terms of income and industry-specific consumer expenditure. It is necessary to incorporate the industry market size too, because the same growth rate could represent completely different realities according to the initial market size. The potential of each country depends on the growth potential and also on the initial market size.

On the third step, indicators of responsiveness and growth potential are combined with aggregate measures such as GDP (Gross Domestic Product) growth rate, country risk, or other measure critical to the specific industry country level indicator (for example, for umbrella industry the rainfall rate). Key indicators are then plotted on a chart (see figure 2). Subsequently, each potential country will be represented by a circle according to its specific degree of attractiveness; the diameter of the circles will be drawn in accordance with the country's related industry market size.

*Figure 2. Four Clusters of FMOA Tool*
*Source: Ozturk et al, 2015, 129*

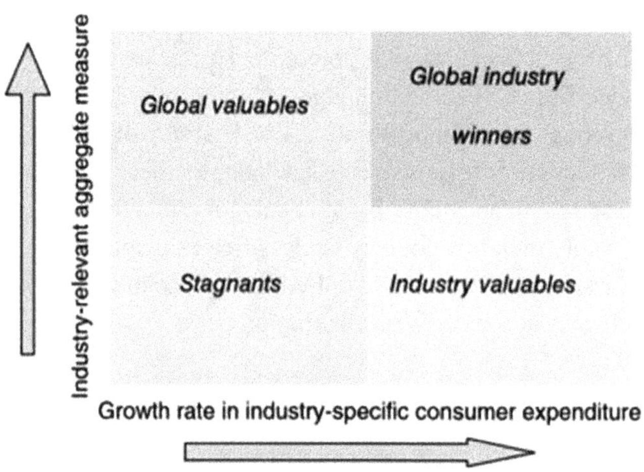


According to FMOA tool, countries are classified as belonging to one of the four clusters: global valuables, global industry winners, stagnants, and industry valuables. "Global Industry Winners (high growth in expenditure and high ranking in the selected aggregate measure), Global Valuables (low growth in expenditure and high ranking in the selected aggregate measure), Industry Valuables (high growth in expenditure and low ranking in the selected aggregate measure), and Stagnants (low growth in expenditure and low ranking in the selected aggregate measure)" (Ozturk et al, 2015, 129). The global industry winners are the most favorable markets and, in opposition, the stagnants are the least attractive one. Both methodologies proposed by Andersen & Buvik (2002) and Ozturk et al. (2015) are however considered to be excessively time-consuming and costly (Rahman, 2001; Musso & Francioni, 2014; Ellis, 2000; Harms & Schiele, 2012, amongst others). To this extent, Papadopoulos and Martín (2011, 133) point out that the systematic approach in IMS is a bounded rational process as "the rationality of decision makers is constrained by their cognitive limitations, their limited amount of time for decision making, the market information they have, and the imperfections of available decision-making models". Additionally, it is important to note that according to the United Nations, there are 193 countries worldwide, so the process of obtaining related macro-economic information is very complex. Even more complex and cumbersome is the process of generating industry-specific information and forecasts. Papadopoulos and Martin (2011, 134) claim that "IMS is inherently difficult in practice". In addition, when going abroad firms face a different culture. In spite of the idea of world *hamburguerization* markets are still very different from each other and "distance still matters". As Musso & Francioni (2014) point out the use of systematic approach is limited by the difficulty that firms often face in accessing relevant information and knowledge. This is especially significant considering that firms typically possess scarce and limited resources. Furthermore, this approach is not only deemed to be too costly and time-consuming, but it also tends to ignore the specificity of firm's business sector and the strategic and experimental context in which the firm operates (Papadopoulos et al, 2002; Annushkina & Trinka Colonel, 2013; Gripsrud & Benito, 2005).

In order to overcome the drawbacks of direct data collection and analysis, several authors (e.g. Kobrin, 1979; Cavusgil, 1985) propose an alternative approach - the *Opportunistic Approach* - based on the Uppsala Model (Johanson and Vahlne, 1977). The Uppsala Model predicts that firms benefit from internationalizing in an incremental way i.e. firms should select first psychically and geographically close markets and only later on should move to moderately closer markets. In other words, firms can overcome internationalization inherent uncertainty and risk by adopting a very gradual process based on experimental knowledge.

Traditionally, the incremental stages model dominated all other approaches towards explaining internationalization (Johanson, 1966; Forsgren & Kinch, 1970; Hornell & Vahlne, 1972). This model is based on organizing learning processes. Firms must acquire experiential knowledge that allows them to take small, incremental steps in order to enter into new markets (Johanson and Vahlne, 1977).

As market knowledge increases, the internationalizing firm ventures from geographically and/or psychically close countries to successively more distant ones. Psychic distance is a dominant concept in this model; it is defined as "factors, such as differences in language, cultures and business practices that prevent and disturb the flow of information between the firm and the market" (Arenius, 2005, p. 115). So, psychic distance has a positive relation with the degree of complexity of inherent information flows between the firm and its markets. According to the traditional Uppsala model, experiential learning is mandatory to get the necessary relevant knowledge to overcome the psychic distance. It is important to note that "experience itself can never be transmitted, it produces a change—frequently a subtle change—in individuals and cannot be separated from them" (Johanson & Vahlne, 1977, p. 30). Firms must learn how to internationalize internationalizing. However, this gradual process is very time- and cost-consuming. Firms tend to start their internationalization process on nearby markets and then gradually move to more psychically distant markets by increasing their commitment and improving their understanding of the foreign markets (Arenius, 2005) (see figure 3). For example, a firm from Bolivia will start its internationalization to Paraguay, and then move to Spain.

Arenius (2005) argues that in the incremental stages model the psychic distance affects the speed at which technology-based firms penetrate in selected foreign markets. In other words, due to psychic distance the penetration process of new ventures in far-out markets requires more time and therefore increases the costs of internationalization. On the other hand, if the firm possesses social capital i.e. the required amount and quality of external networks the market penetration can be speeded up and consequently the costs of psychic distance reduced. In any case, the acquisition of information and knowledge about foreign markets occurs by experimental learning through the firm's own operations.

*Figure 3. International Market Selection according to Uppsala Model*

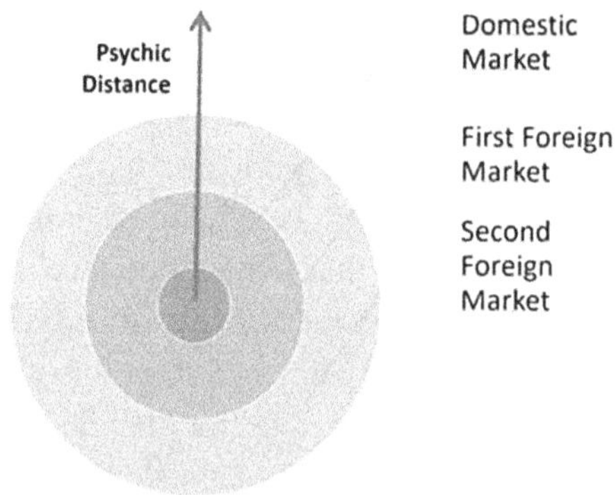


In summary, in the incremental stage model firms choose first the market (starting by a nearby market) and not the partner, and they tend not to evaluate the potential of each of the alternative markets. Firms select a market because it is psychically near. So, "when using this model, the decision-maker will focus on incremental alteration of existing conditions, without knowing or even paying attention to how close to the optimal alternative the chosen incremental really is" (Andersen and Buvik, 2002, 350).

## RELATIONAL APPROACH

Several other authors (e.g. Agdal & Axelsson, 2002; Moen et al., 2014; Andersen & Buvik, 2002) argue that firms can also gain valuable knowledge about foreign markets by using information that is disseminated through their existing network system. According to Sharma & Bolmsterno (2003), firm's ties provide a framework for sharing knowledge and also for promoting the dissemination of knowledge. To this extent, firms can overcome the limitations of direct data collection by relying on their network system. This system acts as a source of knowledge fostering information and experience flows. This allows the firms to learn with their contacts and therefore to acquire second-hand knowledge (Silva et al., 2012).

In the same line of thought, Hakansson and Snehota (1989) claim that "no business is an island". The individual internationalization process is dependent on the internationalization process of firms' network[1]. If a firm is connected to a highly international network, it is easier to get access to contacts, knowledge, and opportunities. Therefore, this firm will not have to select the closest market to start its internationalization process; the firm will use the knowledge disseminated by their external network to select the market with higher potential of expansion. Often, knowledge about potential partners is available in the network too and, in these situations firms do not select countries. Instead, they select partners or they are selected by partners. "The parties to a relationships have privileged access to certain information and knowledge as such information and knowledge is transmitted via relationships" (Schweizer, Vahlne & Johanson, 2010, 366).

It is important to note that according to the network approach to internationalization, firms can be differentiated into four different categories (see figure 4).

*Figure 4. Network approach of internationalization*

| | | Degree of market (network) internationalisation | |
|---|---|---|---|
| | | low | high |
| Degree of company internationalisation | low | early starter | late starter |
| | high | lonely international | international among others |

In the case of an early starter the process is very similar to one described in the Uppsala model. These firms are not internationalized and neither is their network. The early starter has little knowledge of foreign markets and it cannot use its relationships in the home country to obtain this knowledge (Hintu et al., 2002; Hadley and Wilson, 2003; Johanson and Mattson, 1988). "Implementing a project abroad requires a heavy commitment of resources to obtain knowledge and to make the quantitative and qualitative adjustments required by the foreign market" (Łuczak, Małys, Ratajczak-Mrozek, Szczepański, Soniewicki, Dymitrowski, & Deszczyński,, 2012, 33). So, in this situation the internationalization will be gradual, and firms will prefer to start the internationalization process by the closest country (with less psychic distance).

In the lonely international case, firms have already begun the internationalization process without the support of their network. Usually they are going step by step at the beginning of the process, but as this process develops, firms start establishing connections and building up networks. So, in this situation firms tend to use their own expanding relations to get access to new markets, to obtain knowledge, and to establish new contacts. International market selection will be done according to the knowledge and contacts that firms acquire with time.

The late starter is a firm in the starting point of its internationalization but connected to an internationalized network. This situation could be split into two. In the first scenario, the knowledge required to internationalize is quite banal and everybody could have access to it easily. This could be beneficial if the market is not too saturated. In some sectors it is difficult to find a firm without any kind of international presence. Knowledge is available to everyone, and a new firm does not consider as a very risky strategy the international expansion. In the second scenario, however, the more appealing markets tend to be already saturated and in this scenario firms must internationalize into not so obvious or more distant markets. In this case, firms are able to access to some degree of internationalization knowledge, but they cannot get access to the knowledge about these more distant and unexplored markets.

Finally, in the case of international among others firms can use second-hand knowledge from their own international network or from indirect contacts (contacts from her network), which could result in the selection of different international markets. This is the most favorable situation, since firms can get access to privileged information that flows in its own network and in its network's network (for example, a firm can know about an opportunity in a determined country via a buyer which is already there).

"We may conclude that, according to the network model of internationalization, the internationalization process is neither linear nor sequential, as it is in the case of the stage-based models" (Łuczak et al. 2012, 35). Rather, the network model is a self-feeding process (Figure 5). At the beginning of any new internationalization process firms have some knowledge and some contacts (the amount depends on its own level of initial internationalization and on its network level of internationalization). As the process develops firms get more first-hand knowledge and more contacts. These contacts disseminate knowledge, which flows through the network. So as the process develops firms get access to more and more knowledge (first and second-hand knowledge).

*Figure 5. The Internationalization Process on the Basis of Experience and Relationships Development*
*Source: Silva et al, 2012, 147*

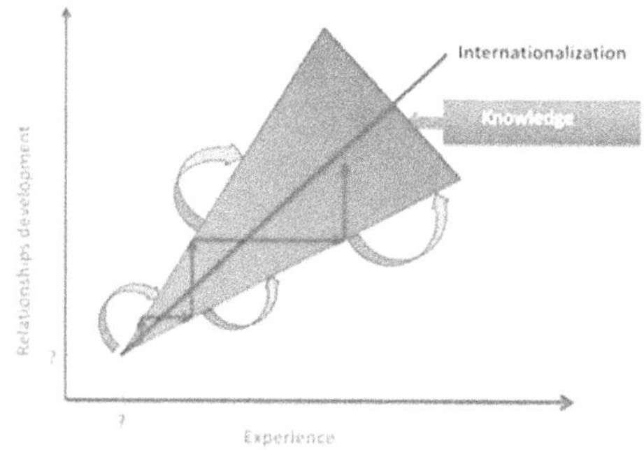


Moreover, it is important to note that not only the firms possess networks but also managers have their own networks as well. The agents responsible for the decisions regarding international expansion are the managers (firms are an abstraction, indeed), so managers' own experience and contacts have a huge impact in all internationalization process, namely in international market selection (Shin, Seidle & Okhmatovskiy, 2016). More, "while both international experience and nationality diversity [of the management team] are likely to influence international decision-making, they lead to different preferences and strategic choices" (Nielsen and Nielsen, 2011, 185).

During their lives managers accumulate experience and contacts. "Thus, given the different experiences, backgrounds and, consequently, given the different capacities and qualities [that entrepreneurs can bring] to process [and considering also] the different relationships and social capital, each entrepreneur will influence in many different ways the internationalization of the company" (Moutinho, 2010, 70).

"Each person's idiosyncratic prior knowledge of markets, of the marketing process, and of customer problems creates a knowledge corridor that allows her or him to recognize certain opportunities" (Schweizer et al, 2010, 347). At the same time, firms can use managers' social capital to establish contacts and privileged knowledge which flows through personal networks. So, firms select some markets based on managers' knowledge and contacts, and this is other type of relational international market selection.

According to all these approaches namely systematic, experimental and relational, the acquisition of knowledge is a fundamental element to the process of internationalization. Firms use:

- internal knowledge
  - first-hand knowledge – as firms go international they learn more and more about all the process through their own operations in the foreign markets.
  - personal knowledge – managers could transfer their knowledge to their firms. This knowledge is the result of the story of their lives (they could be foreigners, they could have study abroad, they could have previous international experience, …);
- external knowledge – resulting from others experience.
  - Business are not an island - firms are not alone, they have customers, suppliers, partners, … and all these agents are connected in a not boundary network. Knowledge flows in this network.

- Acquired knowledge – firms can acquire directly knowledge from institutional or specialized commercial organizations. "These include chambers of commerce, banks, trade associations, consultancy/research agencies, trade publications, and government outlets, as well as technology-based services" (Fletcher & Harris, 2012, 635).
- People are not an island – during their lives managers have developed many contacts. All organizational contacts are mediated by people. When people move from one business to other they pass their own contacts to new business. Very often managers use their social capital as organizational capital to connect to other organizations, to benefit from knowledge and/or to get access to new opportunities.

## MIMETIC APPROACH

### Social Learning or Herding Behavior

Bikhchandan et al. (1998) also point out that direct gathering and analysis might be too costly or even unaffordable especially for small and medium-sized companies (SME)[2]. Furthermore, they also agree that direct data collection is a time-consuming process stressing that it might lead companies to forgone profitable investments or at least to lose valuable outcomes from their investments. However, these authors propose an alternative approach for acquisition of knowledge that does not rely necessarily on the presence of a network system.

According to Bikhchandan et al. (1998) firms take decisions regarding internationalization by adopting a herding behavior i.e. they imitate the actions of similar companies believing that previous trends convey information about the quality of business alternatives. Romano (2009) points out that informational herding takes place because of the externalities attributed to the information conveyed by the actions of previous agents are strong enough to override firms own private information. Indeed, as Bikhchandan et al. (1998) suggest firms might be led to act contrary to what is signaled by their own private information set due to *observational* or *social learning*. These authors stress the social learning applies to situations when the payoff is the same (for instance, the benefits from expanding to a cross-border market) even when the initial information is different (for instance, some firms already operate cross-border whereas others not). Generally speaking, social learning allows the rational processing of information acquired by observing the actions of related market players and evaluating their consequences. Bikhchandan et al. (1998) distinguish two scenarios where social learning or herding behavior might occur. (1) The observable-signals scenario where both private signals and actions of predecessors are observable and (2) the observable-actions scenario where only the actions of predecessors are observable. In the observable-signals scenario, as soon as a firm acts, not only its action is publicly observed but also the private information underpinning this action is publicly disclosed. In this scenario, other firms will benefit from the information conveyed and will adjust their behavior accordingly. As all past signals are publicly observable, information keeps accumulating and eventually all firms will adopt the same behavior which would be the correct one. In the observable-actions scenario, however, firms tend also to mimic the behavior of predecessors but this behavior is very often the incorrect one i.e. the one leading to a lower outcome. In any case, Bikhchandan et al. (1998) stress that although a firm's action generates a weaker positive externality in an observable-actions scenario compared to an observable-signals scenario as long as this action is informative it will foster social learning.

## Informational Cascade

Romano (2009) emphasizes, however, that social learning might to be a rather slow and inefficient process because a large amount of private information is not publicly disclosed which hinders the manager's decision process. In the extreme, herd behavior might lead to informational cascade in which firms' decisions do not convey any new information to other market participants generating a complete information blockage. In this situation, Bernando & Welch (2001) states that irrationally overconfident entrepreneurs, who place heavier weight in their own information relative to those of others play an extraordinary useful role in disseminating information to the market. However, rational agents acting in their own self-interest will always take uninformative imitative actions (Bikhchandan et al., 1998).

Smith & Sorensen (2000) highlight the importance of distinguish the concepts of herd behavior and informational cascade. Thus, whereas a herd takes place when firms act alike after sometime, an informational cascade occurs when consistently firms ignore their private information in their decision-making. In other words, in a herd all the firms take an identical action but some could have acted differently if the private information obtained had been different. In an information cascade the reliance in public information conveyed by the action of others is so strong that overrides any private signal. Thus, an informational cascade implies a herd behavior but the inverse is not always true (Bikhchandan et al., 1998). In the context of international market selection, informational cascade behavior might occur only if the distribution of private information among firms is bounded i.e. no individual firm has stronger private signals than those of others (Smith & Sorensen, 2000). In the case when there is a firm with a stronger, more reliable set of private information (a successful or more experienced firm in the field) the informational cascade will not occur because this firm will benefit from acting first revealing its stronger private information and allowing effective social learning process to take place (Romano, 2009). Bikhchandan et al. (1998) stress that agents that possess superior information have less incentive to wait and see the actions of informational inferior agents, because there is a cost per unit of time of delaying a decision. To this extent, these authors defend that "fashion leaders" can trigger mimicking behavior by disseminating superior private information through their publicly observable actions.

## Institutional Isophormism (or Social Legitimacy)

DiMaggio & Powell (1983) refer to mimetic isophormism as the process by each institutions model their behavior on the behavior of those companies perceived to be legitimated or more successful. In this case, the mimicking behavior is encouraged not necessarily by dissemination of previously private information but by the desire of companies to improve their position and to acquire legitimacy including social legitimacy. As Bresser and Millonig (2003) point out firms mimicking behavior is shaped by isomorphic pressures coming from shared values and norms within the same institutional environment. Therefore, by showing alignment with other organizations in a given institutional context, firms gain legitimacy from the external environment which allows them to benefit from social acceptance and resources. This in turn increases the firms' likelihood of survival in an increasingly competitive environment (Suchman, 1995; Scott, 2001; Li & Ding, 2013). In the context of internationalization, several studies provide evidence that firms tend to imitate competitors' foreign expansion strategies in particular with regards to market entry (Guillén, 2002; Delios, Guar and Makino, 2008), choice of entry mode (Davis, Desai and Francis, 2000; Li, Yang and Yue, 2007) and local operational strategy (Salomon & Wu, 2002). According to Li and Ding (2013) the more prevalent and successful internationalization practices are within an industry, the more reliable and legitimate these practices are considered to be. This according to institutional isophormism theory explains why companies tend to imitate the behavior of successful firms. Moreover, recent research (e.g. Child and Rodrigues, 2005; Li and Yao, 2010; Yang et al., 2009) shows that firms in emerging countries are more sensitive than their counterparties in developed countries to the pressures of mimetic isomorphism due to the volatile and fast changing character of emerging markets (Li, Poppo and Zhou, 2008). In particular, Li and Yao (2010) show that when the risk of government interference is significant, emerging market firms tend to imitate the entry decision of their local rivals in order to avoid failure which is a fairly likely scenario in a highly uncertain and competitive environment.

## Rivalry-Based Theories

Lieberman and Asaba (2006: 374) note that "firms imitate others in an effort to maintain their relative position or to neutralize the aggressive actions of rivals". More specifically, when firms with comparable resources endowments and market positions face intense rivalry they can follow either differentiation or homogeneous strategies (Baum & Haveman, 1997; Deephouse, 1999; Gimeno & Chen, 1998). Lieberman and Asaba (2006) point out that firms that pursue differentiation strategies (with regards to resources and market positions) are less likely to be imitated and are able to obtain higher profits if these strategies turn out to be successful. However, this outcome is uncertain. Therefore, in order to reduce the intensity of competition or to mitigate risk, firms often choose homogeneous strategies in which they mimic the behavior of close competitors. Multimarket contact studies (e.g. Bernheim & Whinston, 1990; Karnani & Wernerfelt, 1985; Leahy & Pavelin, 2003) reinforce the idea that firms adopt homogeneous behavior to avoid retaliatory attacks from competitors that operate in similar markets around the world. More specifically, Lieberman and Asaba (2006) point out that multimarket contact literature propose two ways to justify the adoption of homogeneous behavior among rival companies. On one hand, firms might wish to retaliate against an aggressive move of a rival in one market by adopting the same move in another market. On the other hand, firms might wish to imitate rivals' entry decisions in order to increase the level of multimarket contact. In any case, in highly competitive contexts, retaliatory actions that punish deviant strategies will enforce tacit collusion among rivals fostering cooperation and matching behavior (Lieberman and Asaba, 2006). Knickerbocker (1973) argues that this matching behavior is likely to be related to the need to mitigate risks rather than to decrease rivalry's intensity. To this extend, this author defends that rival firms pursue "follow-the-leader" behavior to sustain their competitive capabilities i.e. to guarantee that no firm is better or worse off relative to the others. Knickerbocker (1973) describes "follow-the-leader" behavior as the strategy pursued by risk-averse firms that wish to follow their main competitors ("the leader") into a foreign country in order to keep the existing oligopolistic equilibrium. This author stresses that the alternative to imitation is adopting a differentiation strategy but as it was point out before this might turn out to be a very costly and risky strategy. In the context of international market selection, recent studies found evidence that oligopolistic firms adopt "follow-the-leader" strategies with regards to the decision where to locate their operations. Specifically, Ghemewat and Thomas (2008) found that dominant players in the cement industry worldwide locate activities in similar locations in order to sustain collusion in prices. Moreover, Gimeno et al. (2005) used a sample of US telecommunication firms to investigate if mimetic behavior regarding international entry moves was determined by rivalry conditions or by information-based processes. Their results showed that firms competing in the domestic market tend to follow each other to the same foreign markets, while non-competing firms try to avoid each other geographically when selecting international markets. This finding provide strong support to rivalry-based theories in particular to the prediction that imitation is related to the need to preserving existing oligopolistic position in order to decrease risk. As point out by Hansen & Hoenen (2018) the concept of "follow-the-leader" is closely related to herding that occurs when firms from the same industry converge to the same country at the same time without this convergence being guided by economic fundamentals of the location in question. By following the large crowd (herding), the likelihood of serious negative repercussions to each individual firm is low (Lung, 2000).

## Implications of Information- or Rivalry-based Theories on Empirical Research

Lieberman and Asaba (2006) propose three criteria to help distinguishing between information-based conditions and rivalry-based conditions that might lead to empirically observable mimicking behavior. The flowchart in figure 6 summarizes the criteria used by Lieberman and Asaba (2006) criteria to define the potential conditions of mimic behavior in international market context. Thus, the two first criteria - related to market overlap and resources similarity – defines whether the leader and the follower operate as rivals. Indeed, if firms possess similar resources and overlap in terms of product lines and geographic market they will tend to be close rivals. On the other hand, if firms differ in terms of market, size or resources, information-based motives are more likely to explain mimetic behavior rather than rivalry-based motives. In particular, if firms operate in highly uncertain environments managers will be more likely to match the behavior of non-competing firms as they believe that the actions of others convey superior information about the quality of internationalization strategies. Therefore, Lieberman and Asaba (2006) point out that the third criterion to distinguish between the two types of imitation's motives is the degree of uncertainty of the environment in which firms operate In summary, the flowchart in figure 6 shows that if asymmetry (with regards to market, size or resources) among firms prevails then information-based motives for imitation should dominate. If firms are close rivals then the dominant criterion should be the degree of environment uncertainty. To this extend, if high uncertainty prevails then firms adopt homogeneous behavior either for information or rivalry-based reasons. If firms operate in a low uncertainty environment, rivalry-based reasons for imitation should prevail. Finally, Lieberman and Asaba (2006) add that both multimarket contact and firms´ risk aversion can further contribute for increasing the prevalence of rivalry-based motives in determining imitation strategies.

*Table 1. The holistic perspective on the IMS phenomenon*

<table>
<tr><th>Theoretical View</th><th>IMS Approach</th><th colspan="2">Key Drivers</th><th>Knowledge Acquisition</th></tr>
<tr><td>International Business</td><td>Systematic</td><td colspan="2">Market-seeking characteristics</td><td>Mandatory</td></tr>
<tr><td rowspan="2">Networking</td><td>Relational Active</td><td rowspan="2">Partners regarded as assets</td><td>Searching for stakeholders</td><td>Mandatory</td></tr>
<tr><td>Relational Passive</td><td>Following stakeholders</td><td>Not acquired</td></tr>
<tr><td>Mimetic</td><td>Mimetic</td><td colspan="2">Bandwagon effect</td><td>Not acquired</td></tr>
</table>

Source: Silva et al, 2018, 595

## RECENT TRENDS IN INTERNATIONAL MARKET SELECTION

Sánchez and Ferrá (2019) argue that it is crucial to develop a methodology that would establish a bridge between systematic and non-systematic approaches and that would reflect the decision-making of managers when selecting the most attractive market for international expansion. To this extent, these authors conducted a study on a sample of exporting companies from the food-processing sector located in the region of Lleida, Spain. The focus of this study is to answer three main questions: what are the external determinants that affect the selection of the most attractive foreign market, what are the differentiating characteristics of the primary target markets and whether companies follow either a systematic or non-systematic approach on their selection of preferential markets. The first step was to obtain information about the five relevant criteria proposed by Whitelock and Jobber (2004) as the main determinants for establishing *country clusters* and for setting *country ranks*. Although some of these criteria are traditionally used in systematic approach models namely country specificities, market factors and competitiveness intensity in the target market other criteria such as psychic distance and knowledge of the market obtained through experience are closely related to non-systematic approach models. In Sánchez and Ferrá (2019) study country specificities include political stability, market opportunities, economic development, cultural unity and legal and geographic barriers (Papadopoulos and Jansen 1994); market factors comprise market size and growth rate, follow customers' location choice and potential of market demand (Whitelock and Jobber, 2004 and Papadopoulos et al., 2002). Finally, psychic distance is assessed by the geographic and cultural distance and by the level of linguistic barriers (Dow and Karunaratna, 2006; Sheng and Mullen, 2011). Applying a principal components analysis (PCA) procedure, Sánchez and Ferrá (2019) show that the main external factors that determine the selection of the most attractive foreign markets are: high level of economic development and low level of risk of target country and high degree of competitive advantage offered by the target market. The latter is affected to a large extent by the degree of cultural proximity with the potential foreign markets (Sánchez and Ferrá, 2019). Moreover, Sánchez and Ferrá (2019) study allows for the identification of country and rank clusters that share common characteristics in terms of degree of attractiveness to an exporting firm. Finally, as Sánchez and Ferrá (2019) point out, their study contributes for the development of a methodology that can be applied worldwide to any industrial sector. This methodology depends only on secondary information that is reliable and easily accessible by business managers which brings objectivity and homogeneity to the decision process. Most importantly, this methodology bridges the gap between systematic and non-systematic literature and provides a framework that facilitates and enlightens the decision regarding international market selection.

Following a similar line of thought, Silva et al. (2018) present a holistic approach to international market selection by proposing a framework that considers a network of dimensions from systematic, relational and mimetic literature. Silva et al. (2018) develop an exploratory study based on the analysis of three case studies of Portuguese firms that selected Poland as the desirable exporting market. This study relies mostly on data obtained through unstructured interviews with the founders and chairmen of the sampled companies although additional information is also retrieved from newspaper articles and companies' websites. The findings of the study show that different companies use different strategies to select and penetrate in the desirable market. Thus, the larger firm in the sample followed a systematic approach to acquire relevant information and knowledge regarding the potential markets. This firm selected Poland as the target market due to its potential of development and large population, removal of some legal and institutional barriers and relative low risk of penetration, in particular for this company considering its solid financial situation and availability of resources. The second firm analysed followed a relational approach in selecting Poland as its desirable foreign market. As a SME firm, this company strived to follow its client to an international market, capitalising on the close relationship it maintained with its main client. Typically, this proximity with clients operations and strategies is stronger for the case of smaller companies compared to larger companies (Fabian and Molina, 2009). Finally, the third firm analysed decided to select Poland as the most attractive foreign market based solely on the observed success of other Portuguese companies that had previously expanded to Poland. Due to its small size, this firm could not spend many resources or time to adopt a systematic approach and therefore relied on informational cascade process to legitimize its decision of international market selection. Silva et al. (2018) emphasise that there is no unique or best approach with regard to the selection of the most appropriate international market. Depending on the characteristics of the exporting firm and of the market in which it operates, a rational decision of market selection might rely on systematic, related or mimetic factors (see Figure 7).

*Figure 6. Environmental Conditions to distinguish between Information-based and Rivalry-based Mimetic Approach*
**Source:** *Adapted from Lieberman and Asaba, 2006, 376.*

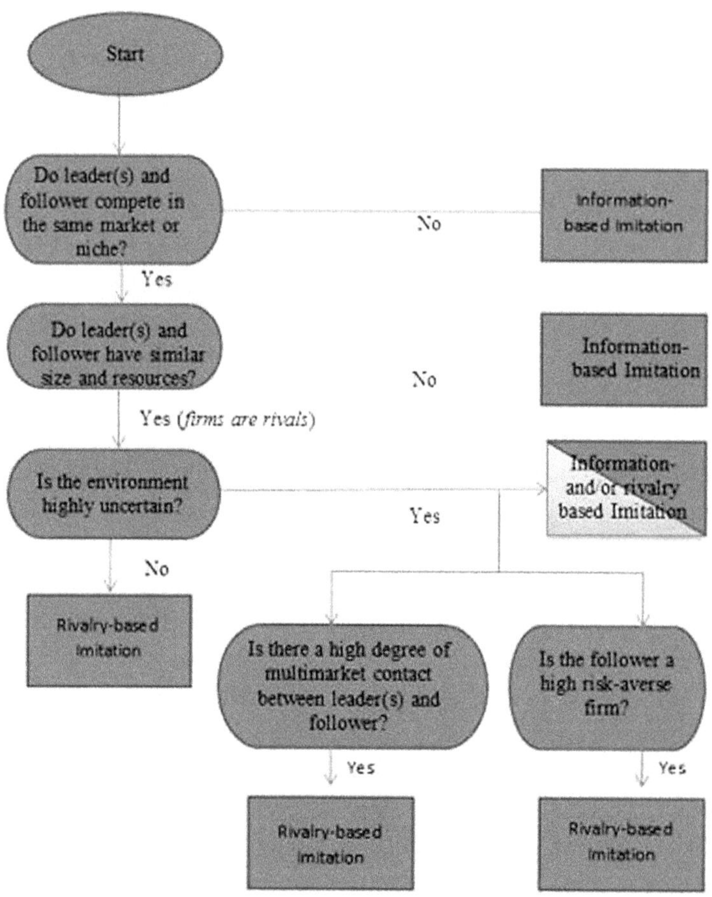

In an era of fast development in communication technologies, Gonçalves (2020) and Gonçalves and Smith (2019) stresses the importance of developing a new conceptual framework for market internationalization that takes into account new integrated communication technology strategies in conjunction with the traditional networking models of foreign market selection such as the Uppsala model. To this extent, Gonçalves (2020, 1) points out that "current internationalization theories have failed to provide a comprehensive framework of the effects of networking and network relationships on the internationalization process, especially the role of the Internet, the web, and social media." Gonçalves and Smith (2019) run an exploratory study based on data collected from a qualitative online survey and semi-structured interviews to a group of senior management executives from a sample of multinational enterprises (MNE) in Angola and Mozambique. This study shows that many multinational enterprises chose to internationalise not only based on existing network relationships but also by relying on web-enabled digital and virtual resources such as Internet, social media and web-based professional community of practices. A holistic approach that takes into account the important role played by web-enabled digital resources represents a step forward in the ever evolving research on international market selection process.

## CONCLUSION

The process of international market selection is pivotal in all internationalization strategies. It could be said that the success of internationalization is dependent on the adequacy of international market selection.

Literature defends that firms must analyse markets in a systematic and formalized way. However, this is a very time and cost-consuming process, not affordable to the majority of firms.

So, according to the Uppsala model firms try to get knowledge in an incremental way. They learn how internationalize, internationalizing. To this extent, firms select markets, step by step, going from the closest (psychic) market to more distant (psychic) ones. International market selection is based on the experimental knowledge – first-hand knowledge. This process assumes that firms live in isolation. However, in reality, firms are connected in a very complex network. Knowledge flows in this network. Firms can therefore use this second-hand knowledge to help them selecting the most attractive and appropriate foreign markets. Firms could also use the entrepreneur's knowledge, transforming social capital in organizational capital.

Very often, firms tend to follow the leader or they follow the herd. Firms select the same market, imitating a validated behaviour. In this situation, there is a homogeneity of selection and a cascade effect will appear. Most recent studies on the process of internationalization suggest that there is no unique approach with regard to international market selection. A holistic perspective should be adopted to best support internationalization strategies in the current globalized and diversified business world.

## REFERENCES

Agndal, H., & Axelsson, B. (2002). Internationalisation of the firm – The influence of relationship sediments. In V. Havila, M. Forsgren, & H. Håkansson (Eds.), *Critical perspectives on internationalisation* (pp. 437–456). Pergamon.

Andersen, O., & Buvik, A. (2002). Firms' internationalization and alternative approaches to the international customer/market selection. *International Business Review*, *11*(3), 347–363. doi:10.1016/S0969-5931(01)00064-6

Andersen, P. H., & Strandskov, J. (1997). International market selection: A cognitive mapping perspective. *Journal of Global Marketing*, *11*(3), 65–84. doi:10.1300/J042v11n03_05

Annushkina, O. E., & Trinca Colonel, R. (2013). Foreign market selection by Russian MNEs-beyond a binary approach? *Critical Perspectives on International Business*, *9*(1/2), 58–87. doi:10.1108/17422041311299950

Arenius, P. (2005). The psychic distance postulate revised: From market selection to speed of market penetration. *Journal of International Entrepreneurship*, *3*(2), 115–131. doi:10.100710843-005-4203-6

Astley, W. G., & Brahm, R. (1989). Organizational designs for post-industrial strategies: The role of interorganizational collaboration. In C. C. Snow (Ed.), *Strategy, organization design, and human resource management* (pp. 233–270). JAE.

Baum, J. A., & Haveman, H. A. (1997). Love thy neighbor? Differentiation and agglomeration in the Manhattan hotel industry, 1989–1990. *Administrative Science Quarterly*, *42*(2), 304–338. doi:10.2307/2393922

Bernardo, A., & Welch, I. (2001). On the evolution of overconfidence and entrepreneurs. *Journal of Economics & Management Strategy*, *10*(3), 301–330. doi:10.1162/105864001316907964

Bernheim, B. D., & Whinston, M. D. (1990). Multimarket contact and collusive behavior. *The RAND Journal of Economics*, *21*(1), 1–26. doi:10.2307/2555490

Bikhchandani, S., Hirshleifer, D., & Welch, I. (1998). Learning from the behavior of others: Conformity, fads, and informational cascades. *The Journal of Economic Perspectives*, *12*(3), 151–170. doi:10.1257/jep.12.3.151

Bresser, R., & Millonig, K. (2003). Institutional capital: Competitive advantage in light of the new institutionalism in organization theory. *Schmalenbach Business Review*, *55*(3), 220–241. doi:10.1007/BF03396675

Cavusgil, S. T. (1985). Guidelines for export market research. *Business Horizons*, *28*(6), 27–33. doi:10.1016/0007-6813(85)90082-5

Child, J., & Rodriguez, S. B. (2005). The Internationalization of Chinese Firms: A Case for Theoretical Extension? *Management and Organization Review*, *1*(3), 381–410. doi:10.1111/j.1740-8784.2005.0020a.x

Davis, P., Desai, A., & Francis, J. (2000). Mode of International Entry: An Isomorphism Perspective. *Journal of International Business Studies*, *31*(2), 239–258. doi:10.1057/palgrave.jibs.8490904

Deephouse, D. L. (1999). To be different, or to be the same? It's a question (and theory) of strategic balance. *Strategic Management Journal*, *20*(2), 147–166. doi:10.1002/(SICI)1097-0266(199902)20:2<147::AID-SMJ11>3.0.CO;2-Q

Delios, A., Gaur, A. S., & Makino, S. (2008). The timing of international expansion: Information, rivalry and imitation among Japanese firms, 1980–2002. *Journal of Management Studies*, *45*(1), 169–195.

DiMaggio, P., & Powell, W. (1983). The Iron Cage revisited: Institutional isomorphism and colective rationality in organizational fields. *American Sociological Review*, *48*(2), 147–160. doi:10.2307/2095101

Dow, D., & Karunaratna, A. (2006). Developing a Multidimensional Instrument to Measure Psychic Distance Stimuli. *Journal of International Business Studies*, *37*(5), 578–602. doi:10.1057/palgrave.jibs.8400221

Ellis, P. (2000). Social ties and foreign market entry. *Journal of International Business Studies*, *31*(3), 443–469. doi:10.1057/palgrave.jibs.8490916

Erramilli, M. K., & Rao, C. P. (1990). Choice of Foreign Market Entry Mode by Service Firms: Role of Market Knowledge. *International Marketing Review*, *7*(5), 60–72.

Fabian, A. P. F., Molina, H., & Labianca, G. (2009). Understanding Decisions to Internationalize by Small and Medium-sized Firms Located in an Emerging Market. *Management International Review*, *49*(5), 537–563. doi:10.100711575-009-0007-6

Fletcher, M., & Harris, S. (2012). Knowledge acquisition for the internationalization of the smaller firm: Content and sources. *International Business Review*, *21*(4), 631–647. doi:10.1016/j.ibusrev.2011.07.008

Forsgren, M., & Kinch, N. (1970). The adaptation of the firm to changes in surrounding systems. Department of Business Studies, Uppsala.

Ghemawat, P., & Thomas, C. (2008). Strategic Interaction Across Countries and Multinational Agglomeration: An Application to the Cement Industry. *Management Science*, *54*(12), 1–32. doi:10.1287/mnsc.1080.0917

Gimeno, J., & Chen, M. J. (1998). The dynamics of competitive positioning: A pair-wise perspective. Academy of Management Proceedings, 1–8.

Gimeno, J., Hoskisson, R. E., Beal, B. D., & Wan, W. P. (2005). Explaining the clustering of international expansion moves: A critical test in the U.S. telecommunications industry. *Academy of Management Journal*, *48*(2), 297–319. doi:10.5465/amj.2005.16928411

Gonçalves, M. V. (2020). *A Holistic Approach to Emerging and Frontier MNE's Internationalization: A New Conceptual Research Framework*. Paper presented at the Conference on Academic and Business Collaboration across Borders: A Focus on Emerging and Developing Countries, Casablanca, Morocco.

Gonçalves, M. V., & Smith, E. C. (2019). Internationalisation strategies of African MNEs: A case analysis of Angolan and Mozambican enterprises. *International Journal of Export Marketing*, *3*(1), 59–76. doi:10.1504/IJEXPORTM.2019.101809

Gripsrud, G., & Benito, G. (2005). Internationalization in retailing: Modelling the pattern of foreign market entry. *Journal of Business Research*, *58*(12), 1672–1680. doi:10.1016/j.jbusres.2004.11.003

Guillén, M. (2002). Structural inertia, imitation, and foreign expansion: South Korean firms and business groups in China, 1987–1995. *Academy of Management Journal*, *45*(3), 509–525. doi:10.5465/3069378

Hadley, R. D., & Wilson, H. M. (2003). The network model of internationalisation and experimental knowledge. *International Business Review*, *12*(6), 697–717. doi:10.1016/j.ibusrev.2003.01.001

Håkansson, H., & Snehota, I. (1989). No business is an island: The network concept of business strategy. *Scandinavian Journal of Management*, *5*(3), 187–200. doi:10.1016/0956-5221(89)90026-2

Hansen, M. W., & Hoenen, A. K. (2018). Global Oligopolistic Competition and Foreign Direct Investment: Revisiting and Extending the Literature. *Critical Perspectives on International Business*, *12*(4), 369–387. doi:10.1108/cpoib-03-2014-0017

Harms, R., & Schiele, H. (2012). Antecedents and consequences of effectuation and causation in the international new venture creation process. *Journal of International Entrepreneurship*, *10*(2), 95–116. doi:10.100710843-012-0089-2

Hintu, S., Forsman, M., & Kock, S. (2002). Mission Impossible? Internaionalization without Social Networks. *Nordic Workshop on Interorganisational Research*.

Hörnell, E., & Vahlne, J. E. (1972). *The deciding factors on the choice of subsidiary sales company as the channel for exports*. Academic Press.

Johanson, J., & Mattson, G. (1988). Internationalization in industrial systems-A network approach in global Competition. In *Prince Bertil Symposium at the Institute of International Business*. Stockholm School of Economics.

Johanson, J., & Vahlne, J. E. (1977). The internationalization process of the firm: A model knowledge development and increasing foreign market commitments. *Journal of International Business Studies*, *8*(1), 23–32. doi:10.1057/palgrave.jibs.8490676

Johansson, H. (1966). *Foreign Ownership in Norwegian Enterprises* [Utenländske eierintressen i norske bedrifter]. Academic Press.

Karnani, A., & Wernerfelt, B. (1985). Multiple point competition. *Strategic Management Journal*, *6*(1), 87–96. doi:10.1002mj.4250060107

Knickerbocker, F. T. (1973). *Oligopolistic reaction and multinational enterprise*. Harvard Business School Press. doi:10.1002/tie.5060150205

Kobrin, S. J. (1979). Political risk: A review and reconsideration. *Journal of International Business Studies*, *10*(1), 67–80. doi:10.1057/palgrave.jibs.8490631

Leahy, D., & Pavelin, S. (2003). Follow-my-leader FDI and tacit collusion. *International Journal of Industrial Organization*, *21*(3), 439–453. doi:10.1016/S0167-7187(02)00091-7

Li, F., & Ding, D. Z. (2013). The effect of institutional isomorphic pressure on the internationalization of firms in an emerging economy: Evidence from China. *Asia Pacific Business Review*, *19*(4), 506–525. doi:10.1080/13602381.2013.807602

Li, J. J., Poppo, L., & Zhou, K. Z. (2008). Do Managerial Ties in China Always Produce Value? Competition, Uncertainty, and Domestic vs. Foreign Firms. *Strategic Management Journal*, *29*(4), 383–400. doi:10.1002mj.665

Li, J. T., Yang, J. Y., & Yue, D. R. (2007). Identity, community, and audience: How wholly owned foreign subsidiaries gain legitimacy in China. *Academy of Management Journal, 50*(1), 175–190. doi:10.5465/amj.2007.24162209

Li, J. T., & Yao, K. (2010). The role of reference groups in international investment decisions by firms from emerging economies. *Journal of International Management, 16*(2), 143–153. doi:10.1016/j.intman.2010.03.005

Lieberman, M., & Asaba, S. (2006). Why do firms imitate each other? *Academy of Management Review, 31*(2), 366–385. doi:10.5465/amr.2006.20208686

Łuczak, M., Małys, Ł., Ratajczak-Mrozek, M., Szczepański, R., Soniewicki, M., Dymitrowski, A., & Deszczyński, B. (2012). *The development of business networks in the company internationalisation process*. Wydawnictwo Uniwersytetu Ekonomicznego w Poznaniu.

Lung, Y. (2000). Is the Rise of Emerging Countries as Automobile Producers an Irreversible Phenomenon? In J. Humphrey, Y. Lecler, & M. Salerno (Eds.), *Global Strategies and Local Realities: The Auto Industry in Emerging Markets*. London & St Martin's Press. doi:10.1057/9780333977712_2

Michailova, S., & Wilson, H. I. (2008). Small firm internationalization through experientiallearning: The moderating role of socialization tactics. *Journal of World Business, 43*(2), 243–254. doi:10.1016/j.jwb.2007.11.002

Moen, Ø., Gavlen, M., & Endrese, I. (2004). nternationalization of small, computer softwarefirms: Entry forms and market selection. *European Journal of Marketing, 8*(9/10), 1236–1251. doi:10.1108/03090560410548951

Moutinho, R. F. A. Ch. M. S. B. (2010), *International New Ventures Não Tecnológicos* (PhD Dissertation). School of Economics and Management of University of Porto.

Musso, F., & Francioni, B. (2014). International strategy for SMEs: Criteria for foreign marketsand entry modes selection. *Journal of Small Business and Enterprise Development, 21*(2), 301–312. doi:10.1108/JSBED-10-2013-0149

Nielsen, B. B., & Nielsen, S. (2011). The role of top management team international orientation in international strategic decision-making: The choice of foreign entry mode. *Journal of World Business, 46*(2), 185–193. doi:10.1016/j.jwb.2010.05.003

Ohmae, K. (1989). Managing in a borderless world. *Harvard Business Review, 67*(May-June), 152–161. PMID:10292934

Ozturk, A., Joiner, E., & Cavusgil, S. T. (2015). Delineating Foreign Market Potential: A Tool for International Market Selection. *Thunderbird International Business Review, 57*(2), 119–141. doi:10.1002/tie.21686

Papadopoulos, N., Chen, H., & Thomas, D. R. (2002). Toward a tradeoff model for internationalmarket selection. *International Business Review, 11*(2), 165–192. doi:10.1016/S0969-5931(01)00054-3

Papadopoulos, N., & Denis, J. E. (1988). Inventory, taxonomy and assessment of methods for international market selection. *International Marketing Review, 5*(3), 38–51. doi:10.1108/eb008357

Papadopoulos, N., & Jansen, D. (1994). Country and method-of-entry selection for international expansion: International distributive arrangements revisited. *Dimensions of International Business, 11*, 31–52.

Papadopoulos, N., & Martín Martín, O. (2011). International market selection and segmentation: Perspectives and challenges. *International Marketing Review, 28*(2), 132–149. doi:10.1108/02651331111122632

Rahman, S. (2001). The international market selection process: A study of successful Australian international firms. *Journal of International Marketing and Exporting, 6*(2), 150–160.

Romano, M. G. (2009). Informational cascades in financial economics: A review. *Giornale degli Economisti e Annali di Economia, 68*(122), 81–109.

Salomon, R., & Wu, Z. (2012). Institutional distance and local isomorphism strategy. *Journal of International Business Studies, 43*(4), 343–367. doi:10.1057/jibs.2012.3

Sánchez, P. C., & Ferrá, B. E. (2019). Clusters of exporting priority countries. *Cuadernos de Gestión, 19*(1), 147–174. doi:10.5295/cdg.170733pc

Schweizer, R., Vahlne, J. E., & Johanson, J. (2010). Internationalization as an entrepreneurial process. *Journal of International Entrepreneurship, 8*(4), 343–370. doi:10.100710843-010-0064-8

Scott, R. (1991). Unpacking Institutional Arguments. In W. Powell & P. DiMaggio (Eds.), The New Institutionalism in Organizational Analysis (pp. 164–182). Academic Press.

Sharma, D., & Blomstermo, A. (2003). The internationalization process of Born Globals: A network view. *International Business Review, 12*(6), 739–753. doi:10.1016/j.ibusrev.2003.05.002

Sheng, S. Y., & Mullen, M. R. (2011). A hybrid model for export market opportunity analysis. *International Marketing Review, 28*(2), 163–182. doi:10.1108/02651331111122650

Shin, D., Seidle, R., & Okhmatovskiy, I. (2016). Making the foreign familiar: The influence of top management team and board of directors characteristics on the adoption of foreign practices. *Journal of World Business, 51*(6), 937–949. doi:10.1016/j.jwb.2016.09.003

Silva, S., Meneses, R., & Radomska, J. (2018). A holistic perspective on the international market selection phenomenon. *Journal for East European Management Studies, 23*(4), 579–602. doi:10.5771/0949-6181-2018-4-579

Silva, S., Pacheco, E., Meneses, R., & Brito, C. (2012). The importance of second-hand knowledge in the revised Uppsala Model: Can European textiles producers export to China? *Journal of Global Marketing, 25*(3), 141–160. doi:10.1080/08911762.2012.741963

Smith, L., & Sorensen, P. (2000). Pathological Outcomes of Observational Learning. *Econometrica, 68*(2), 371–398. doi:10.1111/1468-0262.00113

Suchman, M. (1995). Managing Legitimacy: Strategic and Institutional Approaches. *Academy of Management Review, 20*(3), 571–610. doi:10.5465/amr.1995.9508080331

Whitelock, J., & Jobber, D. (2004). An evaluation of external factors in decision of UK industrial firms to enter a new non-domestic market: An exploratory study. *European Journal of Marketing, 38*(11/12), 1437–1455. doi:10.1108/03090560410560182

Yang, X., Lim, Y., Sakurai, Y., & Seo, S. (2009). Comparative analysis of internationalization of Chinese and Korean firms. *Thunderbird International Business Review*, *51*(1), 37–51. doi:10.1002/tie.20243

## ADDITIONAL READING

Andersen, O., & Buvik, A. (2002). Firms' internationalization and alternative approaches to the international customer/market selection. *International Business Review*, *11*(3), 347–363. doi:10.1016/S0969-5931(01)00064-6

Brouthers, L. E., & Nakos, G. (2005). The role of systematic international market selection on small firms' export performance. *Journal of Small Business Management*, *43*(4), 363–381. doi:10.1111/j.1540-627X.2005.00142.x

Delerue, H., & Lejeune, A. (2012). Internationalization of biotechnology start-ups: Geographic location and mimetic behaviour. *International Small Business Journal*, *30*(4), 388–405. doi:10.1177/0266242611402565

Herzenstein, M., Dholakia, U. M., & Andrews, R. L. (2011). Strategic herding behavior in peer-to-peer loan auctions. *Journal of Interactive Marketing*, *25*(1), 27–36. doi:10.1016/j.intmar.2010.07.001

Mersland, R., Nyarko, S. A., & Sirisena, A. B. (2020). A hybrid approach to international market selection: The case of impact investing organizations. *International Business Review*, *29*(1), 101624 (1-12).

Qi, X., Chan, J. H., Hu, J., & Li, Y. (2020). Motivations for selecting cross-border e-commerce as a foreign market entry mode. *Industrial Marketing Management*, *89*, 50–60. doi:10.1016/j.indmarman.2020.01.009

Vahlne, J. E. (2020). Development of the Uppsala model of internationalization process: From internationalization to evolution. *Global Strategy Journal*, *10*(2), 239–250. doi:10.1002/gsj.1375

## KEY TERMS AND DEFINITIONS

**Herding Behavior:** Occurs when firms from the same industry converge to a behavior at the same time, and this Convergence is not guided by economic fundamentals. Firms are just following the large crowd (herding).

**IMS-Mimetic Approach:** Companies decide where to go following the options of those companies perceived to be successful or following the high number of companies. It is not about access to knowledge; it is about mimicking behavior.

**IMS-Relational Approach:** Companies select where to go according to their network knowledge and contacts.

**Informational Cascade:** Is a situation where firms sequentially take decisions. The first one chooses an option based on information. In the next step, firms observe this option, and as they believe that the first one is well informed, so they imitate it. In the next step, firms observe the imitators, believing they have good information and imitate them. This process repeats for a long time.

**Mimetic Isomorphism or Social Legitimacy:** Is the process by which an institution models its behavior on the behavior of those companies perceived to be successful. In this case, mimicking behavior is encouraged not necessarily by dissemination of previously private information but by the desire of companies to improve their position and to acquire legitimacy, including social legitimacy.

**Rivalry-Based Theories:** Is the process by which institution imitates their rival to maintain its competitive position.

**Second-Hand Knowledge:** Firms are part of a very complex network; and knowledge flows in this network. This knowledge developed outside the firm is second-hand knowledge.

## ENDNOTES

1 In the very first approach, the concept of network in the internationalization process overlaps with the concept of market.

2 Ellis (2000) and Harms & Schiele (2012) studies provide evidence of adoption of alternative approaches to traditional systematic methods to support firms' foreign direct investment decisions.

# Section 4
# Innovation Drivers

# Chapter 9
# The Impact of ICTs and Business Strategy on Innovation Activities:
## Empirical Evidence From Japanese SMEs

**Hiroki Idota**
*Kindai University, Japan*

**Sheikh Abu Taher**
*Jahangirnagar University, Bangladesh*

**Masatsugu Tsuji**
*Kobe International University, Japan*

## ABSTRACT

*This research explores factors of innovation and clarifies the effects of information and communication technologies (ICTs) on innovation process. Analysis is based on a mail survey conducted in February 2012 to March 2012 on 3,959 Japanese SMEs. The number of valid responses was 647 (16.3%) and is used as a sample for the analysis. Based on the data, logit analysis is employed for product and process innovation to answer the following three research questions: (1) What are factors promoting innovation? (2) How ICTs affect innovation? and (3) Which affect SMEs with higher ICT use to realize innovation? As a result, (1) the factors such as R&D expenditures, leadership of top management, motivation of employees, ICT index, effects of ICTs are extracted. (2) Sharing information and shortening the R&D process are the effects which ICTs perform to innovation. (3) These effects are greater to SMEs with higher ICT index. The new finding of this chapter lies in results such that ICTs affect innovation through sharing information and shortening the R&D period.*

DOI: 10.4018/978-1-7998-1843-4.ch009

## INTRODUCTION

Recent digital transformation and the long-term recession termed by "Lost two decades" force Japanese SMEs (small and medium-sized enterprises) to change drastically the business process and develop continuously new products and services. Without achieving these, it is impossible for them to survive. The further empowerment of SMEs to enhance innovation is required. This is difficult and time-consuming task. There are many factors behind the promotion of innovation in an economy, as endogenous economic growth theory emphasizes, i.e. capital, labor and technology. In reality, it is difficult to raise these factors and promote economic development in the entire economy, but it is more difficult for SMEs to improve the innovation which do not necessarily own sufficient resources for innovation.

There are many sources for promoting innovation, including technological ability, managerial organization to enhance the flow of information and ideas related to innovation, orientation of top management toward innovation, human resources such as engineers, and workers at the job shop as well as related to R&D. Moreover, since SMEs do not own sufficient resources for innovation inside the firms, they have to absorb the necessary technology and information from outside such as large firms, universities, regional research institutions, and business organizations. SMEs thus have to obtain and mobilize these factors and resources from outside and assimilate them into innovation. To achieve innovation, current SMEs have larger advantages than those in the past, because of Information and Communication Technologies (ICTs). In the age of the information society, SMEs also can make full use of ICTs to achieve innovation (Lee & Xia, 2006; Idota, et al 2012; Shigeno, Matsuzaki, and Tsuji, 2018; Ueki and Tsuji, 2019). The main theme of this paper is how ICTs enhance innovation. As seen in what follows, various ICTs can contribute to innovation while simply introducing ICTs do not automatically create innovation. But for SMEs, ICT is essential. In this context, this paper focuses on ICT use and the process or transmission mechanism of ICTs contribution to innovation.

ICTs can be categorized in terms of their functionality in the innovation process; the mediation of communications and information flow, and system, devises, and equipment in the manufacturing process. In the former, communication is divided into those inside and outside the firms. The examples of internal use of ICTs for communications are groupware, intra-SNS (Social Networking Service), ERP (Enterprise Resources Planning), whereas external uses for exchanging information are e-commerce such as B2B and B2C, EDI (Electronic Data Interchange), SCM (Supply Chain Management), CRM (Customer Relationship Management), social SNS, and so on. CAD/CAM (Computer-aided Design/ Computer-aided Manufacturing) and Industry 4.0 are examples of ICTs used for production.

These explained factors are known as tools of innovation but less analysis were conducted how and why ICTs contribute to innovation. In addition, this paper is interested to whether there is difference in ICT use between SMEs with high and low ICT use or not. Therefore, based on the aim and objective of the paper, the research questions (RQ) are summarized as follows:

**RQ1:** What are the factors inside the firm to promote innovation?
**RQ2:** How do ICTs have effect on innovation?
**RQ3:** Which effect do SMEs with higher ICT use realize for innovation?

The paper consists of the following sections; the next section presents the survey of previous literature. Section 3 clarifies the framework of the analysis while factors promoting innovation are examined in Section 4. Section 5 conducts statistical analysis and identifies significant factors. The contents of the regional industrial policy and estimation results are presented in Section 6. Discussions and conclusion are presented in the final section.

## LITERATURE REVIEW

One of the benefits deriving from the use of ICTs comes from efficient and effective use of existing knowledge enabled by ICTs to create new knowledge. This section surveys previous studies on the roles of ICTs and other factors in the innovation process. This paper discusses roles of ICTs for promoting innovation in the perspectives of tools as well as the functionality of ICTs such as obtaining and sharing information or applying information for innovation. In so doing, this literature review consists of two parts; theoretical foundation of ICTs on innovation and roles of particular ICTs on innovation. The latter contains recent development of ICTs to innovation.

### ICTs as Foundations of Innovation

#### Innovation Capability and ICT

Absorptive capacity is widely accepted by innovation literature which is defined by Cohen and Levinthal (1990) as "a firm's ability to recognize the value of new information, assimilate it, and apply it to commercial ends." Cohen and Levinthal (1990) and Zahra and George (2002) also recognize the innovation process as a learning process consisting four dimensions such as acquisition, assimilation, transformation, and exploitation of information. In this context, ICTs can contribute promoting innovations, since ICTs can enhance the development of capacities necessary for achieving innovations; SMEs can utilize ICTs to search and access knowledge outside the firm at the stage of acquisition. At the next stage, it assimilates the knowledge through its own managerial resources and transforms it into new knowledge which process is known as "knowledge management." ICTs can enhance this process more efficiently (Nicolas & Acosta, 2010; Omona, van der Weide, & Lubega, 2010; Ologbo & Nor, 2015). For example, ICTs enable the sharing of information among R&D teams, which shortens the time required for results, or assists in transforming tacit knowledge to explicit knowledge (Polanyi, 1966; Nonaka & Takeuchi, 1996). From these functionalities, ICTs are termed by "IT capability" (Karimi, Somers, & Bhattacherjee, 2007).

#### ICTs Use for Obtaining and Sharing External Information

ICTs facilitate in searching and accessing external information. Current innovations rely on more complicated technologies and broader ranges of knowledge and information. In this environment, firms have to combine new and existing knowledge in more innovative ways to develop products and services which are new to the market and gain higher customer satisfaction. In these days, it is much more difficult to achieve breakthrough innovations simply by utilizing internal resources such as technologies and knowledge and own R&D capability. Therefore, external information becomes much more important for innovation. To access and obtain external information, open innovation becomes indispensable, which is defined by collaboration with organizations that own cutting-edge information outside the firm such as universities and research institutions (Chesbrough, 2003). ICTs assist firms to search and access to knowledge and communicate and collaborate for the creation of new knowledge. ICTs thus make more communication channels available and enable faster access to knowledge sources (Alavi & Leidner, 2001).

Open innovation is thus a key concept of channels to firms which consists of the intellectual and transaction channels (Tsuji et al, 2016; 2017). The former is used for collaboration with universities and research institutions, whereas the latter is for transferring information from customers and suppliers via transactions or the supply chain (Pietrobelli & Rabellotti, 2011). The intimate collaboration between automobile assemblers and parts suppliers is a typical example (Dyer & Nobeoka, 2000; Todo, Matous, & Inoue, 2016). SCM enables information flows on orders, claims or improvements to interact much more efficiently.

### ICTs for Sharing Internal Information

Even if ICTs support firms in accessing and sharing external knowledge, SMEs are required to own sufficient absorptive capacity for communicating and sharing external information to achieve innovations.

Firms create and accumulate different knowledge through daily operations. Examples of technological knowledge include the blueprints of products and production machines, CAD/CAM data and records on machine operation, maintenance or problems. Effective use of this internal technological knowledge may assist firms to identify and assess technologies that they lack and need to obtain externally to shorten the product development period. Reengineering by ICTs in the 1990s performed the same roles (Davenport and Short, 1990; Hammer and Champy, 1993; Davenport, 1993; Davenport,1994; Brockhoff, Korch, and Pearson; 1997). Current similar technologies are found in supercomputers, 3D printers, and Building Information Modeling (BIM) in the construction industry, and so on. Supercomputers, for example, can speed up product development by making it possible to avoid the fabrication of prototypes, since this can be replaced by computer simulation (Ueki and Tsuji, 2019).

### ICTs for Sharing Information in the Market

Even if firms own high level technologies, they cannot always make a profit from investments in R&D. Firms need to grasp market demands and customer needs. Firms accumulate and update such information through their ordinal sales activities and direct interactions with customers. Recently, social media have been widely utilized. For producing new products, it is better to learn consumers' needs (Rodriguez, Peterson, & Vijaykumar, 2012; Idota, Bunno, & Tsuji, 2017). Social media are also used for constructing mutual trust with consumers and enhancing the value for consumers (Noone, McGuire, & Rohlfs, 2011; Kate & Pavan, 2012). Thus, social media has become an effective means for obtaining potential customers, sales improvement, and the improvement of brand image (Luo & Zhang, 2013; Kim & Ko, 2012).

## Recent Innovations Promoted by New ICTs

### Social Media and Innovation

Social media such as Twitter, blogs, Facebook, Instagram, and others have become popular in all economies. A number of firms recognize social media as communication tools outside as well as inside the firm. Social media was originally used for sharing information for internal company work such as schedules, meetings, and on sales data among colleagues in the office. Besides, firms have come to recognize that social media as strategic means to collect information on promoting marketing and sales force, ideas of new products, and consumer needs for developing new goods and services (Idota et al., 2017; 2019). Kaplan and Haenlein (2010) classify six types of social media. Rodriguez et al. (2012) clarifies that social media influences positively on sales promotion since it is beneficial for firms in learning from consumers as well as in developing a new market and in constructing mutual trust with consumers (Noone et al., 2011; Kate & Pavan, 2012). Through social media, consumers exchange information related to product improvement and new marketing strategies (Haavisto, 2012). Consumer involvement to the social media context has three dimensions of consumer brand engagement; cognitive processing, affection and activation (Brandão et al., 2019). Social media thus develop Customer Relationship Management (CRM) (Malthouse et al., 2013). The word-of-mouth communication in social media is useful to obtain potential customers, sales improvement, and improvements in brand image (Luo & Zhang, 2013; Hausmann, 2012). By analyzing 111 peer reviewed papers available at EBSCO host and Scopus databases, Bhimani et al. (2019) conclude that social media is mediator and potential drivers of innovation through extensive use of the knowledge within and across organization boundaries. On the other hand, Malthouse et al., (2013) point out negative aspects of social media, indicating that social media may become double-edged swords to firms.

## IoT and Innovation

The Internet of Things (IoT) is the current phase of Internet revolution and has been transforming the traditional innovation process into new one by making use of sufficient information and data on consumers, firms and markets in the real time. IoT is a basis of Industry 4.0 which is expected as a new dimension of manufacturing. IoT is never imagined without ICTs development which is related to various sensors collecting data and communications devices via wireless or wire-line such as Smartphone. Equipment and machine in the factory are operated without human assistance; Robot with AI can replace with human engineers and workers which shifts the form of traditional process innovation (Andrea et al., 2016; Bilgeret et al., 2019). Agriculture which is supposed to be far away from ICTs has been restructured and becomes high tech industry, which is due to ICTs (Karl et al., 2014; Alan et al., 2016; Paul, 2019). These observations show that IoT promotes process innovation. On the other hand, IoT is not necessarily welcomed by consumers; they may show resistance to smart devices. Zied and Inès (2018) find that perceived complexity of IoT to consumers is a main barrier by employing structural equations modeling.

## Big Data and Innovation

Similar to IoT, due to the development of wireless devices such as Smartphone, social media, e-commerce, and so on, huge amount of data can be saved and stored which can be utilized for business purposes. Such big data is allowing companies to create new processes or business models to serve customers in new ways. So-called GAFA (Google, Apple, Facebook, and Amazon) are typical examples which have been expanding new business models. What kind of characteristics of big data leverages competitive competency or innovation become a center of academic research while Lee (2018), Maryam and Goran (2019), and Jaime et al. (2019) identify those are three Vs of big data; Volume, Velocity, and Variety. Yuanzhu, et al. (2017) analyze merits of big data in the traditional framework of innovation and discuss it facilities to reduce lead time and costs of innovation through efficient connections to consumers and trade partners. Michael et al., (2017) focus on how big data transforms R&D process by interviews and case studies. Big data is relevant for not only large companies but also SMEs, since the latter can access to big data through open innovation with large firms or universities (Rasquals et al., 2018). The age of big data has just started but new ICT such as 5G mobile phones will surely accelerate toward the data driven economy while more research will be expected to analyze how bid data transform the innovation ecosystem.

## FACTORS PROMOTING INNOVATION AND HYPOTHESES

In the previous section, the paper emphasizes the roles of ICTs in the innovation process. ICTs are important factors to promote innovation which are termed by innovation capability. To clarify the importance of factors, let us describe authors' framework of the innovation process shown in Figure 1. For firms, particularly SMEs, to achieve innovation, new information on technology, consumers, and market are necessary which exists outside the firm such as universities and other large firms (Chesbrough, 2003). Then they have to obtain information through open innovation network, for example. They absorb it, assimilate with domestic resources, transform to new ideas, and create innovation. Cohen and Levinthal (1990) who initiated this describe the process as Acquisition → Assimilation → Transforming → Exploitation. In this innovation process, capability to absorb information and R&D are keys to success of innovation. In this study, the former is referred to internal innovation capability which are equivalent to factors promoting innovation. More concretely, internal innovation capability includes capabilities related to factors such as technologies that the company own, human resources (human factor), organizational form (organization), and leadership. Authors utilize this concept in the series of papers and field researches (Tsuji et al. 2016, 2017, and 2018; Ogawa et al., 2018).

*Figure 1.*
*Source: Tsuji et al. 2016, 2017, 2018, and Ogawa 2018*

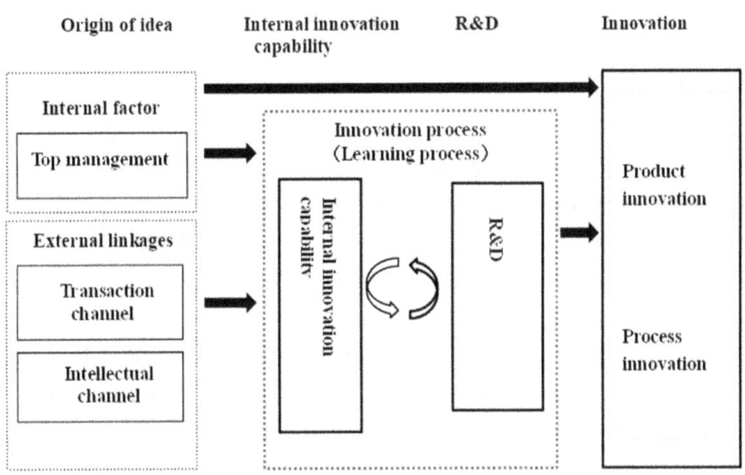


In addition to ICT as innovation capability, this section focuses the following factors and R&D.

## Level of Technology

Since innovation is more or less related to the technological novelty, technological capability of firms is also essential. The number of patents registered engineers with higher education degrees such as postgraduate or higher and ISO9000 series are used as proxies for firms' potentiality of developing new technologies.

## Top Management

The role of top management is essential for all decision-makings which determine the future of firms. Top management has to own leadership, knowledge, ideas, and experience, and they are also capable of managing all aspects of a firm, including marketing, HR, financing, and so on. The business development strategy adopted by SMEs is also important for advancing innovation which is aimed at radical or incremental innovation depends on firm's resources. Top management takes both of risks and gains into consideration for innovation strategy. When they face problems in the innovation process, their capability of problem solving is also a factor to promote innovation (Iansiti, 1994; Thomke & Fujimoto, 2000; Sharp & Gadde, 2008).

## Human Resources

Ability, motivation, morale, and work ethics of employees are indispensable for innovation. SMEs suffer from the shortage of skilled engineers, and innovation success depends on ability of engineers and workers. SMEs in other economies practice various schemes of HRM (Human resource management) which include OJT (on-the-job training), OFFJT (off-the-job training), job rotations, pairing with skilled workers, and vocational education in high school. The main form of training is OJT. Basically, senior workers teach and train the new employees on a man-to-man and face-to-face basis. They follow the training manual and repeat frequently. The reports of the procedure, materials, and reasons for success or failure are saved and stored for future references (Jensen et al., 2007; Thomä, 2017; Tsuji et al., 2017).

## R&D

R&D is one of the important elements of innovation and therefore, numerous papers in this issue were accumulated. For example, regarding the autonomy of R&D team (Argyres & Silverman, 2004) and leadership (Hirst & Mann, 2004; Berson & Linton, 2005; Zheng et al., 2010) were discussed. The ratio of R&D investment to the amount of sales as a proxy of R&D capabilities is often used (Thomä, 2017; Lee & Walsh, 2016).

Regarding R&D in SMEs, there are two categories of R&D: traditional R&D and non-R&D. The former is conducted by R&D sections or units, whereas the latter is without formal units. Jensen et al. (2007) defines the former as the science, technology and innovation (STI) mode and the latter as the doing, using, and interacting (DUI) mode. SMEs are too small to establish specific sections or teams for R&D.

## Size of Firms

The size of firms in terms of the number of employees and capital is an important factor. Although this concept is primitive, it is crucial for firms to establish an R&D unit and plan the R&D budget, for example. R&D is not a simple activity but requires engineers and other personnel as well as large amount of fund. To achieve innovation, a certain number of employees and funds for R&D and other relevant activities are matter.

This paper does not explore all the above factors for empirical study and the variables used in the estimation will be explained in the section of construction of variables.

# DATA AND CONSTRUCTION OF VARIABLES

This paper is based on a mail survey conducted in February 2012 to March 2012 on top management of 3,959 innovative Japanese SMEs on the industries including manufacturing, service, information processing service and construction. The samples were selected as follows: From the lists of *Teikoku* Data Bank, 3,959 firms were selected comprise to manufacturing, construction, information and communications, and service industries. The criteria of the selection are that sample firms have to satisfy the following conditions: (i) unlisted; (ii) the number of employees is more than 20, (iii) earning positive profits in the recent three terms, that is, one year and half, and (iv) the positive growth of sales. The reason of these limitations is to reduce the number of samples in the appropriate size. The valid number of responses is 647 and the response rate is 16.2%.

## Firm Characteristics

### Years of Operation

Table 1 shows the years of operation; firms with 30-49 years of operation are 219 (35.0%), which is the largest. And it is concentrated on 10-70 years. These indicate that sample SMEs may not contain start-ups or ventures.

*Table 1. Years of operation*

| Years of Operation | Freq. | % |
|---|---|---|
| Less than 10 year | 36 | 5.8 |
| 10-30 year | 170 | 27.2 |
| 30-49 year | 219 | 35.0 |
| 50-69 year | 140 | 22.4 |
| 70-99 year | 49 | 7.8 |
| More than 100 year | 12 | 1.9 |
| Total | 626 | 100.0 |

Source: Authors

## Size of SMEs

As for the size of responding firms, the amount of capital and the number of capital full time employees are used. Table 2 shows that less than JPY10 million is 170 (26.6%), which is the largest. Table 3 shows the number of full-time employees; less than 50 employees occupied more than two thirds, implying most of sample firms are small.

*Table 2. Amount of capital*

| Capital (JPY) | Freq. | % |
|---|---|---|
| Less than10 million | 170 | 26.6 |
| 10-15 million yen | 23 | 3.6 |
| 15-20 million yen | 92 | 14.4 |
| 20-25 million yen | 35 | 5.5 |
| 25-30 million yen | 80 | 12.5 |
| 30-40 million yen | 52 | 8.2 |
| 40-50 million yen | 67 | 10.5 |
| 50-100 million yen | 86 | 13.5 |
| More than 100 million | 33 | 5.2 |
| Total | 638 | 100.0 |

Source: Authors

*Table 3. Number of full time employees*

| Full Time Employees | Freq. | % |
|---|---|---|
| 1-20 | 78 | 12.6 |
| 21-30 | 176 | 28.3 |
| 31-40 | 111 | 17.9 |
| 41-50 | 81 | 13.0 |
| 51-60 | 41 | 6.6 |
| 61-70 | 26 | 4.2 |
| 71-80 | 29 | 4.7 |
| 81-90 | 12 | 1.9 |
| 91-100 | 14 | 2.3 |
| 101-200 | 43 | 6.9 |
| 201-300 | 8 | 1.3 |
| 301-600 | 2 | 0.3 |
| Total | 621 | 100.0% |

Source: Authors

## R&D Expenditures

In the questionnaire, instead of amount of R&D, its trend was asked, namely R&D expenditures in the recent three years. Table 4 shows "leveling off" is 251 (57.3%), which is the largest. And 131 (29.9%) replied "increase," which is the next largest.

*Table 4. Change in R&D expenditures in the recent three years*

| Increase or Decrease in R&D Expense for Recent Three Years | Freq. | % |
|---|---|---|
| Decrease in R&D expenditures | 56 | 12.8 |
| Leveling off R&D expenditures | 251 | 57.3 |
| Increase in R&D expenditures | 131 | 29.9 |

Source: Authors

## Summary of Sample SMEs

The summary statistics is shown in Table 5, which indicates the industry of sample SMEs; 357 firms (56%) belong to manufacturing, 184 (29%) to construction, 53 (8%) to information, 38 (6%) to the service industry, and 14 (2%) to others.

539 firms (83.3%) recruited mid-career employees in the recent three years, indicating that Japanese SMEs face the labor shortage and they have to hire this category of employee.

*Table 5. Characteristics of respondents*

| Variable | Freq. | Mean | S. D. | Min | Max |
|---|---|---|---|---|---|
| The period of operation (logarithm) | 626 | 3.56 | 0.67 | 0.00 | 5.06 |
| Capital (logarithm) | 638 | 7.85 | 1.02 | 2.30 | 11.14 |
| Manufacturing | 640 | 0.56 | 0.50 | 0.00 | 1.00 |
| Information | 640 | 0.08 | 0.28 | 0.00 | 1.00 |
| Service | 640 | 0.06 | 0.24 | 0.00 | 1.00 |
| Construction | 639 | 0.29 | 0.45 | 0.00 | 1.00 |
| Other industry | 640 | 0.02 | 0.15 | 0.00 | 1.00 |
| Changes in R&D expenses for recent three years | 438 | 2.17 | 0.63 | 1.00 | 3.00 |
| Number of mid-career hiring employees for recent three years | 539 | 6.64 | 9.53 | 0.00 | 100.00 |

Source: Authors

## ICT Use

Table 6 shows the questions and replies related to the types of ICT use. The most common use of ICT is CMC (Computer-Mediated Communication) (84.5%), while the lowest is SCM (2.7%). ICT systems such as design management system (CAD/CAM), product management, and sales management are connected to SMEs'missions and the mostly widespread. Groupware and internal SNS for sharing information inside SMEs are also widely used, while SCM and general SNS for connecting with outside firm or customer is not widespread in the sample firms.

*Table 6. ICT use*

| Variable | Freq. | % | S. D. |
|---|---|---|---|
| Sales management system | 232 | 37.4 | 0.48 |
| Product management system | 260 | 41.9 | 0.49 |
| Design management system | 376 | 60.5 | 0.49 |
| ERP (Enterprise Resource Planning) | 36 | 5.8 | 0.23 |
| Groupware | 139 | 22.4 | 0.42 |
| CTI (Computer Telephony Integration) | 19 | 3.1 | 0.17 |
| SCM (Supply Chain Management) | 17 | 2.7 | 0.16 |
| CMC (Computer-Mediated Communication) | 525 | 84.5 | 0.36 |
| Internal SNS (Social Networking Service) | 81 | 13.0 | 0.34 |
| General SNS (Social Networking Service) | 30 | 4.8% | 0.21 |

Note: multiple answers are permitted.
Source: Authors

## ICT Index

One of the aims of this paper is to construct an index of ICT use. In so doing, four types of ICT use such as; (1) the sales management system, (2) groupware, (3) internal SNS, and (4) SCM are focused.

The rationale for this is as follows. The sales management system by ICTs fulfills the basic mission and then it is utilized by all industries. As for product innovation, demand and needs of customers can be obtained by the above system. Process innovation improves routine works related to core business management in a single firm.

Groupware and internal SNS are also necessity for ICTs to share information among workers inside the firm. Sharing information inside the firm is an important basis for communications not only in the process of creating new products and services but also for the improvement of the business process, as seen already in the previous sections.

SCM is indispensable to construct the network with partners of transactions outside the firms and becomes an important tool for collecting customer needs for improving supply chain process. SMEs supply parts and components to large firms in the distribution networks which are channels not only for the smooth flow physical commodities but also for exchanging information on innovation. Process innovation is aimed to raise customer satisfaction and to enhance customer's values continuously, since claims or proposals for improvement from customers and consumers.

Based on the above discussions, an index which indicates the degree of ICT use is constructed as follows: point is provided according to importance of these ICT use, that is, ICT more commonly used indicates that it is rather easy for SMEs to adopt it, and therefore it obtains a small point. One point is provided for ICT which use exceeds 30% of respondents. ICT use with the diffusion rate of 10-30% has two points, while ICT with less than 10% diffusion rate owns three points. Since one SME may have several types of ICT uses, all indices are added in order to calculate the maturity level of ICT for each SME. The final distribution of point is shown in Table 7, which is varying from 0 to eight points, but ICT use among Japanese SMEs is not advanced yet.

*Table 7. ICT index*

| ICT Index | Freq. | % |
|---|---|---|
| 0 point | 278 | 43.0 |
| 1 | 148 | 22.9 |
| 2 | 90 | 13.9 |
| 3 | 63 | 9.7 |
| 4 | 18 | 2.8 |
| 5 | 17 | 2.6 |
| 6 | 3 | 0.5 |
| 7 | 1 | 0.2 |
| 8 | 3 | 0.5 |
| N/A | 26 | 4.0 |
| Total | 647 | 100.0 |

Source: Authors

## Achievement of Innovation: Objective Variables

Innovation is categorized by two types; product innovations which associates with the creation of new products and services, and process innovations with increasing productivity and efficiency of business works. Regarding the achievement of innovation for recent five years, 428 (67.2%) replied they achieved product innovation, while 308 (48.9%) as process innovation (Table 8). Two types of innovation are taken as objective variables in estimation.

*Table 8. Achieving innovation in the recent five years*

| Variable | Freq. | % | S. D. |
|---|---|---|---|
| Product innovation | 428 | 67.2 | 0.47 |
| Process innovation | 308 | 48.9 | 0.50 |

Source: Authors

## Factor Analysis

The questionnaire includes various questions which ask SMEs' management and ICT use. Hence, it is necessary to identify specific variables, which promote innovation and are referred to as "factors" in what follows. These factors are not observed directly, which is referred to as latent variables, whereas other variables are observed as replies of questions, for example, which are termed by observed variables. Since there is correlation between these two variables, factor analysis is used for finding how observed variables influence latent variables. Factor analysis is one of multivariate statistical methods used to examine the relationship between observed variables such as responses to questions and unobserved latent variables that create a commonality. Factor analysis is widely used in social sciences such as psychology, business, and economics. Factor analysis searches for such joint variations from unobserved latent variables. The observed variables are assumed to be expressed as linear combinations of the factors and error terms.

## Managerial Trait of SMEs

Table 9 indicates questions regarding managerial trait of SMEs' top management and employees. The former asked its orientation of business strategy, and leadership and participation in innovation, whereas the letter contains their morale and motivation, and the atmosphere of the office. These questions are answered in the Likert five scales. The averages of all questions are over 3.5 point, which are larger than 2.5 of medium number.

*Table 9. Managerial trait of SMEs*

| Variables | Freq. | Mean | S. D. | Min | Max |
|---|---|---|---|---|---|
| Top manager voluntarily shows the idea and decides a new business. | 641 | 3.71 | 0.99 | 1 | 5 |
| Top manager takes leading to do new business. | 641 | 3.89 | 0.96 | 1 | 5 |
| Top manager positively participates in the project. | 609 | 3.81 | 1.15 | 1 | 5 |
| Employee understands the target of the firm. | 644 | 3.97 | 0.73 | 1 | 5 |
| Employee is proud of his/her firm. | 644 | 3.84 | 0.71 | 1 | 5 |
| Employee understands the strong point of the firm. | 644 | 3.93 | 0.68 | 1 | 5 |
| There is atmosphere that consults the colleague easily. | 641 | 3.78 | 0.77 | 1 | 5 |
| Employee understands the scene for which the in-house product is used. | 639 | 3.91 | 0.84 | 1 | 5 |
| Even if it is unrelated to him/her, the employee helps the others' work. | 641 | 3.65 | 0.81 | 1 | 5 |

Source: Authors

To specify latent variables from the above replies to questions, factor analysis is conducted by maximum likelihood method (Varimax Rotation). The result is shown in Table 10, in which two factors are extracted. Since the first factor consists of the employee's boast and understanding, and atmosphere of the office and so on, it is termed by "Motivation of employees." As for the second factor, top management' presenting his/her ideas, leadership of the top manager and top manager's participation in project are extracted, and therefore it is referred to as "Leadership of top management."

*Table 10. Factor analysis of management trait of sample SMEs*

| Management Behavior | Common Factors | |
|---|---|---|
| | Motivation of Employees | Leadership of Top Management |
| Employee is proud of the firm. | .751 | .068 |
| Employee understands the strong point of the firm. | .724 | .095 |
| Employee understands the target of the firm. | .696 | .113 |
| Even if it is unrelated to him/her, the employee helps the others' work. | .616 | .011 |
| There is atmosphere that consults the colleague easily. | .613 | .050 |
| Employee understands the scene for which the product is used. | .523 | .108 |
| Top manager takes leading to do new business. | .023 | .907 |
| Top manager voluntarily shows the idea and decides a new business. | -.003 | .827 |
| Top manager positively participates in the project. | .258 | .398 |
| Eigen Value | 2.668 | 1.706 |
| Rotated Factor Pattern (%) | 29.641 | 18.959 |
| Cumulative Proportion (%) | 48.601 | |
| Cronbach's α | .817 | .720 |

Source: Authors

## Effects of ICT Use

Since one of the objectives of this paper is to identify how ICTs effect on innovation, questions about these were prepared which include performances or effects such as on R&D, sharing information, activating communications, and obtaining information in the market. Table 11shows the effects of ICT use. These questions are answered in the Likert five scales in the same way as Table 9. Among effects, "Sharing information and knowledge inside the firm" has 3.66 point, and "Activation of communications with customer" 3.52 point on the average. Thus, they have high point, and averages of all questions are larger than 2.8 point. These characteristics are commonly recognized as the role of ICTs in the R&D or innovation process.

*Table 11. Effects of ICT use*

| Variables | Freq. | Mean | S. D. | Min | Max |
|---|---|---|---|---|---|
| Shortening of R&D period for innovation | 601 | 2.83 | 1.13 | 1 | 5 |
| Usefulness of PR for products | 612 | 3.14 | 1.26 | 1 | 5 |
| Easiness of awareness of customer's needs | 608 | 3.16 | 1.07 | 1 | 5 |
| Activation of communications inside the firm | 611 | 3.29 | 1.09 | 1 | 5 |
| Activation of communications with customers | 613 | 3.52 | 1.00 | 1 | 5 |
| Sharing information and knowledge inside the firm | 609 | 3.66 | 1.00 | 1 | 5 |
| Sharing information and knowledge with customers | 612 | 3.39 | 0.93 | 1 | 5 |

Source: Authors

To specify factors for innovation, factor analysis is conducted to questions shown in Table 12 again by the same maximum likelihood method. Two common factors were extracted, namely the first factor contains "Sharing information and knowledge inside the firm" and "Activation of communications," which is termed by "Sharing information by ICT use." Since the second factor consists of "Shortening the product development period," "Easiness of awareness of customer's needs," and "Usefulness of PR for goods," which is termed by "Shortening R&D process by ICT use," since the effect on R&D is the greatest.

*Table 12. Factor analysis on the effect of ICT use*

| Effects of ICT Use | Common Factors | |
|---|---|---|
| | Sharing Information | Shortening R&D Process |
| Sharing information and knowledge with customers | .804 | .254 |
| Sharing information and knowledge inside the firm | .735 | .219 |
| Activation of communications with customers | .725 | .313 |
| Activation of communications inside the firms | .626 | .332 |
| Shortening of R&D period for innovation | .245 | .745 |
| Easiness of awareness of customer's needs | .417 | .590 |
| Usefulness of PR for goods | .174 | .570 |
| Eigen Value | 2.368 | 1.549 |
| Rotated Factor Pattern (%) | 33.828 | 22.130 |
| Cumulative Proportion (%) | 55.957 | |
| Cronbach's α | .858 | .719 |

Source: Authors

## RESULTS OF ESTIMATION

In this section, to answer RQs of this paper, logit regression analysis is conducted, since the outcome variables are expressed in terms of binary variable.

### Answer RQ1: Factors Promoting Innovation

"Achievement of innovation" is used for the dependent variable, while the explanatory variables contain ICT index, business resources, managerial trait and effect of ICT use, besides firms' characteristics. Estimation was conducted to product and process innovation separately.

#### Product Innovation

The estimation result is shown in Table 13 for product innovation. As a result, significant variables are "Capital" ($p<0.00$), "Number of mid-career employees recruited in the recent three years" ($p<0.02$) and "Change in R&D expenditures in the recent three years" ($p<0.00$), "Leadership of top management" (p<0.00) became positively significant in case of product innovation. Regarding effect of ICT use, only "Shortening R&D process by ICT use" (p<0.01) is significant. Among these variables, the marginal effect of "Leadership of top management" is the greatest, implying that the role of top management is important. This is consistent with authors' results of field surveys and estimations. For example, owners SMEs are engineers and own accumulated skills and experiences and thus take a lead in R&D for innovation (Tsuji, et al, 2017 and 2018). The ICT index, however, is not significant, which can be explained from Table 6. Among questions there, "Product management system" and "Design management system" seem to related product innovation, since production and design are closely related to product innovation. However, their diffusion rates seem high; accordingly, their contributions to the index become small.

*Table 13. Effects of ICT use on promoting product innovation*

| Product Innovation | Coeff. | S. E. | Z- Value | P-Value | Sig. | Marginal Effect |
|---|---|---|---|---|---|---|
| The period of operation | -0.014 | 0.279 | -0.05 | 0.96 | | -0.002 |
| Capital | 0.565 | 0.190 | 2.98 | 0.00 | *** | 0.073 |
| Number of mid-career recruit for recent three years | 0.075 | 0.033 | 2.26 | 0.02 | ** | 0.010 |
| ICT index | 0.166 | 0.121 | 1.38 | 0.17 | | 0.021 |
| Change in R&D expenses for recent three years | 0.930 | 0.264 | 3.52 | 0.00 | *** | 0.121 |
| Motivation of employees | 0.086 | 0.171 | 0.50 | 0.62 | | 0.011 |
| Leadership of top management | 0.884 | 0.193 | 4.58 | 0.00 | *** | 0.115 |
| Sharing information by ICT use | 0.039 | 0.186 | 0.21 | 0.84 | | 0.005 |
| Shortening R&D process by ICT use | 0.413 | 0.197 | 2.10 | 0.04 | ** | 0.054 |
| Manufacturing | -0.777 | 1.767 | -0.44 | 0.66 | | -0.101 |
| Information | 0.074 | 1.941 | 0.04 | 0.97 | | 0.010 |
| Service | -0.595 | 1.778 | -0.33 | 0.74 | | -0.077 |
| Construction | -1.574 | 1.787 | -0.88 | 0.38 | | -0.204 |
| Constant | -4.770 | 2.470 | -1.93 | 0.05 | * | |

Number of observations=335
LR chi2 (12)=103.63
Prob > chi2=0
Log likelihood=-135.74112
Pseudo $R^2$=0.2763
Note: *, **, and *** indicate the significance level at 10%, 5%; and 1%, respectively.
Source: Authors

## Process Innovation

Table 14 shows the estimation result of process innovation. "Number of mid-career employees recruited in the recent three years" (p< 0.07), "ICT index" (p<0.01), "Change in R&D expenditures in the recent three years" (p<0.00), "Motivation of employees" (p<0.01) and "Leadership od top management" (p<0.02) became positively significant. In addition, both of effects of ICT use such as "Sharing information by ICT use" (p<0.01) and "Shortening R&D process by ICT use" (p<0.01) also are significant.

In contrast with product innovation, process innovation is related to mainly improvement, which will be achieved by collaboration among related personnel and sections, and thus "Sharing information by ICTs" becomes significant. The result of ICT index seems to be the similar reason, since "Internal SNS" which consist of the index is less diffused in practice, implying larger effect on process innovation.

*Table 14. Effect of ICT use on promoting process innovation*

| Process Innovation | Coeff. | S. E. | Z-Value | P-Value | Sig. | Marginal Effect |
|---|---|---|---|---|---|---|
| Period of operation | -0.032 | 0.219 | -0.15 | 0.88 | | -0.006 |
| Capital | -0.135 | 0.139 | -0.97 | 0.33 | | -0.026 |
| Number of mid-career recruit for recent three years | 0.032 | 0.015 | 2.07 | 0.04 | ** | 0.006 |
| Manufacturing | 0.962 | 1.091 | 0.88 | 0.38 | | 0.188 |
| Information | -0.198 | 1.213 | -0.16 | 0.87 | | -0.039 |
| Service | 1.049 | 1.175 | 0.89 | 0.37 | | 0.205 |
| Construction | 1.067 | 1.124 | 0.95 | 0.34 | | 0.208 |
| ICT index | 0.180 | 0.095 | 1.89 | 0.06 | * | 0.035 |
| Change in R&D expenses for recent three years | 0.589 | 0.206 | 2.87 | 0.00 | *** | 0.115 |
| Motivation of employees | 0.209 | 0.143 | 1.46 | 0.14 | | 0.041 |
| Leadership of top management | 0.246 | 0.154 | 1.60 | 0.11 | | 0.048 |
| Sharing information by ICTs | 0.570 | 0.169 | 3.38 | 0.00 | *** | 0.111 |
| Shortening R&D process by ICTs | 0.517 | 0.169 | 3.07 | 0.00 | *** | 0.101 |
| Manufacturing | 0.962 | 1.091 | 0.88 | 0.38 | | 0.188 |
| Information | -0.198 | 1.213 | -0.16 | 0.87 | | -0.039 |
| Service | 1.049 | 1.175 | 0.89 | 0.37 | | 0.205 |
| Construction | 1.067 | 1.124 | 0.95 | 0.34 | | 0.208 |
| Constant | -1.235 | 1.773 | -0.70 | 0.49 | | |

Number of observation=334
LR chi2 (12)=74.56
Prob > chi2=0
Log likelihood=-191.32594
Pseudo $R^2$=0.1631
Note: *, **, and *** indicate the significance level at 10%, 5%; and 1%, respectively
Source: Authors

## Answer to RQ2: Effect of ICT Use on Innovation

Here RQ2 is examined; that is, RQ2: How ICTs have effect on innovation. Factor analysis shown in Table 12 identifies two effects such as "Sharing information by ICT use" and "Shortening R&D process by ICT use." Tables 13 and 14 have an answer. For product innovation, only the former becomes significant (Table 13), whereas for process innovation, both of them are significant (Table 14). The reason for this is already provided, that is, product innovation is more or less related to technological aspects, and accordingly simple sharing information may not be sufficient.

## Answer to RQ3: Which Effect SMEs With Higher ICT Use Realize for Innovation

Similar to RQ2, factor analysis extracts two effects such as "Sharing information" and "Shortening R&D period." A natural question is whether SMEs with higher ICT index make use these two better than those with lower index. In other words, SMEs with advanced ICT use is expected to have better utilization in performances or effects. In so doing, the cross terms such that "Sharing information*ICT index" and "Shortening R&D period*ICT index" are focused to answer RQ3. These cross terms imply what kind of benefits from ICTs SMEs with higher ICT index realize. Although Table 13 indicates that "Sharing information by ICT use" and "ICT index" are not significant, these are added to the cross-terms.

The results of logit estimation are shown in Table 15 and 16 for product and process innovation, respectively. Although ICT index was not significant, the cross term (Shortening R&D process*ICT index)" became positively significant ($p<0.04$) for product innovation, whereas both the cross terms (Sharing information by ICT use*ICT index)" ($p<0.01$) and (Shortening R&D process*ICT index)" ($p<0.05$) became positively significant for process innovation. Based on these results, it is confirmed that SMEs with the more developed level of ICT yield the larger effect of ICTs on innovation through these functionalities.

*Table 15. Effectiveness of ICT use; cross term analysis of product innovation*

| Product Innovation | Coeff. | S. E. | Z-Value | P-Value | | Marginal Effect |
|---|---|---|---|---|---|---|
| Period of operation | -0.080 | 0.276 | -0.29 | 0.77 | | -0.010 |
| Capital | 0.571 | 0.189 | 3.02 | 0.00 | *** | 0.074 |
| Number of mid-career recruit for recent three years | 0.074 | 0.033 | 2.21 | 0.03 | ** | 0.010 |
| ICT index | 0.166 | 0.135 | 1.23 | 0.22 | | 0.022 |
| Cross term (Sharing information by ICTs*ICT index) | 0.026 | 0.122 | 0.21 | 0.83 | | 0.003 |
| Cross term (Shortening R&D process by ICTs*ICT index) | 0.312 | 0.153 | 2.04 | 0.04 | ** | 0.041 |
| Change in R&D expenses for recent three years | 0.928 | 0.264 | 3.51 | 0.00 | *** | 0.121 |
| Motivation of employees | 0.100 | 0.168 | 0.59 | 0.55 | | 0.013 |
| Leadership of top management | 0.881 | 0.194 | 4.54 | 0.00 | *** | 0.115 |
| Manufacturing | -0.893 | 1.816 | -0.49 | 0.62 | | -0.116 |
| Information | -0.094 | 1.997 | -0.05 | 0.96 | | -0.012 |
| Service | -0.768 | 1.824 | -0.42 | 0.67 | | -0.100 |
| Construction | -1.880 | 1.838 | -1.02 | 0.31 | | -0.244 |
| Constant | -4.432 | 2.508 | -1.77 | 0.08 | * | |

Number of observations=335
LR chi2 (12)=103.74
Prob > chi2=0
Log likelihood=-135.68558
Pseudo R2=0.2766
Note: *, **, and *** indicate the significance level at 10%, 5%; and 1%, respectively.
Source: Authors

The above difference with respect to "Sharing information by ICT use" in two innovation processes may be due to types of innovation. Product innovation is more related to R&D activities or technological matters and accordingly less enhanced by sharing information, whereas since process innovation contains improving quality, design, and packaging, for example, these can be achieved by discussions and exchanging ideas among related sections or personnel.

*Table 16. Effectiveness of ICT use; cross term analysis of process innovation*

| Process Innovation | Coeff. | S. E. | Z-Value | P-Value | | Marginal Effect |
|---|---|---|---|---|---|---|
| The period of operation | -0.112 | 0.217 | -0.51 | 0.61 | | -0.023 |
| Capital | -0.095 | 0.137 | -0.69 | 0.49 | | -0.019 |
| Number of mid-career recruit for recent three years | 0.031 | 0.015 | 2.09 | 0.04 | ** | 0.006 |
| ICT index | 0.141 | 0.103 | 1.37 | 0.17 | | 0.029 |
| Cross term (Sharing information by ICTs*ICT index) | 0.277 | 0.108 | 2.58 | 0.01 | ** | 0.056 |
| Cross term (Shortening R&D process by ICTs*ICT index) | 0.213 | 0.108 | 1.98 | 0.05 | ** | 0.043 |
| Changes in R&D expenses for recent three years | 0.604 | 0.202 | 2.99 | 0.00 | *** | 0.123 |
| Motivation of employees | 0.274 | 0.138 | 1.99 | 0.05 | ** | 0.056 |
| Leadership of top management | 0.273 | 0.150 | 1.81 | 0.07 | * | 0.055 |
| Manufacturing | 0.904 | 1.048 | 0.86 | 0.39 | | 0.183 |
| Information | -0.319 | 1.190 | -0.27 | 0.79 | | -0.065 |
| Service | 0.896 | 1.134 | 0.79 | 0.43 | | 0.182 |
| Construction | 0.773 | 1.077 | 0.72 | 0.47 | | 0.157 |
| Constant | -1.178 | 1.747 | -0.67 | 0.50 | | |

Number of observations=334
LR chi2 (12)=64.3
Prob > chi2=0
Log likelihood=-196.45514
Pseudo $R^2$=0.1406
Note: *, **, and *** indicate the significance level at 10%, 5%; and 1%, respectively.
Source: Authors

## DISCUSSION AND CONCLUSION

This paper constructed an ICT index according to the level of ICT use, and examined whether innovation is promoted by SMEs with the higher ICT index. The estimation results extracted factors of innovation such as size of firms, R&D expenditures, Leadership of top management, Motivation of employees, which are more or less consistent with authors' previous studies (Idota et al 2012; Tsuji et al, 2016, 2017, 218) and previous literature (Jensen et al., 2007; Thomä, 2017). The novelty of the paper, however, lies in examining the functionality of ICT use and its relationship with ICT index. Two functionalities such as sharing information and shortening R&D period are extracted by rigorous regression analysis. ICTs contribute to shortening the R&D was already cognized as "reengineering," when ICTs were emerging (Davenport and Short, 1990; Hammer & Champy, 1993; Davenport, 1993; Davenport, 1994; Brockhoff, Korch, & Pearson; 1997). This paper demonstrates by regression analysis.

It should be discussed on the direction of future research. The construction of the ICT index in this paper is rather primitive and it needs to be elaborated further by using AHP (Analytical hierarchy process), for example (Ogawa et al. 2018). Another use of the index is to match it with business strategy, that is, how business strategy is different according to the different level of the ICT use. Furthermore, by making use of the index, the suitable strategic policy can be proposed according to the maturity level of ICT so that SMEs can engage in innovation properly.

ICTs have been continuously developing in the various ways and used by SMEs in the age of digital transformation. The amount of data becomes tremendously huge and is termed by big data. To analyze big data, AI has been utilizing and the areas in which ICTs are expected to use have been enlarging. The data and ICT use in this paper should be update for searching new direction of ICT use.

## ACKNOWLEDGMENT

The first and third authors are partly supported by JSPS grants titled "Business Innovation Strategy by Social Media" (Grant number c-24530435). Financial supports are gratefully acknowledged.

## REFERENCES

Alan, M., Armando, P., Benedetta, C., & Giuseppe, R. (2016). Evaluating the innovation of the Internet of Things. *Business Process Management Journal*, *22*(2), 341–356.

Alavi, M., & Leidner, D. E. (2001). Knowledge management and knowledge management systems: Conceptual foundations and research issues. *Management Information Systems Quarterly*, *25*(1), 107–136. doi:10.2307/3250961

Andrea, C., Giacomo, M., & Matteo, P. M. (2016). The Internet of Things in manufacturing innovation processes. *Business Process Management Journal*, *22*(2), 383–402.

Argyres, N. S., & Silverman, B. S. (2004). R&D, organization structure, and the development of corporate technological knowledge. *Strategic Management Journal*, *25*(8-9), 929–958. doi:10.1002mj.387

Berson, Y., & Linton, J. D. (2005). An examination of the relationships between leadership style, quality, and employee satisfaction in R&D versus administrative environments. *R & D Management*, *35*(1), 51–60. doi:10.1111/j.1467-9310.2005.00371.x

Bhimani, H., Mention, A. L., & Barlatier, P. J. (2019). Social media and innovation: A systematic literature review and future research directions. *Technological Forecasting and Social Change*, *144*, 251–269. doi:10.1016/j.techfore.2018.10.007

Bilgeri, D., Gebauer, H., Fleisch, E., & Wortmann, F. (2019). Driving process innovation with IoT field data. *MIS Quarterly Executive*, *18*(3), 191–207. doi:10.17705/2msqe.00016

Brandão, A., Pinho, E., & Rodrigues, P. (2019). Antecedents and consequences of luxury brand engagement in social media. *Spanish Journal of Marketing-ESIC*, *23*(2), 163–183. doi:10.1108/SJME-11-2018-0052

Brockhoff, K. K., Korch, G., & Pearson, A. W. (1997). Business process re-engineering: Experiences in R&D. *Technology Analysis and Strategic Management*, *9*(2), 163–178. doi:10.1080/09537329708524277

Chesbrough, H. W. (2003). *Open innovation: the new imperative for creating and profiting from technology*. Harvard Business School Press.

Cohen, W. M., & Levinthal, D. A. (1990). Absorptive capacity: A new perspective on learning and innovation. *Administrative Science Quarterly*, *35*(1), 128–152. doi:10.2307/2393553

Davenport, T. (1993). *Process Innovation: Reengineering work through information technology*. Harvard Business School Press.

Davenport, T. (1995). *Reengineering – The Fad That Forgot People*. Fast Company.

Davenport, T., & Short, J. (1990). The new industrial engineering: Information technology and business process redesign. *Sloan Management Review*, *31*(4), 1–31.

Dyer, J., & Nobeoka, K. (2000). Creating and managing a high-performance knowledge-sharing network: The Toyota case. *Strategic Management Journal*, *21*(3), 345–367. doi:10.1002/(SICI)1097-0266(200003)21:3<345::AID-SMJ96>3.0.CO;2-N

Haavisto, P. (2012). *Social media discussion forums and product innovation - The way forward?* Retrieved from https://journals.uic.edu/ojs/index.php/fm/article/view/3984/3332

Hausmann, A. (2012). Creating 'buzz': Opportunities and limitations of social media for arts institutions and their viral marketing. *International Journal of Nonprofit and Voluntary Sector Marketing*, *17*(3), 173–182. doi:10.1002/nvsm.1420

Hirst, G., & Mann, L. (2004). A model of R&D leadership and team communication: The relationship with project performance. *R & D Management*, *34*(2), 147–160. doi:10.1111/j.1467-9310.2004.00330.x

Iansiti, M., & Clark, K. B. (1994). Integration and dynamic capability: Evidence from product development in automobiles and mainframe computers. *Industrial and Corporate Change*, *3*(3), 557–605. doi:10.1093/icc/3.3.557

Idota, H., Bunno, T., & Tsuji, M. (2017). How social media enhances product innovation in Japanese firms. *Journal of Socionetwork Strategies*, *11*(1), 33–45. doi:10.100712626-017-0006-1

Idota, H., Ogawa, M., Bunno, T., & Tsuji, M. (2012). An empirical analysis of organizational innovation generated by ICT in Japanese SMEs. In S. Allegrezza & A. Dubrocard (Eds.), *Internet Econometrics* (pp. 259–287). Palgrave Macmillan. doi:10.1057/9780230364226_12

Idota, H., Taher, S. A., Bunno, T., & Tsuji, M. (2019). Conducting product innovation by using social media among Japanese firms. *STI Policy and Management Journal*, *4*(2), 153–166. doi:10.14203/STIPM.2019.176

Jaime, G., Octav, N., Iulia, G., & Gheorghe, G. (2019). Big data analytics in industry 4.0: Sustainable industrial value creation, manufacturing process innovation, and networked production structures. *Journal of Self-Governance & Management Economics*, *7*(3), 34–40. doi:10.22381/JSME7320195

Jensen, M. B., Johnson, B., Lorenz, E., Lundvall, B. Å., & Lundvall, B. A. (2016). Forms of knowledge and modes of innovation. *The learning economy and the economics of hope,* 155-182.

Kaplan, A. M., & Haenlein, M. (2010). Users of the world, unite! The challenges and opportunities of social media. *Business Horizons, 53*(1), 59–68. doi:10.1016/j.bushor.2009.09.003

Karimi, J., Somers, M. T., & Bhattacherjee, A. (2007). The role of information systems resources in ERP capability building business process outcomes. *Journal of Management Information Systems, 24*(2), 221–260. doi:10.2753/MIS0742-1222240209

Karl, P., Michael, B., & Eivor, O. (2014). Dialogical strategies for orchestrating strategic innovation networks: The case of the Internet of Things. *Information and Organization, 24*(2), 106–127. doi:10.1016/j.infoandorg.2014.05.001

Kate, V., & Pavan, S. (2012). Social media and revenue management; where should the two meet*? Journal of Technology Management for Growing Economies.*, *3*(1), 33–46. doi:10.15415/jtmge.2012.31002

Kim, A. J., & Ko, E. (2012). Do social media marketing activities enhance customer equity? An empirical study of luxury fashion brand. *Journal of Business Research, 65*(10), 1480–1486. doi:10.1016/j.jbusres.2011.10.014

Lee, G., & Xia, W. (2006). Organizational size and IT innovation adoption: A meta-analysis. *Information & Management, 43*(8), 975–985. doi:10.1016/j.im.2006.09.003

Lee, H. L. (2018). Big Data and the innovation cycle. *Production and Operations Management, 27*(9), 1642–1646. doi:10.1111/poms.12845

Luo, X., & Zhang, J. (2013). How do consumer buzz and traffic in social media marketing predict the value of the firm? *Journal of Management Information Systems, 30*(2), 213–238. doi:10.2753/MIS0742-1222300208

Malthouse, E. C., Haenlein, M., Skiera, B., Wege, E., & Zhang, M. (2013). Managing customer relationships in the social media era: Introducing the social CRM house. *Journal of Interactive Marketing, 27*(4), 270–280. doi:10.1016/j.intmar.2013.09.008

Maryam, G., & Goran, C. (2019). Does big data enhance firm innovation competency? The mediating role of data-driven insights. *Journal of Business Research, 104*, 69–84. doi:10.1016/j.jbusres.2019.07.006

Michael, B., Jeffrey, A., David, L. J., & Diego, K. (2017). Big data and the future of R&D Management: The rise of big data and big data analytics will have significant implications for R&D and innovation management in the next decade. *Research Technology Management, 60*(5), 43–50. doi:10.1080/08956308.2017.1348135

Nicolas, C. L., & Acosta, P. S. (2010). Analyzing ICT adoption and use effects on knowledge creation: An empirical investigation in SMEs. *International Journal of Information Management, 30*(6), 521–528. doi:10.1016/j.ijinfomgt.2010.03.004

Nonaka, I., & Takeuchi, H. (1996). *Knowledge Creating Companies.* Oxford University Press.

Noone, B. M., McGuire, K. A., & Rohlfs, K. V. (2011). Social media meets hotel revenue management: Opportunities, issues and unanswered questions. *Journal of Revenue and Pricing Management, 10*(4), 293–305. doi:10.1057/rpm.2011.12

Ogawa, M., Ueki, Y., Idota, H., Bunno, T., & Tsuji, M. (2018). Internal innovation capacity and external linkages in firms of ASEAN economies focusing on endogeneity. *STI Policy and Management Journal, 3*(2), 97–117. doi:10.14203/STIPM.2018.135

Ologbo, A. C., & Nor, K. M. (2015). Knowledge management processes and firm innovation capability: A theoretical model. *Asian Social Science, 11*(8), 10–17. doi:10.5539/ass.v11n18p10

Omona, W., van der Weide, T., & Lubega, J. (2010). Using ICT to enhance knowledge management in higher education: A conceptual framework and research agenda. *International Journal of Education and Development Using Information and Communication Technology, 6*(4), 83–101.

Pasquale, D. V., Alberto, D. M., Messeni, P. A., Umberto, P., & Salvatore, P. (2018). Big data for open innovation in SMEs and large corporations: Trends, opportunities, and challenges. *Creativity and Innovation Management, 27*(1), 6–22. doi:10.1111/caim.12224

Paul, M. (2019). Reconceptualizing value innovation for industry 4.0 and the industrial Internet of Things. *Journal of Business and Industrial Marketing, 34*(6), 1203–1209. doi:10.1108/JBIM-11-2018-0348

Polanyi, P. (1966). *The Tacit Dimension*. Chicago University Press.

Rodriguez, M., Peterson, R. M., & Vijaykumar, K. (2012). Social media's influence on business-to-business sales performance. *Journal of Personal Selling & Sales Management, 32*(3), 365–378. doi:10.2753/PSS0885-3134320306

Thomä, J. (2017). DUI mode learning and barriers to innovation-A case from Germany. *Research Policy, 46*(7), 1327–1339. doi:10.1016/j.respol.2017.06.004

Thomke, S., & Fujimoto, T. (2000). The effect of front-loading problem-solving on product development performance. *Journal of Product Innovation Management: An International Publication of the Product Development & Management Association, 17*(2), 128–142. doi:10.1111/1540-5885.1720128

Todo, Y., Matous, P., & Inoue, H. (2016). The strength of long ties and the weakness of strong ties: Knowledge diffusion through supply chain networks. *Research Policy, 45*(9), 1890–1906. doi:10.1016/j.respol.2016.06.008

Tsuji, H., Shigeno, H., Ueki, Y., Idota, H., & Bunno, T. (2017). Characterizing R&D and HRD in the innovation process of Japanese SMEs: Analysis based on field study. *Asian Journal of Technology Innovation, 35*(2), 367–385. doi:10.1080/19761597.2017.1385987

Tsuji, M., Idota, H., Ueki, Y., Shigeno, H., & Bunno, T. (2016). Connectivity in the Technology Transfer Process among Local ASEAN Firms. *Contemporary Economics, 10*(3), 193–203. doi:10.5709/ce.1897-9254.209

Tsuji, M., Ueki, Y., Shigeno, H., Idota, H., & Bunno, T. (2018). R&D and non-R&D in the innovation process among firms in ASEAN countries: Based on firm-level survey data. *European Journal of Management and Business Economics, 27*(2), 198–214. doi:10.1108/EJMBE-02-2018-0030

Ueki, Y. & Tsuji, M. (2019). The Roles of ICTs in Product Innovation in Southeast Asia. *The Review of Socionetwork Strategies, 13*(1), 79–95.

Yuanzhu, Z., Hua, T. K., Guojun, J., Leanne, C., & Minglang, T. (2017). A big data framework for facilitating product innovation processes. *Business Process Management Journal, 23*(3), 518–536. doi:10.1108/BPMJ-11-2015-0157

Zahra, S. A., & George, G. (2002). Absorptive capacity: A review, reconceptualization, and extension. *Academy of Management Review, 27*(2), 185–203. doi:10.5465/amr.2002.6587995

Zied, M., & Inès, C. (2018). Consumer resistance to innovation in services: Challenges and barriers in the Internet of Things era. *Journal of Product Innovation Management, 35*(5), 780–807. doi:10.1111/jpim.12463

# Section 5
# Digital Drivers

# Chapter 10
# Trust in E-Commerce:
## The Importance of the Experience and Relationship With This New Sales System – New Business Commerce

**Paula Rodrigues**
https://orcid.org/0000-0003-2967-2583
*Research Centre in Organizations, Markets and Industrial Management (COMEGI), BRU-IUL, Lusíada University of Porto, Portugal*

## ABSTRACT

*E-commerce is a reality of the 21st century. This type of business is nothing more than the conversion of any offline business in its online version. Understanding the online consumer has been a challenge for managers around the world. In this sense, the authors intend to verify how consumer experience with e-commerce and social media usage influences consumer trust in this new type of sales system. Another objective of this research is to understand if anxiety caused by the consumer perceived risk about the information sharing on the internet affects the trust in e-commerce. The data are collected through an online structured questionnaire and a quantitative methodology of structural equation modeling is used. The results obtained show that consumption experience with e-commerce and social media usage has a positive effect on trust in internet shopping. However, consumption experience has a stronger effect on trust in internet shopping than social media usage. But it can conclude that anxiety does not have a moderate effect on consumer trust in e-commerce and social media usage.*

## INTRODUCTION

The theme of e-commerce in everything is linked to the management and the marketing and it is to the managers of these two areas that it has been putting more challenges over the last decades.

One of the weaknesses of the Internet, on which e-commerce is based, makes security one of the major problems consumers encounter when shopping online (Abyad, 2017; Ashraf, Thongpapanl & Spyrapoulous, 2016; Suh & Han, 2003). This is because consumers, in general, can not control the

DOI: 10.4018/978-1-7998-1843-4.ch010

security of the personal and financial information they send to the buying sites (Abyad, 2017; Corbitt, Thanasankit & Yi, 2003). And this may leave to a lack of trust in this kind of commerce.

Companies with an Internet presence in Portugal increase from 25.8% in 2003 to 62.7% in 2018 (Pordata, 2018). However, little is known about Portuguese consumer behavior in terms of experience with e-commerce, social media usage, trust in e-commerce and anxiety in use e-commerce.

The principal objective of this research is to analyse the antecedents which lead consumers to trust on purchase in e-commerce, testing the moderating effect of anxiety with this kind of new commerce. The antecedents are divided into two types: (1) consumer experience with e-commerce and (2) the influence of social media usage in the consumer trust in e-commerce. It was carried out this analysis in the north of Portugal and only consider in the sample consumers with experience in e-commerce, who have at least one re-purchase and are thinking about continuing to purchase on e-commerce and are frequent users of at least one social media. This research derives from technology acceptance model (TAM), along with the concepts of consumers experience with e-commerce, social media usage, anxiety and trust in e-commerce. The novelty of the research is the analyses of the moderate effect of anxiety in the relationship between the consumer experience with e-commerce, the influence of social media in e-commerce and consumer trust in e-commerce.

The structure of this chapter is as follows. First, is done a literature review of trust in Internet shopping, with a focus on two antecedents – consumer experience with e-commerce and social media usage – and a moderator variable – anxiety with the discussion of the objective of the research and the propose of the conceptual model. Second, the methodology of the research is presented followed by the analysis and results. Then, the discussion and conclusions are discussed. Finally, the theoretical and managerial implication is discussed, limitations and future research are presented.

## THEORETICAL BACKGROUND

### Trust in Internet Shopping

Trust can be define as a belief in the reliability, truth, and ability of the exchange party that has been recognized as one of the reasons consumers refrain from electronic purchases (Gefen, Karahanna & Straub, 2003).

There are significant differences between traditional commerce, established in a face-to-face relationship, and e-commerce. In e-commerce, transactions can be performed at any time, however, they are not instantaneous, and consumers do not have automatic access to the product (Kim, Ferrin & Rao, 2008; Ortinou, Babin, & Chebat, 2013). In this way, trust in e-commerce becomes the trust that consumers can have in the transaction process (Kim et al., 2008, Kim, Song, Braynov & Rao, 2005). As in e-commerce, the consumer can not physically verify the product, it must be confident that whoever is selling will supply the product with the expected quality (Abyad, 2017; Ortinou et al., 2013).

Lynch, Kent and Srinivasan (2001) in their cross-national study conducted in 12 different countries, came to the conclusion that there are three factors that influence consumers' online shopping: quality, affection, and trust.

In an initial phase, trust is generated from the website and the characteristics of the website (Chen, Teng, Yu, & Yu, 2015). Chen and Dhillon (2003) argue that in e-commerce, the website is the only means of the company communicating with its consumers. Urban, Sultan, and Qualls (2000) defend that there are three ways to gain the trust of consumers through websites: trust in the Internet and in the specific website, trust in the information that is transmitted on the website and trust that is generated by the services provided.

Trust translate the conviction that what is promised by the seller is guaranteed and that the seller will not take advantage of the situation of consumer vulnerability (Abyad, 2017; Geyskens, Steenkamp & Kumar, 1996, Hernández, Jiménez & Martin, 2010).

Beldad et al. (2010) have made a literature review on the antecedents of trust in commercial and non-commercial websites and classified them into three main categories: (1) customer-based antecedents; (2) website-based antecedents and (3) organization/company-based antecedents.

*Table 1. Antecedents of trust in e-commerce*

| Antecedents | Variables |
|---|---|
| Customer-based | Users' experience with technologies; used for the transaction or user's tendency to trust |
| Websites | Quality of website used or quality of information |
| Organization/Company | Customers' experience with online organizations |

There are a number of others factors that contribute to trust in e-commerce, namely, quality, customer support, timely delivery, convincing product presentation, reasonable and clear transaction prices and transparent and reliable privacy policies (Achuthan, 2016; Agarwal & Yadav, 2015; Benlian, Montréal, & Hess, 2012; Hoffman & Novak, 1996; Reichheld & Schefter, 2000).

Given that e-commerce is a form of new business activity, this implies greater uncertainty and greater risk in relation to traditional commerce (Abyad, 2017, Hernández et al., 2010, Lee & Turban, 2001). As such, trust becomes a critical factor, having an important role in the relationship between the consumer and the seller (Christodoulides & Michaelidou, 2011, Fung & Lee, 1999). Doney and Cannon (1997) consider trust as a deciding factor for online shopping. Also, Quelch and Klein (1996) argued that in the initial phase of the Internet, trust was a critical factor in the purchase process by this means.

## Consumer Experience With E-Commerce

Nowadays, researchers reinforced that consumer experience was a critical component of the value creation process (Bhattacharya et al., 2019; Martin et al., 2015; Prahalad & Ramaswamy, 2004) and attempted to understand the different components of consumer experience: sensorial, emotional, cognitive, lifestyle, pragmatic and relational (Gentile, Spiller & Noci, 2007), which can be influenced by marketer-controlled technologies (Majra, Saxena, Jha, & Jagannathan, 2016).

Academic research shows that online consumer experience still an emergent fill and is evolving (Bhattacharya, Srivastava & Verma, 2019; McLean & Wilson, 2016). By another side, online consumer experience is a critical component of value creation process (Bhattacharya et al., 2019; Martin et al., 2015; Prahalad & Ramaswamy, 2004; Rose, Hair & Clark, 2011), and as a multidimensional variable it is composed of a consumer's cognitive, affective, social and physical response to the online offers of the retailers (Bhattacharya et al., 2018; Verhoef et al., 2009).

The first research on online consumer experience was based on the concept of flow. This concept refers to psychological consumer motivation and is characterized by a sensation of loose online navigation, lack of self-consciousness and enjoyment (Hoffman & Novak, 1996; Martin et al., 2015; Novak, Hoffman & Yung, 2000). Lemon and Verhoef (2016:71) define consumer experience as a "multidimensional construct focusing on a customer's cognitive, emotional, behavioral, sensorial, and social response to a firm's offering during the customer's entire purchase journey". Trust may be particularly important in the e-commerce consumer experience given the absence of physical contact with the product and with the seller.

The understanding of consumer behavior is an important aspect for the success of e-commerce. However, the consumer behavior on the Internet changes as they acquire experience with e-commerce (Falk, Hammerschmidt & Schepers, 2010; Vijayasarathy, 2004; Yu et al., 2005; Wang, Minor, & Wei, 2011). Chiu et al. (2004) posit that positive experiences with online shopping affect consumers' sense of trust and making the e-retailers more reliable. Gefen et al. (2008) also found that trust is important for consumers, independently their level of experience. For Pappas et al. (2014), consumer experience with e-commerce has a moderate effect on trust. This is also defended by Jin, Park, and Kim (2008) work's because they posit that trust seems to be more important when consumers have less informed about the seller and never have done a purchase by e-commerce.

According to Bart et al. (2005) more consumer knowledge and experience with the Internet can increase confidence in using e-commerce trust. Others studies have found that high levels of consumers' Internet experience affect consumers' tendency to trust in technology and e-commerce (Corbitt, Thanasanki & Yi, 2003). Then, it can be posited that:

**Hypothesis One**: Consumption experience (CE) with e-commerce has a positive effect on trust in Internet shopping (TIS)

## Social Media Usage

The advancement of the Internet has facilitated the realizations of purchases between consumers and international brands/companies. Social media is changing the business model and defining how companies communicate with their consumers (Rapp et al., 2013). Social media usage refers to the use of social media tools (Facebook, Instagram, Twitter, and others) to increase consumer engagement, create value from consumer interactions and increase business performance (Zhang & Li, 2019). Twitter is the social media most used by brands and companies as microblogging, followed by Facebook and YouTube (Zhan, Barnes, Zhao & Zhang, 2018). In their research, Zhang et al. (2018) report that in the USA, 253 international brands were observed to use Twitter and it was concluded that more than half used this social media to establish relationships with their consumers. Social media enable consumers to generate content and have social interaction online via social platforms (Chen et al., 2015).

Several studies have examined the variables the lead individuals to adopt and use social media trough TAM (Lee, 2010; Shin, 2010), however, few approaches have focused on the importance of perceived risk and trust in this process (Shin, 2010).

Social networking sites and online communities are effective Internet technology for sharing information and for social interaction (Hajli, 2013; Lu & Hsiao, 2010), and this became central in e-commerce when consumers have access to many different sources of information and experiences (Fue, Li & Wenyu,

2009; Mueller et al., 2011). Then, it can be posited that social media is a new stream in e-commerce, which encourages the social interaction of consumers (Hajli, 2013).

Social media offers consumers the possibility to obtain more information about the organizations, brands, products and services and make better buying decisions (Mueller et al., 2011). Several authors, posit that social media creating social networking environments and motivating consumers to use them lead to engagement with the consumers and increasing consumer trust and loyalty (Hogg, 2010; Park et al., 2010; Spaulding, 2010).

The influence of social media usage can be seen of the point of view of consumers or sellers. Regarding consumers, social media usage can engage consumers, increase corporate reputation, lead to positive word of mouth and improve consumer-brand relationship (Dijkmans et al., 2015; Hudson et al., 2016). However, the effect of social media usage on trust in e-commerce has not been subject to an in depth examination.

Wu, Chen, and Chung (2010) suggest that networking of consumers through social media provides share values, leading to a positive effect on trust. For Lu, Zhao and Wang (2010) online platforms where consumers have social interactions, given that a possible source of trust in e-commerce. By another side, social relationship of consumers generated through social media uses affect positively the perceived trust on e-commerce (Pan & Chiou, 2011; Purnawirawan, De Pelsmacker & Dens, 2012; Weisberg, Te'eni & Arman, 2011). Hence, it was postulated this hypothesis:

**Hypothesis Two**: Social media usage (SMU) have a positive effect on trust in Internet shopping (TIS)

## Moderate Effects of Anxiety

Consumer anxiety, can be seen as a negative sensations initiated by the potentially harmful future events, and has a negative effect on well-being of consumers live (Jackson, 2010). According with Arkin and Ruck (2007), anxiety is an unpleasant emotional state, characterized by apprehension, tension, and worry, and occurs in response as a threat to a self-preservation goal (Arkin & Ruck, 2007). Anxiety is also defined as felling of worry and nervousness, and in the case of consumer anxiety arise from a sense of threat in the context of consumption and uncertainty reduction or risk avoidance (Alkis et al., 2017; Liu, Ang & Lwin, 2003). According with Liu et al. (2013) individuals with a high privacy avoid sharing their personal information online. Research of consumer anxiety has demonstrated several antecedent of that emotion (Table 2).

Information security in an online context remains a dominant subject in research when it comes to e-commerce (Yao & Liao, 2011). Everyone is concerned with the security of personal data of the consumers and even the consumers themselves are aware that there are implications for providing their data for the companies (Park & Kim, 2003; Kim, Ferrin & Rao, 2008; Suh & Han, 2003). This makes consumers feel anxious when they have to choose which buy something by e-commerce or by traditional commerce. Consider Thomas and Tsai (2012: 327) work, "individual's dispositional anxiety toward a task can also affect the feeling of difficulty". Prior research has found that anxiety encourages attentional vigilance (Hanin, 2010), selective attention to and processing of anxiety-related stimuli (Quigley et al., 2012), motivates effort in seeking information (Locander & Hermann, 1979) and soliciting advice from others (Gino, Brook, & Schweitzer, 2012).

*Table 2. Consumer Anxiety Studies*

| Antecedents Variables | Authors |
|---|---|
| Individuals choices that increases perceptions of uncertainty and risk | Locander & Hermann (1979) |
| Impulsive buying | Gardner & Rook (1988) |
| Exposure to fear appeals | Sego & Stout (1994) |
| Consumers' familiarity obtained from ongoing usage and past experience | Kuhlmeier & Knight (2005) |
| Perception of self-efficacy | Meuter et al. (2003); Gelbrich & Sattler (2014) |
| Potential negative evaluations from others | Alkis et al. (2017) |
| The degree of awareness of and sensitivity to the reactions of others to one's own behavior | Piamphongsant & Mandhachitara (2008) |
| Service or website quality and trust | Hwang & Kim (2007); Yao & Liao (2011) |

As anxiety can be consider as a negative emotion experienced in the present but in regard to a goal-incongruent future outcome, it is possible to consider the following hypotheses:

**Hypothesis Three**: Anxiety (A) moderated negatively the relation between consumption experience (CE) with e-commerce and trust in Internet shopping (TIS)

**Hypothesis Four**: Anxiety (A) moderated negatively the relation between social media usage (SMU) and trust in Internet shopping (TIS)

Based on the previous literature review, the conceptual model and the research hypotheses are presented in figure 1.

*Figure 1. Conceptual Model*

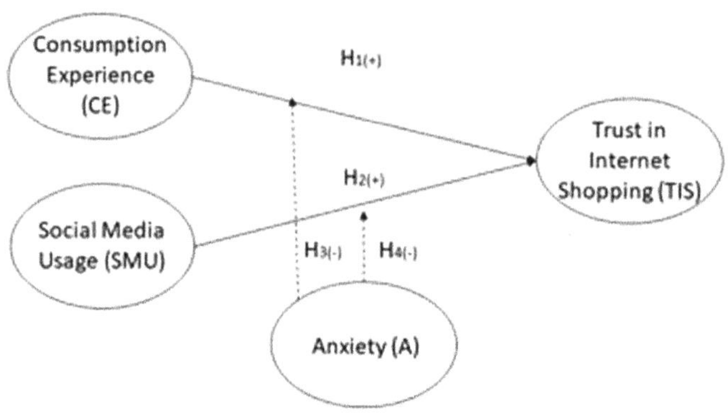

## METHODOLOGY

This study follows a quantitative methodology. It was used as a survey by questionnaire to measure relationships between constructs on the conceptual model, about Portuguese consumer perceptions about e-commerce. We use a convenience sample with data obtained by Google Drive and distributed in different social media platform. The questionnaire are divided in two parts: one to collected social-demographic variables and the other to collect data with respect to the constructs used in the conceptual model. The research follows the two-step structural equation modeling methodology recommended by Anderson and Gerbing (1988) and using SPSS/AMOS 21 software. The measurement model is developed according to the constructs considered in the theory and then to estimate the causal relations that validate or not the hypotheses raised. The relevant constructs in the theoretical model have operationalized measures from existing literature, advocated by Podsakoff et al. (2003) as a procedural method to reduce the common method bias. It was used, Clarkson, Janiszewski and Cinelli (2013) scale to measure consumer experiences with e-commerce, Rapp, Britelspacher, Grewal, and Hughes (2013) scale adapted it was used to measure social media usage, Rose, Clark, Samouel and Hair (2012) scale was used to measure trust in Internet shopping and Thomas and Tsai (2012) scale was used to measure anxiety. All the variables were measured by 5-point Likert scales. The respondents could choose between "Totally Disagree" (1) and "Totally Agree" (5).

## RESULTS

The data collection was done through an online structured questionnaire, in the north of Portugal. It was distributed by the main social networks (Facebook and LinkedIn) and by email, during March 2019. A total of 143 valid questionnaires were obtained. Of the 143 respondents, 64.3% are female and 35.7& are male, 76.2% are between the ages of 20 and 35, 18.6% over than 35 and 5.6% below the 20 years old, 37.1% had higher education and 60.1% had secondary education.

To evaluate the measurement model was performed a CFA by maximum likelihood estimation method and using AMOS 21.0., to evaluate the measurement model. Data analysis for the measurement model was carried out in two steps: (1) evaluate data normality and multicollinearity and (2) evaluate the reliability and the three types of the validity of the constructs. All parameter estimates were considered in the empirical analyses, the statistical test of significance has a cut-off value of $p < 0.01$ and, this criterion was selected to maintain consistency across all the tests (Trafimow & Earp, 2017).

In the first step, to verify the data normality, it was found the skewness and kurtosis values of all constructs. The skewness values were within the suggested range of –2.00 to +2.00, while kurtosis values were between the suggested range of –7.00 and + 7.00 (Curran, West, & Finch, 1996). The analysis of the data shows that skewness and kurtosis are above these values.

The multicollinearity among the indicators was verified. The Variance Inflation Factor (VIF) was used to evaluate multicollinearity. With VIF of all items ranging between 2.06 and 3.47, below the common cut off of 5, the outcomes show minimal collinearity among the indicators. It can be assumed that multicollinearity is not violated (Chin, 2010).

The measurement model's psychometric values are: $X^2/df = 2.371$, RMSEA = 0.098, CFI = 0.939; TLI = 0.919; IFI = 0.940 (Table 1). For all constructs, Cronbach's alpha is above of 0.858 and CR values are greater than 0.922 and AVE value are greater than 0.794. All standardized factor loading are significant at $p < 0.001$ (Table 3).

*Table 3. Measurement Model Statistics*

| Construct | Itens | Means | SD | Factor Loading [a] | CR | AVE | α |
|---|---|---|---|---|---|---|---|
| Consumption Experiences (Clarkson, Janiszewski & Cinelli, 2013) | CE1: The experience with the e-commerce resolve any uncertainty | 3.31 | 0.906 | 0.800 | 0.928 | 0.813 | 0.875 |
| | CE2: The experience with the e-commerce increase the confidence for this type of commerce | 3.49 | 0.821 | 0.843 | | | |
| | CE3: The experience with the e-commerce increase the ability to defended the preference for this type of commerce | 3.62 | 0.934 | 0.871 | | | |
| Social Media Usage (Rapp, Britelspacher, Grewal, & Hughes, 2013) | SMU1: My relationship with e-commerce is enhanced by social media | 3.48 | 1.060 | 0.687 | 0.922 | 0.799 | 0.861 |
| | SMU2: I use social media to follow sales and promotions | 3.61 | 1.014 | 0.877 | | | |
| | SMU3: I use social media to keep current on events and trends in e-commerce | 3.57 | 0.990 | 0.914 | | | |
| Trust in Internet Shopping (Rose, Clark, Samouel & Hair, 2012) | TIS1: Internet shopping is reliable | 3.74 | 0.853 | 0.834 | 0.956 | 0.844 | 0.920 |
| | TIS2: I can rely on Internet vendors to keep the promises that they make | 3.73 | 0.971 | 0.878 | | | |
| | TIS3: Internet shopping can be trusted, there are no uncertainties | 3.50 | 1.106 | 0.838 | | | |
| | TIS4: Internet shopping is a trustworthy experience | 3.73 | 0.949 | 0.898 | | | |
| Anxiety (Thomas & Tsai, 2012) | A1: I feel anxious about purchasing by e-commerce | 2.62 | 1.113 | 0.678 | 0.919 | 0.794 | 0.858 |
| | A2: I feel nervous about purchasing by e-commerce | 2.36 | 0.953 | 0.933 | | | |
| | A3: I feel worried about purchasing by e-commerce | 2.51 | 0.895 | 0.854 | | | |

Goodness of Adjustment:
Chi-square = 139.896, df = 59, $X^2/df = 2.371$, RMSEA = 0.098, CFI = 0.939, TLI = 0.919, IFI = 0.940
Note: a: $p < 0.001$

The squared correlation between constructs did not exceed the average variance extracted in any of the cases, indicating that the model meets the criterion for discriminant validity among latent variables (Fornell & Larcker, 1981). Hence, it can be concluded that all latent variables have convergent and discriminant validity (Table 3 and 4). To control the common method bias, Harman's single factor test is the most widely used statistical control test in the literature (Podsakoff et al., 2003). The Harman test was performed, for all constructs it was verified that there are no common method bias problems. The result was 23.3%, (< 50% cut off point) of total variance explained by a single factor. Still, in line with Podsakoff et al. (2003), respondents were not informed about the object of the study and it was guaranteed to them that their responses would be confidential and anonymous, that there were no right or wrong answers and the research was support on earlier validated scales.

*Table 4. Discriminant Validity*

| AVE | | CE | SMU | TIS | A |
|---|---|---|---|---|---|
| 0.813 | CE | **0.902**[a] | | | |
| 0.799 | SMU | 0.555* | **0.894**[a] | | |
| 0.844 | TIS | 0.802* | 0.663* | **0.914**[a] | |
| 0.794 | A | -0.076* | 0.156* | 0.048* | **0.891**[a] |

a Square root of AVE in the diagonal
*Correlation is significant at level 0.01 (bilateral)

Structural Equation Modelling (SEM) using maximum likelihood estimation and the bootstrapping method was conducted to test the validity of the model and the hypotheses. The psychometric structural model's values are: $X^2/df = 2.377$; RMSEA = 0.098; CFI = 0.935; TLI = 0.919; IFI = 0.936, and this allow us to conclude that the model fit was good.

$R^2$ value measures the structural model's predictive power and must exceed 0.1 value (Falk & Miller, 1992). The explained percentage of trust in Internet shopping, in this case, is $R^2 = 0.712$. The results obtained in the estimation of the proposed conceptual model show that in respect to consumption experience with the e-commerce has a positive effect on the trust on Internet shopping ($\beta = 0.549$; $p < 0.001$) validated H1. The same occurs in the hypothesis H2, when the social media usage has a positive effect on the trust on Internet shopping ($\beta = 0.246$; $p < 0.001$) validated H2. It can conclude that consumption experience has a stronger effect on trust in Internet shopping than social media usage.

To test the hypotheses H3 and H4 it was used the Hayes (2018) procedure with bootstrapping (Table 5).

*Table 5. Influence of Anxiety in Consumption Experience and Social Media Usage*

| Anxiety | Coefficient | SE | t | p | LLCI | ULCI |
|---|---|---|---|---|---|---|
| CE | 0.083 | 0.072 | 1.148 | 0.253 | -0.059 | 0.225 |
| SMU | 0.107 | 0.069 | 1.547 | 0.124 | -0.029 | 0.243 |

The anxiety has no statistical influence on consumption experience with e-commerce ($p > 0.05$). The consumer trust in e-commerce is not affected by the possible anxiety that they may have and therefore H3 is rejected. The same occurs by the hypothesis H4. Anxiety has no statistical influence on social media usage ($p > 0.05$). Then, it can conclude that anxiety does not have a moderate effect on consumer trust in e-commerce and in social media usage.

## DISCUSSION

The principal objective of this study is to analyze the antecedents which lead consumers to trust on e-commerce, testing the moderating effect of anxiety with this can of new commerce. The results obtained in the estimation of the proposed model show that consumption experience with e-commerce has a positive effect on the trust in e-commerce. These results are in line with the results found by Chiu et al. (2004) and Gefen et al. (2008). By another side, confirmed what the TAM theory posits that the use and experience of the technology have a strong influence on consumer behavior on e-commerce (Hajli, 2013). Another result obtained was the positive effect of social media use on trust on e-commerce. This results re-enforced the results obtained by Wu et al. (2010) and Lu et al. (2010) that networking of consumers through social media usage provides share values, increasing trust in e-commerce. Thus, the interaction that consumers made in social media platforms may increase the trust in e-commerce by the sharing information with others consumers as defended by Pan and Chiou (2011), Purnawirawan et al. (2012) and Weisberg et al. (2011). This may be explain yet by the fact that the majority of the respondents in the sample belongs to an age group very accustomed to used social media platforms.

An interesting result obtained in this study was that anxiety does not have a moderate effect on consumer trust in e-commerce and social media usage. This can be explained by the TAM theory. Consumers are very familiar with the new technologies, with Internet and social media in such a way that they do not feel anxiety in its use. In this case, our sample are constituted for individual with 20 at 35 years old, that is a cohort very familiar with new technologies, social media, Internet and e-commerce (Jordaan et al., 2011).

## SOLUTIONS AND RECOMMENDATIONS

The management implication of this research confirms that Abyad (2017) advocates that in order for consumers to feel secure, e-commerce must implement sophisticated and developed security mechanisms so that companies can defend their business and consumers. By another hand, maintaining trust in e-commerce through consumer experience with e-commerce and social media for online vendors is the main managerial implication of this research. Relationship on social media sites must support trust-building mechanism in e-commerce. Also, e-vendors may encourage consumers to use social media to develop relations with the business and establish the co-creation process and then re-enforced trust.

## FUTURE RESEARCH DIRECTIONS

Future research should pay attention to a representative sample of the population study for better understanding the role of the moderate effect of the anxiety. Or another vein of research is the separation of the sample by different cohorts to verify if the behaviors of the different consumers segments are identical or not.

Another factors like customer satisfaction, information quality of websites, source credibility, website quality and consumer generated content such as online consumer reviews may be utilize as variables to explain consumer trust on e-commerce.

## CONCLUSION

Several studies about consumers' trust in e-commerce show that consumers who are younger, better educated, with higher incomes, less anxious about technologies are generally more inclined to accept this kind of new commerce (Meutet et al. 2003; Nilson, 2007).

Business progressively acknowledge the potential importance of the online social media as a marketing instruments and as tools permitting observing and analysing consumer behaviour. During the trust building on e-commerce, social media usage can facilitate communication and increase the consumer experience of information exchange and cooperation.

By other side, the increasing consumer experience with Internet and technologies allowing the companies to adopt new form to let him informing the consumer about they offer, what are they doing, share information with consumers, allowing even co-creation process and with this facilitating the new forms of commerce.

This research has some limitations. The results of the research should be generalized with caution, as it was carried out only in Portugal. Some other variables must be considered in the model to a better understanding despite the positive results found between consumer experience and social media user in trust in e-commerce, this kind of commerce is still used in Portugal. For future work, it would be interesting to replicate the study in other cultural realities to analyze the aspects of values and culture in consumer behavior in e-commerce.

## ACKNOWLEDGMENT

This work is supported by national funding's of FCT - Fundação para a Ciência e a Tecnologia, I.P., in the project «UIDB/04005/2020».

## REFERENCES

Abyad, A. (2017). Importance of Consumer Trust in e-commerce. *Middle East Journal of Business*, *12*(3), 20–24. doi:10.5742/MEJB.2017.92971

Achuthan, S. (2016). E-commerce Buying Behavior in India: The Role of Website Features in E-loyalty. *South Asian Journal of Management*, *23*(1), 56–88.

Agarwal, A., & Yadav, V. K. (2015). Impact of Technology in E-Retailing Operations: A Consumer Perspective. *Procedia: Social and Behavioral Sciences*, *189*, 252–258. doi:10.1016/j.sbspro.2015.03.220

Alkis, Y., Kadirhan, Z., & Sat, M. (2017). Development and validation of social anxiety scale for social media users. *Computers in Human Behavior*, *72*, 296–303. doi:10.1016/j.chb.2017.03.011

Anderson, J. C., & Gerbing, D. W. (1988). Structural equation modeling in practice: A review and recommended two-step approach. *Psychological Bulletin*, *103*(3), 411–423. doi:10.1037/0033-2909.103.3.411

Arkin, R. M., & Ruck, L. (2007). Anxiety. In R. F. Baumeister & K. D. Vohs (Eds.), *Encyclopedia of Social Psychology* (pp. 42–43). Sage. doi:10.4135/9781412956253.n24

Ashraf, A. R., Thongpapanl, N., & Spyropoulou, S. (2016). The Connection and Disconnection between E-commerce Businesses and Their Customers: Exploring the Role of Engagement, Perceived Usefulness, and Perceived Ease-of-use. *Electronic Commerce Research and Applications*, *20*, 69–86. doi:10.1016/j.elerap.2016.10.001

Bart, Y., Shankar, V., Sultan, F., & Urban, G. L. (2005). Are the drivers and role of online trust the same for all web sites and consumers? A large-scale exploratory empirical study. *Journal of Marketing*, *69*(4), 133–152. doi:10.1509/jmkg.2005.69.4.133

Benlian, A., Montréal, H. E. C., & Hess, T. (2012). Differential Effects of Provider Recommendation and Consumer Reviews In E-commerce Transaction: An Experimental Study. *Journal of Management Information Systems*, *29*(1), 1–47. doi:10.2753/MIS0742-1222290107

Bhattacharya, A., Srivastava, M., & Verma, S. (2019). Customer experience in online shopping: A strutural modeling approach. *Journal of Global Marketing*, *32*(1), 3–16. doi:10.1080/08911762.2018.1441938

Chen, J., Teng, L., Yu, Y., & Yu, X. (2015). The effect of online information sources on purchase intentions between consumers with high and low susceptibility to informational influence. *Journal of Business Research*, *69*(2), 467–475. doi:10.1016/j.jbusres.2015.05.003

Chen, S., & Dhillon, G. (2003). Interpreting dimensions of consumer trust in e-commerce. *Information Technology and Management*, *4*(2-3), 303–318. doi:10.1023/A:1022962631249

Chin, W. W. (2010). How to write up and report PLS analyses. In V. Esposito Vinzi, W. W. Chin, J. Henseler, & H. Wang (Eds.), *Handbook of partial least squares: Concepts, methods and applications* (pp. 655–690). Springer. doi:10.1007/978-3-540-32827-8_29

Chiu, C. M., Lin, H. Y., Sun, S. Y., & Hsu, M. H. (2009). Understanding customers' loyalty intentions towards online shopping: An integration of technology acceptance model and fairness theory. *Behaviour & Information Technology*, *28*(4), 347–360. doi:10.1080/01449290801892492

Christodoulides, G., & Michaelidou, N. (2011). Shopping motives as antecedents of e-satisfaction and e-loyalty. *Journal of Marketing Management*, *27*(1–2), 181–197.

Clarkson, J. J., Janiszewski, C., & Cinelli, M. D. (2013). The desire for consumption knowledge. *The Journal of Consumer Research*, *39*(6), 1313–1329. doi:10.1086/668535

Corbitt, B. J., Thanasankit, T., & Yi, H. (2003). Trust and e-commerce: A study of consumer perceptions. *Electronic Commerce Research and Applications*, *2*(3), 203–215. doi:10.1016/S1567-4223(03)00024-3

Curran, P. J., West, S. G., & Finch, J. F. (1996). The robustness of test statistics to nonnormality and specification error in confirmatory factor analysis. *Psychological Methods*, *1*(1), 16–29. doi:10.1037/1082-989X.1.1.16

Dijkmans, C., Kerkhof, P., & Beukeboom, C. J. (2015). A stage to engage: Social media use and corporate reputation. *Tourism Management*, *47*(5), 58–67. doi:10.1016/j.tourman.2014.09.005

Falk, R. F., & Miller, N. B. (1992). *A primer for soft modelling*. University of Akron Press.

Falk, T., Hammerschmidt, M., & Schepers, J. J. (2010). The service quality-satisfaction link revisited: Exploring asymmetries and dynamics. *Journal of the Academy of Marketing Science, 38*(3), 288–302. doi:10.100711747-009-0152-2

Fornell, C., & Larcker, D. F. (1981). Evaluating structural equation models with unobservable variables and measurement error. *JMR, Journal of Marketing Research, 8*(1), 39–50. doi:10.1177/002224378101800104

Fue, Z., Li, H., & Wenyu, D. (2009). Social factors in user perceptions and responses to advertising in online social networking communities. *Journal of Interactive Advertising, 10*(1), 1–13. doi:10.1080/15252019.2009.10722159

Fung, R. K. K., & Lee, M. K. O. (1990). Electronic commerce trust: Exploring the antecedents factors. *Proceedings of the Association for Information Systems Americas Conference*, 489-491.

Gardner, M. P., & Rook, D. W. (1988). Effects of impulse purchases on consumers' affective states. NA -Advances in Consumer Research, (15), 127-130.

Gefen, D., Karahanna, E., & Straub, D. W. (2003). Inexperience and experience with online stores: The importance of TAM and trust. *IEEE Transactions on Engineering Management, 50*(3), 307–321. doi:10.1109/TEM.2003.817277

Gelbrich, K., & Sattler, B. (2014). Anxiety, crowding, and time pressure in public self-service technology acceptance. *Journal of Services Marketing, 28*(1), 82–94. doi:10.1108/JSM-02-2012-0051

Gentile, C., Spiller, N., & Noci, G. (2007). How to sustain the customer experience: An overview of experience components that co-create value with the customer. *European Management Journal, 25*(5), 395–410. doi:10.1016/j.emj.2007.08.005

Geyskens, I., Steenkamp, J.-B. E. M., & Kumar, N. (1998). Generalization about trust in marketing channel relationships using meta-analysis. *International Journal of Research in Marketing, 15*(3), 223–248. doi:10.1016/S0167-8116(98)00002-0

Gino, F., Brooks, A., & Schweitzer, M. E. (2012). Anxiety, Advice, and the Ability to Discern: Feeling Anxious Motivates Individuals to Seek and Use Advice. *Journal of Personality and Social Psychology, 102*(3), 497–512. doi:10.1037/a0026413 PMID:22121890

Hair, J. F., Anderson, R. E., Tatham, R. L., & Black, W. C. (2006). *Multivariate Data Analysis* (6th ed.). Pearson, Prentice-Hall.

Hajli, M. (2013). A research framework for social commerce adoption. *Information Management & Computer Security, 21*(3), 144–154. doi:10.1108/IMCS-04-2012-0024

Hanin, Y. L. (2010). Coping with Anxiety in Sport. In A. R. Nicholls (Ed.), *Coping in Sport: Theory, Methods, and Related Constructs* (pp. 159–175). Nova Science Publishers.

Hernández, B., Jiménez, J., & Martín, M. J. (2010). Customer behavior in electronic commerce: The moderating effect of e-purchasing experience. *Journal of Business Research, 63*(9–10), 964–971. doi:10.1016/j.jbusres.2009.01.019

Hoffman, D. L., & Novak, T. P. (1996). Marketing in hypermedia computer-mediated environments: Conceptual foundations. *Journal of Marketing*, *60*(3), 50–68. doi:10.1177/002224299606000304

Hogg, T. (2010). Inferring preference correlations from social networks. *Electronic Commerce Research and Applications*, *9*(1), 29–37. doi:10.1016/j.elerap.2009.04.006

Hudson, S., Huang, L., Roth, M. S., & Madden, T. J. (2016). The influence of social media interactions on consumer– brand relationships: A three-country study of brand perceptions and marketing behaviors. *International Journal of Research in Marketing*, *33*(1), 27–41. doi:10.1016/j.ijresmar.2015.06.004

Hwang, Y., & Kim, D. J. (2007). Customer self-service systems: The effects of perceived Web quality with service contents on enjoyment, anxiety, and e-trust. *Decision Support Systems*, *43*(3), 746–760. doi:10.1016/j.dss.2006.12.008

Jackson, P. (2010). Food stories: Consumption in an age of anxiety. *Cultural Geographies*, *17*(2), 147–165. doi:10.1177/1474474010363844

Jin, B., Park, J. Y., & Kim, J. (2008). Cross-cultural examination of the relationships among firm reputation, e-satisfaction, e-trust, and e-loyalty. *International Marketing Review*, *25*(3), 324–337. doi:10.1108/02651330810877243

Jordaan, Y., Ehlers, L., & Grove, J. M. (2011). Advertising credibility across media channels: Perceptions of generation Y consumers. *Communicare*, *30*(1), 1–20.

Kim, D. J., Ferrin, D. L., & Rao, H. R. (2008). A trust-based consumer decision-making model in electronic commerce: The role of trust, perceived risk, and their antecedents. *Decision Support Systems*, *44*(2), 544–564. doi:10.1016/j.dss.2007.07.001

Kim, D. J., Song, Y. I., Braynov, S. B., & Rao, H. R. (2005). A multidimensional trust formation model in B-to-C e-commerce: A conceptual framework and content analyses of academia/practioner perspective. *Decision Support Systems*, *40*(2), 143–165. doi:10.1016/j.dss.2004.01.006

Kuhlmeier, D., & Knight, G. (2005). Antecedents to internet-based purchasing: A Multinational study. *International Marketing Review*, *22*(4), 460–473. doi:10.1108/02651330510608460

Lee, K. O. M., & Turban, E. (2001). A trust model for consumer Internet shopping. *International Journal of Electronic Commerce*, *6*(1), 75–91. doi:10.1080/10864415.2001.11044227

Lee, M. (2010). *The effect of cognitive absorption and network externalities on technology acceptance: an empirical study of social networking sites in Indonesia. Theses and dissertations*. Business Administration Department, University of Ming Chuan.

Lemon, K. N., & Verhoef, P. C. (2016). Understanding customer experience throughout the customer journey. *Journal of Marketing, 80*, 69–96.

Liu, C., Ang, R. P., & Lwin, M. O. (2013). Cognitive, personality, and social factors associated with adolescents' online personal information disclosure. *Journal of Adolescence*, *36*(4), 629–638. doi:10.1016/j.adolescence.2013.03.016 PMID:23849657

Locander, W. B., & Hermann, P. W. (1979). The effect of self-confidence and anxiety on information seeking in consumer risk reduction. *JMR, Journal of Marketing Research, 16*(2), 268–274. doi:10.1177/002224377901600211

Lu, H.-P., & Hsiao, K.-L. (2010). The influence of extro/introversion on the intention to pay for social networking sites. *Information & Management, 47*(3), 150–157. doi:10.1016/j.im.2010.01.003

Lu, Y., Zhao, L., & Wang, B. (2010). From virtual community members to c2c e-commerce buyers: Trust in virtual communities and its effect on consumers' purchase intention. *Electronic Commerce Research and Applications, 9*(4), 346–360. doi:10.1016/j.elerap.2009.07.003

Lynch, P. D., Kent, R. J., & Srinivasan, S. S. (2001). The global Internet shopper: Evidence from shopping tasks in twelve countries. *Journal of Advertising Research, 41*(3), 15–23. doi:10.2501/JAR-41-3-15-23

Majra, H., Saxena, R., Jha, S., & Jagannathan, S. (2016). Structuring technology applications for enhanced customer experience: Evidence from Indian air travellers. *Global Business Review, 17*(2), 351–374. doi:10.1177/0972150915619813

Martin, J., Mortimer, G., & Andrews, L. (2015). Re-examining online customer experience to include purchase frequency and perceived risk. *Journal of Retailing and Consumer Services, 25*, 81–95. doi:10.1016/j.jretconser.2015.03.008

McLean, G., & Wilson, A. (2016). Evolving the online customer experience… is there a role for online customer support? *Computers in Human Behavior, 60*, 602–610. doi:10.1016/j.chb.2016.02.084

Meuter, M. L., Ostrom, A. L., Bitner, M. J., & Roundtree, R. (2003). The influence of technology anxiety on consumer use and experiences with self-service technologies. *Journal of Business Research, 56*(11), 899–906. doi:10.1016/S0148-2963(01)00276-4

Mueller, J., Hutter, K., Fueller, J., & Matzler, K. (2011). Virtual worlds as knowledge management platform - a practice-perspective. *Information Systems Journal, 21*(6), 479–501. doi:10.1111/j.1365-2575.2010.00366.x

Nilsson, D. (2007). A cross-cultural comparison of self-service technology use. *European Journal of Marketing, 41*(3/4), 367–381. doi:10.1108/03090560710728381

Novak, T. P., Hoffman, D. L., & Yung, Y. F. (2000). Measuring the customer experience in online environments: A structural modeling approach. *Marketing Science, 19*(1), 22–42. doi:10.1287/mksc.19.1.22.15184

Ortinau, D. J., Babin, B. J., & Chebat, J. C. (2013). Development of new empirical insights in consumer-retailer relationships within online and offline retail environments: Introduction to the special issue. *Journal of Business Research, 66*(7), 795–800. doi:10.1016/j.jbusres.2011.06.003

Pan, L.-Y., & Chiou, J.-S. (2011). How much can you trust online information? Cues for perceived trustworthiness of consumer-generated online information. *Journal of Interactive Marketing, 25*(2), 67–74. doi:10.1016/j.intmar.2011.01.002

Pappas, I. O., Pateli, A. G., Giannakos, M. N., & Chrissikopoulos, V. (2014). Moderating effects of online shopping experience on customer satisfaction and repurchase intentions. *International Journal of Retail & Distribution Management, 42*(3), 187–204. doi:10.1108/IJRDM-03-2012-0034

Park, B., Ahn, S. K., & Kim, H. J. (2010). Blogging: Mediating impacts of flow on motivational behaviour. *Journal of Research in Interactive Marketing*, *4*(1), 6–29. doi:10.1108/17505931011033533

Park, C., & Kim, Y. (2003). Identifying key factors affecting consumer purchase behavior in an online shopping context. *International Journal of Retail & Distribution Management*, *31*(1), 16–29. doi:10.1108/09590550310457818

Piamphongsant, T., & Mandhachitara, R. (2008). Psychological antecedents of career women's fashion clothing conformity. *Journal of Fashion Marketing and Management*, *12*(4), 438–455. doi:10.1108/13612020810906119

Podsakoff, P. M., MacKenzie, S. B., Lee, J.-Y., & Podsakoff, N. P. (2003). Common method biases in behavioral research: A critical review of the literature and recommended remedies. *The Journal of Applied Psychology*, *88*(5), 879–903. doi:10.1037/0021-9010.88.5.879 PMID:14516251

Pordata. (2018). Access 19 May 2019, https://www.pordata.pt/Portugal/Empresas

Prahalad, C. K., & Ramaswamy, V. (2004). Co-creation experiences: The next practice in value creation. *Journal of Interactive Marketing*, *18*(3), 5–14. doi:10.1002/dir.20015

Purnawirawan, N., De Pelsmacker, P., & Dens, N. (2012). Balance and sequence in online reviews: How perceived usefulness affects attitudes and intentions. *Journal of Interactive Marketing*, *26*(4), 244–255. doi:10.1016/j.intmar.2012.04.002

Quigley, L., Nelson, A. L., Carriere, J., Smilek, D., & Purdon, C. (2012). The Effects of Trait and State Anxiety on Attention to Emotional Images: An Eye-Tracking Study. *Cognition and Emotion*, *26*(8), 1390–1411. doi:10.1080/02699931.2012.662892 PMID:22646929

Rapp, A., Britelspacher, L., Grewal, D., & Hughes, D. (2013). Understanding social media effects across seller, retailer, and consumer interactions. *Journal of the Academy of Marketing Science*, *41*(5), 547–566. doi:10.100711747-013-0326-9

Reichheld, F. F., & Schefter, P. (2000). E-loyalty: Your secret weap-on on the web. *Harvard Business Review*, *78*(4), 105–114.

Rose, S., Clark, M., Samouel, P., & Hair, N. (2012). Online customer experience in e-Retailing: An empirical model of antecedents and outcomes. *Journal of Retailing*, *88*(2), 308–322. doi:10.1016/j.jretai.2012.03.001

Rose, S., Hair, N., & Clark, M. (2011). Online customer experience: A review of the business-to-consumer online purchase context. *International Journal of Management Reviews*, *13*(1), 24–39. doi:10.1111/j.1468-2370.2010.00280.x

Sego, T., & Stout, P. A. (1994). Anxiety associated with social issues: The development of a scale to measure an antecedent construct. NA - Advances in Consumer Research, (21), 601-606.

Shin, D. H. (2010). The effects of trust, security and privacy in social networking: A security-based approach to understand the pattern of adoption. *Interacting with Computers*, *22*(5), 428–438. doi:10.1016/j.intcom.2010.05.001

Spaulding, T. J. (2010). How can virtual communities create value for business. *Electronic Commerce Research and Applications*, *9*(1), 38–49. doi:10.1016/j.elerap.2009.07.004

Suh, B., & Han, I. (2003). The impact of customer trust and perception of security control on the acceptance of electronic commerce. *International Journal of Electronic Commerce*, *7*(3), 135–161. doi:10.1080/10864415.2003.11044270

Thomas, M., & Tsai, C. I. (2012). Psychological distance and subjective experience: How distancing reduces the feeling of difficulty. *The Journal of Consumer Research*, *39*(2), 324–340. doi:10.1086/663772

Trafimow, D., & Earp, B. D. (2017). Null hypothesis significance testing and type 1 error: The domain problem. *New Ideas in Psychology*, *45*, 19–27. doi:10.1016/j.newideapsych.2017.01.002

Urban, G. L., Sultan, F., & Quall, W. J. (2000). Placing trust at the center of your Internet strategy. *MIT Sloan Management Review*, (1), 39–48.

Verhoef, P. C., Lemon, K. N., Parasuraman, A., Roggeveen, A., Tsiros, M., & Schlesinger, L. A. (2009). Customer experience creation: Determinants, dynamics and management strategies. *Journal of Retailing*, *85*(1), 31–41. doi:10.1016/j.jretai.2008.11.001

Vijayasarathy, L. R. (2004). Predicting consumer intentions to use on-line shopping: The case for an augmented technology acceptance model. *Information & Management*, *41*(6), 747–762. doi:10.1016/j.im.2003.08.011

Wang, Y. J., Minor, M. S., & Wei, J. (2011). Aesthetics and the online shopping environment: Understanding consumer responses. *Journal of Retailing*, *87*(1), 46–58. doi:10.1016/j.jretai.2010.09.002

Weisberg, J., Te'eni, D., & Arman, L. (2011). Past purchase and intention to purchase in e-commerce: The mediation of social presence and trust. *Internet Research*, *21*(1), 82–96. doi:10.1108/10662241111104893

Wu, J.-J., Chen, Y.-H., & Chung, Y.-S. (2010). Trust factors influencing virtual community members: A study of transaction communities. *Journal of Business Research*, *63*(9-10), 1025–1032. doi:10.1016/j.jbusres.2009.03.022

Yao, C., & Liao, S. (2011). Measuring the antecedent effects of service cognition and internet shopping anxiety on consumer satisfaction with e-tailing service. *Management & Marketing*, *6*(1), 57–78.

Yu, J., Ha, I., Choi, M., & Rho, J. (2005). Extending the TAM for a t-Commerce. *Information & Management*, *42*(77), 965–976. doi:10.1016/j.im.2004.11.001

Zhang, C.-B., & Li, Y. (2019). How social media usage influences B2B customer loyalty: Roles of trust and purchase risk. *Journal of Business and Industrial Marketing*, *34*(7), 1420–1433. doi:10.1108/JBIM-07-2018-0211

Zhang, K. Z. K., Barnes, S. J., Zhao, S. J., & Zhang, H. (2018). Can consumers be persuaded on brand microblogs? An empirical study. *Information & Management*, *55*(1), 1–15. doi:10.1016/j.im.2017.03.005

## KEY TERMS AND DEFINITIONS

**Consumer Anxiety:** Can be seen as a negative feeling triggered by the potentially harmful future events, and has a negative effect on well-being of consumers live.

**Consumer Experience:** Online consumer experience is a critical component of value creation process and as a multidimensional variable it is composed of a consumer's cognitive, affective, social and physical response to the online offers of the retailers.

**E-Commerce:** Transactions can be performed at any time, with the use of the Internet however, they are not instantaneous, and consumers do not have automatic access to the product.

**Social Media Usage:** Enable consumers to generate content and have social interaction online via social platforms.

**Trust:** Can be define as a belief in the reliability, truth, and ability of the exchange party that has been recognized as one of the reasons consumers refrain from electronic purchases.

# Chapter 11
# Siemens' Value-Driver Tree in Digitalization

**Cozmiuc Claudia Diana**
*University of the West Timisoara, Romania*

## ABSTRACT

*This chapter is a descriptive and explicative case study about value creation at Siemens in an uncertain and in a certain environment. Siemens has implemented economic value-added-based management since 1998. The empirical data analysis highlights value creation at Siemens at the beginning of the innovation lifecycle, when the environment is uncertain, and at the end of the innovation lifecycle, when contracts are signed, and the environment becomes predictable. Innovation is first placed in open networks, in which start-ups are essential, to which venture capital is allocated using business models. This is the ideation stage of the product lifecycle, when competitive advantage, the essence of value creation in both theory and the Siemens example, is created. Innovation matures, and Siemens closes contracts with customers about existing customer offerings. These contracts are managed as projects and funded with equity and debt. This is the stage when sufficient data exists to plan economic value added, the focus of Siemens' corporate governance.*

## INTRODUCTION

This paper illustrates how Siemens reconciles Economic Value Added with digitalization in a simple coherent approach that is tied to several other chapters from the same author. The purpose of this chapter is to explore, analyze and then synthesize the key value drivers and related decisions in Siemens' digitalization strategy, in the context of a world reference case (Siemens) in Economic Value Added centered management and the business context of digital transformation and disruption. The chapter is a descriptive case study. The literature review shows mainstream literature in digital transformation and managing value. The referenced sources in digital transformation refer to the works of consultants in digitalization. A second literature review is performed about value based management and comprises mainstream literature. The topic – strategy is extensive and an exhaustive literature review is too lengthy.

DOI: 10.4018/978-1-7998-1843-4.ch011

The empirical data analysis is an extensive study from sources such as annual reports, presentation, chapters in Siemens magazines, other Siemens website sources. Alhough the paper resides on an incomparably broader reference list, only main sources are cited therein. The paper shows how Siemens reconciles New Economy tools such as digitalization, business eco-systems, open innovation, intangible assets, business models, venture capital with mainframe value indicator Economic Value Added. Siemens' digitalization strategy is a framework for both New Economy and classical tools in strategic management. This paper is conducted on one of the most proeminent value based management practitioners worldwide, Siemens and may serve as example to other companies, academics. The paper finds that Siemens' key value drivers are core technology, business technology, customer industry know-how and the customer value they create, measured as key performance indicators or return on customer investment. This value driver tree shows how Siemens' digital offerings are created across all organizational systems and decisions.

## BACKGROUND

The Industrial Economy is transforming in the Knowledge Economy in several progressive stages. Digital technology has inflicted several waves of fast and high-scale change to the Industrial Economy (IBM Institute for Value Analysis, 2011; IDC, 2017a). These changes may be represented as the decades of the Knowledge Economy (IBM Institute for Business Value Analysis, 2011): in the 1990s, the emergence of the Knowledge Economy, with digital products and infrastructure; in the 2000s, digital distribution and web strategy; since 2010, digital transformation of business models.

Digital technology, created by digitization, may be defined as the IDC's third platform. The third platform comprises cloud, big data analytics, social business, mobility and technology accelerators which consist of robotics, natural interfaces, 3D printing, Internet of Things, cognitive systems, next generation security (IDC, 2017b). Digital technology may bear different names and classifications. For exemple, digitalization technology in manufacturing is called Industrie 4.0 or the Industrial Internet and comprises big data and analytics, autonomous robots, simulation, vertical and horizontal integration, Industrial Internet of Things, cyber security, cloud, additive manufacturing, augmented reality (Boston Consulting Group, 2015). Digitalization technology transforms individual industries (World Economic Forum, 2019).

Digitalization is defined (CapGemeni, 2013; Gartner, 2019; The Global Center for Business Transformation, 2019; IBM Institute for Business Value Analysis, 2011; IDC, 2017a) as the use of digital technologies to change a business model and provide value-creating opportunities or improve performance quantifiably.

According to IBM (2011), digital transformation is the pervasive degree of economic impact digital technology has on functions, industries, society. IDC (2017a) describes digital transformation as the use of digital technologies in ways that were never anticipated. Innovations driven by digital technologies are expected to bring about unprecedented business transformation, representing the biggest industry shakeout since the Industrial Revolution. According to Accenture (2019), digital transformation turns every business into a digital business. Companies face the digital imperative to harness the power of digital technologies to become more effective, innovative and disruptive. Cisco (2019) defines digital transformation as the application of technology to build new business models, processes, software, and systems that results in more profitable revenue, greater competitive advantage, and higher efficiency. According to IScoop (2019), digital transformation is the profound transformation of business and organizational activities, processes, competencies and models to fully leverage the changes and opportunities of a mix of digital technologies and their accelerating impact across society in a strategic and prioritized way, with present and future shifts in mind. The Global Center for Digital Business Transformation (2019) identifies and defines digital business transformation as a journey to adopt and deploy digital technologies and business models to improve performance quantifiably. Digital transformation (CapGemeni, 2013) is the use of technology to radically improve performance or reach of enterprises – via change customer relationships, internal processes, and value propositions, the blocks of digital transformation. These blocks of digital transformation may be used to assess digital maturity. The emergence of the New Economy at all stages has brought volatility, uncertainty, complexity and ambiguity (Berinto, 2014a, 2014b; Bennet & Lemoine, 2014).

Digital disruption (Capgemeni, 2015, 2016; Casadesus-Masanell & Ricart, 2011; Girotra & Netessine, 2014; Grossman, 2016; Kavadias, Ladas, & Loch, 2016; The Global Center for Digital Business Transformation, 2015; Ovans, 2015; Westerman, Bonnet & McAfee, 2014) occurs when digital technology (IDC, 2017b) replace incumbents' business models in industries with new business models. Digital disruption, especially the shift from pipelines to platforms, impacts all industries in a digital vortex (Blank, 2013; Bonchek & Choudary, 2013; Girotra & Netessine, 2014; Grossman, 2016; The Global Center for Digital Business Transformation, 2015; Van Alstyne, Parker, & Choudary, 2016; Westerman, Bonnet, & McAfee, 2014). According to the Global Center for Digital Business Transformation DBT (2019) digital disruption is the effect of digital technologies and business models on a company's current value proposition, and its resulting market position. According to DBT, the digital transformation will impact all industries in a digital vortex. Whereas, in the Industrial Economy, product lifecycles are long and stable, in the Knowledge Economy, product lifecycles are short and given by cycles of innovation and re-innovation (Powell & Snellman, 2004).

*Figure 1. Blocks of the digital transformation*
*(source: CapGemeni, 2013)*

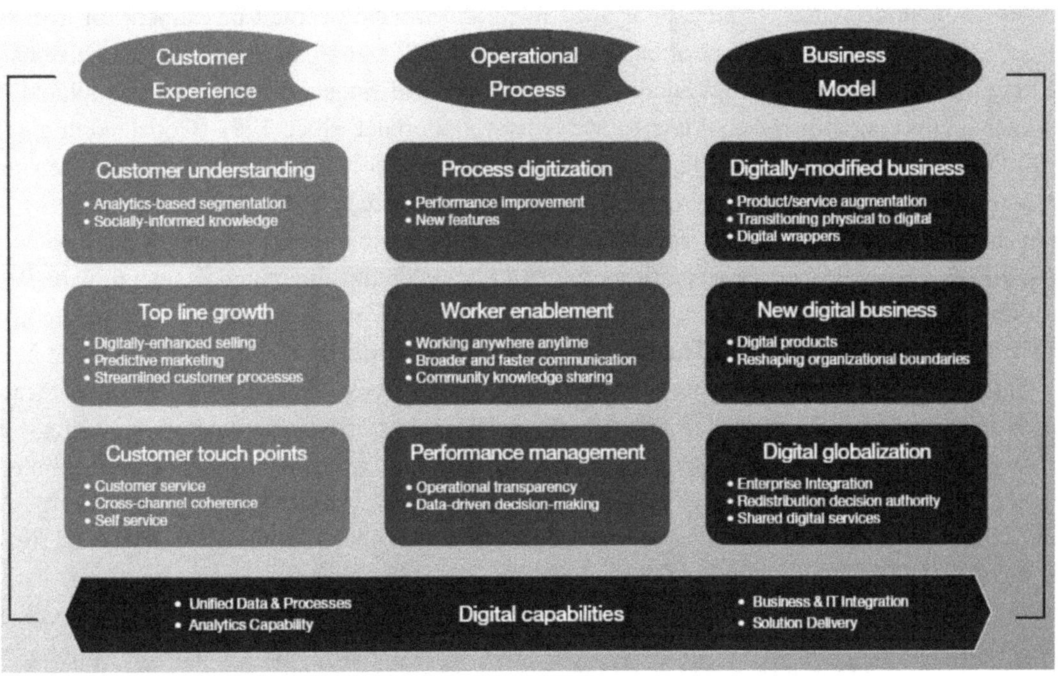

## MAIN FOCUS OF THE CHAPTER

### Issues, Controversies, Problems

Siemens has started its journey to digitalization in 2013, combining innovation with customer knowledge for customer value proposition. The key issue in this article is how customer value is created, proposed and delivered. Siemens uses internal start-ups and networks for ideation and innovation, approves ideas based on business models and funds them with enture capital. This is the lean start-up method in internal environment. This article explores the key value drivers of customer value in Siemens' philosophy and the way they are created in the organization and delivered in customer outcome contracts.

### Value Driver Definition and Relationship to Value Decisions and Value Indicators

In value based management, value drivers are the factors which create shareholder or stakeholder value in the generic formulas of value indicators. In the 1990s, several consultancy firms engaged in the war of metrics and proposed several value indicators: Shareholder Value Added for LEK Consulting (Rappaport, 1986), Economic Value Added for Stern and Stewart (Stewart, 1991), CFROI for Holt Associates (Madden, 1999, 2010), Cash Value Added for Holt Associates (Madden, 1999, 2010) or Boston Consulting Group (Boston Consulting Group, 2008), Total Shareholder Return for Boston Consulting Group (Boston Consulting Group, 2008). In value based management, value drivers may also be defined as the objectives of company decisions in creating long-term and short term shareholder value. In Rappaport's approach in 1986, value drivers are the objectives of competitive advantage, operational, investment and financing decisions that create Shareholder Value Added on the long-run (Rappport, 1986). Value drivers are the duration of competitive advantage; sales growth, operating profit margin, income tax rate for operational decisions; fixed capital investment and working capital investment for investment decisions; equity and debt in the cost of capital (Rappport, 1986). In this view, strategic decisions refer to the long-term and involve capital allocation (investment and financing decisions and related value drivers) for future operations. According to Mc Kinsey's approach since 1994 (Copeland et al, 1994, 2000; Koller et al, 2005, 2010a, 2010b, 2015), value drivers are decisions' objectives to create value to be measured when strategy is executed. Value drivers are performance indicators, and managing value drivers is performance management. Value drivers also form the link between strategy and a company's intrinsic value on capital markets. Valuation bridges strategic management and financial management. In this view, strategy is the long-term value driver and as strategy is progressively implemented, value drivers become shorter term oriented and achieve value. In the Balanced Scorecard (Kaplan & Norton, 1992), value drivers are learning and growth, internal perspective, customer perspective key performance indicators that create future value represented by financial key performance indicators. In strategic management, value drivers are driven from strategy, refer to the future and are used to value and implement strategy (Arnold, 1998; Black et al, 1998; Kaplan & Norton, 1992, 2004; KPMG, 1999; Leahy, 2000; Martin & Petty, 2000; Mc Taggart et al, 1994). In valuation (Wendee, 2011), value drivers are defined as any variable that impacts a company's value to potential buyers and may constitute a large list in an extensive literature review. Across value based management 1990s literature and as in the Balanced Scorecard approach, value drivers are used to allign the organization to strategy and thereby implement it.

The transition to the Knowledge Economy shows the emergence of a new resource, intangible assets (Daum, 2003; Edvinsson & Malone, 1997; Stewart, 1991). Studies show that, by 2000, intangible assets dramatically shift to the greater part of company value and form the main source of value creation (Daum, 2003; Edvinsson, 2002; Lev, 2001; Lev & Daum, 2004; Lev & Gu, 2016; Stegmann, 2009). Strategy maps (Kaplan & Norton, 2004) are an overview about the firm grounded on intangible assets. There are several definitions of intangible assets. In financial accounting, IAS 38, intangible assets may be classified as customer lists, customer relations, supplier relations, marketing rights, research, development, patents, computer software, databases and trade secrets, trademarks, trade dress, newspaper mastheads, internet domains, video and audiovisual material, mortgage servicing rights, licensing, royalty and standstill agreements, import quotas, franchise agreements. In financial accounting, intangible assets need to be controlled by the entity, whereas in management a broader definition is accepted (Petrisor & Cozmiuc, 2015). Intangible assets may be understood as capitals: intellectual capital (Lev, 2001, 2004; Lev & Gu, 2016), which comprises the intangible value of a business, covering its people (human capital), the value relating to its relationships (relational capital), and everything that is left when the employees go home (structural capital), of which intellectual property is but one component. Another type of intangible assets are the activities that preceed operations (Damodaran, 2007): research and development, marketing, supply chain management. This type of intangible asset may be a project or series of projects, programs (International Organization for Standardization, 2017; Project Management Institute, 2013). Projects are allocated capital based on a mixture of strategic and financial criteria and in practicing organizations by a project management board which reviews all these criteria (International Organization for Standardization, 2017; Project Management Institute, 2013). In this view, projects are temporary endevours to create a unique product, service or result. Projects are capital expenditures, allocation or investment. Operation are repetitive efforts to deliver services or results. Their costs are operational expenditure. Intangible assets may explain companies' value (Stegmann, 2009).

The New Economy is shaped as networks (Chesbrough, 2001; Gossain & Kandiah, 1998; Kothandaraman & Wilson, 2001; Kelly, 1997; Moore, 2006; Prahalad & Krishnan, 2008) or eco-systems (Ben Letaifa, 2014; Gossain & Kandiah, 1998; Moore, 2006), where value creation and capture are different from the logic of the Industrial Economy. Business models may be products in traditional value chains or platforms in networks; in this view, business models are a synthesis which highlights traditional value chains, supply side economics, or products when compared to networks, demand side economics, or platforms (Van Alstyne, Parker, & Choudary, 2016).

The new VUCA environment also impacts financing decisions via real options (Luehrman, 1998). In a certain environment, strategy is a detailed plan for action valued via the net present value of discounted cash flow. In a VUCA world, strategy is a decision tree with several options (Koller et al, 2005, 2010a, 2010b, 2015). These options are modeled using call options or put options (Damodaran, 2010, 2011, 2012).

With Kaplan and Norton (2004), value drivers are the hypotheses that shape strategy. Strategy maps comprise customer value proposition, internal activities, capital resources are non-financial value drivers, while revenue, cost and assets financial value drivers (Kaplan & Norton, 1992, 2004). Business models work at the very early discovery stage in strategy as hypotheses (Blank, 2013; McGrath & MacMillan, 1995; Girotra & Netessine, 2013). Already in 1995, McGrath and MacMillan theorized discovery driven planning: in an uncertain world, stages of discovery and testing hypotheses preceed the business plan, suitable for a certain environment. One way to represent business models is the business model canvas (Osterwalder & Pigneur, 2010). With the business model canvas, a new tool in strategic management comprises the value drivers in strategy maps plus customer related drivers – customer segments, customer relationships and customer channels and external resources such as partners. Moreover, business models canvas is intended to illustrate and explain value creation, proposition and capture (Osterwalder & Pigneur, 2010). The elements of the business model canvas are consistent with the value driver definition as any factor that impacts value creation. A series of chapters in Harvard Business Review (Blank, 2013; Bonchek & Choudary, 2013; Casadesus-Masanell & Ricart, 2011; Eyring et al, 2011; Ferry, 2017; Girotra & Netessine, 2013; Grossman, 2016; Kavadias et al, 2016; Johnson et al, 2008; Ladd, 2016; Ovans, 2015; Pisano, 2015; Satell, 2017a, 2017b; Van Alstyne et al, 2016) argue in favor of business models as the new tool to conceptualize competitive advantage, a major form of innovation, one of the drivers of digital disruption and digital transformation, the goal start-ups should produce, a means to fund start-ups later on. Business models, the new tool in strategic management, are managed in internal or external start-ups (Blank, 2013). Start-ups may be defined as (Blank, 2013) a temporary organization designed to search for a repeatable and scalable business model. An alternative definition for a start-up (Ries, 2011) is a human institution designed to deliver a product or a service under conditions of extreme uncertainty (Ries, 2011). At this stage, the product is a pivot (Ries, 2010, pp. 6). The subsequent stage is the execution of the business model, which involves a plan about the how cash flow will be generated. As the cost of developing a digital startup has fallen from approximately $5 million in 2000 to $5,000 as of 2013 (Capgemeni, 2016), the lean start-up movement is taking the world by storm (Blank, 2013; Girotra & Netessine, 2013; The Global Center for Digital Business Transformation, 2015; Grossman, 2016). Traditionally, venture capital has been used to finance start-ups or business development efforts (Kaplan Financial Limited, 2012a, 2012b). Venture capital is a type of private equity, a form of financing that is provided by firms or funds to small, early-stage, emerging firms that are deemed to have high growth potential, or which have demonstrated high growth (in terms of number of employees, annual revenue, or both). The lean start-up movement is closely tied to venture capital (Blank, 2013). Already since the proposal of open innovation (Chesbrough, 2002), one network business model, venture capital is recommended.

## EMPIRICAL EVIDENCE: KEY VALUE DRIVERS IN SIEMENS' DIGITALIZATION STRATEGY

### About Siemens

Siemens is a large industrial global European based engineering company founded in 1847. Since then, Siemens has acted as a large conglomerate with a portfolio of products that has changed throughout time. In 1998, Siemens has wide variety of businesses and business types. In 1998, Siemens' portfolio comprises groups in energy, industry, information and communications, transportation, healthcare, lighting, household appliances. Since 2010, Siemens has focused its portfolio on key sectors industry, energy, infrastructure and cities (Siemens, 2014d, pp. 4; 2016, pp. 4). In the future, 2020 onwards, Siemens scale up and will tap adjacent markets. Siemens has large or medium business customers, with whom it engages in contracts that report sales per contract or won orders. Siemens supplies products, services, solutions, capital assets, constructions in customer specific contracts. Siemens is organized in Managing Board and Supervisory Board. Siemens' Management Board comprises members from

Siemens' businesses, regions, corporate functions. Siemens' research and development activities are organized in a Central Technology Department and in business specific departments. Siemens manages customers via key account managers and Siemens Management Consulting. Key account managers are organized on customer markets as third organizational dimension. A Corporate Supply Chain Management organization is responsible for global supply networks, supplier involvement across the product lifecycle, global direct and indirect purchasing contracts, supplier related innovation. Siemens has 298 factories worldwide. Siemens' financial management is centered on Economic Value Added. Performance management bridges strategy, financial management, human resource management. Siemens is a global company, present in 190 countries, with targets to locate business unit management outside Germany, to be active in emerging countries, in innovation hubs, in large business centers.

With reference to the topic of this chapter, Siemens' value based management practice is cited by the proponents of the Economic Value Added model (Stern, Shiely, & Ross, 2003) as one of the most proeminent cases worlwide. Siemens' Economic Value Added approach has been the topic of a past chapter at Emerald (Zhao, 2004). Digitalizaton at Siemens is a Harvard Business Review case study in 2018 (Collins & Junker, 2018). As follows, secondary data about Siemens is explored, analyzed, induced and grouped close to the Siemens original and following key value drivers as criterium to select statements. Whereas the statements belong to Siemens, their selection is based to the relevance of the key value driver approach.

## Value Based Management – A Holistic Management Program 1998-2020

Since 1998 to date, Siemens implements value based management as a framework that overarches strategic management and financial management. In 1998, Siemens begins to implement value based management (Siemens, 1998, pp. 6) in several stages which show progressive scope of the management systems deliberately subordinated to value creation. To begin with, value based management is one of several management programs named top+ (Siemens, 1998, pp. 6), a ten-point program which comprises portfolio measures and financial and capital measures (Siemens, 1998, pp. 7; Siemens, 1999, pp. 8). In the following years, the EVA centered value based management is renamed Operation 2003 (2002), Siemens Management System (2003, 2004), Fit4More (2004-2007), Fit42010 (2008, 2009), Siemens One (2010 onwards). These programs are all centered on value, involve financial value drivers or performance metrics as goals or targets, and non-financial value drivers as strategic directions.

Corporate Governance is the basis for all decision making and control processes and comprises responsible, value-based management and monitoring focused on long-term success, goal-oriented and efficient cooperation between the Managing and Supervisory Boards, respect for the interests of our shareholders and employees, transparency and responsibility in all entrepreneurial decisions and an appropriate risk management system (Siemens, 2010, pp. 88).

Sustainable value is measured via Economic Value Added, the ultimate corporate governance objective for Siemens 1998 – 2018. Economic Value Added is computed by a formula which summarizes the Profit and Loss statement, the Balance Sheet, the weighted average cost of capital. A business creates value when it recovers its cost of capital and furthermore delivers EVA in line with capital market requirements (Siemens, 2001, pp. 51). The elements of that formula are financial value drivers and performance metrics. Performance is driven by non-financial measures.

*Figure 2. Overview about financial and non-financial value drivers*
*(source: Siemens, 1998; Dr Thomas, 2013)*

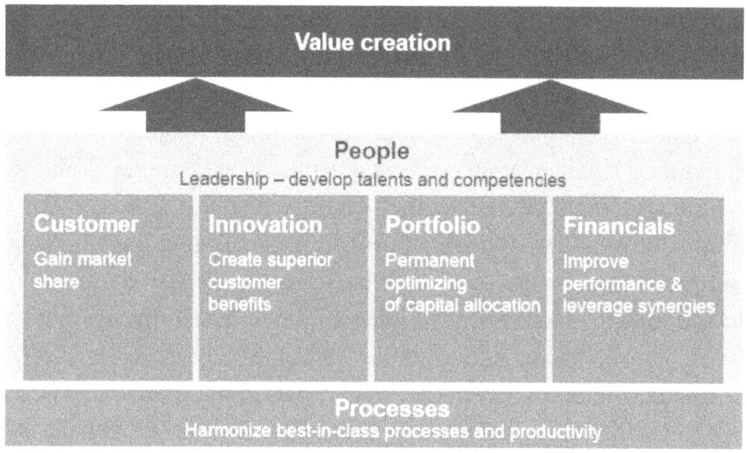


Since 2005, Siemens' non-financial value drivers comprise the strategic directions of Fit4More, Fit42010, Siemens One. Amonst these non-financial value drives have been innovation and customer proxmity, included in operational excellence in the Fit4More and Fit42010 programs and later as strategic directions in Siemens One. Siemens calls goal setting about value drivers performance management (DrThomas, 2013). Since its beginning, value based management involves clear goals about performance, concrete measures and rigurous consequences (Siemens, 1998, pp. 6). Siemens calls this approach business excellence (Siemens, 2002b, pp. 20 – 30). In the One Siemens strategic management framework, strategy, organization, performance management direct personnel behavior and transform environmental input into output (Dr Thomas, 2013, pp. 13). In performance management, the most important value driver is investment in tangible assets, intangible assets and portfolio activities (Dr Thomas, 2013, pp. 22). Value at Siemens is created in investment cycles, that begin with capital allocation, continue with growth, profitability and generate cash flow that allows self-financing new investment (Dr Thomas, 2013, pp. 21). Performance metrics are the basics of Siemens' global performance management process (Siemens, 2006, pp. 25), which involve the appraisal of all employees based on performance and the compensation of management based on the same criterium. Siemens has practiced competitor benchmarking since 1998, and incorporated benchmarking as hurdle rates for its performance metrics progressively in Fit4More, Fit42010 and eventually reaching all strategic performance indicators in Siemens One, the current group strategy since 2010 overarching 2020+. One Siemens is centered on value, and comprises three strategic directions: focus on innovation driven markets; get closer to customers; use the power of Siemens.

## The Siemens One Group Strategy and the Role Digitalization Plays

The first strategic direction is focusing on innovation-driven markets, comprising three focus areas: be a pioneer in technology-driven markets; strengthen portfolio; provide a leading environmental portfolio. In 2013, Siemens defines its activities alongside key technologies electrification, automation and digitalization (Siemens, 2013a, pp. 98). In 2014, Vision 2020, and in Vision 2020+, Siemens defines its portfolio alongside key technologies electrification, automation and digitalization (Siemens, 2014e, pp.

14, 15). The three technologies define what all Siemens' businesses have in common, long-term trends that define Siemens' markets, the territory for competition, the requirements of customers, partners and society (Siemens, 2014d, pp. 15). Siemens is a leader in electrification, automation, and exploits the opportunities offered by digitalization (Siemens, 2017e, pp. 14). On structural level, innovation is achieved by the research and development department, which at Siemens comprises the Corporate Technology department for core technology and business specific departments. Research and development is organized in two directions: customer focus, divisions' responsibility; core technology leadership, the responsibility of the Corporate Technology department. While businesses spend research and development on future versions of existing products and solutions, the Corporate Technology department works with businesses to develop group technology and innovation strategy (Siemens, 2014d, pp. 218). Beginning 2014, according to Siemens, technology leadership stems from key competences in electrification, automation and digitalization across all Siemens customer industries or domains (Siemens, 2014d, pp. 12, 13). In 2015, the Corporate Technology department is focused on key activities in an electrification, automation and digitalization (Siemens, 2015b, pp. 140). The goal of Corporate Technology is to secure the technological base and future of Siemens (Siemens, 2014d, pp. 5).

Focusing on innovation-driven markets is Siemens' primary strategic direction out of three more. This strategy is complemented by the second strategic direction in Siemens One, getting closer to Siemens' customers and entails intensifying Siemens' customer focus, expanding service business, growing in emerging markets (Siemens, 2010, pp. 43). Customer focus involves customer loyalty from one project to another and even recommending Siemens to other prospective customers; this is measured via the net promoter score. This strategic direction also brings value drivers such as sales growth in emerging markets; empowering regional companies to make decisions on their own; enduring brand loyalty in emerging markets, via the net promoter score; establishing local service networks that bring higher return on investment via low capital employed; intangible assets such as customer knowledge (gaining a detailed understanding of customers' processes and of their customers' processes), customer relationships; high customer tailoring of Siemens' products (Siemens, 2010, pp. 43 – 46). Customer proximity is the responsibility of key account managers, which report to Vertical Market Management Boards, for vertical markets or individual industries, and Market Development Boards, for cross-industry solutions (Siemens, 2012, pp. 18). Key account managers have targets for won orders, that is the sales brought by new customer contracts, and for customer loyalty and relationship, measured via the net promoter score (Siemens, 2011, pp. 166). In the Siemens One strategy, innovation and customer focus are key non-financial value drivers.

The two main strategic directions in Siemens One show that innovation and customer focus complement each other in creating customer solutions. In Vision 2020 (Siemens, 2017e, pp. 3), Siemens' strategy for 2020 onwards is to scale up, based on innovation, customer and market focus, and digitalization. Beyond 2020, in Vision 2020+ (Siemens, 2018b, pp. 24), the two strategic priorities in Siemens One, focus on electrification, automation and digitalization and customer focus, remain and receive targets for measurable growth (in sales and in the net promoter score).

## Stages in Siemens' Digitalization Strategy

At Siemens, core technologies electrification, automation and digitalization are types of products, services or solutions Siemens' businesses provide (Siemens, 2018c, pp. 11). In Siemens' digitalization strategy and in a series of other statements, digitalization refers to digital services, vertical software,

Internet of Things integration and Webs of Systems. Today, digital platforms all businesses share are Synalitics for digital services, Product Lifecycle Management software for vertical software, Internet of Things consulting and integration (Cozmiuc & Petrisor, 2018c; Siemens, 2015a, pp. 2-4; 2018, pp. 13). Core technologies electrification, automation and digitalization are shared by Siemens' businesses and may be an alternative classification to their offerings – products, services, solutions, constructions.

At Siemens, digital services connect Siemens' customers' devices to the digital platform Synalitics and generate data via sensors (Siemens, 2016c, pp. 8). This data is converted into smart data using the smart data principle, a combination of domain, context and device know-how (Siemens, 2016c, pp. 16 – 18). Data from Siemens' devices is processed using data analytics, business intelligence and business innovation to customer value. Customer benefits include performance increase, energy saving, cost reduction and risk avoidance and security. Data analytics may refer to the past, and be descriptive and informs; analyzes, via diagnostic and predictive analytics; prescriptive, describing future decisions and actions (Siemens, 2016c, pp. 9, 10). Vertical software Product Lifecycle Management is another customer offering Siemens classifies as digitalization. This is especially true in the Industry businesses, where Product Lifecycle Management software is a key technology component in Industry 4.0 (Cozmiuc & Petrisor, 2018c; Siemens, 2017d). Product Lifecycle Management software is a generic technology adapted to industry, energy and buildings. Internet of Things integration is a management consulting service to Siemens' customers, conducted by strategy consulting Siemens Management Consulting (Siemens, 2018c, pp. 13). It is intended to achieve Internet of Things integration across Siemens' businesses. Cyber-physical systems and Webs of Systems are another digital offering at Siemens, not yet reported but possible to exist again or in the future (Cozmiuc & Petrisor, 2018b).

*Figure 3. Siemens' digitalization strategy and Siemens' customer offerings in digitalization*
*(source: Siemens, 2015)*

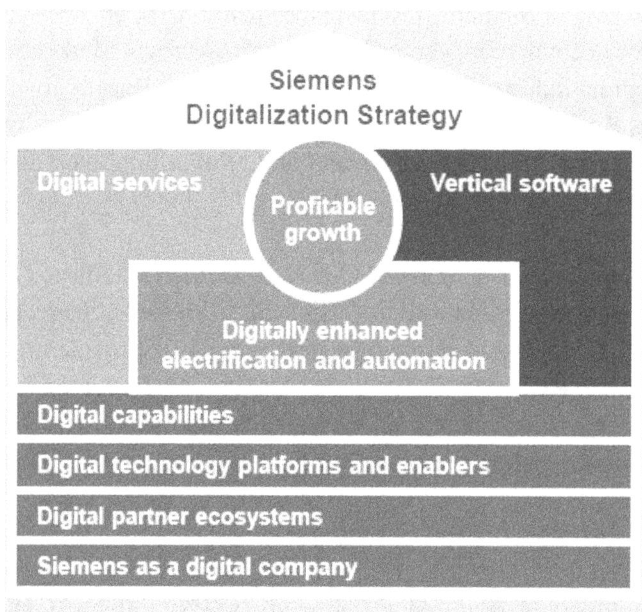

Siemens' digitalization strategy (Siemens, 2015a, pp. 2-3) consists of the digital foundation, the digital business opportunities thereby created, and tailoring core digitalization technology to businesses and customer industries. Siemens' digital foundation shows the open innovation strategy that comprises busines eco-ecosystems, internal capabilities and results in the platforms and enablers that underpin digital offerings. Several Siemens other presentations converge to show digitaliation offerings are created by blending core technology, business technology and customer industry know-how to achieve a concrete customer proposition, quantified as performance indicator or return on investment. Siemens' achievements in digitalization: digital services, vertical software, cyber-physical systems and Webs of Systems (Siemens, 2016d, pp. 6; 2017e, pp. 19) reflect the core technology plus business technology plus customer industry know-how equals customer value (performance indicators or return on investment) strategy. The platform for digital services, Synalitics, blends analytics know-how, context know-how and domain know-how to deliver customers performance in the form of improved performance, energy savings, cost reductions, risk minimization, quality improvement (Siemens, 2016c, pp. 16). Siemens calls this combination the smart data to business principle (Siemens, 2016c, pp. 5-9). Vertical software, Smart Innovation including Product Lifecycle Management software, is a core technology adapted to Siemens' businesses and furthermore customer processes and customer industry know-how (Cozmiuc & Petrisor, 2018c). Contracts stipulate concrete return on the investment the customer makes. The formula for cyber-physical systems accross Webs of Systems combines the same: technology with domain context for return on customer investment (Cozmiuc & Petrisor, 2018b; Siemens, 2015c, pp. 4-11; 2016d, pp. 22, 23). Technology comprises smart networked devices (Siemens, 2016, pp. 10). Domain and context comprise domain-specific requirements, cross-domain integration and semantics (Siemens, 2016d, pp. 10). Web of Systems therefore become smart networked systems for industries and critical infrastructures (Siemens, 2016d, pp. 4-11).

The foundation in Siemens' digitalization strategy is open innovation in core technology, that involves external networks and internal capabilities and creates digital technology platforms and enablers (Siemens, 2015c). Innovation in core technology electrification, automation and digitalization and in business technology is supported by the open innovation strategy. Open innovation is the core group strategy since 2008. Open Innovation is the task of the Corporate Technology Department (Siemens, 2013a, pp. 218). At Siemens, open innovation comprises crowd development, development of user stories and customer insights; validation of existing data-driven service business ideas; development of new data-driven business opportunities (high level); common description of ideas based on proven BizMo™ methodology; community idea generation, evaluation, discussion and maturation, Siemens' knowledge management system, Corporate Memory, division boards that compile knowledge about past projects as part of Corporate Memory, market information compiled by market boards, project Technoweb, blogs, microblogs, wikis, customer relationshp management, corporate memory, the Internet, Internet, publications, TechnoForum, a Web of Knowledge with world-class partners, crowdsourcing of ideas, the Siemens Innovation Fund, eco-systems of partners, innovation producing suppliers (Cozmiuc & Petrisor, 2018a). Open innovation at Siemens is a large topic that may constitute the topic of an individual much lager chapter (Cozmiuc & Petrisor, 2018a). Siemens' innovation partners form business eco-systems, another pillar of Siemens' digital foundation in its digitalization strategy (Siemens, 2015a pp. 11). Innovation occurs in several stages: ideation, concept and selection, technology development, market launch (Siemens, 2011, pp. 36). In a technology Siemens uses internally as well, ideation, realization, utilization are stages of product lifecycle (Siemens, 2018a, pp. 14). In 2013, Siemens works in an Enterprise 2.0 mode, that blends network structures with centralized project and portfolio offices (Siemens, 2013b, pp. 7, 8). In

2017, Siemens places its key technology innovation in start-up organization next 47, also called Innovation AG and previously called Siemens Venture Capital. Siemens Venture Capital identifies (Siemens, 2019c) and finances young companies worldwide during their start-up phase, and provides established companies with additional capital for their growth plans during the expansion phase. Venture capital is important because it assumes the high risk involved by innovations. Siemens is rated among the top ten venture capital providers in the world. Siemens next 47 supports start-ups along the entire venture lifecycle: incubation, acceleration, growth, transfer and exit (Siemens, 2016a, pp. 8). Next47 will be established as an independent entity which offers freedom to experiment, to innovate and to grow in an early stage of the market development (Siemens, 2016a, pp. 8). To that end, Siemens uses all available options: builds, buys and partners to enable tomorrow's successful and profitable companies (Siemens, 2016b, pp. 4). Siemens' dedicated team of experts forms a bridge between the start-up world and the Siemens ecosystem (Siemens, 2016a, pp. 16). Within next 47, there are three organizations that manage start-ups: Technology to Business, Novel Businesses, Technology Accelerator (Siemens, 2016a, pp. 15). Siemens Technology to Business brings externally developed technologies and turns them into innovative Siemens products and technologies. Siemens Novel Businesses takes disruptive business opportunities and transforms them into innovative Siemens businesses. Siemens Technology Accelerator turns innovative Siemens technologies and exists them into innovative businesses outside Siemens. Siemens places future core technology in start-ups, such as artificial intelligence, autonomous machines, connected e-mobility, distributed electrification, blockchain applications. In Siemens' digitalization strategy, internal effort spent for innovation is called digital capabilities (Siemens, 2015a, pp. 7). From a performance management perspective, in Siemens' annual reports, innovation has been measured deliberately in the One Siemens strategy by the annual research and development expenditure; number of research and development staff, in all and by categories; number of patents or similar achievements. In the past decade, Siemens has been ranked by Boston Consulting Group as one of the most innovative companies in the world.

*Figure 4. Siemens' innovation lifecycle*
*(source: Siemens, 2011)*

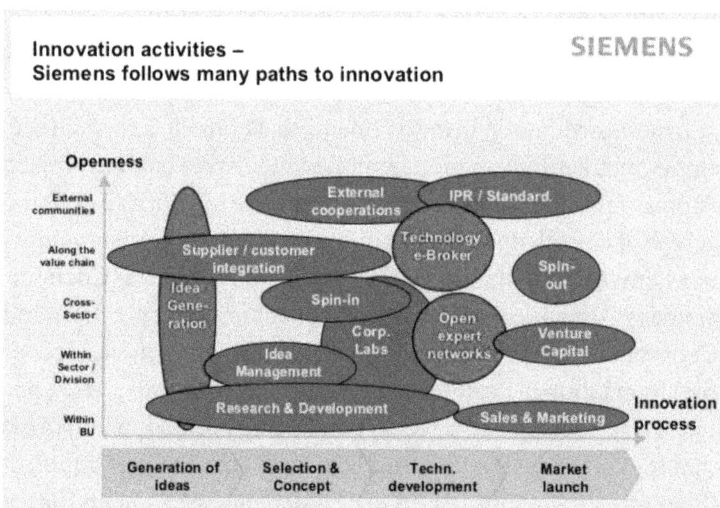

Siemens achieves technology invention in open networks. Siemens complements technology invention with business models. Siemens asserts innovation in the 21st century is created not just by new technologies. Business models also have what it takes to turn the rules of entire industries on their head (Siemens, 2017b). Technology invention and business models are the criteria used by Siemens to select innovation ideas in internal and external idea contests. At the concept and selection stage of the innovation lifecycle, the Open Co-Ideation guideline shapes innovation processes (Siemens, 2014b). According to Siemens, the method has been used since 2009 (Siemens, 2014b). Open Co-Ideation involves several steps to choose ideas (Siemens, 2014b, pp. 17). The first step new ideas by community (guided within predefined framework). The next steps are idea discussion and maturation (supported by expert moderators) and idea pre-selection (through community and expert rating). The fourth step is validation (supported by expert moderators). The next steps are final selection of winner ideas (by high level management jury) and implementation. The Open Co-Ideation concept comprises three parts: the technology view, the business view and the customer value proposition view they create (Siemens, 2014b, pp. 20). The technology view refers to core technology electrification, automation, digitalization.

The business view comprises business intelligence and business innovation (Siemens, 2014b). The customer value proposition view includes business intelligence and business innovation. Customer value proposition may comprise key performance indicators or return on investment. Ideas may also be selected that create value for Siemens. Open Co-Ideation is used by Siemens to approve and finance new ideas (Siemens, 2014b). The universal idea language is BizMo, the Siemens framework for business models (Siemens, 2014b). BizMo is the Siemens framework to innovate business models (Siemens, 2014b, pp. 20), and comprises the revenue module (how to generate business volume), the customer module (who are customers), the value proposition module (what is customer value), the investment and finance module (how to obtain capital), the cost module (what are expenses), the delivery module (how to be achieved).

The concept and selection stage is the stage when Siemens decide show to use ideas from its internal or external network. For example, venture capital may be used to spin in start-ups, to scale start-ups into full companies or to sell them to venture funds (Cozmiuc & Petrisor, 2018a).

In the past, Siemens used venture capital for special external partnerships but currently only uses it to finance start-ups at all their lifecycle stages (Siemens, 2019c).

As ideas digitalization ideas mature, they become technology platforms and enablers al businesses used. Other sources show Siemens' digitalization strategy as a two-stepped approach (Siemens, 2016c, pp. 19). In Siemens, digitalization strategy, Siemens builds on common technology platforms, that provide the latest technology for all Siemens businesses; reduce technical complexity in the company; leverage synergies through scaling; ensure faster development (Siemens, 2016c, pp. 19). In order to bring this technology to business, Siemens uses customer proximity of operating units to develop applications; this brings know-how about the large installed bases of products and systems; deep know-how of customer processes and challenges; many existing applications that already generate value for customers (Siemens, 2016c, pp. 19). The digitalization strategy enables Siemens to create today's achievements in digitalization, digital platforms all businesses share, like digital services and vertical software. Siemens' digitalization strategy furthermore includes Siemens' customer focus to tailor customer offerings, using Siemens' large installed base and customer access, Siemens' being the trusted partner for critical processes, Siemens' deep vertical know-how (Siemens, 2015a, pp. 3). Taken together, technology innovation and customer focus enable Siemens to propose customer concrete value, via performance indicators such as increased productivity and flexibility, shorter time-to-market, improved uptimes and lifetimes (Siemens, 2015a, pp. 2). Customer outcomes are included in customer contracts and comprise performance indicators with defined levels, such as higher availability, lower costs, increased performance, more security or return on investment for the whole solution (Siemens, 2016c, pp. 10). Siemens calls this "technology go to market". An even more advanced type of customer contract is network platforms (Siemens, 2016c, pp. 14). Siemens leverages digital technology trends for concrete customer benefits (Siemens, 2016c, pp. 5). Siemens' digital platform, Synalitics, provides tailored digital services to all Siemens businesses (Siemens, 2016c, pp. 11). Product Lifecycle software (Cozmiuc & Petrisor, 2018c) is essential to Industry 4.0 in manufacturing. The technology may also be used in energy, buildings. Cyber-physical systems and Webs of Systems are key technology in manufacturing, Industry 4.0, and also in energy, as energy grids, and in smart cities.

As products, services or solutions are tailored to customers, projects are used. In the Enterprise 2.0 organization (Siemens, 2013b, pp. 7, 8) and in the Siemens innovation lifecycle (Siemens, 2011, pp. 36), as ideas mature, projects are used in a Project and Portfolio Management organization structure (Siemens, 2014c, pp. 9-11). Projects are contracts with Siemens' customers (Siemens, 2019b) to supply existing products, services and solutions in large or medium-sized orders. Projects have phases, work-packages, milestones, plans that show how customer offerings are tailored to individual customers and marketed (Siemens, 2014c, pp. 11). Projects are approved by Portfolio Management Offices (Siemens, 2013b, pp. 7, 8; 2014c, pp. 9-11) and financed by Siemens Financial Services using debt and equity capital (Siemens, 2019a). Siemens (Siemens, 2014a, pp. 7-15) shows concrete examples of how smart data was used in projects in various Siemens businesses with individual customers: energy, healthcare, mobility, smart cities.

It is also at this stage Siemens provides Internet of Things integration services. More recently, Siemens Management Consulting has given customer tailoring a new strategic edge (Siemens, 2018c, pp. 13). Siemens Management Consulting Services are customer market specific. They provide a holistic customer offering: consulting, design and prototyping, implementation (Siemens, 2018c, pp. 13). It is a dedicated unit for customer's digital transformation and Internet. Siemens Management Consulting relies on Siemens' global access to customer assets, on its installed base and vertical domain know-how (Siemens, 2018c, pp. 13).

Siemens' digitalization strategy also involves Siemens' own assessment about its digital readiness. This is Siemens' digital master plan, and includes: digital strategy; offering and business models; business plans including investment; go to market sales concept; customers and partners; well trained resources already mentioned in this chapter. Digitalization also involves roll out and headquarter support, branding, tailor made digital events, data base for use cases. Siemens' digital foundation transforms Siemens into a digital company (Siemens, 2015a, pp. 4).

## SOLUTIONS AND RECOMMENDATIONS

Siemens uses customer proximity and know-how to tailor technology solutions to customers' needs for superior value contribution. Siemens' strengths lies in the technology offered and the customer value this creates and delivers. This creates customer loyalty for Siemens' solutions. Siemens works in the business to business sector, where customer knowledge is gained via business contacts in an opaque environment, rather than on open markets. Customer relations, knowledge and loyalty are a significant strength to build on. Siemens Management Consulting could keep even closer relationships with customers and offer them tailored solutions not only from Siemens' portfolio but also from competitors or adjacent solutions, while Siemens knows customers' needs best. Siemens as a large incumbent has the advantage of customer knowledge and relationships, and Siemens may capitalize on this advantage using all means. Siemens' past experience for example in aerospace shows detailed knowledge of customer manufacturing lines and the ability to provide finesse solutions. As Siemens has shifted business model from selling products to prodividing solutions, they should stay close to customers and become their expert providers. An argument in this respect is above 20% in Siemens' Net Promoter Score in 2018, and goal to improve it as Siemens' strategy is customer loyalty.

## FUTURE RESEARCH DIRECTIONS

At Siemens, the product lifecycle begins with ideations in open networks. Business models are approved using venture capital. Siemens practices the lean start-up method for ideation stage and uses networks, business models, venture capital to manage innovation. Business models may be understood as hypotheses about the pivot product. Some of the key issues that arise here include intellectual property management for ideas generated in internal start-ups, reconciliation with project management techniques, integration of venture capital with debt and equity, organizational structure and management, importance of intangible assets in contemporary environment, intangible assets recognition and ownership, customer value proposition indicators, role of customer value proposition in competitive advantage.

## CONCLUSION

In summary, Siemens' key value drivers are core technology know-how, business technology know-how, customer industry know-how (intangible assets) and the customer value proposition (key performance indicators or return on investment) of individual products, services and solutions. These value drivers reflect the stages in Siemens' digitalization strategy. The first stage in digitalization is investment in core technology, an intangible asset which has digital plaforms and technology inventions as outcome. The platforms are created in open innovation networks or business eco-systems, where start-ups are financed by venture capital. The next decision is to tailor platforms, using business technology know-how (such as manufacturing) and customer industry know-how (such as automotive manufacturing). Once this investment in intangible assets is performed, innovation in digitalization is outcome; so is the product, service, solution. In the Open Co-Ideation guideline, business models help turn invention into innovation. Another key value driver is value proposition, expressed as performance indicator or return on investment. Siemens approves innovations ideas based on core technology, busines technology, business models and concrete customer value proposition.

These key value drivers are a Siemens mantra and reflect financial value drivers such as investment in the EVA formula, key non-financial value drivers innovation and customer focus, the key strategic directions in Siemens One (the group strategy), the organizational structure, Siemens' digitalization strategy, statements about the way digital services are created, the guideline to approve innovation ideas, the key value drivers on the long-run in performance management, the key value driver in Siemens' philosophy, the value creation cycle in performance management. In the 1990s approach to value drivers, alligning the organization to strategy implements it effectively. Evidence shows Siemens' digitalization strategy paves the way from strategic directions to outcome – innovation, customer offering, customer value.

Siemens' statements about its digitalization strategy highlight digital products, services or solutions. Using 2010s tools, Siemens' digitalization strategy is a business model, and it is using business models that the strategy is approved at Siemens. Customer value proposition is performance or return on investment. Internal resources – core technology, business technology, customer industry know-how and an eco-system of business partners are main costs. Customers are large or medium sized businesses, the administration, and customer relationships are close. Siemens strategy highlights New Economy trends: digitalization is created using networks or business eco-systems in open innovation. Financing reflects decisions under uncertainty, using venture capital in an open network structure. In the Enterprise 2.0 Siemens management model, it is only later on, as ideas mature, that innovation is realized in projects, which are approved using a Portfolio Management Office and equity and debt capital. Both in theory and in the practice of Siemens, networks, business models and venture capital work at early stages of the product lifecycle: ideation, business development, discovery. As ideas mature, planning becomes possible. As in the discovery driven planning model of McGrath and MacMillan in 1995, in an uncertain world, stages of discovery and hypotheses validation are necessary before a business plan can be drawn up.

In conclusion, digitalization and New Economy value based management tools such as venture capital are included in the overall Economic Value Added logic. Innovation life-cycle at Siemens and discovery driven planning may explain this co-existence.

## REFERENCES

Accenture. (2019). *Digital transformation turns every business into a digital business*. Retrieved on May 26th, 2019, from: https://www.accenture.com/ro-en/service-digital-transformation

Arnold, G. (1998). *Corporate Financial Management*. Pitman Publishing.

Ben Letaifa, S. (2014). The uneasy transition from supply chains to ecosystems: The value-creation/value-capture dilemma. *Management Decision*, *52*(2), 278–295. doi:10.1108/MD-06-2013-0329

Bennet, N., & Lemoine, G. J. (2014, Jan.). *What VUCA really means for you. Harvard Business Review*.

Berinto, S. (2014a, Sept.). *A Framework for understanding VUCA. Harvard Business Review*.

Berinto, S. (2014b, Jan.). *What VUCA really means for you. Harvard Business Review*.

Black, A., Wright, P., & Bachman, J. (1998). *In search of Shareholder Value. Managing the Drivers of Performance*. Pitman Publishing.

Blank, S. (2013, May). Why the Lean Start-Up Changes Everything. *Havard Business Review*.

Bonchek, M., & Choudary, S. P. (2013, Jan.). Three Elements of a Successful Platform Strategy. *Harvard Business Review*.

Boston Consulting Group. (2008). *Value creators report*. Retrieved on May 26th, 2019, from: https://www.bcg.com/documents/file15314.pdf

Boston Consulting Group. (2015a). *Industry 4.0: The Future of Productivity and Growth in Manufacturing Industries.* Retrieved on May 26th, from: https://www.bcgperspectives.com/content/articles/engineered_products_project_business_industry_40_future_productivity_growth_manufacturing_industries/?chapter=2

CapGemeni. (2013). *Digital transformation: a roadmap for billion-dollar organizations.* Digital Transformation Review No. 1.

CapGemeni. (2015). *Strategies for the Age of Digital Disruption.* Digital Transformation Review No. 7.

CapGemeni. (2016). *The Digital Strategy Imperative: Steady Long-Term Vision, Nimble Execution.* Digital Transformation Review No. 9.

Casadesus-Masanell, R., & Ricart, J. E. (2011, Jan.). *How to Design a winning business model. Harvard Business Review.*

Chesbrough, H. (2001). Assembling the elephant: A review of empirical studies on the impact of technical change upon incumbent firms. *Research on Technological Innovation, Management and Policy*, *7*, 1–36.

Collins, D. J., & Junker, T. (2018). *Digitalization at Siemens.* Harvard Business School Case 717-428.

Copeland, T. E., Koller, T. M., & Murrin, J. (1994). *Valuation: Measuring and Managing the Value of Companies.* John Wiley & Sons.

Copeland, T. E., Koller, T. M., & Murrin, J. (2000). *Valuation, Measuring and managing the value of companies* (3rd ed.). John Wiley and Sons.

Cozmiuc, D., & Petrisor, P. (2018a). *Innovation in the Age of Digital Disruption: The Case of Siemens. In Handbook of Research on Strategic Innovation Management for Improved Competitive Advantage.* IGI Global. doi:10.4018/978-1-5225-3012-1.ch025

Cozmiuc, D., & Petrisor, P. (2018b, January-March). Industrie 4.0 by Siemens: Steps Made Next. *Journal of Cases on Information Technology*, *20*(1), 31–46. doi:10.4018/JCIT.2018010103

Cozmiuc, D., & Petrisor, P. (2018c, April-June). Industrie 4.0 by Siemens: Steps Made Today. *Journal of Cases on Information Technology*, *20*(2), 30–48. doi:10.4018/JCIT.2018040103

Damodaran, A. (2007). *Return on Capital (ROC), Return on Invested Capital (ROIC), and Return on Equity (ROE): Measurement and Implications.* New York University Stern School of Business.

Damodaran, A. (2010). *Applied Corporate Finance.* Wiley.

Damodaran, A. (2011). *Damodaran on Valuation: Security Analysis for Investment and Corporate Finance.* Wiley.

Damodaran, A. (2012). *Investment Valuation: Tools and Techniques for Determining the Value of Any Asset.* Wiley.

Daum, J. H. (2003). *Intangible Assets and Value Creation.* Wiley.

Edvinsson, L. (2002). *Corporate Longitude - What You Need to Know to Navigate the Knowledge Economy.* Financial Times Prentice Hall.

Edvinsson, L., & Malone, M. (1997). *Intellectual Capital*. Harper Business.

Eyring, M., Johnson, M. W., & Nair, H. (2011, Jan.). *New business models in emerging markets. Harvard Business School.*

Ferry, K. (2017, Mar.). How Organizations Can Thrive in the Digital Economy. *Harvard Business Review*.

Gartner. (2019). *IT Glossary*. Retrieved on May 26th, 2019, from: https://www.gartner.com/it-glossary/digitalization/

Girotra, K., & Netessine, S. (2013). *Business Model Innovation for Sustainability*. INSEAD Working Paper No. 2013/77/TOM.

Global Center for Digital Business Transformation. (2019a). *Digital vortex*. Retrieved on May 26th, 2019, from: https://www.imd.org/dbt/digital-business-transformation/

Global Center for Digital Business Transformation. (2019b). *Orchestrating Transformation*. Retrieved on May 26th, from: https://www.imd.org/research-knowledge/books/orchestrating-transformation/

Gossain, G., & Kandiah, S. (1998). Reinventing value: The new business ecosystem. *Strategy and Leadership*, *26*(5).

Grossman, R. (2016, Mar.). The Industries that are being disrupted the most by digital. *Harvard Business Review*.

IDC. (2017a). *Digital Transformation*. Retrieved on May 26th, 2019, from: https://www.idc.com/promo/thirdplatform/digitaltransformation

IDC. (2017b). *Explore 3rd Platform Transformation*. Retrieved on May 26th, 2019, from: https://www.idc.com/prodserv/3rd-platform/

Institute for Business Value. (2011). *Digital transformation. Creating new business models where digital meets physical*. Retrieved on May 26th, from: https://www-07.ibm.com/sg/manufacturing/pdf/manufacturing/Digital-transformation.pdf

International Organization for Standardization. (2017). *ISO 9000:2015*. Retrieved on May 26th, 2019, from: https://www.iso.org/obp/ui/#iso:std:iso:9000:ed-4:v1:en

IScoop. (2019). *Digital transformation: online guide to digital business transformation*. Retrieved on May 26th, 2019, from: https://www.i-scoop.eu/digital-transformation/

Johnson, M., W., Christensen, C., M., & Kagermann, H. (2008, Dec.). Reinventing your business model. *Harvard Business Review*.

Kaplan, R., & Norton, D. (1992, Jan.). *The Balanced Scorecard – measures that drive performance. Harvard Business Review*.

Kaplan, R., & Norton, D. (2004). *Strategy Maps: Converting Intangible Assets into Tangible Outcomes*. Harvard Business School Press.

Kaplan Financial Limited. (2012a). *Financial Management*. BPP Learning Media.

Kaplan Financial Limited. (2012b). *Advanced Financial Management.* BPP Learning Media.

Kavadias, S., Ladas, K., & Loch, C. (2016, Oct.). The Transformative Business Model. *Harvard Business Review.*

Kelly, K. (1997). New Rules for the New Economy. *Wired Magazine.* Available at https://kk.org/mt-files/books-mt/KevinKelly-NewRules-withads.pdf

Koller, T., Debbs, R., & Huyett, B. (2010). *The Four Cornerstones of Corporate Finance.* John Wiley & Sons.

Koller, T., Goedhart, M., & Wessels, D. (2005). *Valuation: Measuring and Managing the Value of Companies.* John Wiley & Sons.

Koller, T., Goedhart, M., & Wessels, D. (2010). *Valuation: Measuring and Managing the Value of Companies.* John Wiley & Sons.

Koller, T., Goedhart, M., & Wessels, D. (2015). *Valuation: Measuring and Managing the Value of Companies.* John Wiley & Sons.

Kothandaraman, P., & Wilson, D. T. (2001). The future of competition: Value-creating networks. *Industrial Marketing Management, 30*(4), 379–389. doi:10.1016/S0019-8501(00)00152-8

KPMG. (1999). A Core Competency Approach to Valuing Intangible Assets. *International Symposium Measuring and Reporting Intellectual Capital: Experiences, Issues and Prospects Amsterdam.*

Ladd, T. (2016, Mar.). The Limits of the lean start-up method. *Harvard Business Review.*

Leahy, T. (2000, June). Making their Mark. *Business of Finance.*

Lev, B. (2001). *Intangibles: Management, Measurement, and Reporting.* Brookings Institution Press.

Lev, B., & Daum, J. (2004). The dominance of intagible assets: Consequences for enterprise management and corporate reporting. *Measuring Business Excellence, 8*(1), 6–17. doi:10.1108/13683040410524694

Lev, B., & Gu, F. (2016). *The End of and the Path Forward for Investors and Managers.* Wiley.

Luehrman, T. A. (1998, Sept.). *Strategy as a Portfolio of Real Options. Harvard Business Review.*

Madden, B. (2010). *Wealth Creation: a Systems Mindset for Building and Investing in Business for the Long-Term.* John Wiley and Sons. doi:10.1002/9781118267769

Madden, B. J. (1999). *CFROI Valuation (Cash Flow Return On Investment, A Total System Approach To Valuing The Firm).* Butterworth-Heinemann.

Martin, J. D., & Petty, J. W. (2000). Value Based Management – The corporate response to the shareholder revolution. Harvard Business School Press.

McGrath, R., & MacMillan, I. (1995, July). *Discovery-driven planning. Harvard Business Review.*

McTaggart, J. M., Kontes, P. W., & Mankins, M. (1994). *The Value Imperative.* The Free Press.

Moore, J. F. (2006). Business ecosystems and the view from the firm. *Antitrust Bulletin*, *51*(1), 31–76. doi:10.1177/0003603X0605100103

Osterwalder, A., & Pigneur, Y. (2008). *Business Model Generation*. John Wiley and Sons.

Ovans, A. (2015, Jan.). *What Is a Business Model? Harvard Business Review*.

Petrisor, P., & Cozmiuc, D. (2015). The Paradox Of Investment: Constraining Strategy. *Proceedings of the 9th International Management Conference, Management and Innovation For Competitive Advantage*.

Pisano, G., P. (2015, June). You Need an innovation strategy. *Harvard Business Review*.

Powell, W. W., & Snellman, K. (2004). The Knowledge Economy. *Annual Review of Sociology*, *30*(1), 199–220. doi:10.1146/annurev.soc.29.010202.100037

Prahalad, C. K., & Krishnan, M. S. (2008). *The New Age of Innovation: Driving Co-Created Value Through Global Networks*. McGraw-Hill.

Project Management Institute. (2013). *A Guide to the Project Management Body of Knowledge (PM-BOK® Guide)* (6th ed.). Project Management Institute.

Rappaport, A. (1986). *Creating Shareholder Value*. The Free Press.

Ries, E. (2010). *Introduction to Customer Development at the Lean Startup Intensive at Web 2.0 Expo by Steve Blank*. Retrieved on May 26th, from: https://www.slideshare.net/startuplessonslearned/introduction-to-customer-development-at-the-lean-startup-intensive-at-web-20-expo-by-steve-blank

Ries, E. (2011). *The Lean Startup: How Today's Entrepreneurs Use Continuous Innovation to Create Radically Successful Businesses*. Retrieved on May 26th, from: https://www.amazon.com/Lean-Startup-Entrepreneurs-Continuous-Innovation/dp/0307887898

Satell, G. (2017a, Mar.). This Program Uses Lean Startup Techniques to Turn Scientists into entrepreneurs. *Harvard Business Review*.

Satell, G. (2017b, June). The Types of Innovation and the Problems. *Harvard Business Review*.

Siemens. (1998). *Siemens annual report*. Retrieved on May 26th, from: https://www.siemens.com/investor/pool/en/investor_relations/downloadcenter/gb1998_d_1365091.pdf

Siemens. (2002a). *Corporate Responsibility Report 2002*. Retrieved on May 26th, 2019, from: https://www.siemens.com/investor/pool/en/investor_relations/downloadcenter/CR-Report_2002_en.pdf

Siemens. (2002b). *Siemens annual report*. Retrieved on May 26th, 2019, from: https://web.lib.aalto.fi/fi/old/yrityspalvelin/pdf/2002/Esiemens2002.pdf

Siemens. (2006). *Siemens annual report*. Retrieved on May 26th, 2019, from: https://web.lib.aalto.fi/fi/old/yrityspalvelin/pdf/2006/Esiemens2006.pdf

Siemens. (2010). *Siemens annual report*. Retrieved on May 26th, 2019, from: https://www.siemens.com/investor/pool/en/investor_relations/siemens_ar_2010.pdf

Siemens. (2011). *Opening innovation*. Retrieved on May 26th, from: https://www.slideshare.net/heisss/opening-innovation-7436014

Siemens. (2011). *Siemens annual report*. Retrieved on May 26th, 2019, from: https://www.siemens.com/investor/pool/en/investor_relations/siemens_ar_2011.pdf

Siemens. (2012). *Siemens annual report*. Retrieved on May 26th, 2019, from: https://www.siemens.com/investor/pool/en/investor_relations/siemens_ar_2012.pdf

Siemens. (2013a). *Siemens annual report*. Retrieved on May 26th, 2019, from: https://www.siemens.com/annual/13/en/download/pdf/Siemens_AR2013.pdf

Siemens. (2013b). *Innovation in an Enterprise 2.0*. Retrieved on May 26th, 2019, from: https://www.slideshare.net/heisss/innovation-in-an-enterprise-20

Siemens. (2014a). *From big data to smart data*. Retrieved on May 26th, 2019, from: https://w3.siemens.com/topics/global/en/events/hannover-messe/program/Documents/pdf/Smart-Data-to-Business-Michal-Skubacz.pdf

Siemens. (2014b). *Open Co-Ideation @ Siemens. An Innovation approach to connecting an organization's knowledge and creativity*. Retrieved on May 26th, 2019, from: https://studylib.net/doc/18616093/open-co-ideation-%40-siemens

Siemens. (2014c). *PM@Siemens. Integrated Project Management*. Retrieved on May 26th, from: http://ipma.it/ipma_/images/E._Delogu_Siemens_Presentation_Evento_ANIMA-ANIMP_03.05.16.pdf

Siemens. (2014d). *Siemens annual report*. Retrieved on May 26th, 2019, from: https://www.siemens.com/annual/14/en/download/pdf/Siemens_AR2014.pdf

Siemens. (2014e). *Siemens – Vision 2020*. Retrieved on May 26th, 2019, from: https://www.siemens.com/investor/pool/en/investor_relations/financial_publications/speeches_and_presentations/140529_bernstein_ny_presentation.pdf

Siemens. (2015a). *The digital change constant*. Retrieved on May 26th, 2019, from: https://www.siemens.com/press/pool/de/events/2015/corporate/2015-09-analyst-conference/presentation-kayser-e.pdf

Siemens. (2015b). *Siemens annual report*. Retrieved on May 26th, 2019, from: https://www.siemens.com/investor/pool/en/investor_relations/Siemens_AR2015.pdf

Siemens. (2015c). *Web of Systems for a digital world*. Retrieved on May 26th, 2019, from: https://www.siemens.com/press/pool/de/events/2015/corporate/2015-12-internet-of-things/presentation-iot-russwurm_web-of-systems-e.pdf

Siemens. (2016a). *Corporate Technology. Our central research and development unit*. Retrieved on May 26th, 2019, from: https://www.siemens.com/content/dam/internet/siemens-com/global/company/innovation/innovation/corporate-technology/pdf/CT-Standardpresentation_E_March_2017.pdf

Siemens. (2016b). *next47*. Retrieved on May 26th, 2019, from: https://www.siemens.com/press/pool/de/feature/2016/corporate/2016-06-next47/presentation-next47-e.pdf

Siemens. (2016c). *Siemens Digitalization Strategy & Sinalytics Platform*. Retrieved on May 26th, 2019, from: https://www.siemens.com/digitalisierung/public/pdf/Sinalytics-and-Digital-Services-Presentation.pdf

Siemens. (2016d). *We enable digitalization*. Retrieved on May 26th, 2019, from: https://slideplayer.com/slide/13046746/

Siemens. (2017a). *Digitalization @ Siemens*. Retrieved on May 26th, 2019, from: https://www.automationsummit.se/wp-content/uploads/2017/10/7-%E2%80%93-Mimmi-Alladin.pdf

Siemens. (2017b). *Innovations*. Retrieved on May 26th, 2019, from: https://www.siemens.com/global/en/home/company/innovation/pictures-of-the-future/innovations.html

Siemens. (2017c). *Siemens annual report*. Retrieved on May 26th, 2019, from: https://www.siemens.com/investor/pool/en/investor_relations/Siemens_AR2017.pdf

Siemens. (2017d). *Siemens PLM Software: Innovation for the future*. Retrieved on May 26th, 2019, from: http://www.ctecno.cat/wp-content/uploads/2015/09/Siemens-PLM-Innovation-for-the-future-keynote-mi-X17.pdf

Siemens. (2017e). *Siemens Vision 2020 – Focus on profitable growth*. Retrieved on May 26th, 2019, from: https://www.siemens.com/investor/pool/en/investor_relations/financial_publications/speeches_and_presentations/170322_presentation_bofaml_conference.pdf

Siemens. (2018a). *Empowering the Digital Transformation via Digitalization within the Integrated Lifecycle*. Retrieved on May 26th, 2019, from: https://www.nist.gov/sites/default/files/documents/2018/04/09/3se1_deren_siemens_empowering_dig_transf_via_digitalization_in_the_integrated_lifecycle.pdf

Siemens. (2018c). *Vision 2020+ Shaping the future Siemens*. Retrieved on May 26th, 2019, from: https://www.siemens.com/investor/pool/en/investor_relations/financial_publications/speeches_and_presentations/q32018/180802_Press_Analyst_Conference.pdf

Siemens. (2019a). *Project finance*. Retrieved on May 26th, 2019, from: https://new.siemens.com/global/en/products/financing/project-finance.html

Siemens. (2019b). *Project Management made by Siemens*. Retrieved on May 26th, 2019, from: https://w3.siemens.com/mcms/engineering-consulting/en/services_/engineering/project-management/pages/project-management.aspx

Siemens. (2019c). *Siemens Venture Capital*. Retrieved on May 26th, 2019, from: https://www.startus.cc/company/siemens-venture-capital

Stegmann, P. (2009). *Strategic Value Management: Stock Value Creation and the Management of the Firm*. Wiley. doi:10.1002/9781118268087

Stern, G. M., Shiely, J. S., & Ross, J. (2003). *The EVA Challenge. Implementing Value-Added in an Organization*. Wiley.

Stewart, G. B. (1991). *The Quest for Value*. Harper Collins.

Van Alstyne, M. W., Parker, G. G., & Choudary, S. P. (2016, Apr.). Pipelines, platforms, and the new rules of strategy. *Harvard Business Review*.

Wendee, P. M. (2011). A Theory of Value Drivers: a Grounded Theory Study. University of Phoenix.

Westerman, G., Bonnet, D., & McAfee, A. (2014). *Leading Digital: Turning Technology Into Business Transformation*. Harvard Business Review Press.

World Economic Forum. (2019). *An introduction to the Digital Transformation of Industries initiative*. Retrieved on May 26th, from: http://reports.weforum.org/digital-transformation/an-introduction-to-the-digital-transformation-initiative/

Zhao, F. (2004). Siemens' business excellence model and sustainable development. *Measuring Business Excellence*, *8*(2), 55–64. doi:10.1108/13683040410539436

## ADDITIONAL READING

CapGemeni. (2018). *Digital Transformation Review Twelfth Edition. Taking Digital Transformation to the Next Level,* retrieved on July 10th, 2020, from https://www.capgemini.com/wp-content/uploads/2019/02/Report-Digital-%E2%80%93-DTR12.pdf

Collins, D., & Junker, T. (2017, February). Digitalization at Siemens. *Harvard Business Review*.

IDC. (2020). *Worldwide Digital Transformation Strategies*. Retrieved on July 10th, 2020, from https://www.idc.com/getdoc.jsp?containerId=IDC_P32570

Khosrow-Pour, M. (2017). Encyclopedia of Information Science and Technology (4th ed.). (Vols. 1–10). IGI Global.

Lakhani, K. (2013, June). ROpen Innovation at Siemens. *Harvard Business Review*.

Lakhani, K. R., Iansiti, M., & Herman, K. (2014, April). GE and the Industrial Internet. *Harvard Business Review*.

Lal, R., & Johson, S. (2017, February). GE Digital. *Harvard Business Review*.

Shih, W. (2016, May). Building the Digital Manufacturing Enterprise of the Future at Siemens. *Harvard Business Review*.

World Economic Forum. (2016). *World Economic Forum White Paper. Digital Transformation of Industries: In collaboration with Accenture*, retrieved on July 10th, 2020, from https://www.accenture.com/_acnmedia/Accenture/Conversion-Assets/WEF/PDF/Accenture-Digital-Enterprise.pdf

World Economic Forum. (2017). *Digital Transformation Initiative. In collaboration with Accenture*, retrieved on July 10th, 2020, from https://www.accenture.com/_acnmedia/Accenture/Conversion-Assets/WEF/PDF/Accenture-DTI-executive-summary.pdf

## KEY TERMS AND DEFINITIONS

**Customer Value:** The sum total of benefits which a vendor promises a customer will receive in return for the customer's associated payment (or other value-transfer).

**Customer Value Creation:** The organizational processes which lead to benefits for the customers.

**Customer Value Delivery:** The organizational processes that assure the customer receives and acknowledges this value.

**Digitalization:** A series of technologies, mainly defined by IDC's third platform, and their use in organizations and society with a purpose, for example value.

**Value Creation:** The decisions which generate value thoughout the organization.

**Value Driver:** Key performance indicators directly or indirectly linked to shareholder value; in a broad sense, factors which impact value directly or indirectly.

**Value Indicator:** The corporate governance indicator all decisions are aligned to in value-based management, the net present value of discounted cash flow or economic value added.

# Compilation of References


Abyad, A. (2017). Importance of Consumer Trust in e-commerce. *Middle East Journal of Business*, *12*(3), 20–24. doi:10.5742/MEJB.2017.92971

Accenture. (2019). *Digital transformation turns every business into a digital business*. Retrieved on May 26th, 2019, from: https://www.accenture.com/ro-en/service-digital-transformation

Achille, A., Marchessou, S., & Remy, N. (2018). *Luxury in the Age of Digital Darwinism*. Academic Press.

Achuthan, S. (2016). E-commerce Buying Behavior in India: The Role of Website Features in E-loyalty. *South Asian Journal of Management*, *23*(1), 56–88.

Agarwal, A., & Yadav, V. K. (2015). Impact of Technology in E-Retailing Operations: A Consumer Perspective. *Procedia: Social and Behavioral Sciences*, *189*, 252–258. doi:10.1016/j.sbspro.2015.03.220

Agndal, H., & Axelsson, B. (2002). Internationalisation of the firm – The influence of relationship sediments. In V. Havila, M. Forsgren, & H. Håkansson (Eds.), *Critical perspectives on internationalisation* (pp. 437–456). Pergamon.

Alan, M., Armando, P., Benedetta, C., & Giuseppe, R. (2016). Evaluating the innovation of the Internet of Things. *Business Process Management Journal*, *22*(2), 341–356.

Alavi, M., & Leidner, D. E. (2001). Knowledge management and knowledge management systems: Conceptual foundations and research issues. *Management Information Systems Quarterly*, *25*(1), 107–136. doi:10.2307/3250961

Ali, M. R., Nelson, J., & Freedman, M. (2017). *Blockstack: A Decentralized Internet*. Retrieved from https://blockstack.org/whitepaper.pdf

Alkis, Y., Kadirhan, Z., & Sat, M. (2017). Development and validation of social anxiety scale for social media users. *Computers in Human Behavior*, *72*, 296–303. doi:10.1016/j.chb.2017.03.011

AllenD. (2016). *Discovering and Developing the Blockchain Cryptoeconomy*. Retrieved from https://ssrn.com/abstract=2815255

Almeida, D., Santos, M. A. R., & dos e Costa, A. F. B. (2010). Aplicação do coeficiente alfa de Cronbach nos resultados de um questionário para avaliação de desempenho da saúde pública. XXX Encontro Nacional de Engenharia de Produção, Anais da Associação Brasileira de Engenharia de Produção, 1 - 12.

Aloysius, J. A., Hoehle, H., & Venkatesh, V. (2016). Exploiting big data for customer and retailer benefits: A study of emerging mobile checkout scenarios. *International Journal of Operations & Production Management*, *36*(4), 467–486.

Amin, M. N., & Habib, A. (2015). Comparison of Different Classification Techniques Using WEKA for Hematological Data. *American Journal of Engineering Research*, (43), 2320–2847.

Amin, S. H., Razmi, J., & Zhang, G. (2011). Supplier Selection and Order Allocation Based on Fuzzy SWOT Analysis and Fuzzy Linear Programming. *Expert Systems with Applications*, *38*(1), 334–342. doi:10.1016/j.eswa.2010.06.071

Amit, R., & Schoemaker, P. J. (1993). Strategic assets and organizational rent. *Strategic Management Journal*, *14*(1), 33–46. doi:10.1002mj.4250140105

Amit, R., & Zott, C. (2001). Value creation in e-business. *Strategic Management Journal*, *22*(6/7), 493–520. doi:10.1002mj.187

Amit, R., & Zott, C. (2012). Creating value through business model innovation. *Sloan Management Review*, *53*(3), 41–49.

Amit, R., & Zott, C. (2015). Crafting business architecture: The antecedents of business model design. *Strategic Entrepreneur. J.*, *9*(4), 331–350. doi:10.1002ej.1200

Amorim, P., Curcio, E., Almada-Lobo, B., Barbosa-Póvoa, A. P. F. D., & Grossmann, I. E. (2016). Supplier Selection in the Processed Food Industry under Uncertainty. *European Journal of Operational Research*, *252*(3), 801–814. doi:10.1016/j.ejor.2016.02.005

Andersen, O., & Buvik, A. (2002). Firms' internationalization and alternative approaches to the international customer/market selection. *International Business Review*, *11*(3), 347–363. doi:10.1016/S0969-5931(01)00064-6

Andersen, P. H., & Strandskov, J. (1997). International market selection: A cognitive mapping perspective. *Journal of Global Marketing*, *11*(3), 65–84. doi:10.1300/J042v11n03_05

Anderson, C. (2006). *The Long Tail: Why the Future of Business is Selling Less of More*. Hyperion.

Anderson, J. C., & Gerbing, D. W. (1988). Structural equation modeling in practice: A review and recommended two-step approach. *Psychological Bulletin*, *103*(3), 411–423. doi:10.1037/0033-2909.103.3.411

Andrea, C., Giacomo, M., & Matteo, P. M. (2016). The Internet of Things in manufacturing innovation processes. *Business Process Management Journal*, *22*(2), 383–402.

Andriulo, S., Elia, V., & Gnoni, M. G. (2015). Mobile self checkout systems in the FMCG retail sector: A comparison analysis. *International Journal of RF Technologies: Research and Applications*, *6*(4), 207–224. doi:10.3233/RFT-150067

Annushkina, O. E., & Trinca Colonel, R. (2013). Foreign market selection by Russian MNEs-beyond a binary approach? *Critical Perspectives on International Business*, *9*(1/2), 58–87. doi:10.1108/17422041311299950

Antonopoulos, A. (2016). *The Internet of Money*. Merkle Bloom LLC.

Araújo, M.S.G. & Lopes, P.M.P.R. (2014). Virtuous leadership, organizational commitment and individual performance. *Téckhene – Review of Applied Management Studies*, *12*, 3-10.

Arenius, P. (2005). The psychic distance postulate revised: From market selection to speed of market penetration. *Journal of International Entrepreneurship*, *3*(2), 115–131. doi:10.100710843-005-4203-6

Argyres, N. S., & Silverman, B. S. (2004). R&D, organization structure, and the development of corporate technological knowledge. *Strategic Management Journal*, *25*(8-9), 929–958. doi:10.1002mj.387

Arkin, R. M., & Ruck, L. (2007). Anxiety. In R. F. Baumeister & K. D. Vohs (Eds.), *Encyclopedia of Social Psychology* (pp. 42–43). Sage. doi:10.4135/9781412956253.n24

Arnold, G. (1998). *Corporate Financial Management*. Pitman Publishing.

Arnould, E. J., & Price, L. L. (1993). River Magic: Extraordinary Experience and the Extended Service Encounter. *The Journal of Consumer Research*, *20*(1), 24–55. doi:10.1086/209331

Arthur, R. (2019, April 18). Louis Vuitton Becomes Latest Luxury Brand to Launch a Chatbot. *Forbes*.

Ashraf, A. R., Thongpapanl, N., & Spyropoulou, S. (2016). The Connection and Disconnection between E-commerce Businesses and Their Customers: Exploring the Role of Engagement, Perceived Usefulness, and Perceived Ease-of-use. *Electronic Commerce Research and Applications*, *20*, 69–86. doi:10.1016/j.elerap.2016.10.001

Astley, W. G., & Brahm, R. (1989). Organizational designs for post-industrial strategies: The role of interorganizational collaboration. In C. C. Snow (Ed.), *Strategy, organization design, and human resource management* (pp. 233–270). JAE.

Atwal, G., & Williams, A. (2009). Luxury brand marketing–the experience is everything! *Journal of Brand Management*, *16*(5-6), 338–346. doi:10.1057/bm.2008.48

Avolio, B. J. (2007). Promoting more integrative strategies for leadership theory-building. *The American Psychologist*, *62*(1), 25–33. doi:10.1037/0003-066X.62.1.25 PMID:17209677

Azadnia, A. H., Muhamad, Z. M. S., & Wong, K. Y. (2015). Sustainable Supplier Selection and Order Lot-Sizing: An Integrated Multi-Objective Decision-Making Process. *International Journal of Production Research*, *53*(2), 383–408. doi:10.1080/00207543.2014.935827

Baker, W., & Sinkula, J. (2005). Market orientation and the new product paradox. *Journal of Product Innovation Management*, *22*(6), 483–502. doi:10.1111/j.1540-5885.2005.00145.x

Baker, W., & Sinkula, J. (2007). Does market orientation facilitate balanced innovation programs? An organizational learning perspective. *Journal of Product Innovation Management*, *24*(4), 316–334. doi:10.1111/j.1540-5885.2007.00254.x

Bandura, A. (1986). *Social foundations of thought and action: A social cognitive theory*. Prentice-Hall.

Bandyopadhyay & Saha. (2018). *Unsupervised Classification*. Academic Press.

Banzato, C. R., & Sierra, J. C. V. (2016). Implications of Theory and Research on Strategic Leadership: A Critical Review. *Revista Ibero-Americana de Estratégia*, *15*(03), 119–131. doi:10.5585/riae.v15i3.2331

BarnesS. (2017). Understanding Virtual Reality in Marketing: Nature, Implications and Potential. doi:10.2139srn.2909100

Barney, J. B., & Hesterly, W. S. (2010). VRIO framework. *Strategic Management and Competitive Advantage*, 68-86.

Barney, J. (1991). Firm resources and sustained competitive advantage. *Journal of Management*, *17*(1), 99–120. doi:10.1177/014920639101700108

Barney, J. B. (1995). Looking inside for competitive advantage. *The Academy of Management Perspectives*, *9*(4), 49–61. doi:10.5465/ame.1995.9512032192

Barsh, J., Mogelof, J., & Webb, C. (2010). How centered leaders achieve extraordinary results. *The McKinsey Quarterly*.

Bart, Y., Shankar, V., Sultan, F., & Urban, G. L. (2005). Are the drivers and role of online trust the same for all web sites and consumers? A large-scale exploratory empirical study. *Journal of Marketing*, *69*(4), 133–152. doi:10.1509/jmkg.2005.69.4.133

Barwitz, N., & Maas, P. (2018). Understanding the omnichannel customer journey: Determinants of interaction choice. *Journal of Interactive Marketing*, *43*, 116–133. doi:10.1016/j.intmar.2018.02.001

Bass, B. M. (1990). From Transactional to Transformational Leadership: Learning to Share the Vision. *Organizational Dynamics*, *18*(3), 19–32. doi:10.1016/0090-2616(90)90061-S

Batat, W. (2017). *Luxe et expérience client*. Dunod.

Baum, J. A., & Haveman, H. A. (1997). Love thy neighbor? Differentiation and agglomeration in the Manhattan hotel industry, 1989–1990. *Administrative Science Quarterly*, *42*(2), 304–338. doi:10.2307/2393922

Baxendale, S., Macdonald, E. K., & Wilson, H. N. (2015). The impact of different touchpoints on brand consideration. *Journal of Retailing*, *91*(2), 235–253. doi:10.1016/j.jretai.2014.12.008

Becker, J., & Hamburg, C. (1999). Market oriented management: A system based perspective. *Journal of Market Focused Management*, *4*(1), 17–41. doi:10.1023/A:1009804011447

Belegundu, A. D., & Chandrupatla, T. R. (2011). *Optimization Concepts and Applications in Engineering* (2nd ed., Vol. 34). doi:10.1017/CBO9780511975905

Ben Letaifa, S. (2014). The uneasy transition from supply chains to ecosystems: The value-creation/value-capture dilemma. *Management Decision*, *52*(2), 278–295. doi:10.1108/MD-06-2013-0329

Benlian, A., Montréal, H. E. C., & Hess, T. (2012). Differential Effects of Provider Recommendation and Consumer Reviews In E-commerce Transaction: An Experimental Study. *Journal of Management Information Systems*, *29*(1), 1–47. doi:10.2753/MIS0742-1222290107

Bennet, N., & Lemoine, G. J. (2014, Jan.). *What VUCA really means for you. Harvard Business Review.*

Bennett, N., & Lemoine, G. J. (2014a). What a difference a word makes: Understanding threats to performance in a VUCA world. *Business Horizons*, *57*(3), 311–317. doi:10.1016/j.bushor.2014.01.001

Bennett, N., & Lemoine, J. (2014b). What VUCA really means for you. *Harvard Business Review*, *92*(1/2), 27.

Berinto, S. (2014a, Sept.). *A Framework for understanding VUCA. Harvard Business Review.*

Bernardo, A., & Welch, I. (2001). On the evolution of overconfidence and entrepreneurs. *Journal of Economics & Management Strategy*, *10*(3), 301–330. doi:10.1162/105864001316907964

Bernheim, B. D., & Whinston, M. D. (1990). Multimarket contact and collusive behavior. *The RAND Journal of Economics*, *21*(1), 1–26. doi:10.2307/2555490

Berson, Y., & Linton, J. D. (2005). An examination of the relationships between leadership style, quality, and employee satisfaction in R&D versus administrative environments. *R & D Management*, *35*(1), 51–60. doi:10.1111/j.1467-9310.2005.00371.x

Bhattacharya, A., Srivastava, M., & Verma, S. (2019). Customer experience in online shopping: A strutural modeling approach. *Journal of Global Marketing*, *32*(1), 3–16. doi:10.1080/08911762.2018.1441938

Bhimani, H., Mention, A. L., & Barlatier, P. J. (2019). Social media and innovation: A systematic literature review and future research directions. *Technological Forecasting and Social Change*, *144*, 251–269. doi:10.1016/j.techfore.2018.10.007

Bhuiyan, M. S. H., Choudhury, I. A., & Dahari, M. (2014). Monitoring the Tool Wear, Surface Roughness and Chip Formation Occurrences Using Multiple Sensors in Turning. *Journal of Manufacturing Systems*, *33*(4), 476–487. doi:10.1016/j.jmsy.2014.04.005

Biggs, Lloyd, & Wilson. (1986). Graph Theory, 1736-1936. Clarendon Press.

Bikhchandani, S., Hirshleifer, D., & Welch, I. (1998). Learning from the behavior of others: Conformity, fads, and informational cascades. *The Journal of Economic Perspectives*, *12*(3), 151–170. doi:10.1257/jep.12.3.151

Bilgeri, D., Gebauer, H., Fleisch, E., & Wortmann, F. (2019). Driving process innovation with IoT field data. *MIS Quarterly Executive*, *18*(3), 191–207. doi:10.17705/2msqe.00016

Black, A., Wright, P., & Bachman, J. (1998). *In search of Shareholder Value. Managing the Drivers of Performance.* Pitman Publishing.

Blank, S. (2013, May). Why the Lean Start-Up Changes Everything. *Havard Business Review.*

Boal, K. B., & Hooijberg, R. (2000). Strategic leadership research: Moving on. *The Leadership Quarterly, 11*(4), 515–549. doi:10.1016/S1048-9843(00)00057-6

Bonchek, M., & Choudary, S. P. (2013, Jan.). Three Elements of a Successful Platform Strategy. *Harvard Business Review.*

Boston Consulting Group. (2008). *Value creators report.* Retrieved on May 26th, 2019, from: https://www.bcg.com/documents/file15314.pdf

Boston Consulting Group. (2015a). *Industry 4.0: The Future of Productivity and Growth in Manufacturing Industries.* Retrieved on May 26th, from: https://www.bcgperspectives.com/content/articles/engineered_products_project_business_industry_40_future_productivity_growth_manufacturing_industries/?chapter=2

Botes, M., & Pretorius, M. (2020). Exploring management perceptions of competitive versus transient advantage. *Journal of Contemporary Management, 17*(1), 41–63. doi:10.35683/jcm19052.55

Boucher, P. (2017). *How blockchain technology could change our lives.* European Parliamentary Research Service. Retrieved Apr 13, 2017, from https://www.europarl.europa.eu/RegData/etudes/IDAN/2017/581948/EPRS_IDA(2017)581948_EN.pdf

Bouchet, P., & Pulh, M. (2006). *L'expérience Vécue: Un Autre Regard sur l'Analyse du Comportement du Consommateur.* Paper presented at the 5èmes Journées Normandes de Recherche sur la Consommation: Société et consommations, Caen.

Brandão, A., Pinho, E., & Rodrigues, P. (2019). Antecedents and consequences of luxury brand engagement in social media. *Spanish Journal of Marketing-ESIC, 23*(2), 163–183. doi:10.1108/SJME-11-2018-0052

Brandenburg, M., Govindan, K., Sarkis, J., & Seuring, S. (2014). Quantitative Models for Sustainable Supply Chain Management: Developments and Directions. *European Journal of Operational Research, 233*(2), 299–312. doi:10.1016/j.ejor.2013.09.032

Bresser, R., & Millonig, K. (2003). Institutional capital: Competitive advantage in light of the new institutionalism in organization theory. *Schmalenbach Business Review, 55*(3), 220–241. doi:10.1007/BF03396675

Brettel, M., Strese, S., & Flatten, C. T. (2012). Improving the performance of business models with relationship marketing efforts – an entrepreneurial perspective. *European Management Journal, 30*(2), 85–98. doi:10.1016/j.emj.2011.11.003

Brockhoff, K. K., Korch, G., & Pearson, A. W. (1997). Business process re-engineering: Experiences in R&D. *Technology Analysis and Strategic Management, 9*(2), 163–178. doi:10.1080/09537329708524277

Brooks, J. (2015). *Virtual Reality: Advancing Marketing Research… and Visualizing a Better World.* Lieberman Research Worldwide.

Brown, M. E., & Treviño, L. K. (2006). Ethical leadership: A review and future directions. *The Leadership Quarterly, 17*(6), 595–616. doi:10.1016/j.leaqua.2006.10.004

Burke, R. R. (2002). Technology and the customer interface: What consumers want in the physical and virtual store. *Journal of the Academy of Marketing Science, 30*(4), 411–432. doi:10.1177/009207002236914

Cachin, C. (2017). *Blockchain, cryptography, and consensus.* Retrieved from https://www.zurich.ibm.com/~cca/talks/20170622-blockchain-ice.pdf

Çadırcı, T. O., & Köse, Ş. G. (2016). Augmented reality as a tool to enhance the experiential value of online shopping: The future of fashion retailing. In *Handbook of research on global fashion management and merchandising* (pp. 280–304). IGI Global. doi:10.4018/978-1-5225-0110-7.ch012

Cadwalladr, C., & Graham-Harrison, E. (2018). Revealed: 50 million Facebook profiles harvested for Cambridge Analytica in major data breach. *The Guardian, 17*, 22.

CapGemeni. (2013). *Digital transformation: a roadmap for billion-dollar organizations.* Digital Transformation Review No. 1.

CapGemeni. (2015). *Strategies for the Age of Digital Disruption.* Digital Transformation Review No. 7.

CapGemeni. (2016). *The Digital Strategy Imperative: Steady Long-Term Vision, Nimble Execution.* Digital Transformation Review No. 9.

Carter, C. R., Rogers, D. S., & Choi, T. Y. (2015). Toward the Theory of the Supply Chain. *The Journal of Supply Chain Management, 51*(2), 89–97. doi:10.1111/jscm.12073

Casadesus-Masanell, R., & Ricart, J. E. (2011, Jan.). How to design a winning business model. *Harvard Business Review*, 1–9.

Casadesus-Masanell, R., & Ricart, J. E. (2011, Jan.). *How to Design a winning business model. Harvard Business Review.*

Castañeda, J. A., Muñoz-Leiva, F., & Luque, T. (2007). Web Acceptance Model (WAM): Moderating effects of user experience. *Information & Management, 44*(4), 384–396. doi:10.1016/j.im.2007.02.003

Cavallo, M. (2016,). *Accueil: IMODEV - Improving public policies. Sharing economy, sharing information. Are open data addressing us towards a new wikieconomy?* Retrieved on March 12th, 2017, from http://ojs.imodev.org/index.php/RIDDN/article/view/145/201

Cavusgil, S. T. (1985). Guidelines for export market research. *Business Horizons, 28*(6), 27–33. doi:10.1016/0007-6813(85)90082-5

Caywood, C., Schultz, D. E., & Wang, P. (1991). *Integrated Marketing Communications.* Northwestern University Medill School of Journalism.

Cegarra-Navarro, J. G. (2005). An empirical investigation of organizational learning through strategic alliances between SMEs. *Journal of Strategic Marketing, 13*(1), 3–16. doi:10.1080/0965254042000328686

Chandra, S. K. (1993). Sustainability of Social Service Sector Programmes in India. *The Indian Journal of Public Administration, 39*(3), 498–502. doi:10.1177/0019556119930329

Chase & Rademacher. (2008). A Benchmark Study of Optimization Search Algorithms. *Red Cedar,* 1–15.

Chen, J., Teng, L., Yu, Y., & Yu, X. (2015). The effect of online information sources on purchase intentions between consumers with high and low susceptibility to informational influence. *Journal of Business Research, 69*(2), 467–475. doi:10.1016/j.jbusres.2015.05.003

Chen, S., & Dhillon, G. (2003). Interpreting dimensions of consumer trust in e-commerce. *Information Technology and Management, 4*(2-3), 303–318. doi:10.1023/A:1022962631249

Chesbrough, H. (2001). Assembling the elephant: A review of empirical studies on the impact of technical change upon incumbent firms. *Research on Technological Innovation, Management and Policy, 7*, 1–36.

Chesbrough, H. (2007). Business model innovation: It's not just about technology anymore. *Strategy and Leadership, 35*(6), 12–17. doi:10.1108/10878570710833714

Chesbrough, H. W. (2003). *Open innovation: the new imperative for creating and profiting from technology*. Harvard Business School Press.

Chesbrough, H. W., & Rosenbloom, R. S. (2002). The role of the business model in capturing value from innovation: Evidence from Xerox Corporation's technology spinoff companies. *Industrial and Corporate Change, 11*(3), 533–534. doi:10.1093/icc/11.3.529

Child, J., & Rodriguez, S. B. (2005). The Internationalization of Chinese Firms: A Case for Theoretical Extension? *Management and Organization Review, 1*(3), 381–410. doi:10.1111/j.1740-8784.2005.0020a.x

Chin, W. W. (2010). How to write up and report PLS analyses. In V. Esposito Vinzi, W. W. Chin, J. Henseler, & H. Wang (Eds.), *Handbook of partial least squares: Concepts, methods and applications* (pp. 655–690). Springer. doi:10.1007/978-3-540-32827-8_29

Chiu, C. M., Lin, H. Y., Sun, S. Y., & Hsu, M. H. (2009). Understanding customers' loyalty intentions towards online shopping: An integration of technology acceptance model and fairness theory. *Behaviour & Information Technology, 28*(4), 347–360. doi:10.1080/01449290801892492

Choi, S. B., Ullah, S. M. E., & Kwak, W. J. (2015). Ethical Leadership and Followers' Attitudes Toward Corporate Social Responsibility: The Role of Perceived Ethical Work Climate. *Social Behavior and Personality, 43*(3), 353–365. doi:10.2224bp.2015.43.3.353

Choudhary, D., & Shankar, R. (2013). Joint Decision of Procurement Lot-Size, Supplier Selection, and Carrier Selection. *Journal of Purchasing and Supply Management, 19*(1), 16–26. doi:10.1016/j.pursup.2012.08.002

Christidis, K., & Devetsikiotis, M. (2016). Blockchains and smart contracts for the internet of things. *IEEE Access: Practical Innovations, Open Solutions, 4*, 2292–2303. doi:10.1109/ACCESS.2016.2566339

Christodoulides, G., & Michaelidou, N. (2011). Shopping motives as antecedents of e-satisfaction and e-loyalty. *Journal of Marketing Management, 27*(1–2), 181–197.

Chuen, K., & David, L. E. E. (2017). *Fintech Tsunami: Blockchain as the Driver of the Fourth Industrial Revolution*. Academic Press.

Clarkson, J. J., Janiszewski, C., & Cinelli, M. D. (2013). The desire for consumption knowledge. *The Journal of Consumer Research, 39*(6), 1313–1329. doi:10.1086/668535

Cohen, W. M., & Levinthal, D. A. (1990). Absorptive capacity: A new perspective on learning and innovation. *Administrative Science Quarterly, 35*(1), 128–152. doi:10.2307/2393553

Collins, D. J., & Junker, T. (2018). *Digitalization at Siemens*. Harvard Business School Case 717-428.

Colorni, Dorigo, & Maniezzo. (1992). An Investigation of Some Properties of an 'Ant Algorithm.' *Ppsn, 92*, 509–20.

Cong, L. W., He, Z., & Zheng, J. (2017). *Blockchain Disruption and Smart Contracts*. Rtetrieved from https://papers.ssrn.com/sol3/Data_Integrity_Notice.cfm?abid=2985764

Copeland, T. E., Koller, T. M., & Murrin, J. (1994). *Valuation: Measuring and Managing the Value of Companies*. John Wiley & Sons.

Copeland, T. E., Koller, T. M., & Murrin, J. (2000). *Valuation, Measuring and managing the value of companies* (3rd ed.). John Wiley and Sons.

Corbin, J., & Strauss, A. (2008). Basics of Qualitative Research (3rd ed.). Thousand Oaks: Sage.

Corbitt, B. J., Thanasankit, T., & Yi, H. (2003). Trust and e-commerce: A study of consumer perceptions. *Electronic Commerce Research and Applications*, *2*(3), 203–215. doi:10.1016/S1567-4223(03)00024-3

Cozmiuc, D., & Petrisor, P. (2018a). *Innovation in the Age of Digital Disruption: The Case of Siemens. In Handbook of Research on Strategic Innovation Management for Improved Competitive Advantage*. IGI Global. doi:10.4018/978-1-5225-3012-1.ch025

Cozmiuc, D., & Petrisor, P. (2018b, January-March). Industrie 4.0 by Siemens: Steps Made Next. *Journal of Cases on Information Technology*, *20*(1), 31–46. doi:10.4018/JCIT.2018010103

Cozmiuc, D., & Petrisor, P. (2018c, April-June). Industrie 4.0 by Siemens: Steps Made Today. *Journal of Cases on Information Technology*, *20*(2), 30–48. doi:10.4018/JCIT.2018040103

Crosby, M., Nachiapan, P., Verma, S., & Kalyanaraman, V. (2016). Blockchain Technology: Beyond Bitcoin. *Applied Innovation Review*. Retrieved from: http://scet.berkeley.edu/wp-content/uploads/AIR-2016-Blockchain.pdf

Curran, P. J., West, S. G., & Finch, J. F. (1996). The robustness of test statistics to nonnormality and specification error in confirmatory factor analysis. *Psychological Methods*, *1*(1), 16–29. doi:10.1037/1082-989X.1.1.16

D'Arpizio, C., Prete, F., & de Montgolfier, J. (2019). *Luxury Goods Worldwide Market Study, Fall-Winter 2018*. Academic Press.

D'Aveni, R. A. (1998). Waking up to the new era of hypercompetition. *The Washington Quarterly*, *21*(1), 183–195. doi:10.1080/01636609809550302

D'Aveni, R. A., & Gunther, R. E. (1995). *Hypercompetitive rivalries: Competing in highly dynamic environments*. Free Pr.

Damodaran, A. (2007). *Return on Capital (ROC), Return on Invested Capital (ROIC), and Return on Equity (ROE): Measurement and Implications*. New York University Stern School of Business.

Damodaran, A. (2010). *Applied Corporate Finance*. Wiley.

Damodaran, A. (2011). *Damodaran on Valuation: Security Analysis for Investment and Corporate Finance*. Wiley.

Damodaran, A. (2012). *Investment Valuation: Tools and Techniques for Determining the Value of Any Asset*. Wiley.

Daum, J. H. (2003). *Intangible Assets and Value Creation*. Wiley.

Davenport, T. (1993). *Process Innovation: Reengineering work through information technology*. Harvard Business School Press.

Davenport, T. (1995). *Reengineering – The Fad That Forgot People*. Fast Company.

Davenport, T., & Short, J. (1990). The new industrial engineering: Information technology and business process redesign. *Sloan Management Review*, *31*(4), 1–31.

Davezies, Ph. (1998). De la récupération psychique. *Santé et Travail*, *25*, 35–37.

Davidson, S., De Filippi, P., & Potts, J. (2016). *Economics of blockchain*. Retrieved from https://papers.ssrn.com/sol3/papers.cfm?abstract_id=2744751

Davies, B. J., & Davies, B. (2004). Strategic leadership, Advancing the Organization from Planning to Reality. *School Leadership*, *70*(1), 57–38. doi:10.1080/1363243042000172804

Davis, P., Desai, A., & Francis, J. (2000). Mode of International Entry: An Isomorphism Perspective. *Journal of International Business Studies*, *31*(2), 239–258. doi:10.1057/palgrave.jibs.8490904

De Filippi, P., & Reymond, M. (2016). *La Blockchain: comment réguler sans autorité*. Retrieved from https://archive-ouverte.unige.ch/unige:90735

Deephouse, D. L. (1999). To be different, or to be the same? It's a question (and theory) of strategic balance. *Strategic Management Journal*, *20*(2), 147–166. doi:10.1002/(SICI)1097-0266(199902)20:2<147::AID-SMJ11>3.0.CO;2-Q

Delios, A., Gaur, A. S., & Makino, S. (2008). The timing of international expansion: Information, rivalry and imitation among Japanese firms, 1980–2002. *Journal of Management Studies*, *45*(1), 169–195.

Deloitte. (2015). *Omni-channel retail A Deloitte point of view*. Retrieved from https://www2.deloitte.com/content/dam/Deloitte/se/Documents/ /Omni-channel-2015.pdf

Deng, X., Hu, Y., Deng, Y., & Mahadevan, S. (2014). Supplier Selection Using AHP Methodology Extended by D Numbers. *Expert Systems with Applications*, *41*(1), 156–167. doi:10.1016/j.eswa.2013.07.018

Deshpandé, R. (1999). *Developing a Market Orientation*, MSI. *Sage (Atlanta, Ga.)*.

Deshpandé, R., & Farley, J. (1998). Measuring market orientations: Generalization and synthesis. *Journal of Market Focused Management*, *2*(3), 213–232. doi:10.1023/A:1009719615327

Deshpandé, R., Farley, J., & Webster, F. Jr. (1993). Corporate culture, customer orientation and innovativeness in Japanese firms: A quadrat analysis. *Journal of Marketing*, *75*(1), 23–37. doi:10.1177/002224299305700102

Deshpandé, R., & Webster, F. Jr. (1989). Organizational culture and marketing: Defining the research agenda. *Journal of Marketing*, *53*(1), 3–15. doi:10.1177/002224298905300102

Dholakia, U. M., Kahn, B. E., Reeves, R., Rindfleisch, A., Stewart, D., & Taylor, E. (2010). Consumer behavior in a multichannel, multimedia retailing environment. *Journal of Interactive Marketing*, *24*(2), 86–95.

Diamantopoulos, A. (2005). The C-OAR-SE procedure for scale development in marketing: A comment. *International Journal of Research in Marketing, 22*(9).

Diamantopoulos, A., & Hart, S. (1993). Linking market orientation and company performance: Preliminary evidence on Kohli and Jaworski's framework. *Journal of Strategic Marketing*, *1*(2), 93–121. doi:10.1080/09652549300000007

Dijkmans, C., Kerkhof, P., & Beukeboom, C. J. (2015). A stage to engage: Social media use and corporate reputation. *Tourism Management*, *47*(5), 58–67. doi:10.1016/j.tourman.2014.09.005

DiMaggio, P., & Powell, W. (1983). The Iron Cage revisited: Institutional isomorphism and colective rationality in organizational fields. *American Sociological Review*, *48*(2), 147–160. doi:10.2307/2095101

Dobni, C. B., & Luffman, G. (2003). Determining the scope and impact of market orientation profiles on strategy implementation and performance. *Strategic Management Journal*, *24*(6), 577–585. doi:10.1002mj.322

Doty, J., & Fenlason, J. (2015, May-June). It's Not About Trust; It's About Thinking and Judgment. *Military Review*, 78–83.

Dow, D., & Karunaratna, A. (2006). Developing a Multidimensional Instrument to Measure Psychic Distance Stimuli. *Journal of International Business Studies*, *37*(5), 578–602. doi:10.1057/palgrave.jibs.8400221

Drucker, P. F. (1993). *Managing in turbulent times*. Routledge.

Du, B., Guo, S., Huang, X., Li, Y., & Guo, J. (2015). A Pareto Supplier Selection Algorithm for Minimum the Life Cycle Cost of Complex Product System. *Expert Systems with Applications*, *42*(9), 4253–4264. doi:10.1016/j.eswa.2015.01.056

Dulčić, Ž., Gnjidić, V., & Alfirević, N. (2012). From Five Competitive Forces to Five Collaborative Forces: Revised View on Industry Structure-firm Interrelationship. *Procedia: Social and Behavioral Sciences*, *58*, 1077–1084. doi:10.1016/j.sbspro.2012.09.1088

Dyer, J., & Nobeoka, K. (2000). Creating and managing a high-performance knowledge-sharing network: The Toyota case. *Strategic Management Journal*, *21*(3), 345–367. doi:10.1002/(SICI)1097-0266(200003)21:3<345::AID-SMJ96>3.0.CO;2-N

Editora, P. (2016). *Dicionário da Língua Portuguesa*. Porto Editora.

Edvinsson, L. (2002). *Corporate Longitude - What You Need to Know to Navigate the Knowledge Economy*. Financial Times Prentice Hall.

Edvinsson, L., & Malone, M. (1997). *Intellectual Capital*. Harper Business.

Eisenhardt, K. M., & Martin, J. A. (2000). Dynamic capabilities: What are they? *Strategic Management Journal*, *21*(10-11), 1105–1121. doi:10.1002/1097-0266(200010/11)21:10/11<1105::AID-SMJ133>3.0.CO;2-E

Elenkov, D. S., Judge, W., & Wright, P. (2005). Strategic leadership and executive innovation influence: An international multi-cluster comparative study. *Strategic Management Journal*, *26*(7), 665–682. Advance online publication. doi:10.1002mj.469

Elg, U. (2007). Market orientation processes in retailing: A cross-national study. *European Journal of Marketing*, *41*(5/6), 568–589. doi:10.1108/03090560710737615

Ellis, P. (2000). Social ties and foreign market entry. *Journal of International Business Studies*, *31*(3), 443–469. doi:10.1057/palgrave.jibs.8490916

eMarketer. (2016). *Virtual Reality Is an Immersive Medium for Marketers: Marketers should start experimenting sooner rather than later*. Retrieved February 10, 2017 from: https://www.emarketer.com/Article/Virtual-Reality-Immersive-Medium-Marketers/1013526

Eroglu, S. A., Machleit, K., & Barr, T. F. (2005). Perceived retail crowding and shopping satisfaction: The role of shopping values. *Journal of Business Research*, *58*(8), 1146–1153. doi:10.1016/j.jbusres.2004.01.005

Erramilli, M. K., & Rao, C. P. (1990). Choice of Foreign Market Entry Mode by Service Firms: Role of Market Knowledge. *International Marketing Review*, *7*(5), 60–72.

Eskandarpour, M., Dejax, P., Miemczyk, J., & Péton, O. (2015). Sustainable Supply Chain Network Design: An Optimization-Oriented Review. *Omega (United Kingdom)*, *54*, 11–32. doi:10.1016/j.omega.2015.01.006

European Parliament. (2016). Regulation (EU) 2016/679 of the European Parliament and of the Council. *Regulation*, *679*, 2016.

Eyring, M., Johnson, M. W., & Nair, H. (2011, Jan.). *New business models in emerging markets. Harvard Business School.*

Fabian, A. P. F., Molina, H., & Labianca, G. (2009). Understanding Decisions to Internationalize by Small and Medium-sized Firms Located in an Emerging Market. *Management International Review*, *49*(5), 537–563. doi:10.100711575-009-0007-6

Fahimnia, B., Farahani, R. Z., & Sarkis, J. (2013). Integrated Aggregate Supply Chain Planning Using Memetic Algorithm – A Performance Analysis Case Study. *International Journal of Production Research*, *51*(18), 5354–5373. doi:10.1080/00207543.2013.774492

Fahimnia, B., Sarkis, J., & Davarzani, H. (2015). Green Supply Chain Management: A Review and Bibliometric Analysis. *International Journal of Production Economics*, *162*, 101–114. doi:10.1016/j.ijpe.2015.01.003

Falk, R. F., & Miller, N. B. (1992). *A primer for soft modelling*. University of Akron Press.

Falk, T., Hammerschmidt, M., & Schepers, J. J. (2010). The service quality-satisfaction link revisited: Exploring asymmetries and dynamics. *Journal of the Academy of Marketing Science*, *38*(3), 288–302. doi:10.100711747-009-0152-2

Fazlollahtabar, H. (2016). Integration between Fuzzy PROMETHEE and Fuzzy Linear Program for Supplier Selection Problem: Case Study. *Journal of Applied Mathematical Modelling and Computing*, *1*(1), 8.

Ferdman, B. M., Barrera, V., Allen, A., & Vuong, V. (2009, August). Inclusive behaviors and the experience of inclusion. In B. G. Chung (Chair), *Inclusion in organizations: Measures, HR practices, and climate*. Symposium presented at the 69th Annual Meeting of the Academy of Management, Chicago.

Fernandes, T., & Remelhe, P. (2015). How to engage customers in co-creation: Customers' motivations for collaborative innovation. *Journal of Strategic Marketing*, *24*(3-4), 311–326.

Ferry, K. (2017, Mar.). How Organizations Can Thrive in the Digital Economy. *Harvard Business Review*.

Fitza, M. A. (2014). The use of variance decomposition in the investigation of CEO effects: How large must the CEO effect be to rule out chance? *Strategic Management Journal*, *35*(12), 1839–1852. doi:10.1002mj.2192

Fletcher, M., & Harris, S. (2012). Knowledge acquisition for the internationalization of the smaller firm: Content and sources. *International Business Review*, *21*(4), 631–647. doi:10.1016/j.ibusrev.2011.07.008

Flint, G. F. (2000). What is the meaning of competitive advantage? *Advances in Competitiveness Research*, *8*(1), 121–129.

Foley, A., & Fahy, J. (2009). Seeing market orientation through a capabilities lens. *European Journal of Marketing*, *43*(1/2), 13–2. doi:10.1108/03090560910923201

Fornell, C., & Bookstein, F. L. (1982). Two structural equation models: LISREL and PLS applied to consumer exit-voice theory. *JMR, Journal of Marketing Research*, *19*(4), 440–452. doi:10.1177/002224378201900406

Fornell, C., & Larcker, D. F. (1981). Evaluating structural equation models with unobservable variables and measurement error. *JMR, Journal of Marketing Research*, *8*(1), 39–50. doi:10.1177/002224378101800104

Forsgren, M., & Kinch, N. (1970). The adaptation of the firm to changes in surrounding systems. Department of Business Studies, Uppsala.

Foss, N. J., & Saebi, T. (2017). Fifteen years of research on business model innovation. *Journal of Management*, *43*(1), 200–227. doi:10.1177/0149206316675927

Frey, R., Wörner, D., & Ilic, A. (2016). *Collaborative Filtering on the Blockchain: A Secure Recommender System for e-Commerce*. Retrieved from https://aisel.aisnet.org/amcis2016/ISSec/Presentations/36/

Friedman, T. L. (2005). *The World Is Flat: A Brief History of the Twenty-First Century*. Farrar, Straus and Giroux.

Fue, Z., Li, H., & Wenyu, D. (2009). Social factors in user perceptions and responses to advertising in online social networking communities. *Journal of Interactive Advertising*, *10*(1), 1–13. doi:10.1080/15252019.2009.10722159

Fung, R. K. K., & Lee, M. K. O. (1990). Electronic commerce trust: Exploring the antecedents factors. *Proceedings of the Association for Information Systems Americas Conference*, 489-491.

Gabarino, E., & Johnson, M. (1999). The different roles of satisfaction, trust, and commitment in customer relationships. *Journal of Marketing*, *63*(2), 70–87. doi:10.1177/002224299906300205

Ganesh, J., Reynolds, K. E., Luckett, M., & Pomirleanu, N. (2010). Online shopper motivations, and e-store attributes: An examination of online patronage behavior and shopper typologies. *Journal of Retailing*, *86*(1), 106–115. doi:10.1016/j.jretai.2010.01.003

Garcia, D. J., & You, F. (2015). Supply Chain Design and Optimization: Challenges and Opportunities. *Computers & Chemical Engineering*, *81*, 153–170. doi:10.1016/j.compchemeng.2015.03.015

Gardial, S. F., Clemons, D. S., Woodruff, R. B., Schumann, D. W., & Burns, M. J. (1994). Comparing consumers' recall of prepurchase and postpurchase product evaluation experiences. *The Journal of Consumer Research*, *20*(4), 548–560. doi:10.1086/209369

Gardner, M. P., & Rook, D. W. (1988). Effects of impulse purchases on consumers' affective states. NA -Advances in Consumer Research, (15), 127-130.

Gartner. (2019). *IT Glossary*. Retrieved on May 26th, 2019, from: https://www.gartner.com/it-glossary/digitalization/

Gassmann, O., Frankenberger, K., & Csik, M. (2013). *The St. Gallen Business Model Navigator. Working Paper.* University of St. Gallen.

Geem, Z. W., Woo, Z., Kim, J. H. J. H., & Loganathan, G. V. (2001). A New Heuristic Optimization Algorithm: Harmony Search. *Simulation*, *76*(2), 60–68. doi:10.1177/003754970107600201

Gefen, D., Karahanna, E., & Straub, D. W. (2003). Inexperience and experience with online stores: The importance of TAM and trust. *IEEE Transactions on Engineering Management*, *50*(3), 307–321. doi:10.1109/TEM.2003.817277

Gelbrich, K., & Sattler, B. (2014). Anxiety, crowding, and time pressure in public self-service technology acceptance. *Journal of Services Marketing*, *28*(1), 82–94. doi:10.1108/JSM-02-2012-0051

Gensler, S., Verhoef, P. C., & Böhm, M. (2012). Understanding consumers' multichannel choices across the different stages of the buying process. *Marketing Letters*, *23*(4), 987–1003. doi:10.100711002-012-9199-9

Gentile, C., Spiller, N., & Noci, G. (2007). How to sustain the customer experience: An overview of experience components that co-create value with the customer. *European Management Journal*, *25*(5), 395–410. doi:10.1016/j.emj.2007.08.005

Gerdoçi, B., Bortoluzzi, G., & Dibra, S. (2017). Business model design and firm performance: Evidence of interactive effects from a developing economy. *European Journal of Innovation Management*. Doi.org/10.1108/EJIM-02-2017-0012

Geyskens, I., Steenkamp, J.-B. E. M., & Kumar, N. (1998). Generalization about trust in marketing channel relationships using meta-analysis. *International Journal of Research in Marketing*, *15*(3), 223–248. doi:10.1016/S0167-8116(98)00002-0

Ghadimi, Dargi, & Heavey. (2017). Making Sustainable Sourcing Decisions: Practical Evidence from the Automotive Industry. *International Journal of Logistics Research and Applications*.

Ghadimi, P., & Heavey, C. (2014). Sustainable Supplier Selection in Medical Device Industry: Toward Sustainable Manufacturing. Procedia CIRP. doi:10.1016/j.procir.2014.06.096

Ghadimi, P., Toosi, F. G., & Heavey, C. (2018). A Multi-Agent Systems Approach for Sustainable Supplier Selection and Order Allocation in a Partnership Supply Chain. *European Journal of Operational Research*, *269*(1), 286–301. doi:10.1016/j.ejor.2017.07.014

Ghemawat, P., & Thomas, C. (2008). Strategic Interaction Across Countries and Multinational Agglomeration: An Application to the Cement Industry. *Management Science*, *54*(12), 1–32. doi:10.1287/mnsc.1080.0917

Ghorbani, M., Bahrami, M., & Mohammad Arabzad, S. (2012). An Integrated Model For Supplier Selection and Order Allocation; Using Shannon Entropy, SWOT and Linear Programming. *Procedia: Social and Behavioral Sciences, 41*, 521–527. doi:10.1016/j.sbspro.2012.04.064

Gil, A. C. (2008). *Métodos e técnicas de pesquisa social* (6th ed.). Atlas.

Gillard, J. W., & Kvasov, D. E. (2016). Lipschitz Optimization Methods for Fitting a Sum of Damped Sinusoids to a Series of Observations. *Statistics and Its Interface, 10*(1), 59–70. doi:10.4310/SII.2017.v10.n1.a6

Gimeno, J., & Chen, M. J. (1998). The dynamics of competitive positioning: A pair-wise perspective. Academy of Management Proceedings, 1–8.

Gimeno, J., Hoskisson, R. E., Beal, B. D., & Wan, W. P. (2005). Explaining the clustering of international expansion moves: A critical test in the U.S. telecommunications industry. *Academy of Management Journal, 48*(2), 297–319. doi:10.5465/amj.2005.16928411

Gino, F., Brooks, A., & Schweitzer, M. E. (2012). Anxiety, Advice, and the Ability to Discern: Feeling Anxious Motivates Individuals to Seek and Use Advice. *Journal of Personality and Social Psychology, 102*(3), 497–512. doi:10.1037/a0026413 PMID:22121890

Girotra, K., & Netessine, S. (2013). *Business Model Innovation for Sustainability*. INSEAD Working Paper No. 2013/77/TOM.

Glanz, J. (2010). Justice and Caring: Power, Politics and Ethics in Strategic Leadership. *International Studies in Educational Administration, 38*(1), 66–87.

Global Center for Digital Business Transformation. (2019a). *Digital vortex*. Retrieved on May 26th, 2019, from: https://www.imd.org/dbt/digital-business-transformation/

Global Center for Digital Business Transformation. (2019b). *Orchestrating Transformation*. Retrieved on May 26th, from: https://www.imd.org/research-knowledge/books/orchestrating-transformation/

Gomez, M., McLaughlin, E., & Wittink, D. (2004). Customer satisfaction and retail sales performance: An empirical investigation. *Journal of Retailing, 80*(4), 265–278. doi:10.1016/j.jretai.2004.10.003

Gonçalves, M. V. (2020). *A Holistic Approach to Emerging and Frontier MNE's Internationalization: A New Conceptual Research Framework*. Paper presented at the Conference on Academic and Business Collaboration across Borders: A Focus on Emerging and Developing Countries, Casablanca, Morocco.

Gonçalves, M. V., & Smith, E. C. (2019). Internationalisation strategies of African MNEs: A case analysis of Angolan and Mozambican enterprises. *International Journal of Export Marketing, 3*(1), 59–76. doi:10.1504/IJEXPORTM.2019.101809

Gören, H. G. (2018). A Decision Framework for Sustainable Supplier Selection and Order Allocation with Lost Sales. *Journal of Cleaner Production, 183*, 1156–1169. doi:10.1016/j.jclepro.2018.02.211

Gossain, G., & Kandiah, S. (1998). Reinventing value: The new business ecosystem. *Strategy and Leadership, 26*(5).

Grant, R. M. (1991). The resource-based theory of competitive advantage: Implications for strategy formulation. *California Management Review, 33*(3), 114–135. doi:10.2307/41166664

Gray, B. J., & Hooley, G. J. (2002). Market orientation and service firm performance – a research agenda. *European Journal of Marketing, 36*, 980–988. doi:10.1108/03090560210437280

Gray, B., Matear, S., Boshoff, C., & Matheson, P. (1998). Developing a better measure of market orientation. *European Journal of Marketing, 32*(9/10), 884–903. doi:10.1108/03090569810232327

Greenley, G. E. (1995). Market orientation and company performance: Empirical evidence from UK companies. *British Journal of Management*, *6*(1), 1–13. doi:10.1111/j.1467-8551.1995.tb00082.x

Gripsrud, G., & Benito, G. (2005). Internationalization in retailing: Modelling the pattern of foreign market entry. *Journal of Business Research*, *58*(12), 1672–1680. doi:10.1016/j.jbusres.2004.11.003

Grossman, R. (2016, Mar.). The Industries that are being disrupted the most by digital. *Harvard Business Review*.

Grundy, T. (2006). Rethinking and reinventing Michael Porter's five forces model. *Strategic Change*, *15*(5), 213–229. doi:10.1002/jsc.764

Guelfand, G. (2013). *Les études qualitatives: fondamentaux, méthodes, analyse, techniques*. Éditions EMS. doi:10.3917/ems.guelf.2013.01

Guenther, M. (2012). *Intersection: How Enterprise Design Bridges the Gap between Business, Technology, and People*. Newnes.

Guillén, M. (2002). Structural inertia, imitation, and foreign expansion: South Korean firms and business groups in China, 1987–1995. *Academy of Management Journal*, *45*(3), 509–525. doi:10.5465/3069378

Gunasekaran, A., & Ngai, E. W. T. (2014). Expert Systems and Artificial Intelligence in the 21st Century Logistics and Supply Chain Management. *Expert Systems with Applications*, *41*(1), 1–4. doi:10.1016/j.eswa.2013.09.006

Guo, C., & Li, X. (2014). A Multi-Echelon Inventory System with Supplier Selection and Order Allocation under Stochastic Demand. *International Journal of Production Economics*, *151*, 37–47. doi:10.1016/j.ijpe.2014.01.017

Guo, C., & Wang, Y. (2015). How manufacturer market orientation influences B2B customer satisfaction and retention: Empirical investigation of the three market orientation components. *Journal of Business and Industrial Marketing*, *30*(2), 182–193. doi:10.1108/JBIM-03-2012-0042

Gupta, A., & Maranas, C. D. (2003). Managing Demand Uncertainty in Supply Chain Planning. Computers and Chemical Engineering. doi:10.1016/S0098-1354(03)00048-6

Gupta, A., Su, B.-C., & Walter, Z. (2004). An empirical study of consumer switching from traditional to electronic channels: A purchase-decision process perspective. *International Journal of Electronic Commerce*, *8*(3), 131–161. doi:10.1080/10864415.2004.11044302

Gupta, D., & Gupta, V. (2018). Effective Policing in a VUCA Environment: Lessons from a Dark Network. In *Flexible Strategies in VUCA Markets* (pp. 89–111). Springer. doi:10.1007/978-981-10-8926-8_7

Gupta, G., Tan, K. T. L., Ee, Y. S., & Phang, C. S. C. (2018). Resource-based view of information systems: Sustainable and transient competitive advantage perspectives. *AJIS. Australasian Journal of Information Systems*, *22*, 22. doi:10.3127/ajis.v22i0.1657

Gurt, J., Schwennen, C., & Elke, G. (2011). Health-specific leadership: Is there an association between leader consideration for the health of employees and their strain and well-being? *Work and Stress*, *25*(2), 108–127. doi:10.1080/02678373.2011.595947

Gyrard, A. (2014). *Domain knowledge Interoperability to build the Semantic Web of Things.* W3C Web of Things Workshop, Berlin, Germany

Haavisto, P. (2012). *Social media discussion forums and product innovation - The way forward?* Retrieved from https://journals.uic.edu/ojs/index.php/fm/article/view/3984/3332

Hachin, G., Dubois, B., Jourda, M.-C., & Besse, J. (2014). *Expérience Client: les clés pour réussir la transformation*. Academic Press.

Hadley, R. D., & Wilson, H. M. (2003). The network model of internationalisation and experimental knowledge. *International Business Review*, *12*(6), 697–717. doi:10.1016/j.ibusrev.2003.01.001

Hahn, R., Speith, P., & Ince, I. (2018). Business model design in sustainable entrepreneurship: Illuminating the commercial logic of hybrid businesses. *Journal of Cleaner Production*, *176*, 439–451. doi:10.1016/j.jclepro.2017.12.167

Hair, J. F., Anderson, R. E., Tatham, R. L., & Black, W. C. (2006). *Multivariate Data Analysis* (6th ed.). Pearson, Prentice-Hall.

Hair, J., Black, W., Babin, B., & Anderson, R. (2010). *Multivariate Data Analysis: International Version*. Prentice Hall.

Hajli, M. (2013). A research framework for social commerce adoption. *Information Management & Computer Security*, *21*(3), 144–154. doi:10.1108/IMCS-04-2012-0024

Håkansson, H., & Snehota, I. (1989). No business is an island: The network concept of business strategy. *Scandinavian Journal of Management*, *5*(3), 187–200. doi:10.1016/0956-5221(89)90026-2

Hambrick, D. C. (2007). Upper echelons theory: An update. *Academy of Management Review*, *32*(2), 334–343. doi:10.5465/amr.2007.24345254

Hamdan, S., & Cheaitou, A. (2017). Supplier Selection and Order Allocation with Green Criteria: An MCDM and Multi-Objective Optimization Approach. *Computers & Operations Research*, *81*, 282–304. doi:10.1016/j.cor.2016.11.005

Hamel, G. (1998). Opinion: Strategy innovation and the quest for value. *Sloan Management Review*, *39*(2), 7–14.

Hanin, Y. L. (2010). Coping with Anxiety in Sport. In A. R. Nicholls (Ed.), *Coping in Sport: Theory, Methods, and Related Constructs* (pp. 159–175). Nova Science Publishers.

Han, J., Namwoon, K., & Rajendra, K. (1998). Market Orientation and Organizational Performance: Is Innovation a Missing Link? *Journal of Marketing*, *62*(4), 30–45. doi:10.1177/002224299806200403

Hansen, M. W., & Hoenen, A. K. (2018). Global Oligopolistic Competition and Foreign Direct Investment: Revisiting and Extending the Literature. *Critical Perspectives on International Business*, *12*(4), 369–387. doi:10.1108/cpoib-03-2014-0017

Harms, R., & Schiele, H. (2012). Antecedents and consequences of effectuation and causation in the international new venture creation process. *Journal of International Entrepreneurship*, *10*(2), 95–116. doi:10.100710843-012-0089-2

Harris, D. F. (2014). *The complete guide to writing questionnaires: How to get better information for better decisions*. I & M Press.

Harris, L. (1993). Benchmarking against the theory of market orientation. *Journal of Marketing*, *57*(3), 537–545.

Hausmann, A. (2012). Creating 'buzz': Opportunities and limitations of social media for arts institutions and their viral marketing. *International Journal of Nonprofit and Voluntary Sector Marketing*, *17*(3), 173–182. doi:10.1002/nvsm.1420

Helfat, C. E., & Lieberman, M. B. (2002). The birth of capabilities: Market entry and the importance of pre-history. *Industrial and Corporate Change*, *11*(4), 725–760. doi:10.1093/icc/11.4.725

Helfert, G., Ritter, T., & Walter, A. (2001). How does market orientation affect business relationships. *17th IMP conference*.

Henderson, S. (1998). No such thing as market orientation – a call for no more papers. *Management Decision*, *36*(9), 598–609. doi:10.1108/00251749810239487

Herhausen, D., Binder, J., Schoegel, M., & Herrmann, A. (2015). Integrating bricks with clicks: Retailer-level and channel-level outcomes of online–offline channel integration. *Journal of Retailing*, *91*(2), 309–325. doi:10.1016/j.jretai.2014.12.009

Hernandez, K. (2017). *Blockchain for Development–Hope or Hype?* Retrieved from https://opendocs.ids.ac.uk/opendocs/handle/123456789/15

Hernández, B., Jiménez, J., & Martín, M. J. (2010). Customer behavior in electronic commerce: The moderating effect of e-purchasing experience. *Journal of Business Research*, *63*(9–10), 964–971. doi:10.1016/j.jbusres.2009.01.019

He, X., Brouthers, K., & Filatotchev, I. (2018). Market orientation and export performance: The moderation of channel and institutional distance. *International Marketing Review*, *35*(2), 258–279. doi:10.1108/IMR-09-2015-0194

Hintu, S., Forsman, M., & Kock, S. (2002). Mission Impossible? Internaionalization without Social Networks. *Nordic Workshop on Interorganisational Research.*

Hirst, G., & Mann, L. (2004). A model of R&D leadership and team communication: The relationship with project performance. *R & D Management*, *34*(2), 147–160. doi:10.1111/j.1467-9310.2004.00330.x

Hoehle, H., Aloysius, J. A., Chan, F., & Venkatesh, V. (2018). Customers' tolerance for validation in omnichannel retail stores: Enabling logistics and supply chain analytics. *International Journal of Logistics Management*, *29*(2), 704–722. doi:10.1108/IJLM-08-2017-0219

Hoffman, D. L., & Novak, T. P. (1996). Marketing in hypermedia computer-mediated environments: Conceptual foundations. *Journal of Marketing*, *60*(3), 50–68. doi:10.1177/002224299606000304

Hogg, T. (2010). Inferring preference correlations from social networks. *Electronic Commerce Research and Applications*, *9*(1), 29–37. doi:10.1016/j.elerap.2009.04.006

Ho, L. P. K., Nguyen, C. N., Adhikari, R. P., Miles, M. P., & Bonney, L. (2018). Exploring market orientation, innovation, and financial performance in agricultural value chains in emerging economies. *Journal of Innovation and Knowledge*, *3*(3), 154–163. doi:10.1016/j.jik.2017.03.008

Holland, J. H. (1975). *Adaptation in Natural and Artificial Systems*. Academic Press.

Holland, S. (2020). Project Management in an Increasingly Fr (Agile). *WORLD (Oakland, Calif.).*

Hollingworth, P. (2016). *The Light and Fast Organisation: A new way of dealing with uncertainty*. John Wiley & Sons.

Homburg, C., Jozić, D., & Kuehnl, C. (2017). Customer experience management: Toward implementing an evolving marketing concept. *Journal of the Academy of Marketing Science*, *45*(3), 377–401. doi:10.100711747-015-0460-7

Homburg, C., & Pflesser, C. (2000). A Multiple-layer model of market-oriented organizational culture: Measurement issues and performance outcomes. *JMR, Journal of Marketing Research*, *37*(49), 449–462. doi:10.1509/jmkr.37.4.449.18786

Hörnell, E., & Vahlne, J. E. (1972). *The deciding factors on the choice of subsidiary sales company as the channel for exports*. Academic Press.

Horney, N., Pasmore, B., & O'Shea, T. (2010). Leadership Agility: A Business Imperative for a VUCA World. *People & Strategy*, *33*(4), 32–38. Retrieved from www.hrps.org

Horney, N., Pasmore, B., & O'Shea, T. (2010). Leadership agility: A business imperative for a VUCA world. *Human Resource Planning*, *33*(4), 34.

Huang, W. Y., & Dubinsky, A. J. (2014). Measuring customer pre-purchase satisfaction in a retail setting. *Service Industries Journal*, *34*(3), 212–229. doi:10.1080/02642069.2013.778249

Hu, B. (2014). Linking business models with technological innovation performance through organizational learning. *European Management Journal*, *32*(4), 587–595. doi:10.1016/j.emj.2013.10.009

Hu, B., & Chen, W. (2016). Business model ambidexterity and technological innovation performance: Evidence from China. *Technology Analysis and Strategic Management*, *28*(5), 583–600. doi:10.1080/09537325.2015.1122186

Hudson, S., Huang, L., Roth, M. S., & Madden, T. J. (2016). The influence of social media interactions on consumer–brand relationships: A three-country study of brand perceptions and marketing behaviors. *International Journal of Research in Marketing*, *33*(1), 27–41. doi:10.1016/j.ijresmar.2015.06.004

Hult, G., Hurley, R., & Knight, G. (2004). Innovativeness: Its antecedents and impact on business performance. *Industrial Marketing Management*, *33*(5), 429–438. doi:10.1016/j.indmarman.2003.08.015

Hunitie, M. (2018). Impact of strategic leadership on strategic competitive advantage through strategic thinking and strategic planning: A bi-meditational research. *Business: Theory and Practice*, *19*(0), 322–330. doi:10.3846/btp.2018.32

Hunt, S. D., & Lambe, C. J. (2000). Marketing's contribution to business strategy: Market orientation, relationship marketing and resource-advantage theory. *International Journal of Management Reviews*, *2*(1), 17–43. doi:10.1111/1468-2370.00029

Hwang, Y., & Kim, D. J. (2007). Customer self-service systems: The effects of perceived Web quality with service contents on enjoyment, anxiety, and e-trust. *Decision Support Systems*, *43*(3), 746–760. doi:10.1016/j.dss.2006.12.008

Iansiti, M., & Clark, K. B. (1994). Integration and dynamic capability: Evidence from product development in automobiles and mainframe computers. *Industrial and Corporate Change*, *3*(3), 557–605. doi:10.1093/icc/3.3.557

IDC. (2017a). *Digital Transformation*. Retrieved on May 26th, 2019, from: https://www.idc.com/promo/thirdplatform/digitaltransformation

IDC. (2017b). *Explore 3rd Platform Transformation*. Retrieved on May 26th, 2019, from: https://www.idc.com/prodserv/3rd-platform/

Idota, H., Bunno, T., & Tsuji, M. (2017). How social media enhances product innovation in Japanese firms. *Journal of Socionetwork Strategies*, *11*(1), 33–45. doi:10.100712626-017-0006-1

Idota, H., Ogawa, M., Bunno, T., & Tsuji, M. (2012). An empirical analysis of organizational innovation generated by ICT in Japanese SMEs. In S. Allegrezza & A. Dubrocard (Eds.), *Internet Econometrics* (pp. 259–287). Palgrave Macmillan. doi:10.1057/9780230364226_12

Idota, H., Taher, S. A., Bunno, T., & Tsuji, M. (2019). Conducting product innovation by using social media among Japanese firms. *STI Policy and Management Journal*, *4*(2), 153–166. doi:10.14203/STIPM.2019.176

Ilic, A., & Fleisch, E. (2016). *Augmented Reality and the Internet of Things*. Retrieved from https://www.research-collection.ethz.ch/bitstream/handle/20.500.11850/128476/eth-50534-01.pdf

Institute for Business Value. (2011). *Digital transformation. Creating new business models where digital meets physical.* Retrieved on May 26th, from: https://www-07.ibm.com/sg/manufacturing/pdf/manufacturing/Digital-transformation.pdf

International Organization for Standardization. (2017). *ISO 9000:2015*. Retrieved on May 26th, 2019, from: https://www.iso.org/obp/ui/#iso:std:iso:9000:ed-4:v1:en

Ireland, R. D., & Hitt, M. A. (2005). Achieving and maintaining strategic competitiveness in the 21st century: The role of trategic leadership. *The Academy of Management Executive*, *19*(4), 63–77. doi:10.5465/ame.2005.19417908

IScoop. (2019). *Digital transformation: online guide to digital business transformation*. Retrieved on May 26th, 2019, from: https://www.i-scoop.eu/digital-transformation/

IVV. (2018). Instituto do Vinho e da Vinha I. P. *Anuário*. Retrieved from: http://www.ivv.min-agricultura.pt/np4/Anuário

Jackson, P. (2010). Food stories: Consumption in an age of anxiety. *Cultural Geographies*, *17*(2), 147–165. doi:10.1177/1474474010363844

Jaime, G., Octav, N., Iulia, G., & Gheorghe, G. (2019). Big data analytics in industry 4.0: Sustainable industrial value creation, manufacturing process innovation, and networked production structures. *Journal of Self-Governance & Management Economics*, *7*(3), 34–40. doi:10.22381/JSME7320195

Jaleha, A. A., & Machuki, V. N. (2018). Strategic Leadership and Organizational Performance: A Critical Review of Literature. *European Scientific Journal ESJ*, *14*(35), 124–149. doi:10.19044/esj.2018.v14n35p124

Jaworski, B., & Kohli, A. (1993). Market orientation: Antecedents and consequences. *Journal of Marketing*, *57*(3), 53–57. doi:10.1177/002224299305700304

Jaworski, B., Kohli, A., & Sahay, A. (2000). Market-driven versus driving markets. *Academy of Marketing Science Journal*, *28*(1), 45–54. doi:10.1177/0092070300281005

Jensen, M. B., Johnson, B., Lorenz, E., Lundvall, B. Å., & Lundvall, B. A. (2016). Forms of knowledge and modes of innovation. *The learning economy and the economics of hope,* 155-182.

Jiang, P., & Rosenbloom, B. (2005). Customer intention to return online: Price perception, attribute-level performance, and satisfaction unfolding over time. *European Journal of Marketing*, *39*(1/2), 150–174. doi:10.1108/03090560510572061

Jin, B., Park, J. Y., & Kim, J. (2008). Cross-cultural examination of the relationships among firm reputation, e-satisfaction, e-trust, and e-loyalty. *International Marketing Review*, *25*(3), 324–337. doi:10.1108/02651330810877243

Johansen, B. (2012). Leaders make the future: ten new leadership skills for an uncertain world (2nd ed.). San Francisco: Academic Press.

Johanson, J., & Mattson, G. (1988). Internationalization in industrial systems-A network approach in global Competition. In *Prince Bertil Symposium at the Institute of International Business*. Stockholm School of Economics.

Johanson, J., & Vahlne, J. E. (1977). The internationalization process of the firm: A model knowledge development and increasing foreign market commitments. *Journal of International Business Studies*, *8*(1), 23–32. doi:10.1057/palgrave.jibs.8490676

Johansson, H. (1966). *Foreign Ownership in Norwegian Enterprises* [Utenländske eierintressen i norske bedrifter]. Academic Press.

Johnson, M., W., Christensen, C., M., & Kagermann, H. (2008, Dec.). Reinventing your business model. *Harvard Business Review.*

Johnson, G., Scholes, K., & Whittington, R. (2008). *Exploring corporate strategy: text & cases*. Pearson Education.

Johnson, M. W., Christensen, C. M., & Kagermann, H. (2008). Reinventing Your Business Model. *Harvard Business Review*, *86*(12).

Jonsen, K., Maznevski, M. L., & Schneider, S. (2011). Diversity and its not so diverse literature: An international perspective. *International Journal of Cross Cultural Management*, *11*(1), 35–62. doi:10.1177/1470595811398798

Jordaan, Y., Ehlers, L., & Grove, J. M. (2011). Advertising credibility across media channels: Perceptions of generation Y consumers. *Communicare*, *30*(1), 1–20.

Jung, H., Chen, F. F., & Jeong, B. (2008). Decentralized Supply Chain Planning Framework for Third Party Logistics Partnership. *Computers & Industrial Engineering*, *55*(2), 348–364. doi:10.1016/j.cie.2007.12.017

Jung, H., Jeong, B., & Lee, C.-G. (2008). An Order Quantity Negotiation Model for Distributor-Driven Supply Chains. *International Journal of Production Economics*, *111*(1), 147–158. doi:10.1016/j.ijpe.2006.12.054

Kaczorowska-Spychalska, D. (2017). Consumer perspective of omnichannel commerce. *Management*, *21*(2), 95–108. doi:10.1515/manment-2017-0007

Kaleja, P., & Kozlovská, M. (2016). Virtual reality as marketing tool for developer projects. *Czech Journal of Civil Engineering.*, *2016*(1), 64–70.

Kane, E. (2017). *Is Blockchain a General Purpose Technology?* Retrieved from https://ssrn.com/abstract=2932585

Kaplan Financial Limited. (2012a). *Financial Management*. BPP Learning Media.

Kaplan Financial Limited. (2012b). *Advanced Financial Management*. BPP Learning Media.

Kaplan, A. M., & Haenlein, M. (2010). Users of the world, unite! The challenges and opportunities of social media. *Business Horizons*, *53*(1), 59–68. doi:10.1016/j.bushor.2009.09.003

Kaplan, R., & Norton, D. (1992, Jan.). *The Balanced Scorecard – measures that drive performance. Harvard Business Review*.

Kaplan, R., & Norton, D. (2004). *Strategy Maps: Converting Intangible Assets into Tangible Outcomes*. Harvard Business School Press.

Karimi, J., Somers, M. T., & Bhattacherjee, A. (2007). The role of information systems resources in ERP capability building business process outcomes. *Journal of Management Information Systems*, *24*(2), 221–260. doi:10.2753/MIS0742-1222240209

Karl, P., Michael, B., & Eivor, O. (2014). Dialogical strategies for orchestrating strategic innovation networks: The case of the Internet of Things. *Information and Organization*, *24*(2), 106–127. doi:10.1016/j.infoandorg.2014.05.001

Karnani, A., & Wernerfelt, B. (1985). Multiple point competition. *Strategic Management Journal*, *6*(1), 87–96. doi:10.1002mj.4250060107

Kate, V., & Pavan, S. (2012). Social media and revenue management; where should the two meet*? Journal of Technology Management for Growing Economies.*, *3*(1), 33–46. doi:10.15415/jtmge.2012.31002

Katsifarakis, K. L. (2012). *Hydrology, Hydraulics and Water Resources Management: A Heuristic Optimization Approuch*. WIT Press.

Kavadias, S., Ladas, K., & Loch, C. (2016, Oct.). The Transformative Business Model. *Harvard Business Review*.

Keen, C., Wetzels, M., De Ruyter, K., & Feinberg, R. (2004). E-tailers versus retailers: Which factors determine consumer preferences. *Journal of Business Research*, *57*(7), 685–695. doi:10.1016/S0148-2963(02)00360-0

Kelloway, E. K., & Barling, J. (2010). Leadership development as an intervention in occupational health psychology. *Work and Stress*, *24*(3), 260–279. doi:10.1080/02678373.2010.518441

Kelly, K. (1997). New Rules for the New Economy. *Wired Magazine*. Available at https://kk.org/mt-files/books-mt/KevinKelly-NewRules-withads.pdf

Kennedy, J., & Eberhart, R. (1994). Particle Swarm Optimization. *Proceedings of ICNN'95 - International Conference on Neural Networks, 4*(10), 1942–48.

Keskin, G. A. (2015). Using Integrated Fuzzy DEMATEL and Fuzzy C: Means Algorithm for Supplier Evaluation and Selection. *International Journal of Production Research, 53*(12), 3586–3602. doi:10.1080/00207543.2014.980461

Kilic, H. S. (2013). An Integrated Approach for Supplier Selection in Multi-Item/Multi-Supplier Environment. *Applied Mathematical Modelling, 37*(14-15), 7752–7763. doi:10.1016/j.apm.2013.03.010

Kim, H., & Laskowski, M. (2016). *Towards an ontology-driven blockchain design for supply chain provenance*. Retrieved from https://papers.ssrn.com/sol3/papers.cfm?abstract_id=2828369

Kim, A. J., & Ko, E. (2012). Do social media marketing activities enhance customer equity? An empirical study of luxury fashion brand. *Journal of Business Research, 65*(10), 1480–1486. doi:10.1016/j.jbusres.2011.10.014

Kim, D. J., Ferrin, D. L., & Rao, H. R. (2008). A trust-based consumer decision-making model in electronic commerce: The role of trust, perceived risk, and their antecedents. *Decision Support Systems, 44*(2), 544–564. doi:10.1016/j.dss.2007.07.001

Kim, D. J., Song, Y. I., Braynov, S. B., & Rao, H. R. (2005). A multidimensional trust formation model in B-to-C e-commerce: A conceptual framework and content analyses of academia/practioner perspective. *Decision Support Systems, 40*(2), 143–165. doi:10.1016/j.dss.2004.01.006

Kim, J., & Lennon, S. J. (2013). Effects of reputation and website quality on online consumers' emotion, perceived risk and purchase intention: Based on the stimulus-organism-response model. *Journal of Research in Interactive Marketing, 7*(1), 33–56. doi:10.1108/17505931311316734

Kim, S. S., Malhotra, N. K., & Narasimhan, S. (2005). Research note—two competing perspectives on automatic use: A theoretical and empirical comparison. *Information Systems Research, 16*(4), 418–432. doi:10.1287/isre.1050.0070

Kiranyaz, S., Ince, T., & Gabbouj, M. (2014). Optimization Techniques: An Overview. *Adaptation, Learning, and Optimization, 15*, 13–44. doi:10.1007/978-3-642-37846-1_2

Kirca, A., Cavusgil, S., & Hult, G. (2009). The effects of national culture on market orientation: Conceptual framework and research propositions. *International Business Review, 18*(2), 111–118. doi:10.1016/j.ibusrev.2009.02.003

Klein, J. (2002). Beyond competitive advantage. *Strategic Change, 11*(6), 317–327. doi:10.1002/jsc.606

Knickerbocker, F. T. (1973). *Oligopolistic reaction and multinational enterprise*. Harvard Business School Press. doi:10.1002/tie.5060150205

Kobrin, S. J. (1979). Political risk: A review and reconsideration. *Journal of International Business Studies, 10*(1), 67–80. doi:10.1057/palgrave.jibs.8490631

Ko, C., Ma, J., Bartnik, R., Haney, M. H., & Kang, M. (2018). Ethical Leadership: An Integrative Review and Future Research Agenda. *Ethics & Behavior, 28*(2), 104–132. doi:10.1080/10508422.2017.1318069

Kohli, A., & Jaworski, B. (1990). Market Orientation: The Construct, Research Propositions, and Managerial Implications. *Journal of Marketing, 54*(2), 1–18. doi:10.1177/002224299005400201

Kohli, A., Jaworski, B., & Kumar, A. (1993). MARKOR a measure of market orientation. *JMR, Journal of Marketing Research, 30*(4), 467–477. doi:10.1177/002224379303000406

Koller, T., Debbs, R., & Huyett, B. (2010). *The Four Cornerstones of Corporate Finance*. John Wiley & Sons.

Kornelsen, J. (2019). The quest to lead (with) millennials in a VUCA-world: Bridging the gap between generations. In *Leading in a VUCA World* (pp. 27–41). Springer. doi:10.1007/978-3-319-98884-9_2

Kothandaraman, P., & Wilson, D. T. (2001). The future of competition: Value-creating networks. *Industrial Marketing Management*, *30*(4), 379–389. doi:10.1016/S0019-8501(00)00152-8

Kotler, P. (1967). *Marketing Management: Analysis, Planning, and Control*. Prentice-Hall.

Kotler, P. (1988). *Marketing Management*. Prentice Hall.

Kotler, P., & Keller, K. (2017). *Marketing Management, Student Value Edition* (15th ed.). Pearson.

Kotter, J. (2012). How the most innovative companies capitalize on today's rapid-fire strategic challenges-and still make their numbers. *Harvard Business Review*, *90*(11), 43–58. PMID:23155997

KPMG. (1999). A Core Competency Approach to Valuing Intangible Assets. *International Symposium Measuring and Reporting Intellectual Capital: Experiences, Issues and Prospects Amsterdam.*

Kriger, M., & Zhovtobryukh, Y. (2013). Rethinking strategic leadership: Stars, clans, teams and networks. *Journal of Strategy and Management*, *6*(4), 411–432. doi:10.1108/JSMA-09-2012-0051

Kuhlmeier, D., & Knight, G. (2005). Antecedents to internet-based purchasing: A Multinational study. *International Marketing Review*, *22*(4), 460–473. doi:10.1108/02651330510608460

Kulins, C., Leonardy, H., & Weber, C. (2016). A configurational approach in business model design. *Journal of Business Research*, *69*(4), 1437–1441. doi:10.1016/j.jbusres.2015.10.121

Kumar, M., Vrat, P., & Shankar, R. (2006). A Fuzzy Programming Approach for Vendor Selection Problem in a Supply Chain. *International Journal of Production Economics*, *101*(2), 273–285. doi:10.1016/j.ijpe.2005.01.005

Kumar, V., & Venkatesan, R. (2005). Who are the multichannel shoppers and how do they perform?: Correlates of multichannel shopping behavior. *Journal of Interactive Marketing*, *19*(2), 44–62. doi:10.1002/dir.20034

Kurtmollaiev, S. (2020). Dynamic capabilities and where to find them. *Journal of Management Inquiry*, *29*(1), 3–16. doi:10.1177/1056492617730126

Kusunoki, K., Nonaka, I., & Nagata, A. (1998). Organizational capabilities in product development of Japanese firms: A conceptual framework and empirical findings. *Organization Science*, *9*(6), 699–718. doi:10.1287/orsc.9.6.699

Kvasov, D. E., & Mukhametzhanov, M. S. (2018). Metaheuristic vs. Deterministic Global Optimization Algorithms: The Univariate Case. *Applied Mathematics and Computation*, *318*, 245–259. doi:10.1016/j.amc.2017.05.014

Ladd, T. (2016, Mar.). The Limits of the lean start-up method. *Harvard Business Review*.

Lambin, J. J. (1999). *Marketing Estratégico*. McGraw Hill.

Langeard, E., & Eiglier, P. (1987). *Servuction: Le marketing des services*. John Wiley & Sons.

Langerak, F. (2001). Effects of market orientation on the behaviours of salespersons and purchasers, channel relationships, and performance of manufacturers. *International Journal of Research in Marketing*, *18*(3), 221–234. doi:10.1016/S0167-8116(01)00040-4

Lawrence, K. (2013). Developing Leaders in a VUCA Environment. *UNC Executive Development*, 1–15.

Leahy, T. (2000, June). Making their Mark. *Business of Finance*.

Leahy, D., & Pavelin, S. (2003). Follow-my-leader FDI and tacit collusion. *International Journal of Industrial Organization, 21*(3), 439–453. doi:10.1016/S0167-7187(02)00091-7

Leavy, B. (2014). Strategy, organization and leadership in a new "transient-advantage" world. *Strategy and Leadership, 42*(4), 3–13. doi:10.1108/SL-05-2014-0038

Lee, A. H. I., Kang, H. Y., Chun, M. L., & Wan, Y. H. (2013). An Integrated Model for Lot Sizing with Supplier Selection and Quantity Discounts. *Applied Mathematical Modelling, 37*(7), 4733–4746. doi:10.1016/j.apm.2012.09.056

Lee, A. H. I., Kang, H. Y., & Ter Chang, C. (2009). Fuzzy Multiple Goal Programming Applied to TFT-LCD Supplier Selection by Downstream Manufacturers. *Expert Systems with Applications, 36*(3), 6318–6325. doi:10.1016/j.eswa.2008.08.044

Lee, C. K. H. (2018). A Review of Applications of Genetic Algorithms in Operations Management. *Engineering Applications of Artificial Intelligence, 76*(May), 1–12. doi:10.1016/j.engappai.2018.08.011

Lee, G., & Xia, W. (2006). Organizational size and IT innovation adoption: A meta-analysis. *Information & Management, 43*(8), 975–985. doi:10.1016/j.im.2006.09.003

Lee, H. L. (2018). Big Data and the innovation cycle. *Production and Operations Management, 27*(9), 1642–1646. doi:10.1111/poms.12845

Lee, K. O. M., & Turban, E. (2001). A trust model for consumer Internet shopping. *International Journal of Electronic Commerce, 6*(1), 75–91. doi:10.1080/10864415.2001.11044227

Lee, M. (2010). *The effect of cognitive absorption and network externalities on technology acceptance: an empirical study of social networking sites in Indonesia. Theses and dissertations.* Business Administration Department, University of Ming Chuan.

Lemon, K. N., & Verhoef, P. C. (2016). Understanding customer experience throughout the customer journey. *Journal of Marketing, 80*, 69–96.

Lev, B. (2001). *Intangibles: Management, Measurement, and Reporting*. Brookings Institution Press.

Lev, B., & Daum, J. (2004). The dominance of intagible assets: Consequences for enterprise management and corporate reporting. *Measuring Business Excellence, 8*(1), 6–17. doi:10.1108/13683040410524694

Lev, B., & Gu, F. (2016). *The End of and the Path Forward for Investors and Managers*. Wiley.

Levine, R., Locke, C., Searls, D., & Weinberger, D. (2011). *The cluetrain manifesto*. Basic books.

Leybourn, E. (2013). *Directing the Agile organisation: A lean approach to business management*. IT Governance Ltd.

Liao, C. N., & Hsing, P. K. (2011). An Integrated Fuzzy TOPSIS and MCGP Approach to Supplier Selection in Supply Chain Management. *Expert Systems with Applications, 38*(9), 10803–10811. doi:10.1016/j.eswa.2011.02.031

Lieberman, M., & Asaba, S. (2006). Why do firms imitate each other? *Academy of Management Review, 31*(2), 366–385. doi:10.5465/amr.2006.20208686

Li, F., & Ding, D. Z. (2013). The effect of institutional isomorphic pressure on the internationalization of firms in an emerging economy: Evidence from China. *Asia Pacific Business Review, 19*(4), 506–525. doi:10.1080/13602381.2013.807602

Li, J. J., Poppo, L., & Zhou, K. Z. (2008). Do Managerial Ties in China Always Produce Value? Competition, Uncertainty, and Domestic vs. Foreign Firms. *Strategic Management Journal, 29*(4), 383–400. doi:10.1002mj.665

Li, J. T., Yang, J. Y., & Yue, D. R. (2007). Identity, community, and audience: How wholly owned foreign subsidiaries gain legitimacy in China. *Academy of Management Journal*, *50*(1), 175–190. doi:10.5465/amj.2007.24162209

Li, J. T., & Yao, K. (2010). The role of reference groups in international investment decisions by firms from emerging economies. *Journal of International Management*, *16*(2), 143–153. doi:10.1016/j.intman.2010.03.005

Limayem, M., & Hirt, S. G. (2003). Force of habit and information systems usage: Theory and initial validation. *Journal of the Association for Information Systems*, *4*(1), 3. doi:10.17705/1jais.00030

Lindgreen, A., Vanhamme, J., & Beverland, M. B. (Eds.). (2009). *Memorable Customer Experiences - A Research Anthology*. Gower Publishing Limited.

Lin, H. E., Hsu, I. C., Hsu, A. W., & Chung, H. M. (2020). Creating competitive advantages: Interactions between ambidextrous diversification strategy and contextual factors from a dynamic capability perspective. *Technological Forecasting and Social Change*, *154*, 119952. doi:10.1016/j.techfore.2020.119952

Lin, M.-H., Tsai, J.-F., & Yu, C.-S. (2012). A Review of Deterministic Optimization Methods in Engineering and Management. *Mathematical Problems in Engineering*, *2012*, 1–15. doi:10.1155/2012/756023

Lipskier, V. (2018). *D.N.V.B.: Les surdouées du commerce digital (Digitally Natives Vertical Brands)*. Maxima Laurent du Mesnil.

Liu, C., Ang, R. P., & Lwin, M. O. (2013). Cognitive, personality, and social factors associated with adolescents' online personal information disclosure. *Journal of Adolescence*, *36*(4), 629–638. doi:10.1016/j.adolescence.2013.03.016 PMID:23849657

Li, Z. (2013). An Integrated Model of Material Supplier Selection and Order Allocation Using Fuzzy Extended AHP and Multiobjective Programming. *Mathematical Problems in Engineering*, 1–14.

Locander, W. B., & Hermann, P. W. (1979). The effect of self-confidence and anxiety on information seeking in consumer risk reduction. *JMR, Journal of Marketing Research*, *16*(2), 268–274. doi:10.1177/002224377901600211

Lo, H. W., Liou, J. J. H., Wang, H. S., & Tsai, Y. S. (2018). An Integrated Model for Solving Problems in Green Supplier Selection and Order Allocation. *Journal of Cleaner Production*, *190*, 339–352. doi:10.1016/j.jclepro.2018.04.105

Lucas, C., Mirhassani, S. A., Mitra, G., & Poojari, C. A. (2001). An Application of Lagrangian Relaxation to a Capacity Planning Problem under Uncertainty. *The Journal of the Operational Research Society*, *52*(11), 1256–1266. doi:10.1057/palgrave.jors.2601221

Łuczak, M., Małys, Ł., Ratajczak-Mrozek, M., Szczepański, R., Soniewicki, M., Dymitrowski, A., & Deszczyński, B. (2012). *The development of business networks in the company internationalisation process*. Wydawnictwo Uniwersytetu Ekonomicznego w Poznaniu.

Luehrman, T. A. (1998, Sept.). *Strategy as a Portfolio of Real Options. Harvard Business Review*.

Lu, H.-P., & Hsiao, K.-L. (2010). The influence of extro/introversion on the intention to pay for social networking sites. *Information & Management*, *47*(3), 150–157. doi:10.1016/j.im.2010.01.003

Lukas, B., & Farrell, O. (2000). The effect of market orientation on product innovation. *Journal of the Academy of Marketing Science*, *28*(2), 239–247. doi:10.1177/0092070300282005

Lung, Y. (2000). Is the Rise of Emerging Countries as Automobile Producers an Irreversible Phenomenon? In J. Humphrey, Y. Lecler, & M. Salerno (Eds.), *Global Strategies and Local Realities: The Auto Industry in Emerging Markets*. London & St Martin's Press. doi:10.1057/9780333977712_2

Luo, X., & Zhang, J. (2013). How do consumer buzz and traffic in social media marketing predict the value of the firm? *Journal of Management Information Systems, 30*(2), 213–238. doi:10.2753/MIS0742-1222300208

Lu, Y., Zhao, L., & Wang, B. (2010). From virtual community members to c2c e-commerce buyers: Trust in virtual communities and its effect on consumers' purchase intention. *Electronic Commerce Research and Applications, 9*(4), 346–360. doi:10.1016/j.elerap.2009.07.003

Lynch, P. D., Kent, R. J., & Srinivasan, S. S. (2001). The global Internet shopper: Evidence from shopping tasks in twelve countries. *Journal of Advertising Research, 41*(3), 15–23. doi:10.2501/JAR-41-3-15-23

Mack, O., & Khare, A. (2015). Perspectives on a VUCA world. In O. Mack, A. Khare, A. Krämer, & T. Burgartz (Eds.), *Managing in a VUCA World.* Springer.

Madden, B. (2010). *Wealth Creation: a Systems Mindset for Building and Investing in Business for the Long-Term.* John Wiley and Sons. doi:10.1002/9781118267769

Madden, B. J. (1999). *CFROI Valuation (Cash Flow Return On Investment, A Total System Approach To Valuing The Firm).* Butterworth-Heinemann.

Mafakheri, F., Breton, M., & Ghoniem, A. (2011). Supplier Selection-Order Allocation: A Two-Stage Multiple Criteria Dynamic Programming Approach. *International Journal of Production Economics, 132*(1), 52–57. doi:10.1016/j.ijpe.2011.03.005

Maison, D. (2018). *Qualitative Marketing Research: Understanding Consumer Behaviour.* Routledge. doi:10.4324/9780429467028

Majra, H., Saxena, R., Jha, S., & Jagannathan, S. (2016). Structuring technology applications for enhanced customer experience: Evidence from Indian air travellers. *Global Business Review, 17*(2), 351–374. doi:10.1177/0972150915619813

Malewska, K., & Sajdak, M. (2015). The Intuitive Manager and the Concept of Strategic Leadership. *Management, 18*(2), 44–58. doi:10.2478/manment-2014-0041

Malthouse, E. C., Haenlein, M., Skiera, B., Wege, E., & Zhang, M. (2013). Managing customer relationships in the social media era: Introducing the social CRM house. *Journal of Interactive Marketing, 27*(4), 270–280. doi:10.1016/j.intmar.2013.09.008

Maman, A.-F. (2011). Memorable Customer Experiences–A Research Anthology. *Journal of Consumer Marketing, 28*(3), 241–242. doi:10.1108/07363761111127680

Markides, C.C. (2013). Business model innovation: what can the ambidexterity literature teach us? *The Academy of Management Perspectives, 27*(4), 313–323.

Martin, J. D., & Petty, J. W. (2000). Value Based Management – The corporate response to the shareholder revolution. Harvard Business School Press.

Martin, J., Mortimer, G., & Andrews, L. (2015). Re-examining online customer experience to include purchase frequency and perceived risk. *Journal of Retailing and Consumer Services, 25*, 81–95. doi:10.1016/j.jretconser.2015.03.008

Maryam, G., & Goran, C. (2019). Does big data enhance firm innovation competency? The mediating role of data-driven insights. *Journal of Business Research, 104*, 69–84. doi:10.1016/j.jbusres.2019.07.006

Mathwick, C., Malhotra, N., & Rigdon, E. (2001). Experiential value: Conceptualization, measurement and application in the catalog and Internet shopping environment☆. *Journal of Retailing, 77*(1), 39–56. doi:10.1016/S0022-4359(00)00045-2

Matsumo, K., Mentzer, J. T., & Rentz, J. O. (2000). A refinement and Validation of the MARKOR Scale. *Journal of the Academy of Marketing Science*, *28*(4), 527–539. doi:10.1177/0092070300284005

Mattinen, J. (2016). *Intensifying buyer personas using an inbound marketing strategy*. Academic Press.

Mazur, B. (2010, November). Cultural Diversity in Organizational Theory and Practice. *Journal of Intercultural Management*, *2*(2), 5–15.

McCarthy, E. (1960). *Basic Marketing: A Managerial Approach*. Lisa Firth.

McCauley, C. D. (2010). Concepts of Leadership. In E. Biech (Ed.), The ASTD Leadership Handbook (5th ed., pp. 1–13). Campus.

McGrath, R. (2013b). Continuous reconfiguration in the transient advantage economy. *Strategy and Leadership*, *41*(5), 17–22. doi:10.1108/SL-05-2013-0039

McGrath, R. G. (2013a). Transient advantage. *Harvard Business Review*, *91*(6), 62–70.

McGrath, R., & MacMillan, I. (1995, July). *Discovery-driven planning. Harvard Business Review.*

McLean, G., & Wilson, A. (2016). Evolving the online customer experience… is there a role for online customer support? *Computers in Human Behavior*, *60*, 602–610. doi:10.1016/j.chb.2016.02.084

McTaggart, J. M., Kontes, P. W., & Mankins, M. (1994). *The Value Imperative*. The Free Press.

Meuter, M. L., Ostrom, A. L., Bitner, M. J., & Roundtree, R. (2003). The influence of technology anxiety on consumer use and experiences with self-service technologies. *Journal of Business Research*, *56*(11), 899–906. doi:10.1016/S0148-2963(01)00276-4

Michael, B., Jeffrey, A., David, L. J., & Diego, K. (2017). Big data and the future of R&D Management: The rise of big data and big data analytics will have significant implications for R&D and innovation management in the next decade. *Research Technology Management*, *60*(5), 43–50. doi:10.1080/08956308.2017.1348135

Michailova, S., & Wilson, H. I. (2008). Small firm internationalization through experientiallearning: The moderating role of socialization tactics. *Journal of World Business*, *43*(2), 243–254. doi:10.1016/j.jwb.2007.11.002

Midgen, T. (2015). (Un)Ethical leadership: What can Educational Psychology Services learn? *Educational and Child Psychology*, *32*(4), 81–94.

Miller, D. (2019). The Resource-Based View of the Firm. In Oxford Research Encyclopedia of Business and Management. doi:10.1093/acrefore/9780190224851.013.4

Mishra, R. (2014). *Omni-channel Retailing: When it becomes a commodity, what then?* Academic Press.

Mitchell, V.-W., & Harris, G. (2005). The importance of consumers' perceived risk in retail strategy. *European Journal of Marketing*, *39*(7/8), 821–837. doi:10.1108/03090560510601789

Moen, Ø., Gavlen, M., & Endrese, I. (2004). nternationalization of small, computer softwarefirms: Entry forms and market selection. *European Journal of Marketing*, *8*(9/10), 1236–1251. doi:10.1108/03090560410548951

Moghaddam, K. S. (2015). Fuzzy Multi-Objective Model for Supplier Selection and Order Allocation in Reverse Logistics Systems under Supply and Demand Uncertainty. *Expert Systems with Applications*, *42*(15–16), 6237–6254. doi:10.1016/j.eswa.2015.02.010

Moore, J. F. (2006). Business ecosystems and the view from the firm. *Antitrust Bulletin*, *51*(1), 31–76. doi:10.1177/0003603X0605100103

Mor Barak, M. E. (2011). *Managing diversity: Toward a globally inclusive workplace*. Sage.

Morgan, N., & Vorhies, D., (2018). The business performance outcomes of market orientation culture and behaviors. *Innovation and Strategy, 15*, 259-286.

Morris, C. (2016). *Virtual reality and the new sales experience*. Retrieved from: https://www.campaignlive.com/article/virtual-reality-new-sales-experience/1392253

Mosteller, J., Donthu, N., & Eroglu, S. (2014). The fluent online shopping experience. *Journal of Business Research*, *67*(11), 2486–2493. doi:10.1016/j.jbusres.2014.03.009

Moutinho, R. F. A. Ch. M. S. B. (2010), *International New Ventures Não Tecnológicos* (PhD Dissertation). School of Economics and Management of University of Porto.

Mueller, J., Hutter, K., Fueller, J., & Matzler, K. (2011). Virtual worlds as knowledge management platform - a practice-perspective. *Information Systems Journal*, *21*(6), 479–501. doi:10.1111/j.1365-2575.2010.00366.x

Muneer, M. (2019). Knowledge Sharing is Key to Win in the Transient Advantage Era. *NHRD Network Journal*, *12*(2), 87–96. doi:10.1177/2631454119832391

Muniz, A., & Schau, H. (2007). Vigilante Marketing and Consumer-created Communications. *Journal of Advertising*, *36*(3), 187–202.

Musso, F., & Francioni, B. (2014). International strategy for SMEs: Criteria for foreign marketsand entry modes selection. *Journal of Small Business and Enterprise Development*, *21*(2), 301–312. doi:10.1108/JSBED-10-2013-0149

Nakamoto, S. (2008). *Bitcoin: A Peer-to-Peer Electronic Cash System*. Retrieved from https://bitcoin.org/bitcoin.pdf

Nandram, S. S., & Bindlish, P. K. (2017). Introduction to VUCA. In *Managing VUCA Through Integrative Self-Management* (pp. 3–14). Springer. doi:10.1007/978-3-319-52231-9_1

Narver, J., & Slater, S. (1990). The effect of a market orientation on business performance. *Journal of Marketing*, *54*(4), 20–35. doi:10.1177/002224299005400403

Narver, J., Slater, S., & MacLachlan, D. (2004). Responsive and proactive market orientation and new-product success. *Journal of Product Innovation Management*, *21*(5), 334–347. doi:10.1111/j.0737-6782.2004.00086.x

NASIG. (2012). *NASIG Communication. Newsletter*. Retrieved from http://tigerprints.clemson.edu/cgi/viewcontent.cgi?article=1385&context=nasig

Neslin, S. A., Grewal, D., Leghorn, R., Shankar, V., Teerling, M. L., Thomas, J. S., & Verhoef, P. C. (2006). Challenges and opportunities in multichannel customer management. *Journal of Service Research*, *9*(2), 95–112. doi:10.1177/1094670506293559

Newman, N. (2014). Apple iBeacon technology briefing. *Journal of Direct, Data and Digital Marketing Practice*, *15*(3), 222–225.

Nezhad, Abbas, Roghanian, & Azadi. (2013). A Fuzzy Goal Programming Approach to Solve Multi-Objective Supply Chain Network Design Problems. *International Journal of Industrial Engineering Computations*.

Ngo, L., & O'Cass, A. (2012). In search of innovation and customer-related performance superiority: The role of market orientation, marketing capability, and innovation capability interactions. *Journal of Product Innovation Management*, *5*(5), 861–877. doi:10.1111/j.1540-5885.2012.00939.x

Nicolas, C. L., & Acosta, P. S. (2010). Analyzing ICT adoption and use effects on knowledge creation: An empirical investigation in SMEs. *International Journal of Information Management*, *30*(6), 521–528. doi:10.1016/j.ijinfomgt.2010.03.004

Nielsen, B. B., & Nielsen, S. (2011). The role of top management team international orientation in international strategic decision-making: The choice of foreign entry mode. *Journal of World Business*, *46*(2), 185–193. doi:10.1016/j.jwb.2010.05.003

Nilsson, D. (2007). A cross-cultural comparison of self-service technology use. *European Journal of Marketing*, *41*(3/4), 367–381. doi:10.1108/03090560710728381

Nonaka, I., & Takeuchi, H. (1996). *Knowledge Creating Companies*. Oxford University Press.

Noone, B. M., McGuire, K. A., & Rohlfs, K. V. (2011). Social media meets hotel revenue management: Opportunities, issues and unanswered questions. *Journal of Revenue and Pricing Management*, *10*(4), 293–305. doi:10.1057/rpm.2011.12

Novak, T. P., Hoffman, D. L., & Yung, Y. F. (2000). Measuring the customer experience in online environments: A structural modeling approach. *Marketing Science*, *19*(1), 22–42. doi:10.1287/mksc.19.1.22.15184

Nunnally, J. C., & Bernstein, I. H. (1994). *Psychometric Theory* (3rd ed.). McGraw-Hill.

O'Reilly, C. A. III, & Tushman, M. L. (2013). Organizational ambidexterity: Past, present, and future. *The Academy of Management Perspectives*, *27*(4), 324–338. doi:10.5465/amp.2013.0025

Ogawa, M., Ueki, Y., Idota, H., Bunno, T., & Tsuji, M. (2018). Internal innovation capacity and external linkages in firms of ASEAN economies focusing on endogeneity. *STI Policy and Management Journal*, *3*(2), 97–117. doi:10.14203/STIPM.2018.135

Ohmae, K. (1989). Managing in a borderless world. *Harvard Business Review*, *67*(May-June), 152–161. PMID:10292934

OIV. (2018). *OIV Statistical Report on World Vitiviniculture*. Retrieved from: ttp://www.oiv.int/fr/normes-et-documents-techniques/analyses-statistiques/situation-annuelle

Okati, Mosavi, & Behroozi. (2017). A Comparison between Different Meta-Heuristic Techniques in Power Allocation for Physical Layer Security. *Iranian Journal of Electrical and Electronic Engineering*.

Oliver & Webber. (1982). Supply-Chain Management: Logistics Catches up with Strategy. *The Roots of Logistics*.

Ologbo, A. C., & Nor, K. M. (2015). Knowledge management processes and firm innovation capability: A theoretical model. *Asian Social Science*, *11*(8), 10–17. doi:10.5539/ass.v11n18p10

Omona, W., van der Weide, T., & Lubega, J. (2010). Using ICT to enhance knowledge management in higher education: A conceptual framework and research agenda. *International Journal of Education and Development Using Information and Communication Technology*, *6*(4), 83–101.

Ortinau, D. J., Babin, B. J., & Chebat, J. C. (2013). Development of new empirical insights in consumer-retailer relationships within online and offline retail environments: Introduction to the special issue. *Journal of Business Research*, *66*(7), 795–800. doi:10.1016/j.jbusres.2011.06.003

Osterwalder, A., & Pigneur, Y. (2008). *Business Model Generation*. John Wiley and Sons.

Ovans, A. (2015, Jan.). *What Is a Business Model? Harvard Business Review*.

Ozturk, A., Joiner, E., & Cavusgil, S. T. (2015). Delineating Foreign Market Potential: A Tool for International Market Selection. *Thunderbird International Business Review*, *57*(2), 119–141. doi:10.1002/tie.21686

Paksoy, T., & Ter Chang, C. (2010). Revised Multi-Choice Goal Programming for Multi-Period, Multi-Stage Inventory Controlled Supply Chain Model with Popup Stores in Guerrilla Marketing. *Applied Mathematical Modelling*, *34*(11), 3586–3598. doi:10.1016/j.apm.2010.03.008

Palladan, A. A., Abdulkadir, K. B., & Chong, Y. W. (2016). Strategic Leadership : A Sine Qua Non Toward Revitalizaing Nigerian Public Tertiary Institutions. *International Journal of Economics. Commerce and Management*, *IV*(9), 253–264.

Pan, L.-Y., & Chiou, J.-S. (2011). How much can you trust online information? Cues for perceived trustworthiness of consumer-generated online information. *Journal of Interactive Marketing*, *25*(2), 67–74. doi:10.1016/j.intmar.2011.01.002

Pan, W.-T. (2012). A New Fruit Fly Optimization Algorithm: Taking the Financial Distress Model as an Example. *Knowledge-Based Systems*, *26*, 69–74. doi:10.1016/j.knosys.2011.07.001

Papadopoulos, N., Chen, H., & Thomas, D. R. (2002). Toward a tradeoff model for internationalmarket selection. *International Business Review*, *11*(2), 165–192. doi:10.1016/S0969-5931(01)00054-3

Papadopoulos, N., & Denis, J. E. (1988). Inventory, taxonomy and assessment of methods for international market selection. *International Marketing Review*, *5*(3), 38–51. doi:10.1108/eb008357

Papadopoulos, N., & Jansen, D. (1994). Country and method-of-entry selection for international expansion: International distributive arrangements revisited. *Dimensions of International Business*, *11*, 31–52.

Papadopoulos, N., & Martín Martín, O. (2011). International market selection and segmentation: Perspectives and challenges. *International Marketing Review*, *28*(2), 132–149. doi:10.1108/02651331111122632

Pappas, I. O., Pateli, A. G., Giannakos, M. N., & Chrissikopoulos, V. (2014). Moderating effects of online shopping experience on customer satisfaction and repurchase intentions. *International Journal of Retail & Distribution Management*, *42*(3), 187–204. doi:10.1108/IJRDM-03-2012-0034

Park, B., Ahn, S. K., & Kim, H. J. (2010). Blogging: Mediating impacts of flow on motivational behaviour. *Journal of Research in Interactive Marketing*, *4*(1), 6–29. doi:10.1108/17505931011033533

Park, C., & Kim, Y. (2003). Identifying key factors affecting consumer purchase behavior in an online shopping context. *International Journal of Retail & Distribution Management*, *31*(1), 16–29. doi:10.1108/09590550310457818

Pasquale, D. V., Alberto, D. M., Messeni, P. A., Umberto, P., & Salvatore, P. (2018). Big data for open innovation in SMEs and large corporations: Trends, opportunities, and challenges. *Creativity and Innovation Management*, *27*(1), 6–22. doi:10.1111/caim.12224

Pati, R. K., Nandakumar, M. K., Ghobadian, A., Ireland, R. D., & O'Regan, N. (2018). Business Model Design–performance Relationship under External and Internal Contingencies: Evidence from SMEs in an Emerging Economy. *Long Range Planning*, *51*(5), 750–769. doi:10.1016/j.lrp.2018.01.001

Pattanayak, D., Koilakuntla, M., & Punyatoya, P. (2017). Investigating the influence of TQM, service quality and market orientation on customer satisfaction and loyalty in the Indian banking sector. *International Journal of Quality & Reliability Management*, *34*(3), 362–377. doi:10.1108/IJQRM-04-2015-0057

Paul, M. (2019). Reconceptualizing value innovation for industry 4.0 and the industrial Internet of Things. *Journal of Business and Industrial Marketing*, *34*(6), 1203–1209. doi:10.1108/JBIM-11-2018-0348

Pazaitis, A., De Filippi, P., & Kostakis, V. (2017). *Blockchain and Value Systems in the Sharing Economy: The Illustrative Case of Backfeed*. Academic Press.

Perelman, M. (1994). Retrospectives: Fixed capital, railroad economics and the critique of the market. *The Journal of Economic Perspectives*, *8*(3), 189–195.

Petrisor, P., & Cozmiuc, D. (2015). The Paradox Of Investment: Constraining Strategy. *Proceedings of the 9th International Management Conference, Management and Innovation For Competitive Advantage.*

Piamphongsant, T., & Mandhachitara, R. (2008). Psychological antecedents of career women's fashion clothing conformity. *Journal of Fashion Marketing and Management*, *12*(4), 438–455. doi:10.1108/13612020810906119

Pilkington, M. (2015). *Blockchain technology: principles and applications*. Retrieved from https://papers.ssrn.com/sol3/Papers.cfm?abstract_id=2660

Pina e Cunha, M. P., Gomes, E., Mellahi, K., Miner, A. S., & Rego, A. (2020). Strategic agility through improvisational capabilities: Implications for a paradox-sensitive HRM. *Human Resource Management Review*, *30*(1), 100695. doi:10.1016/j.hrmr.2019.100695

Pine, B. J. II, & Gilmore, J. H. (1999). *The Experience Economy: Work is Theatre & Every Business a Stage*. Harvard Business Press.

Pisano, G., P. (2015, June). You Need an innovation strategy. *Harvard Business Review*.

Podsakoff, P. M., MacKenzie, S. B., Lee, J.-Y., & Podsakoff, N. P. (2003). Common method biases in behavioral research: A critical review of the literature and recommended remedies. *The Journal of Applied Psychology*, *88*(5), 1939–1854. doi:10.1037/0021-9010.88.5.879 PMID:14516251

Polanyi, P. (1966). *The Tacit Dimension*. Chicago University Press.

Pordata. (2018). Access 19 May 2019, https://www.pordata.pt/Portugal/Empresas

Porter, M. E. (1989). How competitive forces shape strategy. In *Readings in strategic management* (pp. 133–143). Palgrave. doi:10.1007/978-1-349-20317-8_10

Porter, M. E. (1991). *Michael E. Porter on competition and strategy*. Harvard Business School Press.

Porter, M. E. (2008). *Competitive strategy: Techniques for analyzing industries and competitors*. Simon and Schuster.

Powaga, K. (2008). Integrated customer measurement. *Marketing News*, *42*, 26–31.

Powell, W. W., & Snellman, K. (2004). The Knowledge Economy. *Annual Review of Sociology*, *30*(1), 199–220. doi:10.1146/annurev.soc.29.010202.100037

Prahalad, C. K., & Krishnan, M. S. (2008). *The New Age of Innovation: Driving Co-Created Value Through Global Networks*. McGraw-Hill.

Prahalad, C. K., & Ramaswamy, V. (2004). Co-creation experiences: The next practice in value creation. *Journal of Interactive Marketing*, *18*(3), 5–14. doi:10.1002/dir.20015

Project Management Institute. (2013). *A Guide to the Project Management Body of Knowledge (PMBOK® Guide)* (6th ed.). Project Management Institute.

Pröllochs, N., & Feuerriegel, S. (2020). Business analytics for strategic management: Identifying and assessing corporate challenges via topic modeling. *Information & Management*, *57*(1), 103070. doi:10.1016/j.im.2018.05.003

Purnawirawan, N., De Pelsmacker, P., & Dens, N. (2012). Balance and sequence in online reviews: How perceived usefulness affects attitudes and intentions. *Journal of Interactive Marketing*, *26*(4), 244–255. doi:10.1016/j.intmar.2012.04.002

Qian, C., Yu, K., & Gu, H. (2020). Flexibility mechanisms in a dynamic distribution network. *Journal of Business & Industrial Marketing*. ahead-of-print.

Quigley, L., Nelson, A. L., Carriere, J., Smilek, D., & Purdon, C. (2012). The Effects of Trait and State Anxiety on Attention to Emotional Images: An Eye-Tracking Study. *Cognition and Emotion*, *26*(8), 1390–1411. doi:10.1080/02699931.2012.662892 PMID:22646929

Quigley, T. J., & Hambrick, D. C. (2015). Has the "cEO effect" increased in recent decades? A new explanation for the great rise in America's attention to corporate leaders. *Strategic Management Journal*, *36*(6), 821–830. doi:10.1002mj.2258

Rahman, S. (2001). The international market selection process: A study of successful Australian international firms. *Journal of International Marketing and Exporting*, *6*(2), 150–160.

Raisch, S., & Birkinshaw, J. (2008). Organizational ambidexterity: Antecedents, outcomes, and moderators. *Journal of Management*, *34*(3), 375–409. doi:10.1177/0149206308316058

Ramirez, S. (2018). *Shoppers Want More Personalised Technology In-Stores and Online*. Luxury Society.

Ramos, P., Martins, F. V., & Barandas, H. (2012). Differences in the market orientation impact on business relationships between wine producers and intermediaries: a PLS application. *Proceedings of the 41st EMAC Conference, 172.*

Rapp, A., Britelspacher, L., Grewal, D., & Hughes, D. (2013). Understanding social media effects across seller, retailer, and consumer interactions. *Journal of the Academy of Marketing Science*, *41*(5), 547–566. doi:10.100711747-013-0326-9

Rappaport, A. (1986). *Creating Shareholder Value*. The Free Press.

Rayna, T., Striukova, L., & Darlington, J. (2015). Co-creation and user innovation: The role of online 3D printing platforms. *Journal of Engineering and Technology Management*, *37*, 90–102.

Reber, R., Schwarz, N., & Winkielman, P. (2004). Processing fluency and aesthetic pleasure: Is beauty in the perceiver's processing experience? *Personality and Social Psychology Review*, *8*(4), 364–382. doi:10.120715327957pspr0804_3 PMID:15582859

Regis, R. G., & Wild, S. M. (2015). CONORBIT: Constrained Optimization by Radial Basis Function Interpolation in Trust Regions. *Mathematics and Computer Science Division*, (October), 1–29.

Rego, A., & Cunha, M. P. e. (2010). Organisational justice and citizenship behaviors: A study in the Portuguese cultural context. *Applied Psychology*, *59*(3), 404–430. doi:10.1111/j.1464-0597.2009.00405.x

Reichheld, F. F., & Schefter, P. (2000). E-loyalty: Your secret weap-on on the web. *Harvard Business Review*, *78*(4), 105–114.

Reinders, M. J., Frambach, R. T., & Dabholkar, P. A. (2007). Forced adoption of self-service technologies: An exploration of antecedents and consequences of consumers' perceived decisional control. *Marketing Theory and Applications*, 85.

Reynolds, W. H. (1965). A stochastic-model of opinion solidification. *Journal of Advertising Research*, *5*(3), 20–23.

Richardson-Greenfield, P. (2016). *Force Usage of Self-Technology (SST) in a Retail Service Setting and the Moderating Effect of Shopping Value*. Paper presented at the AMA Summer Educators Conference, Atlanta, GA.

Ries, E. (2010). *Introduction to Customer Development at the Lean Startup Intensive at Web 2.0 Expo by Steve Blank*. Retrieved on May 26th, from: https://www.slideshare.net/startuplessonslearned/introduction-to-customer-development-at-the-lean-startup-intensive-at-web-20-expo-by-steve-blank

Ries, E. (2011). *The Lean Startup: How Today's Entrepreneurs Use Continuous Innovation to Create Radically Successful Businesses*. Retrieved on May 26th, from: https://www.amazon.com/Lean-Startup-Entrepreneurs-Continuous-Innovation/dp/0307887898

Rifkin, J. (2014). *A Sociedade do Custo Marginal Zero*. Bertrand.

Ringle, C. M., Wende, S., & Will, A. (2005). *SmartPLS 2.0*. www.smartpls.de

Rodrigues, D. (2012). Cyberethics of Business Social Networking. In Information Resources Management Association (Eds.), E-Marketing: Concepts, Methodologies, Tools, and Applications (pp. 756-781). Hershey, PA: IGI Global.

Rodrigues, D. Tavares, J. Lopes, J. (2014). Manifold-Marketing: A new marketing archetype for the information age, applied to the adoption of oral contraceptives and other drugs by end-users. Lusíada. *Economia & Empresa, 2*(17), 59-80.

Rodrigues, D. (2011). Cyberethics of Business Social Networking. In M. Cruz-Cunha, P. Gonçalves, N. Lopes, E. Miranda, & G. Putnik (Eds.), *Handbook of Research on Business Social Networking: Organizational, Managerial, and Technological Dimensions* (pp. 314–338). Business Science Reference.

Rodrigues, D. F., Lopes, J. C., & Tavares, J. F. (2013). Manifold Marketing: A New Marketing Archetype for the Information Age, Applied to the Adoption of Oral Contraceptives and Other Drugs by End-Users. *Proceedings of the Third Annual Conference of International Network of Business & Management Journals (INBAM 2013).*

Rodriguez, M., Peterson, R. M., & Vijaykumar, K. (2012). Social media's influence on business-to-business sales performance. *Journal of Personal Selling & Sales Management, 32*(3), 365–378. doi:10.2753/PSS0885-3134320306

Romano, M. G. (2009). Informational cascades in financial economics: A review. *Giornale degli Economisti e Annali di Economia, 68*(122), 81–109.

Rose, D. (2008, June). The information-seeking funnel. In *National Science Foundation workshop on Information-Seeking Support Systems (ISSS)* (pp. 32-36). Academic Press.

Rose, S., Clark, M., Samouel, P., & Hair, N. (2012). Online customer experience in e-Retailing: An empirical model of antecedents and outcomes. *Journal of Retailing, 88*(2), 308–322. doi:10.1016/j.jretai.2012.03.001

Rose, S., Hair, N., & Clark, M. (2011). Online customer experience: A review of the business-to-consumer online purchase context. *International Journal of Management Reviews, 13*(1), 24–39. doi:10.1111/j.1468-2370.2010.00280.x

Rosinha, A. J. P. E. (2009). *Conhecimento tácito em contexto militar:(inclusões na promoção do desenvolvimento de competências de comando). Conhecimento tácito em contexto militar: Incursões na promoção do desenvolvimento de competências de comando*. Retrieved from http://repositorio.ul.pt/bitstream/10451/967/10/20686_ulsd057394_td_parte2_11.pdf%5Cnhttp://repositorio.ul.pt/handle/10451/967

Rossiter, J. (2002). The C-OAR-SE procedure for scale development in marketing. *International Journal of Research in Marketing, 19*(4), 305–335. doi:10.1016/S0167-8116(02)00097-6

Rouyendegh, Daneshvar, & Saputro. (2014). Supplier Selection Using Integrated Fuzzy TOPSIS and MCGP: A Case Study. *Procedia: Social and Behavioral Sciences.*

Rowe, W. G. (2001). Creating wealth in organizations: The role of strategic leadership. *The Academy of Management Executive, 15*(1), 81–94. doi:10.5465/ame.2001.4251395

Rubino, J. (2014). Bricks and clicks. *CFA Institute Magazine, 25*(4), 30–32.

Ruekert, R. (1992). Developing a market orientation: An organizational strategy perspective. *International Journal of Research in Marketing, 9*(3), 225–245. doi:10.1016/0167-8116(92)90019-H

Saleh, A. A., Al Attar, A. M., Hemeida, A. M., & Ibrahim, A. A. (2018). Comparison of Different Optimization Techniques for Optimal Allocation of Multiple Distribution Generation. *Proceedings of 2018 International Conference on Innovative Trends in Computer Engineering, ITCE 2018*. 10.1109/ITCE.2018.8316644

Salomon, R., & Wu, Z. (2012). Institutional distance and local isomorphism strategy. *Journal of International Business Studies*, *43*(4), 343–367. doi:10.1057/jibs.2012.3

Sánchez, P. C., & Ferrá, B. E. (2019). Clusters of exporting priority countries. *Cuadernos de Gestión*, *19*(1), 147–174. doi:10.5295/cdg.170733pc

Sanzo, M., Santos, M., Vásquez, R., & Álvaréz, L. (2003). The effect of market orientation on buyer–seller relationship satisfaction. *Industrial Marketing Management*, *32*(4), 327–345. doi:10.1016/S0019-8501(01)00200-0

Sarkar, S., Lakha, V., Ansari, I., & Maiti, J. (2017). Supplier Selection in Uncertain Environment: A Fuzzy MCDM Approach. *Advances in Intelligent Systems and Computing*, *458*, v–vi.

Satell, G. (2017a, Mar.). This Program Uses Lean Startup Techniques to Turn Scientists into entrepreneurs. *Harvard Business Review*.

Satell, G. (2017b, June). The Types of Innovation and the Problems. *Harvard Business Review*.

Schaefers, T., Lawson, S. J., & Kukar-Kinney, M. (2016). How the burdens of ownership promote consumer usage of access-based services. *Marketing Letters*, *27*(3), 569–577.

Schmidt, B., Loerbroks, A., Herr, R., Wilson, M., Jarczok, M., Litaker, D., Mauss, D., Bosch, J., & Fischer, J. (2014). Associations Between Supportive Leadership and Employees Self-Rated Health in an Occupational Sample. *International Journal of Behavioral Medicine*, *21*(5), 750–756. doi:10.100712529-013-9345-7 PMID:24072350

Schneider, S., & Spieth, P. (2013). Business model innovation: Towards an integrated future research agenda. *International Journal of Innovation Management*, *17*(1), 1–34. doi:10.1142/S136391961340001X

Schoemaker, P., Heaton, S., & Teece, D. (2018). Innovation, Dynamic Capabilities, and Leadership. *BerkeleyHaas*, *61*(1), 15–42.

Schoemaker, P., Krupp, S., & Howland, S. (2013). *Strategic leadership: the essential skills. Harvard Business Review*. January-February.

Schwab, K. (2016). *The fourth industrial revolution: a Davos reader*. Council on Foreign Relations.

Schwab, K. (2017). *The fourth industrial revolution*. Crown Business.

Schweizer, R., Vahlne, J. E., & Johanson, J. (2010). Internationalization as an entrepreneurial process. *Journal of International Entrepreneurship*, *8*(4), 343–370. doi:10.100710843-010-0064-8

Scott, R. (1991). Unpacking Institutional Arguments. In W. Powell & P. DiMaggio (Eds.), The New Institutionalism in Organizational Analysis (pp. 164–182). Academic Press.

Sego, T., & Stout, P. A. (1994). Anxiety associated with social issues: The development of a scale to measure an antecedent construct. NA - Advances in Consumer Research, (21), 601-606.

Selim, H., Araz, C., & Ozkarahan, I. (2008). Collaborative Production-Distribution Planning in Supply Chain: A Fuzzy Goal Programming Approach. *Transportation Research Part E, Logistics and Transportation Review*, *44*(3), 396–419. doi:10.1016/j.tre.2006.11.001

Setak, M., Sharifi, S., & Alimohammadian, A. (2012). Supplier Selection and Order Allocation Models in Supply Chain Management: A Review. *World Applied Sciences Journal*, *18*(1), 55–72.

Shao, Z. (2019). Interaction effect of strategic leadership behaviors and organizational culture on IS-Business strategic alignment and Enterprise Systems assimilation. *International Journal of Information Management*, *44*, 96–108. Advance online publication. doi:10.1016/j.ijinfomgt.2018.09.010

Sharif, M. M., & Scandura, T. A. (2014). Do perceptions of ethical conduct matter during organizational change? Ethical leadership and employee involvement. *Journal of Business Ethics*, *124*(2), 185–196. doi:10.100710551-013-1869-x

Sharma, D., & Blomstermo, A. (2003). The internationalization process of Born Globals: A network view. *International Business Review*, *12*(6), 739–753. doi:10.1016/j.ibusrev.2003.05.002

Sharma, S., & Vredenburg, H. (1998). Proactive corporate environmental strategy and the development of competitively valuable organizational capabilities. *Strategic Management Journal*, *19*(8), 729–753. doi:10.1002/(SICI)1097-0266(199808)19:8<729::AID-SMJ967>3.0.CO;2-4

Sheng, S. Y., & Mullen, M. R. (2011). A hybrid model for export market opportunity analysis. *International Marketing Review*, *28*(2), 163–182. doi:10.1108/02651331111122650

Shen, X.-L., Li, Y.-J., Sun, Y., & Wang, N. (2018). Channel integration quality, perceived fluency and omnichannel service usage: The moderating roles of internal and external usage experience. *Decision Support Systems*, *109*, 61–73. doi:10.1016/j.dss.2018.01.006

Shiguemoto, A. L., & Armentano, V. A. (2010). A Tabu Search Procedure for Coordinating Production, Inventory and Distribution Routing Problems. *International Transactions in Operational Research*, *17*(2), 179–195. doi:10.1111/j.1475-3995.2009.00741.x

Shin, D. H. (2010). The effects of trust, security and privacy in social networking: A security-based approach to understand the pattern of adoption. *Interacting with Computers*, *22*(5), 428–438. doi:10.1016/j.intcom.2010.05.001

Shin, D., Seidle, R., & Okhmatovskiy, I. (2016). Making the foreign familiar: The influence of top management team and board of directors characteristics on the adoption of foreign practices. *Journal of World Business*, *51*(6), 937–949. doi:10.1016/j.jwb.2016.09.003

Shin, Y. (2012). CEO ethical leadership, ethical climate, climate strength, and collective organizational citizenship behavior. *Journal of Business Ethics*, *108*(3), 299–312. doi:10.100710551-011-1091-7

Shin, Y., Sung, S. Y., Choi, J. N., & Kim, M. S. (2015). Top management ethical leadership and firm performance: Mediating role of ethical and procedural justice climate. *Journal of Business Ethics*, *129*(1), 43–57. doi:10.100710551-014-2144-5 PMID:26430288

Siemens. (1998). *Siemens annual report*. Retrieved on May 26th, from: https://www.siemens.com/investor/pool/en/investor_relations/downloadcenter/gb1998_d_1365091.pdf

Siemens. (2002a). *Corporate Responsibility Report 2002*. Retrieved on May 26th, 2019, from: https://www.siemens.com/investor/pool/en/investor_relations/downloadcenter/CR-Report_2002_en.pdf

Siemens. (2002b). *Siemens annual report*. Retrieved on May 26th, 2019, from: https://web.lib.aalto.fi/fi/old/yrityspalvelin/pdf/2002/Esiemens2002.pdf

Siemens. (2006). *Siemens annual report*. Retrieved on May 26th, 2019, from: https://web.lib.aalto.fi/fi/old/yrityspalvelin/pdf/2006/Esiemens2006.pdf

Siemens. (2010). *Siemens annual report.* Retrieved on May 26th, 2019, from: https://www.siemens.com/investor/pool/en/investor_relations/siemens_ar_2010.pdf

Siemens. (2011). *Opening innovation.* Retrieved on May 26[th], from: https://www.slideshare.net/heisss/opening-innovation-7436014

Siemens. (2011). *Siemens annual report.* Retrieved on May 26th, 2019, from: https://www.siemens.com/investor/pool/en/investor_relations/siemens_ar_2011.pdf

Siemens. (2012). *Siemens annual report.* Retrieved on May 26th, 2019, from: https://www.siemens.com/investor/pool/en/investor_relations/siemens_ar_2012.pdf

Siemens. (2013a). *Siemens annual report.* Retrieved on May 26th, 2019, from: https://www.siemens.com/annual/13/en/download/pdf/Siemens_AR2013.pdf

Siemens. (2013b). *Innovation in an Enterprise 2.0.* Retrieved on May 26th, 2019, from: https://www.slideshare.net/heisss/innovation-in-an-enterprise-20

Siemens. (2014a). *From big data to smart data.* Retrieved on May 26th, 2019, from: https://w3.siemens.com/topics/global/en/events/hannover-messe/program/Documents/pdf/Smart-Data-to-Business-Michal-Skubacz.pdf

Siemens. (2014b). *Open Co-Ideation @ Siemens. An Innovation approach to connecting an organization's knowledge and creativity.* Retrieved on May 26th, 2019, from: https://studylib.net/doc/18616093/open-co-ideation-%40-siemens

Siemens. (2014c). *PM@Siemens. Integrated Project Management.* Retrieved on May 26th, from: http://ipma.it/ipma_/images/E._Delogu_Siemens_Presentation_Evento_ANIMA-ANIMP_03.05.16.pdf

Siemens. (2014d). *Siemens annual report.* Retrieved on May 26th, 2019, from: https://www.siemens.com/annual/14/en/download/pdf/Siemens_AR2014.pdf

Siemens. (2014e). *Siemens – Vision 2020.* Retrieved on May 26th, 2019, from: https://www.siemens.com/investor/pool/en/investor_relations/financial_publications/speeches_and_presentations/140529_bernstein_ny_presentation.pdf

Siemens. (2015a). *The digital change constant.* Retrieved on May 26th, 2019, from: https://www.siemens.com/press/pool/de/events/2015/corporate/2015-09-analyst-conference/presentation-kayser-e.pdf

Siemens. (2015b). *Siemens annual report.* Retrieved on May 26th, 2019, from: https://www.siemens.com/investor/pool/en/investor_relations/Siemens_AR2015.pdf

Siemens. (2015c). *Web of Systems for a digital world.* Retrieved on May 26th, 2019, from: https://www.siemens.com/press/pool/de/events/2015/corporate/2015-12-internet-of-things/presentation-iot-russwurm_web-of-systems-e.pdf

Siemens. (2016a). *Corporate Technology. Our central research and development unit.* Retrieved on May 26th, 2019, from: https://www.siemens.com/content/dam/internet/siemens-com/global/company/innovation/innovation/corporate-technology/pdf/CT-Standardpresentation_E_March_2017.pdf

Siemens. (2016b). *next47.* Retrieved on May 26th, 2019, from: https://www.siemens.com/press/pool/de/feature/2016/corporate/2016-06-next47/presentation-next47-e.pdf

Siemens. (2016c). *Siemens Digitalization Strategy & Sinalytics Platform.* Retrieved on May 26th, 2019, from: https://www.siemens.com/digitalisierung/public/pdf/Sinalytics-and-Digital-Services-Presentation.pdf

Siemens. (2016d). *We enable digitalization.* Retrieved on May 26th, 2019, from: https://slideplayer.com/slide/13046746/

Siemens. (2017a). *Digitalization @ Siemens*. Retrieved on May 26th, 2019, from: https://www.automationsummit.se/wp-content/uploads/2017/10/7-%E2%80%93-Mimmi-Alladin.pdf

Siemens. (2017b). *Innovations*. Retrieved on May 26th, 2019, from: https://www.siemens.com/global/en/home/company/innovation/pictures-of-the-future/innovations.html

Siemens. (2017c). *Siemens annual report*. Retrieved on May 26th, 2019, from: https://www.siemens.com/investor/pool/en/investor_relations/Siemens_AR2017.pdf

Siemens. (2017d). *Siemens PLM Software: Innovation for the future*. Retrieved on May 26th, 2019, from: http://www.ctecno.cat/wp-content/uploads/2015/09/Siemens-PLM-Innovation-for-the-future-keynote-mi-X17.pdf

Siemens. (2017e). *Siemens Vision 2020 – Focus on profitable growth*. Retrieved on May 26th, 2019, from: https://www.siemens.com/investor/pool/en/investor_relations/financial_publications/speeches_and_presentations/170322_presentation_bofaml_conference.pdf

Siemens. (2018a). *Empowering the Digital Transformation via Digitalization within the Integrated Lifecycle*. Retrieved on May 26th, 2019, from: https://www.nist.gov/sites/default/files/documents/2018/04/09/3se1_deren_siemens_empowering_dig_transf_via_digitalization_in_the_integrated_lifecycle.pdf

Siemens. (2018c). *Vision 2020+ Shaping the future Siemens*. Retrieved on May 26th, 2019, from: https://www.siemens.com/investor/pool/en/investor_relations/financial_publications/speeches_and_presentations/q32018/180802_Press_Analyst_Conference.pdf

Siemens. (2019a). *Project finance*. Retrieved on May 26th, 2019, from: https://new.siemens.com/global/en/products/financing/project-finance.html

Siemens. (2019b). *Project Management made by Siemens*. Retrieved on May 26th, 2019, from: https://w3.siemens.com/mcms/engineering-consulting/en/services_/engineering/project-management/pages/project-management.aspx

Siemens. (2019c). *Siemens Venture Capital*. Retrieved on May 26th, 2019, from: https://www.startus.cc/company/siemens-venture-capital

Silva, S., Meneses, R., & Radomska, J. (2018). A holistic perspective on the international market selection phenomenon. *Journal for East European Management Studies*, *23*(4), 579–602. doi:10.5771/0949-6181-2018-4-579

Silva, S., Pacheco, E., Meneses, R., & Brito, C. (2012). The importance of second-hand knowledge in the revised Uppsala Model: Can European textiles producers export to China? *Journal of Global Marketing*, *25*(3), 141–160. doi:10.1080/08911762.2012.741963

Slater, S., & Narver, J. (1994). Does competitive environment moderate market orientation-performance relationship? *Journal of Marketing*, *58*(1), 46–55. doi:10.1177/002224299405800104

Smith, L., & Sorensen, P. (2000). Pathological Outcomes of Observational Learning. *Econometrica*, *68*(2), 371–398. doi:10.1111/1468-0262.00113

Smutkupt, P., Krairit, D., & Esichaikul, V. (2010). Mobile Marketing: Implications for Marketing Strategies. *International Journal of Mobile Marketing*, *5*(2), 126–139.

Snow, C. C., Fjeldstad, Ø. D., Lettl, C., & Miles, R. E. (2010). Organizing Continuous Product Development and Commercialization: The Collaborative Community of Firms Model. *Journal of Product Innovation Management*, *28*(1), 3–16.

Sodenkamp, M. A., Tavana, M., & Di Caprio, D. (2016). Modeling Synergies in Multi-Criteria Supplier Selection and Order Allocation: An Application to Commodity Trading. *European Journal of Operational Research*, *254*(3), 859–874. doi:10.1016/j.ejor.2016.04.015

Solis, B. (2015). *X: The experience when business meets design*. John Wiley & Sons.

Spaulding, T. J. (2010). How can virtual communities create value for business. *Electronic Commerce Research and Applications*, *9*(1), 38–49. doi:10.1016/j.elerap.2009.07.004

Staw, B. M. (1981). The escalation of commitment to a course of action. *Academy of Management Review*, *6*(4), 577–587. doi:10.5465/amr.1981.4285694

Stead, J. G., & Stead, W. E. (2019). Why Porter Is Not Enough: Economic Foundations of Sustainable Strategic Management. In *Rethinking Strategic Management* (pp. 67–85). Springer. doi:10.1007/978-3-030-06014-5_4

Stegmann, P. (2009). *Strategic Value Management: Stock Value Creation and the Management of the Firm*. Wiley. doi:10.1002/9781118268087

Stern, G. M., Shiely, J. S., & Ross, J. (2003). *The EVA Challenge. Implementing Value-Added in an Organization*. Wiley.

Stewart, G. B. (1991). *The Quest for Value*. Harper Collins.

Suchman, M. (1995). Managing Legitimacy: Strategic and Institutional Approaches. *Academy of Management Review*, *20*(3), 571–610. doi:10.5465/amr.1995.9508080331

Suh, B., & Han, I. (2003). The impact of customer trust and perception of security control on the acceptance of electronic commerce. *International Journal of Electronic Commerce*, *7*(3), 135–161. doi:10.1080/10864415.2003.11044270

Takayama, K., Kaplan, M., & Cook-Sather, A. (2017, Summer/Fall). Advancing Diversity and Inclusion. *Liberal Education*, 22–29.

Tapscott, D., & Tapscott, A. (2016). *Blockchain Revolution: How the technology behind Bitcoin is changing money, business, and the world*. Penguin.

Tenenhaus, M., Amato, S., & Esposito, V. (2004). *A global goodness-of-fit index for PLS structural equation modelling*. Paper presented at the XLII SIS Scientific Meeting, CLEUP, Padova.

Tenenhaus, M., Vinzi, V. E., Chatelin, Y.-M., & Lauro, C. (2005). PLS Path Modelling. *Computational Statistics & Data Analysis*, *48*(1), 159–205. doi:10.1016/j.csda.2004.03.005

Terblanche, N. S., & Boshoff, C. (2006). A generic instrument to measure customer satisfaction with the controllable elements of the in-store shopping experience. *South African Journal of Business Management*, *37*(3), 1–15. doi:10.4102ajbm.v37i3.603

The Economist. (2015, Oct. 31). Blockchains: The great chain of being sure about things. *The Economist*.

Theodossiou, Karakatsanis, & Kougias. (2014). The History of Optimization. Applications in Water Resources Management. *Conference of the Hellenic Hydrotechnical Association (H.H.A)*.

Thomä, J. (2017). DUI mode learning and barriers to innovation-A case from Germany. *Research Policy*, *46*(7), 1327–1339. doi:10.1016/j.respol.2017.06.004

Thomas, M., & Tsai, C. I. (2012). Psychological distance and subjective experience: How distancing reduces the feeling of difficulty. *The Journal of Consumer Research*, *39*(2), 324–340. doi:10.1086/663772

Thomke, S., & Fujimoto, T. (2000). The effect of front-loading problem-solving on product development performance. *Journal of Product Innovation Management: An International Publication of the Product Development & Management Association, 17*(2), 128–142. doi:10.1111/1540-5885.1720128

Thurlby, B. (1998). Competitive forces are also subject to change. *Management Decision, 36*(1), 19–24. doi:10.1108/00251749810199202

Todo, Y., Matous, P., & Inoue, H. (2016). The strength of long ties and the weakness of strong ties: Knowledge diffusion through supply chain networks. *Research Policy, 45*(9), 1890–1906. doi:10.1016/j.respol.2016.06.008

Toledo, M., Fabiano, C., De Oliveira, L., Rodrigo, D. F. P., França, P. M., & Morabito, R. (2014). A Genetic Algorithm/Mathematical Programming Approach to Solve a Two-Level Soft Drink Production Problem. *Computers & Operations Research, 48*, 40–52. doi:10.1016/j.cor.2014.02.012

Trafimow, D., & Earp, B. D. (2017). Null hypothesis significance testing and type 1 error: The domain problem. *New Ideas in Psychology, 45*, 19–27. doi:10.1016/j.newideapsych.2017.01.002

Tsuji, H., Shigeno, H., Ueki, Y., Idota, H., & Bunno, T. (2017). Characterizing R&D and HRD in the innovation process of Japanese SMEs: Analysis based on field study. *Asian Journal of Technology Innovation, 35*(2), 367–385. doi:10.1080/19761597.2017.1385987

Tsuji, M., Idota, H., Ueki, Y., Shigeno, H., & Bunno, T. (2016). Connectivity in the Technology Transfer Process among Local ASEAN Firms. *Contemporary Economics, 10*(3), 193–203. doi:10.5709/ce.1897-9254.209

Tsuji, M., Ueki, Y., Shigeno, H., Idota, H., & Bunno, T. (2018). R&D and non-R&D in the innovation process among firms in ASEAN countries: Based on firm-level survey data. *European Journal of Management and Business Economics, 27*(2), 198–214. doi:10.1108/EJMBE-02-2018-0030

Ueki, Y. & Tsuji, M. (2019). The Roles of ICTs in Product Innovation in Southeast Asia. *The Review of Socionetwork Strategies, 13*(1), 79–95.

United Nations Development Programme. (2017). *Background of the Sustainable Development Goals*. United Nations Development Programme.

Urban, G. L., Sultan, F., & Quall, W. J. (2000). Placing trust at the center of your Internet strategy. *MIT Sloan Management Review*, (1), 39–48.

Van Alstyne, M. W., Parker, G. G., & Choudary, S. P. (2016, Apr.). Pipelines, platforms, and the new rules of strategy. *Harvard Business Review*.

Varmesan, O., & Friess, P. (Eds.). (2016). Internet of Things: Converging Technologies for Smart Environments and Integrated Ecosystems. River Publishers.

Varsei, M., & Polyakovskiy, S. (2015). Sustainable Supply Chain Network Design: A Case of the Wine Industry in Australia. *Omega (United Kingdom), 66*, 236–247.

Vega-Vázquez, M., Cossío-Silva, F.-J., & Revilla-Camach, M.-A. (2016). Entrepreneurial orientation–hotel performance: Has market orientation anything to say? *Journal of Business Research, 69*(11), 5089–5094. doi:10.1016/j.jbusres.2016.04.085

Venkatesan, R., Kumar, V., & Ravishanker, N. (2007). Multichannel shopping: Causes and consequences. *Journal of Marketing, 71*(2), 114–132. doi:10.1509/jmkg.71.2.114

Vera, D., & Crossan, M. (2004). Strategic leadership and organizational learning. *Academy of Management Review, 29*(2), 222–240. doi:10.5465/amr.2004.12736080

Verhoef, P. C., Neslin, S. A., & Vroomen, B. (2005). *Browsing versus buying: determinants of customer search and buy decisions in a multi-channel environment.* University of Groningen, Groningen, working paper.

Verhoef, P. C., Kannan, P. K., & Inman, J. J. (2015). From multi-channel retailing to omni-channel retailing: Introduction to the special issue on multi-channel retailing. *Journal of Retailing*, *91*(2), 174–181. doi:10.1016/j.jretai.2015.02.005

Verhoef, P. C., Lemon, K. N., Parasuraman, A., Roggeveen, A., Tsiros, M., & Schlesinger, L. A. (2009). Customer experience creation: Determinants, dynamics and management strategies. *Journal of Retailing*, *85*(1), 31–41. doi:10.1016/j.jretai.2008.11.001

Verhoef, P. C., Neslin, S. A., & Vroomen, B. (2007). Multichannel customer management: Understanding the research-shopper phenomenon. *International Journal of Research in Marketing*, *24*(2), 129–148. doi:10.1016/j.ijresmar.2006.11.002

Vijayasarathy, L. R. (2004). Predicting consumer intentions to use on-line shopping: The case for an augmented technology acceptance model. *Information & Management*, *41*(6), 747–762. doi:10.1016/j.im.2003.08.011

Viniportugal. (2018). *Viniportugal Estatísticas*. Retrieved from: https://www.viniportugal.pt/Estatisticas

Wade, M., Macaulay, J., Noronha, A., & Barbier, J. (2019). Orchestrating Transformation – How to Deliver Winning Performance with a Connected Approach to Change. Global Center for Digital Business Transformation, IMD, Lausanne, Switzerland.

Wagner, H. M., & Whitin, T. M. (1958). Dynamic Version of the Economic Lot Size Model (Vol. 5). Academic Press.

Wan, T., & Hoblitzell, M. (2014). Bitcoin's promise goes far beyond payments. *Harvard Business Review*.

Wan, Xu, & Dong. (2017). Supplier Selection Using ANP and ELECTRE II in Interval 2-Tuple Linguistic Environment. *Information Sciences, 385–386*, 19–38.

Wang, W., Qiu, L., Kim, D., & Benbasat, I. (2016). Effects of rational and social appeals of online recommendation agents on cognition-and affect-based trust. *Decision Support Systems*, *86*, 48–60. doi:10.1016/j.dss.2016.03.007

Wang, Y. J., Minor, M. S., & Wei, J. (2011). Aesthetics and the online shopping environment: Understanding consumer responses. *Journal of Retailing*, *87*(1), 46–58. doi:10.1016/j.jretai.2010.09.002

Ware, N. R., Singh, S. P., & Banwet, D. K. (2014). A Mixed-Integer Non-Linear Program to Model Dynamic Supplier Selection Problem. *Expert Systems with Applications*, *41*(2), 671–678. doi:10.1016/j.eswa.2013.07.092

Weisberg, J., Te'eni, D., & Arman, L. (2011). Past purchase and intention to purchase in e-commerce: The mediation of social presence and trust. *Internet Research*, *21*(1), 82–96. doi:10.1108/10662241111104893

Wei, Z., Zhao, J., & Zhang, C. (2014). Organizational Ambidexterity, Market Orientation, and Firm Performance. *Journal of Engineering and Technology Management*, *33*, 134–153. doi:10.1016/j.jengtecman.2014.06.001

Wendee, P. M. (2011). A Theory of Value Drivers: a Grounded Theory Study. University of Phoenix.

Wen, P., & Chen, Ch. (2016). How Does Ethical Leadership Influence Employee's Whistleblowing Intention? Evidence from China. *Social Behavior and Personality*, *44*(8), 1255–1266. doi:10.2224bp.2016.44.8.1255

Weraikat, D., Zanjani, M. K., & Lehoux, N. (2016). Two-Echelon Pharmaceutical Reverse Supply Chain Coordination with Customers Incentives. *International Journal of Production Economics*, *176*, 41–52. doi:10.1016/j.ijpe.2016.03.003

Westerman, G., Bonnet, D., & McAfee, A. (2014). *Leading Digital: Turning Technology Into Business Transformation*. Harvard Business Review Press.

Whitelock, J., & Jobber, D. (2004). An evaluation of external factors in decision of UK industrial firms to enter a new non-domestic market: An exploratory study. *European Journal of Marketing*, *38*(11/12), 1437–1455. doi:10.1108/03090560410560182

Wiggins, R. R., & Ruefli, T. W. (2005). Schumpeter's ghost: Is hypercompetition making the best of times shorter? *Strategic Management Journal*, *26*(10), 887–911. doi:10.1002mj.492

Winston, B., & Patterson, K. (2006). An integrative definition of leadership. *International Journal of Leadership Studies*, *1*(2), 6–66.

Winterhalter, S., Zeschky, M. B., & Gassmann, O. (2016). Managing dual business models in emerging markets: An ambidexterity perspective. *R & D Management*, *46*(3), 464–479. doi:10.1111/radm.12151

Wold, H. (1966). Estimation of principal components and related models by iterative least squares. In P. R. Krishnaiah (Ed.), *Multivariate Analysis* (pp. 391–42). Academic Press.

World Economic Forum. (2019). *An introduction to the Digital Transformation of Industries initiative.* Retrieved on May 26th, from: http://reports.weforum.org/digital-transformation/an-introduction-to-the-digital-transformation-initiative/

Worldpay. (2015). *The Store of the Future and the Role of Omni-Channel Payments in Driving Business Growth.* Retrieved 21 Mar. 2017 from https://www.worldpay.com/sites/default/files/WPUK-Omni-channel-payments-store-of-the-future.pdf

Wu, J.-J., Chen, Y.-H., & Chung, Y.-S. (2010). Trust factors influencing virtual community members: A study of transaction communities. *Journal of Business Research*, *63*(9-10), 1025–1032. doi:10.1016/j.jbusres.2009.03.022

Wu, W. Y., Sukoco, B. M., Chia, Y. L., & Shu, H. C. (2009). An Integrated Multi-Objective Decision-Making Process for Supplier Selection with Bundling Problem. *Expert Systems with Applications*, *36*(2), 2327–2337. doi:10.1016/j.eswa.2007.12.022

Wu, Z., Xia, X., & Wang, B. (2015). Improving Building Energy Efficiency by Multiobjective Neighborhood Field Optimization. *Energy and Building*, *87*, 45–56. doi:10.1016/j.enbuild.2014.10.079

Yang, X., Lim, Y., Sakurai, Y., & Seo, S. (2009). Comparative analysis of internationalization of Chinese and Korean firms. *Thunderbird International Business Review*, *51*(1), 37–51. doi:10.1002/tie.20243

Yao, C., & Liao, S. (2011). Measuring the antecedent effects of service cognition and internet shopping anxiety on consumer satisfaction with e-tailing service. *Management & Marketing*, *6*(1), 57–78.

Yuanzhu, Z., Hua, T. K., Guojun, J., Leanne, C., & Minglang, T. (2017). A big data framework for facilitating product innovation processes. *Business Process Management Journal*, *23*(3), 518–536. doi:10.1108/BPMJ-11-2015-0157

Yu, J., Ha, I., Choi, M., & Rho, J. (2005). Extending the TAM for a t-Commerce. *Information & Management*, *42*(77), 965–976. doi:10.1016/j.im.2004.11.001

Yulk, G. A. (2002). *Leadership in Organizations* (5th ed.). Prentice Hall.

Yu, U.-J., Niehm, L. S., & Russell, D. W. (2011). Exploring perceived channel price, quality, and value as antecedents of channel choice and usage in multichannel shopping. *Journal of Marketing Channels*, *18*(2), 79–102. doi:10.1080/1046669X.2011.558826

Zahra, S. A., & George, G. (2002). Absorptive capacity: A review, reconceptualization, and extension. *Academy of Management Review*, *27*(2), 185–203. doi:10.5465/amr.2002.6587995

Zare-Reisabadi, E., & Hamid Mirmohammadi, S. (2015). Site Dependent Vehicle Routing Problem with Soft Time Window: Modeling and Solution Approach. *Computers & Industrial Engineering*, *90*, 177–185. doi:10.1016/j.cie.2015.09.002

Zelinka, I., Snasel, V., & Abraham, A. (2013). *Handbook of Optimization: From Classical to Modern Approach* (Vol. 38). doi:10.1007/978-3-642-30504-7

Zhang, C.-B., & Li, Y. (2019). How social media usage influences B2B customer loyalty: Roles of trust and purchase risk. *Journal of Business and Industrial Marketing*, *34*(7), 1420–1433. doi:10.1108/JBIM-07-2018-0211

Zhang, J. L., & Ming, Y. Z. (2011). Supplier Selection and Purchase Problem with Fixed Cost and Constrained Order Quantities under Stochastic Demand. *International Journal of Production Economics*, *129*(1), 1–7. doi:10.1016/j.ijpe.2010.08.003

Zhang, K. Z. K., Barnes, S. J., Zhao, S. J., & Zhang, H. (2018). Can consumers be persuaded on brand microblogs? An empirical study. *Information & Management*, *55*(1), 1–15. doi:10.1016/j.im.2017.03.005

Zhang, Q., Shah, N., Wassick, J., Helling, R., & Van Egerschot, P. (2014). Sustainable Supply Chain Optimisation: An Industrial Case Study. *Computers & Industrial Engineering*, *74*(1), 68–83. doi:10.1016/j.cie.2014.05.002

Zhang, W., & Xu, D. (2014). Integrating the Logistics Network Design with Order Quantity Determination under Uncertain Customer Demands. *Expert Systems with Applications*, *41*(1), 168–175. doi:10.1016/j.eswa.2013.07.019

Zhao, F. (2004). Siemens' business excellence model and sustainable development. *Measuring Business Excellence*, *8*(2), 55–64. doi:10.1108/13683040410539436

Zied, M., & Inès, C. (2018). Consumer resistance to innovation in services: Challenges and barriers in the Internet of Things era. *Journal of Product Innovation Management*, *35*(5), 780–807. doi:10.1111/jpim.12463

Zinciri, Çalışmaları, Literatür, Sınıflama, Kocaoğlu, Gümüş, & Kocaoğlu. (2018). *Supply Chain Optimization Studies: A Literature Review and Classification* (Vol. 19). Academic Press.

Zott, C., & Amit, R. (2007). Business model design and the performance of entrepreneurial firms. *Organization Science*, *18*(2), 181–199. doi:10.1287/orsc.1060.0232

Zott, C., & Amit, R. (2008). The fit between product market strategy and business model: Implications for firm performance. *Strategic Management Journal*, *29*(1), 1–26. doi:10.1002mj.642

Zott, C., & Amit, R. (2010). Business model design: An activity system perspective. *Long Range Planning*, *43*(2-3), 216–226. doi:10.1016/j.lrp.2009.07.004

Zott, C., & Amit, R. (2013). The business model: A theoretically anchored robust construct for strategic analysis. *Strategic Organization*, *11*(4), 403–411. doi:10.1177/1476127013510466

# About the Contributors

**Paula Rodrigues** holds a Ph.D. in Management, in Faculty of Economics at the University of Porto, Portugal. She is an Associate Professor in Brand Management at the School of Economics and Management, Lusíada University - North, Portugal. Since 1995, she teaches Brand Management, Consumer Behaviour, Econometrics, Statistic, and Quantitative Methods at the Lusíada University - North. She has published several scientific papers, chapters, and books. Her on-going research projects concern consumer-brand relationships in the field of luxury, tourism and hospitality, and consumer goods.

* * *

**Maria do Rosário Correia** is currently an Assistant Professor of Finance at German University in Cairo. Previously, she held a Senior Lecturer position at University of Northampton, UK. Before this, she has taught in the areas of Accounting and Finance at several High Education Institutions namely University of Middlesex, Kingston University, University of East London (UK) and at Universidade do Porto (Portugal). Maria do Rosario has studied Management and Finance at the Universities of Porto and Strathclyde. She obtained her PhD in Finance degree at University of Strathclyde. Maria do Rosario has published in a number of high-ranked, peer-reviewed journals listed in the Australian Business Deans Council quality list. Her research interests are in the areas of Corporate Finance, Risk Management, Financial Economics and Entrepreneurship. Maria do Rosario won research grants from Austria National Bank and Fundacao para a Ciencia e Tecnologia (FCT).

**Alexandra R. Costa** is a Psychologist and has a PhD in Social Psychology (Cádiz University), an MBA in EGP - Oporto Business School. She has been a teacher of higher education since 1998 and a consultant since 1990. In her professional career, she has taken on several management roles, namely at Porto Polytechnics, direction at a consultant, among others. As a researcher, she has been dedicated to organizational innovation, work satisfaction, academic performance, self-efficacy and engagement. She has participated in national and international scientific meetings, either as an organizer, as a member of the scientific committee or presenting papers.

**Álvaro Dias** is Professor at Universidade Lusófona and ISCTE, both in Lisbon, Portugal, and a Researcher at Universidad de Sevilla, Spain. He got his Ph.D. in Management from Universidad de Extremadura, Spain, after an MBA in International Business. Professor Dias has over 24 years of teaching experience. He has had several visiting positions in different countries and institutions including Brazil, Angola, Spain, Poland, and Finland. He regularly teaches in English, Portuguese, and Spanish at undergraduate, master and doctorate levels, as well as in executive programs. Professor Dias has produced extensive research in the field of Tourism and Management, including books, book chapters, papers in scientific journals and conference proceedings, case studies, and working papers.

**Bruno Ferreira** is a Ph.D. student in Engineering and Industrial Management at Universidade Lusíada - Norte. He holds a BEng and MSc Degree in Electronics and Informatics Engineering and he is currently doing research on the application of artificial intelligence techniques with a doctoral scholarship.

**Lucile Arsov Gouriou** is a French Digital Product Manager. She holds a Master's degree (2007) in engineering from the University of Grenoble and she has worked for more than 10 years as an engineer specialized in numerical modelling. In 2019, she obtained her Executive Advanced Master's degree from the ESSEC Business School. Especially interested in Customer Experience, she focused her thesis on the Customer Experience in the luxury industry.

**Cécilia Goutran** is a graduate of the IMT Atlantique engineering school, specializing in Lean Management and Risk Management, and holds the Mastère SMIB (Strategy and Management of International Business) from ESSEC. She has led strategic projects for major players in the French public service (Veolia, Oui.sncf): management of software assets, optimization of customer service, improvement of the customer experience, definition of a new purchasing strategy. After several professional experiences in consulting firms, Cécilia joined SémioConsult as Consultant specialized in brand identity and analysis of the marketing and communication strategy through semiotics.

**Hiroki Idota** is Professor of Management Information System, Faculty of Economics, Kindai University, Osaka, Japan. Visiting Scholar, CCSR, De Montfort University, UK Ph.D., CISA (Certificated Information System Auditor). His other serves include Board Member, the Japan Society for Information and Management, and the Nippon Urban Management and Local Government Research Association. Received B.A. in Economics from Kwansei Gakuin University; M.A. in Informatics from Kansai University; and Ph.D. in Economics from Osaka University. Major areas of specialty include Management Information System and Management of Technology. Current research focuses on innovation using ICT. Publications include "An empirical analysis of organizational innovation generated by ICT in Japanese SMEs," in S. Allegrezza and S. Dubrocard (Eds.) Internet Econometrics, Palgrave Macmillan, 2012, "Corporate productivity and the stage of ICT development," Information Management Technology, Vol.13, 2012, and Theory and Practice of Information Security Management (in Japanese), Hakuto-Shobo, 2004, which received the Telecom Social Science Encouragement Award by the Telecommunications Advancement Foundation in March 2005.

**Anne-Flore Maman Larraufie** graduated from the Military Academy of Saint-Cyr as an Engineer, got an Advanced Master in Strategy and Management of International Business (SMIB) from ESSEC Business School (France), a Certificate in Advanced Studies at Thunderbird Business School (USA) and finally completed her Ph.D. in Business Administration at ESSEC. After several working experiences in various companies including EADS and LVMH (Guerlain), she decided to set up her own consulting agency SémioConsult®, while teaching in prestigious business schools and Universities all around the world (ESSEC, HEC, Ca' Foscari, Shanghai Normal University, etc.). She also became a delegate of INPI (the French IP-regulating body) for the European Union, and an expert on Made In France &

Luxury for the French Ministry of Economy. She is an expert in luxury, consumer behavior, branding and counterfeiting. She still pursues academic research and publishes in top-tier journals. Dr. Maman is also the Academic Director of the Advanced Master in Strategy and Management of International Business at ESSEC, for the three campuses (two in Paris and one in Singapore), and as such manages yearly more than 300 students and works with an administrative team of 6 people, all spread around the world. She is also the Academic Director of a Master in Management in the Perfume Industry in partnership with ISIPCA.

**Raquel Filipa do Amaral Chambre de Meneses** holds a Ph.D. in Business Science from the University of Porto, where she teaches in the area of strategy and international marketing. She researches in the same area, attending international conferences and having several book chapters, a manual, and papers published in scientific peer review journals. Currently, she is the director of Master in Marketing at the University of Porto.

**Rayssa Quirino** is MSc in Marketing and a Ba in Management. She performed several managerial activities in Brazil and Portugal.

**Paulo Ramos** (Paulo Fonseca de Matos Graça da Silva Ramos). PhD in Business Sciences FEP-UP, MSc Marketing & Product Management Cranfield University, UK, MA International Relations, UM. Assistant Professor at Lusíada University and at Fernando Pessoa University. Guest lecturer: UCP, FC-UP. CBQF Researcher at UCP-ESB. Member of the editorial board of the Management and Business Academy Journal of Organizational Studies and Innovation, UK. Manager and consultant in the private sector.

**Dario Elias Rodrigues** has a PhD in Management Sciences (UL); Marketing Specialization (IPS). Professional career in Marketing with 20 years of work and research on e-business and the digital economy. He gained international experience in the former German multinational Schering AG (now part of Bayer AG) and was the first E-Business manager of the respective Portuguese subsidiary. Later, he assumed the position of Institutional Communication Manager in this company where he worked for 16 years. He is currently a professor as well as author of scientific articles and publicity books in the areas of Marketing and E-Business. It has broadened the scope of its research on the new digital paradigm, with an emphasis on the new implications of blockchain technology, aimed at improving the quality of management and citizens' lives.

**Rui Silva** is an Associated Professor and Head of the Engineering and Technology Faculty at Universidade Lusíada – Norte, Portugal, since 2008. He obtained a Ph.D. in Mechanical/Electrotechnical Engineering from the University of Glamorgan, Uk and his research interests include the fields of industrial management, condition monitoring and artificial intelligence. He was the Principal Investigator of the Research Centre on Engineering and Industrial Management from 2007 to 2018.

**Sheikh Abu Taher** currently holds associate professorship position in the Department of Finance and Banking, Jahangirnagar University, Bangladesh. He completed BS in Finance and Banking from University of Dhaka, Bangladesh and MS and PhD in Policy and Management Informatics from University of Hyogo, Japan (with Japanese Government Scholarship recipient). His research interest mainly focuses on digital economy, digital finance and modeling of future finance industry. He publishes papers in Telematics and Informatics (Elsevier), International Journal of Innovation in the Digital Economy (IGI Global), Informatica Economica, Springer Medical Lecture Series and so on. He has been nominated for several best papers award namely, O.S. Braunstein Best Student Paper Award (Pacific Telecommunication Council, USA) and International Telecommunication Society Best Student Paper Award (ITS Biennial Conference, Japan).

**Isabel Torres** is a Psychologist, Specialist in Occupational, Social and Organizational Psychology, Vocational and Career Development Psychology and Occupational Health. She has a PhD in Work Psychology (FPCEUP - Faculty of Psychology and Educational Sciences of the University of Porto), has been a teacher of higher education since 1995 and a consultant since 1990. In her professional career, she has taken on several management roles, namely, managing an organic unit at a university, technical direction at a consultant, among others. As a researcher, she has been dedicated to occupational health issues, aging at work, as well as knowledge management and creativity in organizations. She has participated in national and international scientific meetings, either as an organizer, as a member of the scientific committee or presenting papers. It is part of the Editorial Committee of Laboreal Magazine (FPCEUP).

**Masatsugu Tsuji**, Ph.D.; Professor of Economics, Faculty of Economics, Kobe International University, and Professor Emeritus of Osaka University. Received B.A. from Kyoto University in 1965; M.A. from Osaka University in 1967; and Ph.D. in Economics from Stanford University, US in 1976. His serves include visiting professors of Carnegie Mellon University, US and National Cheng Kung University, Taiwan; Board of Director, ITS; Editorial Board, JISfTeH. Current research focuses on identifying factors promoting innovation in Japan and ASEAN economies. Publications include Industrial Clusters, Upgrading and Innovation in East Asia, Edward Elagr, 2011, From Agglomeration to Innovation: Upgrading Industrial Clusters in Emerging Economies, Palgrave Macmillan, 2009, Industrial Agglomeration and New Technology, Edward Elgar, 2007. "The Roles of ICTs in Product Innovation in Southeast Asia," Review of Socionetwork Strategies, Vol. 13, No. 1, pp 79–95, 2019.

# Index

www.ingramcontent.com/pod-product-compliance
Lightning Source LLC
LaVergne TN
LVHW080527300926
849162LV00007B/1556